THE MAN BEHIND THE
IRON MASK

Saint-Mars, the gaoler of the Iron Mask. Artist unknown. Private Collection.

THE MAN BEHIND
THE
IRON MASK

JOHN NOONE

Jamais dieu de l'Inde ne subit tant
de métempsycoses et tant d'avatars

Paul de Saint-Victor

ALAN SUTTON
1988

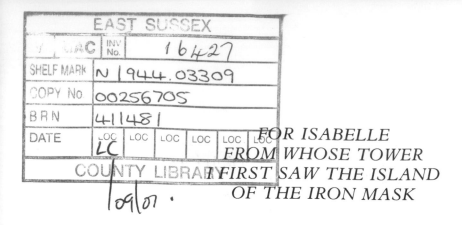
*FOR ISABELLE
FROM WHOSE TOWER
I FIRST SAW THE ISLAND
OF THE IRON MASK*

ALAN SUTTON PUBLISHING
BRUNSWICK ROAD · GLOUCESTER

First published 1988

British Library Cataloguing in Publication Data

Noone, John
The man behind the iron mask.
1. France. Man in the Iron Mask
I. Title
944'.033'0924

ISBN 0-86299-475-6

Cover illustrations: Front: The Mask of Langres, Langres Museum; The Man in
the Velvet Mask; collection of the Comte de Lacour, photograph by
Jean-Pierre Herin. *Back:* The Man in the Iron Mask, engraving by Neuville,
photograph by Viollet.

Typesetting and origination by
Alan Sutton Publishing Limited.
Printed in Great Britain by
WBC Print Limited.

CONTENTS

ACKNOWLEDGEMENTS

I would like to express my thanks to the librarians and custodians of the Bibliothèque Royale in Brussels and of the Bibliothèque Nationale in Paris, to Linda Bull, Librarian at the British Council in Brussels, to Gérard Tisserand, Curator of the Langres Museum, to Grégoire Bahry, Curator of the Armenian Museum of France, to Raoul Verdière and to Gerard Noone.

THE PRINCE IN THE IRON MASK

Lost in subterranean darkness, in cavernous galleries and labyrinthine passageways, a door of massive wood, reinforced with iron, scrapes open on rusted hinges and reveals a vaulted dungeon, dank and bare, where sits the skeleton of a prisoner hung with chains, the bones strung together by rags of clothing, the skull enclosed in an iron mask. Imprisoned in the time of Louis XIV,[1] an iron helmet locked onto his head to hide his face, discovered in the time of Louis XVI,[2] and the melancholy features behind the anonymity of the mask reduced to the anonymity behind the face – to the grimacing bare bone skull.

The scenario is pure fantasy, but in the summer of 1789 when the Paris mob swarmed into the Bastille,[3] slaughtered the guards and liberated the prisoners, there were people ready to believe it. In the popular imagination, the Bastille was the symbol of tyranny and since the mob had met with little resistance from the guards and had found only seven prisoners to release, some sensational invention was needed to satisfy public expectation. The mouldering bones bore witness to the monstrous inhumanity of the despotic rulers of France, of a king's crime against his brother, a queen's crime against her son. What did it matter to the ardent revolutionary that a skeleton in an iron mask had not really been found at all? The Man in the Iron Mask was real enough, his existence had been proved and his identity established long before. For a hundred years he had been the skeleton in the cupboard of the French Royal House and, with the overthrow of their tyranny, the truth could finally be told.

It was Voltaire,[4] scourge of despotism, champion of the underdog, forebear of revolution, who had uncovered the infamy. His bones, refused honourable burial at the time of his death eleven years before, were also found by propagandists of the Revolution, in fact and not in the Bastille, and were transferred in glory to a hero's monument in the Pantheon.[5] His courage in print had been so great that to escape secret agents and hired thugs he had been obliged to live most of his life as a refugee outside of France; yet he, even he, had not dared to publish the entire truth. The account he had given had been spread over various books and the underlying secret revealed only by innuendo. As early as 1738 he had written to his friend the Abbé Dubos, permanent secretary of the French Academy: 'I am well enough informed about the affair of the Man in the Iron Mask who died in the Bastille. I have spoken to people who served him.' From May 1717 until April 1718 he had himself been a prisoner in the Bastille and presumably had persuaded members of the prison staff to talk, but he had spoken also to people in government, to relatives, friends and associates of ministers and officials who had been directly involved with the prisoner.

His first remarks appeared in his *Siècle de Louis XIV* published in Berlin in 1751. After a reference to the death of Cardinal Mazarin,[6] which took place in March 1661, he continued:

Some months after the death of that minister, an event without parallel occurred, and what is no less strange is that all historians are unaware of it. An unknown prisoner, of height above the ordinary, young and of an extremely handsome and noble appearance, was conveyed with the utmost secrecy to the castle on the island of Sainte-Marguerite [7] in the sea off Provence. On the way there this prisoner wore a mask, the chin-piece of which had steel springs to allow him to eat with it on, and the order was to kill him if he took it off. He stayed on the island until 1690 when a trusted officer named Saint-Mars,[8] the governor of Pignerol,[9] was made governor of the Bastille and went to Sainte-Marguerite to get him and conduct him to the Bastille, still wearing the mask . . . This unknown man died in 1703 and was buried at night in the parish church of Saint-Paul. What is doubly astonishing is that when he was conveyed to Sainte-Marguerite, no man of consequence in Europe disappeared.

A second enlarged edition of the *Siècle de Louis XIV* was published the following year and a supplement added the year after that. In the 1752 edition, Voltaire provided more information: 'M. de Chamillart[10] was the last government minister to possess this strange secret. His son-in-law, the second Maréchal de La Feuillade, told me that when his father-in-law lay dying, he begged him on his knees to tell him who this man was, who was only ever known under the name of the Man in the Iron Mask. Chamillart replied that it was a state secret and that he

Print published in 1789 representing the supposed discovery of the skeleton of the Iron Mask in the Bastille. (*Photograph Bibliothèque Nationale*)

had taken an oath never to reveal it.' In the 1753 supplement, Voltaire followed this up with a simple deduction designed to prod his reader towards his own solution of the mystery: 'One has only to ponder the fact that no man of any consequence disappeared at the time, and it is clear that it was a prisoner of the greatest importance whose destiny had always been a secret.'

Finally, in his *Questions sur l'Encyclopédie* published in 1770, Voltaire went as far as he dared, leading his readers on with yet another carefully directed deduction and a further piece of pointed evidence: 'It is clear that if he was not allowed to walk in the courtyard of the Bastille or talk to his physician except in a mask, it was for fear that some too striking resemblance would be recognized in his features . . . As for his age, he himself told the apothecary of the Bastille a few days before his death that he thought he was about sixty years old.' All the information necessary to solve the puzzle was there. The Iron Mask was someone of the highest importance, whose very existence had always been a secret, whose face bore a close resemblance to a well-known person and whose age in 1703 was about sixty years old. In the light of this evidence, a closer consideration of the second factor – the reason for the mask – was enough to bring the reader to the truth which Voltaire had been afraid to publish.

The masked prisoner had been made noticeable by the very means used to render him anonymous. The authorities who forced him to wear the mask must have been aware of this. Clearly, in their estimation he nevertheless attracted less attention with the mask on his face than he would have done without it. The face of the Iron Mask is thus revealed precisely because such pains were taken to hide it. The only face universally recognizable in France at that time was the face of the King, known not only to the many who had actually seen him, whether at court, in procession or on campaign, but to anyone anywhere in the country. No other face, no matter how famous the name of its owner – were he a prince of the blood or a field-marshal, a provincial governor or a president of the Parlement – was known beyond the narrow circle of his own immediate influence. But the profile of the King, engraved as it was on the coins of the realm, was stamped indelibly upon the consciousness of the people.[11] Since the King's face was the only one that was universally known, the only reasonable explanation for covering the prisoner's face from everyone was that he bore such a close resemblance to the King that anyone seeing him would have recognized the likeness and would have supposed that the prisoner was the King; or would have realized the very secret the King wished to hide: that the prisoner was his own flesh and blood, his living image – his identical twin-brother.

The nightmare world of the doomed prince is easy to imagine. His mask was made of riveted iron, padded inside with silk and, being designed especially for him, was a perfect fit. It covered his head like a helmet and locked around his neck. The key was kept by the prison governor and he alone was authorized to use it. To unlock the mask without the key was impossible, and any attempt to wrench or break it off ran the risk of dislocating the wearer's neck or fracturing his skull. It was heavy to wear but not otherwise uncomfortable, and could if necessary be left on the prisoner's head for months at a time. Steel hinges on a spring in the jaw allowed enough movement of the chin-piece for him to eat with it on and, when he lay flat on his bed, the weight was supported well enough to enable him to sleep. The only practical reason for removing the mask at all was to allow his beard and hair to be cut. The prison governor did this personally every month or so, and in between times allowed him the use of a pair of highly polished tweezers with which he could pluck out the odd hairs that discomforted him. No one but the governor ever saw him without the mask. He wore it continuously for more than forty years, wore it even when he was sick and needed to be attended by a physician, was wearing it when he died, and was still wearing it a century later when the face he shared in twinship with Louis XIV had become the face they shared in common with all mankind.

In August 1789, one month after the fall of the Bastille, the identity of the Iron Mask, as insinuated by Voltaire, was finally divulged by Frédéric-Melchior Grimm, a German expatriate journalist living in Paris, who wrote commentaries upon the French intellectual scene for foreign patrons. The secret, he gave his readers to believe, had been closely guarded within the French royal family since the time of Louis XIV, confided as an obligation in conscience with the power of the crown to successive rulers of France. His informant was Jean de La Borde, one-time chief valet of Louis XV.[12] La Borde often questioned his master on the secret of the Iron Mask and Louis XV had told him that he himself had been made to wait until the day he reached his majority before being allowed into the secret, recalling that on that day his friends had pressed around him begging to be told, and that he had replied: 'You cannot know it.' To La Borde he had said the same thing, adding: 'I feel sorry for the man, but his detention did wrong to no one except him and averted great misfortune.'

Apparently Louis XV had been informed by his predecessor in power, the Duc d'Orléans,[13] who had been Regent from the death of Louis XIV in 1715 until his own death in 1723. Unknown to Louis XV, however, the Regent had already betrayed the secret. His daughter, Charlotte de Valois, had persuaded him to disclose it to her. She had passed it on in a letter to her lover, Maréchal de Richelieu,[14] and he had left the letter among his private papers where it had been found by La

Borde. The letter, as quoted by Grimm, began with a short message originally in code: 'Here then is the famous story. I dragged the secret out. I had to pay a horrible price . . .' For Grimm's readers the price the young lady had to pay remained obscure, but the mystery of the Iron Mask was finally elucidated. The Regent had allowed his daughter to read a secret document, the contents of which she reproduced in her letter. This document was a death-bed confession made by an unnamed nobleman, who declared that he had witnessed the birth of the man who later became the Iron Mask, had been his tutor and had shared imprisonment with him until his death.

According to this nobleman's account – as retold by Charlotte de Valois, as reported by La Borde, as revealed by Grimm – the story began in 1638 when Anne of Austria, the wife of Louis XIII,[15] was pregnant. Two shepherds arrived in Paris, demanded an audience with the King, and warned him that his wife would give birth to twin boys who would destroy the kingdom in their conflict over the throne. The King turned for advice to his Prime Minister, Cardinal de Richelieu,[16] the great-uncle of Maréchal de Richelieu, who solved the immediate problem by having the two shepherds locked up in the asylum of Saint-Lazare. At midday on 9 September, the Queen gave birth to a son, Louis XIV, in the presence of all the witnesses normally demanded by law and protocol. But four hours later, while the King was taking his afternoon collation, the midwife, Dame Perronet, came to inform him that the Queen's labour pains had recommenced. The King hurried to her bedside, accompanied by the Chancellor, and, with no one else present except the midwife, the doctor and the nobleman responsible for the secret declaration, saw his wife give birth to a second son 'more handsome and vigorous than the first'. The King had everyone present sign a formal record of what had taken place and swear a solemn oath never to speak of it to anyone, not even to each other, and to reveal it only if the first-born twin should happen to die. The baby was then entrusted to Dame Perronet, who was ordered to pretend that it was the child of some lady at court.

When the child reached boyhood, responsibility for his upbringing was transferred to the nobleman, who took him to live in Dijon. The nobleman might have passed for the boy's father, but the extraordinary deference he always showed caused the young prince to ask questions, which were never answered satisfactorily. As the boy grew older, his curiosity increased, and by the time he was twenty-one his suspicions centred upon the fact that under no circumstances was he ever allowed to see a portrait of the King. Through all this time the nobleman had been in secret correspondence with the King, first with Louis XIII, who died when the boy was five, later with Louis XIV, who was crowned when the boy was sixteen, and also with the Queen, Anne of Austria, and Cardinal Mazarin, who was the successor of Cardinal de Richelieu. Somehow the young man contrived to find or intercept one of these letters and at the same time to persuade a chambermaid, who had become his sweetheart, to procure for him a portrait of Louis XIV. Armed thus with proof that he was the identical twin-brother of the King, he confronted his tutor and informed him that he was leaving at once for Saint-Jean-de-Luz in the South of France, where the court had gathered for the marriage of Louis XIV with Maria-Teresa of Spain. The nobleman had the young prince confined to the house while he informed the King of what had happened. As soon as Louis XIV got the news, he gave orders to have both the prince and the nobleman packed off to prison, first to the island of Sainte-Marguerite in the Bay of Cannes, and later to the Bastille.

Maréchal de Richelieu, among whose papers this supposed letter was found, died at the age of ninety-two, just one year before Grimm's remarkable disclosure was made. Aged nineteen at the time of Louis XIV's death, he had lived through the Regency, the reign of Louis XV and the first fourteen years of the reign of Louis XVI. Born to fortune and to favour, a soldier, diplomat and courtier of the highest rank, illiterate, arrogant, shallow, unscrupulous, dissolute and corrupt, he had made no discernable contribution to government, thought or art in all his long life of influence and power, but coddled by fortune he had outlived the witnesses of his mediocrity and become free in old age to feed his vanity with sensational accounts of his one time political acumen and mettlesome spirit, his military glamour and sexual prowess. The private papers he left behind were important not so much for any particular text they might have provided as for the pretext their mere existence offered. With Richelieu dead and revolution in the air, they could be used as the pretended source of endless bits of gossip or invention about the secrets and scandals of the old regime. The old man's image lent credibility to the pretence, and people believed it simply because they wanted to believe. When the first volumes of his pretended *Mémoires* appeared in 1790, they sold like hot cakes.

The man responsible for this publication was a defrocked priest by the name of Jean-Louis Soulavie, who claimed that Richelieu in the last years of his life had given him access to all his papers, along with the help of the private secretary whose job it had been for twenty-five years to classify them. In fact Soulavie felt as little concern for French history as he did for the Roman Church. The public was eager for sensational disclosures on the crimes and corruptions of the past, and in the pillage of the Revolution there was no shortage of material to satisfy them. Libraries and archives, looted from great houses, could be had by the cartload for next to nothing. Soulavie ran a writing factory where plundered material was sifted through by a team of scribes and hacks, copied, adapted, elaborated, transformed and finally compiled, under his direction, into something that would sell.

After Grimm's disclosure of the letter from the Regent's daughter found in Richelieu's papers, the readers of the *Mémoires* would expect to be treated to a section on the Iron Mask and they could not be disappointed. Grimm moreover had implied that the price paid by the lady to her father for the secret had been in some way shocking. Soulavie could not pass up such an opportunity, and had his Richelieu divulge all: 'At that time it was generally believed that the Regent knew the name of the Mask, the story of his life and the reason for his imprisonment, and so being more curious and daring than anybody else, I attempted, by means of my charming princess whose curiosity was also aroused, to wrest the great secret from him. She always used to repulse the advances of the Duc d'Orléans and show a great aversion for him, but since he was nevertheless passionately in love with her and at the slightest hope of favour would grant her whatever she asked, I persuaded her to let him understand that he would be happy and satisfied if he allowed her to read the *Memoirs of the Iron Mask* which were in his possession.'

The plan worked: in return for making him 'happy and satisfied', the Regent gave his daughter the manuscript she wanted and the next day she sent it to Richelieu with a short message in code. To tease and tantalize his readers, Soulavie reproduced the note without deciphering it, and then seventy pages further on reproduced another note from the same lady in the same code, this time deciphered. Thus he allowed the reader the special thrill of turning back through the book and deciphering the first note for himself. In later editions, even this seventy-page gap was dispensed with so that the titillation could become immediate. With a little adaption to enable the system to work in translation, the note he printed read as follows:

4	1	14	1	21	15	4	1	5	20	8	12	17	21	21	1	11	14	1	15	15	12
H	E	R	E	S	T	H	E	F	A	M	O	U	S	S	E	C	R	E	T	T	O
19	10	12	13	9	15	9	4	20	3	15	12	2	1	15	8	18	21	1	2	5	
K	N	O	W	I	T	I	H	A	D	T	O	L	E	T	M	Y	S	E	L	F	
16	1	5	17	11	19	1	3	15	4	14	1	1	15	9	8	1	21	16	18	8	3
B	E	★	★	★	★	★	★	T	H	R	E	E	T	I	M	E	S	B	Y	M	D[17]

The document referring to the Iron Mask, which was found among Richelieu's papers and published by Grimm, was a letter written by the Regent's daughter reporting information culled from a secret declaration. In Soulavie's book the situation had improved with marvellous illogicality and devastating implausibility: the document, sent to Richelieu by the lady in question and found among his papers, was the secret declaration itself. It bore the following title: *Description of the birth and education of the unfortunate prince sequestrated by the Cardinals de Richelieu and Mazarin and confined by order of Louis XIV. (Written by the tutor of that prince on his death-bed.).* Soulavie reproduced it in its entirety, the same basic story as offered by Grimm, odd details omitted, changed or added, and all padded out to close on two thousand words.

Soulavie's version of the declaration differed from Grimm's only in the following particulars: a) the two shepherds were locked up by the Archbishop of Paris; b) 'the unfortunate prince' was born at half past eight in the evening while the King was at supper. The first chaplain and the Queen's confessor were also present; c) 'the unfortunate prince' cried at birth as if he knew even then the suffering he was to endure. He had birthmarks on his right thigh, his left elbow and the right hand side of his neck; d) it was Cardinal de Richelieu who advised keeping the second twin out of the way but in reserve, though the Queen thought the danger of civil war greatly increased by the medical opinion that the last born of twins was the first conceived. The midwife was threatened with death if she ever betrayed the secret; e) the nobleman's house was in Burgundy, but not actually in Dijon; f) the letter stolen by 'the unfortunate prince' was one from Cardinal Marazin, and it was a young governess of the house who gave 'the unfortunate prince' a portrait of the King; she did it because he was such an accomplished lover; g) the prisons in which 'the unfortunate prince' and the nobleman were confined were not named; h) the nobleman made his death-bed declaration to pacify his soul and to draw attention to the plight of 'the unfortunate prince', who at that time was still alive in prison.

As Soulavie himself remarked in a laboured display of objectivity, there was nothing in the declaration to prove that 'the unfortunate prince' was the Iron Mask, but since the stories of both, fragmentary and bewildering as they were when taken separately, appeared to complete and explain each other when put together, it was reasonable to suppose that they were one and the same. No one eager to accept the *Mémoires* as genuine was likely to refuse such a cautious supposition, and the myth of the Twin in the Iron Mask took its place in popular history, to be developed by romantic souls and exploited by political spirits in the century which followed.

In 1823, Emmanuel de Las Cases, who had been secretary to Napoleon during his exile on Saint Helena, published a journal of conversations with his master, in which for Friday 12 July 1816 he recorded a conversation on the subject of the Iron Mask. Much had been made of the idea, however fanciful, that the last-born of twins is

The Man in the Iron Mask. A romantic nineteenth-century interpretation by Nanteuil. Bibliothèque Arts Déco. (*Photograph Giraudon*)

the first conceived, and that therefore the Iron Mask, though younger than Louis XIV, was the rightful heir to the throne. Louis XIV was a usurper, and the legitimate possession of the crown had devolved upon his progeny only because the Iron Mask had died without children. In the popular myth developed around Napoleon was one ingenious fable which made him the descendant of the Iron Mask. According to this, the governor of the prison of Sainte-Marguerite allowed his daughter to visit the Iron Mask. The young couple fell in love and with the court's permission were married. Since the Iron Mask had no known name, the children of this union were given the name of their mother. That name was *de Bonpart*. The children were secretly moved to Corsica to be raised, and there the difference of language transformed their name from *Bonpart* to *Bonaparte*. Napoleon Bonaparte was of this family, directly descended from the Iron Mask in an unbroken line of eldest sons, and that being so he was the legitimate heir to the French throne. In Napoleon's view the naivity and credulity of the general public was such that to establish such a story and find unscrupulous people in government to sanction it would not have been difficult. Someone else who took part in the conversation remarked that a genealogist had once seriously set about proving it to him, claiming that the record of a marriage between Mlle de Bonpart and the Iron Mask could be seen in the register of some parish church in Marseilles.

Meanwhile the Prince in the Iron Mask had inspired a pantomime, a tragedy, a four-volume novel and, in 1821, a dramatic narrative by Alfred de Vigny entitled *La Prison*. None of this work is remembered today except perhaps de Vigny's poem, three hundred lines of heavily sentimental excitement in verse-couplets, which tells the following story: An old priest clutching the viaticum is led, blindfolded and stumbling, through vast echoing galleries and narrow twisting passageways, to a dungeon dimly lit by torchlight where a mysterious prisoner lies dying. Soldiers remove the blindfold and, addressing the dying man as 'prince', inform him that the priest has arrived. The reaction of the dying man is one of indifference at first, but the priest calls him 'son' and at that he responds with bitterness. The priest exhorts him to confess his sins, sermonizing on penance and the sufferings of Christ, leans forward to peer into the shadows which hide the dying man's face, and is horrified at what he sees:

> A mask without features, a phantasm's head,
> In the torchlight a face made of iron glowed red.

Many years before, the old priest had heard rumours of such a prisoner: a beautiful, noble, sweet-voiced man, royally born and guilty of no crime, condemned from youth to spend his life in prison with his face concealed in a mask. Once one of his fellow monks had found a golden goblet at the foot of the prison tower and had taken it to the prison commander. There had been a message from the masked prisoner scratched into the gold and, because the monk had read it and learned some perilous secret, he had never been seen again. Remembering this, the old priest falls silent. The prisoner speaks: after a life of such unmitigated and unmerited suffering, how can he believe in a just and merciful God:

> I have fed on despair, and my tears wept in vain
> Have rusted the cheeks of the mask of my pain.

The old priest has nothing to say, and the prisoner babbles on in a delirium telling of the girl he never knew and all the longings of his lost life: the sun on his face, the wind in his hair, dreams of mountains and the sea, of rivers and trees and simple love. In a final moment of clarity before he dies, he rejects the viaticum and, with a last despairing gesture, breaks his arm against the prison-wall. The priest stays to pray beside his body throughout the night and in the morning sees it wrapped in its winding-sheet, the face still covered in its iron mask.

It was in 1850 that the story of the Twin in the Iron Mask reached final form and lasting celebrity in another work of fiction, the best-selling novel of Alexandre Dumas, *The Viscount of Bragelonne*. This was the third and last volume of the adventures of his famous Musketeers, d'Artagnan, Athos, Porthos and Aramis. The first two volumes, *The Three Musketeers* in 1844 and *Twenty Years After* in 1845, had been an immense success, and the third book was written for the same readers, reaching the death of d'Artagnan in the last paragraph. The sufferings of the Iron Mask were subsidiary to the deeds and deaths of the Musketeers, just part of the melodrama of French history in which they played key rôles, but it nonetheless was, and still is, the most vivid and elaborate version of the Iron Mask story. This, reduced to eleven short scenes, is how Dumas told it:

Scene One: The bedroom of the Queen Mother in the Royal Palace. Late morning. Anne of Austria, stricken by some secret grief, is talking sadly with her ladies of honour. Enter a mysterious woman in a loo-mask, come to cure her strange complaint. The ladies of honour withdraw and the mysterious woman talks of a terrible secret kept by the Queen Mother since the day her son, the King, was born, twenty-three years ago. On that fateful day she gave birth not just to one son but to two, and in spite of the floods of bitter tears she shed that second child, for reasons of State, for the peace and safety of the realm, was taken from her and hidden away. Shocked at the stranger's knowledge of the secret, the Queen Mother turns pale as death and feels beneath her icy hand the beads of perspiration on her brow. The mysterious woman then removes her mask: it is the Duchesse de Chevreuse, the once bewitchingly beautiful favourite of the Queen Mother, now hideously old and witchlike. After years of banishment she has returned to beg the protection of her one-time friend and mistress. The Queen Mother takes her into her arms and apparently into her confidence; the ill-fated boy, she tells her, died of consumption while still a child.

Scene Two: A prison room on the third floor of the Bertaudière Tower in the Bastille. A starry night sky beyond the bars of the window. Clothes discarded on a leather armchair; supper-dishes untouched on a small table; a young man sprawled disconsolately under the half-drawn curtains of a bed. A man dressed in grey has just entered with a lantern, a distinguished-looking man in late middle age, calm and confident, cold and calculating. It is Aramis, the one-time musketeer, and he has just used the secret powers of the Jesuit Society, of which he is the Father-General, to gain entrance to this room. No one has ever been allowed to see this prisoner. Few people even know that he exists.

Before he was a prisoner here, the young man lived with a nurse and tutor in the confines of a large house and walled garden lost in the country. A house without mirrors, without books of history or literature, without a portrait of the King. In the time he was there a lady of majestic bearing came to see him every month, sometimes accompanied by another lady, once by Aramis, and once by another gentleman. Apart from his former nurse and tutor, his present turnkey and prison governor, these people are the only ones he has ever spoken to in his life. The efforts made to seclude him from the world, the care taken to educate him for that same world, and the respect shown him within the little world in which he lived, made him wonder sometimes about his origin and identity. But he was always told that he was an orphan and that no one had any interest in him.

The incident that transformed his life had occurred eight years previously, soon after his fifteenth birthday. He was sleeping in the hall one day, exhausted after a long lesson of fencing, when he heard his tutor call out in consternation to his nurse. A letter had blown out of a window and fallen down the well. In their agitation the old couple did not realize that he could hear them, and he understood from what they said that they had to retrieve the letter because it was from the Queen. She would want it back to burn, as she did with all the letters they received from her, and they would be in peril of their lives from Mazarin if they could not produce it when next she came. To find someone to help them, someone who would be able to recover the letter without being able to read it, they hurried off to the village, leaving the young man alone in the house.

Urged on then by that impulse which drives a man to his own destruction, he lowered the cord from the windlass and slid down it into the darkness. Plunging into the water, he seized the letter, clambered back up to the courtyard and escaped into the garden. The paper was sodden and torn, the writing almost erased, but what he could read was enough for him to realize that the Queen herself was deeply concerned in his welfare and upbringing, and that the tutor and nurse, who treated him with such respect, were themselves of noble rank. Since the villager who climbed down the well could find nothing, it might have been assumed that the letter had sunk out of sight, but the young man's wet clothes aroused suspicions. When later he was taken ill with a violent fever, brought on by the chill and the excitement of the discovery, these suspicions were borne out. In his delirium he revealed all that had happened. The letter was found and the Queen was informed. The young man was arrested and taken to the Bastille.

What became of the tutor and nurse, the young man does not know, but Aramis does. They were poisoned, he says, and while the young man presses his icy fingers to his clammy brow, his trembling fingers to his beating heart, he goes on to reveal the direful secret of his birth. He produces a mirror and a portrait of Louis XIV to prove it. The resemblance of the young man and his brother, the King, is the God-given instrument of truth and justice, Aramis declares, the weapon which will restore the balance of fate. It was a crime against nature to render different in happiness and fortune brothers conceived and born so much the same. The equilibrium will be restored only when the rôles of prisoner and king have been exchanged. In that high endeavour Aramis intends to liberate the young man from the Bastille.

Scene Three: Deep night under arching foliage in the depths of the Forest of Sénart.[18] A carriage-and-four pulled off the road and hidden in thickets of undergrowth. The horses snuffling as they nibble the young oak shoots. The driver lying silently on a slope beside them. Two figures emerge from the carriage and stand there, black in the darkness, keeping silence too: the young man entranced, feeling the night air on his face, the ecstasy of freedom; Aramis apprehensive, watching him. The young man has a decision to make. Aramis has offered to give him a thousand pistoles,[19] two of his horses and the driver, as servant and guide, to take him far away to a place of safety and obscurity where no one will ever seek him; he can live out his life in ease and liberty close to nature and its honest laws among simple honourable men. Between that and a bid to substitute him for his brother, the King, with the immediate risk of failure, and the lifelong dangers in success, he is to choose. He bows his head and, at last, with a look full of courage and pride, his brow contracted, his jaw clenched, he makes his choice: the crown. Aramis has briefed him with all the information necessary to carry off the impersonation and he is confident that he can do it. Once he has taken his brother's place, Colbert,[20] the King's favourite minister, will be exiled and Fouquet,[21] the minister out of favour, will be restored in office. Aramis will be elevated to the rank of Cardinal and become Prime Minister. Aramis will make him a great king, and he will make Aramis pope, then bound in mutual trust, crown and tiara together, they will establish an empire greater than Charlemagne's.

Scene Four: Vaux-le-Vicomte.[22] Later that night. Aramis and the young man in the Blue Room, seated above a secret trapdoor, looking down through a hidden spyhole in the painted dome which spans the King's chamber below. The King, in sour disgruntled mood, talking with Colbert. He is the guest of Fouquet, whose palatial new home this is, and he feels humiliated by the splendour of the hospitality and entertainment provided for him. The style and wealth of his host fills him with envy. He wants to know where Fouquet has found the money necessary for such a display and Colbert produces a letter which appears to prove that he stole it. There is a deficit in the state accounts of thirteen million francs and the letter written by Mazarin makes it clear that precisely such an amount was taken from the state coffers to be deposited with Fouquet.

Scene Five: Vaux-le-Vicomte. The following night. The King walking in the garden with Colbert. Fouquet's lavish generosity, through all the brilliant festivities of the day, has only made the King more resentful. Deep in the park, the King's mistress, Louise de La Vallière, is waiting for him and, when she discovers that he is about to have Fouquet arrested, she persuades him that he cannot honourably do that so long as he is a guest in Fouquet's house. Colbert bends a look of hatred upon the charming couple as they embrace behind a lime tree; when the young lady leaves, he takes a letter from his pocket and gives it to the King, pretending that she has just dropped it. The King assumes that it must be a love note meant for him, but it is an old letter of admiration and gallantry written to her by Fouquet.

Scene Six: Vaux-le-Vicomte. Later that night. The King in his chamber shuddering with loathing as Fouquet bends to kiss his hand. Through the windows the sky ablaze with fireworks which the King did not wish to see. He wants only to see d'Artagnan,[23] the Captain of the Musketeers, who arrives promptly as soon as everyone else has withdrawn. Handsome, noble d'Artagnan, whose heart is as kind and faithful as it is courageous, whose eyes are as frank and true as they are piercing, whose Gascon blood, tempered with the subtlety and irony of a great spirit, would civilize the most savage tyrant, the most brutal slave. The King wants Fouquet arrested and his rage explodes when d'Artagnan requests the order in writing. He stamps his feet and gnaws his lips, but the order is nonetheless moderated. Fouquet is to be kept under guard pending arrest. There is to be no fuss, no show, and the King will decide in the morning what is to be done with him. When d'Artagnan leaves, the King's frenzy erupts once more. He strides about the room, knocking over the furniture, flings himself onto the bed and rolls from side to side, biting the sheets to smother his tears and groans. When finally he sleeps it is from sheer exhaustion. He dreams that the bed is descending slowly through the floor, and wakes from his dream to find himself in a subterranean passage between the menacing silhouettes of two men, masked and cloaked. As they bundle him away through the darkness, the empty bed lifts slowly back to its original place in the chamber. One of the masked men is of huge stature and vast circumference; he is Porthos: honest, mighty, innocent, gentle, magnificent Porthos. The other man is Aramis.

Scene Seven: Vaux-le-Vicomte. Dawn the next morning. Fouquet alone in his bedroom. D'Artagnan, who has spent the night dozing in an armchair beside him, has gone to the King for further orders. When he returns he is bearing the good news that Fouquet is not to be arrested after all, and he is accompanied by Aramis, who for some extraordinary reason appears to have become the King's confidant overnight. Fouquet is bewildered: he still does not understand why he was put under guard in the first place and, as soon as d'Artagnan has left the room, he asks for an explanation. Aramis tells him how Colbert turned the King against him and how the King's apparent change of mind is in reality a change of kings: the King of yesterday being Fouquet's impacable enemy, the King of today his friend. Confident of Fouquet's collusion, Aramis reveals all: that Louis XIV has an identical twin brother who until yesterday was kept locked up in the Bastille, that last night their places were switched and the King became the prisoner while the prisoner became the King. Fouquet, however, is horrified. Never would he connive at an act of treason against the King, an act of treachery against a guest. Aramis, his eyes bloodshot, his mouth trembling, has plunged his hand into his breast, as though to grasp a dagger, but Fouquet is not intimidated: it is his sacred duty to denounce this execrable crime, he says, and he is ready to die for his honour. When Aramis draws out his hand, his fingers are covered in blood, but he has no weapon. In the passionate anguish of his defeat, he has torn open the flesh of his own breast with his bare hand. Leaving Aramis to make good his escape, Fouquet takes horse to rescue his King from the Bastille.

Scene Eight: Vaux-le-Vicomte. Later that morning. The King's chamber with the shutters half-closed and the King, dressed in hunting costume, receiving his morning visitors. Though the Queen Mother has noticed a slight difference in his voice, the young man is imitating his brother's lofty manner and controlling his own profound feelings so well that not the slightest suspicion has been aroused. The fact that Aramis and Fouquet have not yet appeared surprises him, and while someone is sent to fetch them, he lets it be known that Aramis is now established in his confidence and Fouquet re-established in his favour. The voice of Fouquet is heard from the secret staircase and when the door in the panelling opens, a cry of amazement and horror fills the chamber. Twin Kings, wearing by uncanny chance identical clothes, stand facing each other across the room, both pale as death and trembling, clenching their hands convulsively, their eyes bolting from their heads; then the King who has just entered leaps at one of the shutters and flings it open. Light floods the chamber and the assembly looks on dumbfounded as both Kings kneel at the Queen Mother's feet and beg to be acknowledged as her son. The newly arrived King then turns to d'Artagnan and demands to be recognized. Rousing himself from his shock and wonder, d'Artagnan places his hand on the shoulder of the other King. The choice is made. The triumphant King turns from his rival and sweeps from the room, taking everyone with him except the Queen Mother and Fouquet. Gently, with tragic nobility, the defeated King reproaches his mother for her cruelty. Graciously, with compassion and respect, d'Artagnan and Fouquet ask the young man's forgiveness. Silently, without expression, Colbert appears in the doorway and gives d'Artagnan a written order from the King. The prisoner is to be conducted to the island of Sainte-Marguerite, his face covered with an iron mask, and if he attempts to remove the mask he is to be killed.

Scene Nine: The Harbour of Antibes.[24] Morning sunlight on the sea. Athos and his son, Raoul, together on the quay. Heroic, tragic Athos, the purest and wisest of them all, with his brave, heart-broken son. Betrayed in his love for Louise de La Vallière, Raoul has volunteered for service with the Duc de Beaufort, the Grand Admiral of France, who is leaving Toulon with the fleet on a punitive expedition against Gigelli[25] in North Africa. They are in Antibes to requisition fishing-boats to serve as lighters for the embarkation, and one of the fishermen they talk to has a strange tale to tell. Six days previously, a gentleman he did not know came in the night to hire his boat to go to the island of Saint-Honorat.[26] The stranger had a huge trunk with him and, in spite of the dangers and difficulties of transporting such a thing, insisted on taking it along. In mid-crossing, however, he decided that the approach to Saint-Honorat was too dangerous in the dark and wanted to be landed at Sainte-Marguerite instead. The fisherman, who knew the waters well, was confident that he could make it to Saint-Honorat in safety, but when he refused to change course the stranger drew his sword. Seizing their hatchets, the fisherman and his mate made ready to defend themselves, when the huge trunk sprang open of its own accord and the devil himself climbed out, a phantom whose head was covered in a black mask like a helmet. Terrified, the fisherman and his mate jumped overboard. The stranger thanked the devil and the boat drifted on. When it was found the next day, it was beached and broken on the island of Sainte-Marguerite and the devil, the trunk and the stranger had vanished into thin air. The fisherman went at once to the fortress to tell what had happened, but the governor refused to believe his story and threatened to have him flogged if he persisted in it.

Scene Ten: Island of Sainte-Marguerite. That afternoon. Athos and Raoul in a garden at the foot of the fortress wall. Someone calls out and, looking up, they see a hand at a barred window throw a silver plate towards them. When they pick it up they discover that a message has been scratched into the metal with the point of a knife: 'I am the brother of the King of France – a prisoner today – a madman tomorrow. French gentlemen and Christians, pray to God for the soul and the sanity of the son of your masters.' A musket-ball fired from above strikes the ground at their feet. They are being shot at by two of the prison guards, but with an exclamation of surprise one of their assailants knocks up the musket of the other, and the next moment they are surrounded by soldiers. The governor would have them shot on the spot because the prisoner has made contact with them, but d'Artagnan arrives from the top of the wall in time to save them. They are Spanish, he says, and friends of his: he knows they have not read the prisoner's message because they cannot read a word of French; and taking the plate from them, he scrapes out the writing with the tip of his sword.

Scene Eleven: Island of Sainte-Marguerite. That evening. The ramparts of the fortress in a storm. Dark wracks and wild seas. Thunder and lightning. D'Artagnan, Athos and Raoul have concealed themselves in an angle of the staircase to watch the governor go by with his prisoner. Under the fiery tumult of the exploding heavens, the lambent flash and flicker of lightning reflected, a man clothed all in black stops to look at the storm and breathe its sulphurous fumes; his head is encased in an iron helmet, a mask of iron covering his face, the iron sheathed in fire under the streaming rain. 'Come, sir,' cries the governor impatiently. 'Say, "my lord",' exclaims Athos angrily. 'Say neither,' declares a hollow and dreadful voice from the iron mask. 'Call me the Accursed'.

Not only is this version of the Iron Mask story the one most people know, often it is the only one they know. The novels of Dumas were always bestsellers and when in the twentieth century the cinema came to challenge and supersede the written word, his Musketeer stories were quickly reproduced in the new form. Since 1909 no less than ten films of the Iron Mask have been made – three French, three American, two Italian, one British, one German – and all have used or adapted the story of the twins as told by Dumas, with one actor playing the parts of both Louis XIV and the Iron Mask, as did Richard Chamberlain in 1976; but the star of the cast usually takes the role of d'Artagnan, as did Douglas Fairbanks in 1919 and Jean Marais in 1962. The story of the Iron Mask continues to be part of western popular myth in our own day, as it was part of French political myth two hundred years ago. With the passing of the years the bestseller has prevailed over history to such an extent that it is not perhaps too much of an exaggeration to suggest that by the vast majority of people today, at least outside of France, the illustrious Louis XIV is not likely to be known or remembered except as the monster-brother of the Man in the Iron Mask.

What in the meantime had become of the imaginary skeleton of the Iron Mask found in the Bastille in 1789 is not known. Presumably it was laid to rest in some imaginary tomb, liberated at last from its terrible mask of iron. Certainly the mask itself was not interred with the bones because half a century later it turned up again, discovered in a heap of old iron, far away from Paris, in the little town of Langres, just to the north of Dijon. How it reached Langres was not explained, but it was reasonable to suppose that it had been brought by one of the many scrap-iron merchants who served the booming cutlery industry there. The event was recorded by Paul Lacroix in his *Revue Universelle des Arts* for 1855.

It has been reported in several newspapers that the famous iron mask has been recovered in a heap of scrap-iron at a sale in

Langres. Acquired first of all by a second-hand dealer, it was apparently passed on for a modest sum to a distinguished enthusiast, who having scratched at the thick coating of dust which covered the interior brought to light a little strip of parchment blackened with age on which it was still possible to see some half-erased letters. This strip, carefully washed and treated, revealed the following inscription: 'Anno praesenti 1703 ferream mors avulsit personam quam postnato geminus imponi jusserat fra . . .' (i.e. 'In this year 1703, death removed the iron mask which the twin commanded to be fixed upon his younger bro . . .'). The rest of the inscription is missing; but according to a local newspaper, what there is of it is enough to prove that the mask in question is precisely the one which was used to cover the face of the state prisoner known by the name of the Man in the Iron Mask. This discovery of the famous iron mask, with its beautiful inscription broken off in the middle of the word 'frater', must have been made during carnival-time.

The story of the Mask of Langres, like all good stories, as with the story of the Iron Mask himself, has a basis in truth. An actual mask of iron was found, and still exists today as part of the collection of the Langres Museum. It was donated by a certain Canon Defay, who was the headmaster of a local school, but its provenance beyond that is not known, and it certainly bears no trace of any inscription. The dimensions of the object, as given by the museum, are: 'height 18.3 cms., width 17.3 cms., weight 470 grams'; that is to say, 7.2 inches from top to bottom, 6.8 inches from side to side, and a little more than one pound in weight. The catalogue-card reads as follows: 'Mask of Iron. Hammered plate with cut-out eyes, nostrils and mouth. Formerly painted (traces of pink glaze around eyes and nostrils). Upper rim scalloped. Three holes in form of triangle in middle of forehead. Lower edge pierced with holes along entire length. Keyhole cut into left side of chin. Perforation in each ear-section.'

No doubt the holes around the edge of the mask were made for a web of straps which fastened around the wearer's head. Presumably there was one strap attached to the top of the forehead, with two more attached to the ears, and they met at the back of the head where they were anchored by a fourth strap linking them to a collar which was secured to the chin. What the purpose of the keyhole was, one cannot say. There is no trace of a locking device, and it is difficult to imagine how any such mechanism could have been incorporated into the chin. Perhaps it was added later to suggest a lock which never existed. As it is, the mask appears to be very old and could well be Celtic. Beautiful

The Mask of Langres, 'recovered in a heap of scrap-iron in a sale at Langres' in 1855 and claimed to be 'the one which was used to cover the face of the state prisoner known by the name of the Man in the Iron Mask'. Museum of Langres. (*Photograph Canonge-Art*)

and terrible, with its smoothly ridged features and asymmetric eyes, it defies interrogation. It could have been made for the wearer's protection, a mask of war or of ritual, a defence against physical or spiritual harm. It is not even sure that it was made to cover the face of any living man. It might have been strapped to the head of an image or a corpse, a living god or a dead hero, the face of a totem or a trophy skull. Exhibited today with its startled, staring eyes and gaping, gasping mouth, it siezes the attention and demands an explanation. But its mystery remains as impenetrable as the mystery of the man who, in the popular imagination, was condemned to live out his life in prison, with such a mask on his face.

1. *Louis XIV*: King of France, b. 1638, reigned 1661–1715 after the regency of his mother, Anne of Austria, 1642–1661, and before the regency of his nephew, Philippe, Duc d'Orléans, 1715–1723.
2. *Louis XVI*: King of France, b. 1754, reigned 1774–1793, after the reign of his grandfather Louis XV, 1723–1774. He was deposed and executed during the French Revolution.
3. *Bastille*: French state prison in Paris stormed, captured and destroyed in the early days of the French Revolution.
4. *Voltaire*: pen-name of François-Marie Arouet, 1694–1778. Controversial and influential French writer, best known for his historical and philosophical writings, for his satire and social criticism.
5. *Pantheon*: Neoclassical-style building in Paris, built between 1758 and 1789. Originally intended as a church but secularized under the Revolution to serve as a national temple in honour of great Frenchmen.
6. *Cardinal Jules Mazarin*: Prime Minister and virtual ruler of France under the regency of Anne of Austria.
7. *Sainte-Marguerite*: an island facing the town of Cannes on the French Riviera.
8. *Benigne d'Auvergne de Saint-Mars*, 1626–1708.
9. *Pignerol*: modern town of Pinerolo, south-west of Turin in Piedmont, Italy.
10. *Michel Chamillart*, 1652–1721. Minister of State under Louis XIV from 1699 to 1709.
11. When in 1791 Louis XVI tried to escape the revolutionary forces and flee the country disguised as a valet, he was arrested in a provincial town because a simple postmaster there recognized him from his portrait on the coinage.
12. *Louis XV*: King of France, b. 1710, reigned 1723–1774, great-grandson of Louis XIV.
13. *Philippe, Duc d'Orléans*, 1674–1723, was the son of Louis XIV's only brother.
14. *Armand de Vignerot, Duc de Richelieu*, 1696–1788.
15. *Louis XIII*: King of France, b. 1601, reigned 1617–1643, after the regency of his mother, Marie de Medici, 1610–1617, and before the regency of his widow, Anne of Austria.
16. *Armand Jean du Plessis, Cardinal de Richelieu*: Prime Minister under Louis XIII from 1628 to 1642.
17. *M.D.*: presumably the initials signify *Monsieur le duc*, i.e. her father the Regent.
18. *Forest of Sénart*: south-east of Paris.
19. *Pistole*: Spanish gold coin.

20. *Jean-Baptiste Colbert*, 1619–1683. Finance Minister under Louis XIV from 1665 to 1683.
21. *Nicolas Fouquet*, 1615–1680. Finance Minister under Cardinal Mazarin from 1653 to 1661.
22. *Vaux-le-Vicomte*: château built by Fouquet south-east of Paris.
23. *d'Artagnan*: Dumas based his fictional character upon a real person: Charles de Batz–Castelmore d'Artagnan, 1610–1673.
24. *Antibes*: town close to Cannes on the French Riviera.
25. *Gigelli*: modern town of Djidjelli in Algeria.
26. *Island of Saint-Honorat*: island close to Sainte-Marguerite.

CHAPTER TWO

THE MASKED PRISONER

The report of a mysterious masked man held prisoner in the Bastille had been circulating in French society long before Voltaire began his investigations and though he was the first to get his information into print, he was not the only one to do so, nor was he the first to get it onto paper. The same basic story was told in a letter written while Louis XIV was still alive, forty years before Voltaire published his first account, but not itself published until one hundred and forty years after. It was written by Madame, the Princess Palatine, who was the second wife of Monsieur, Louis XIV's brother, and the mother of the Regent who ruled after Louis XIV's death. She was a big horsy woman who, as the sister-in-law of the King, graced the upper reaches of the court, albeit in hefty graceless fashion, and passed her time into old age collecting geological specimens and palace gossip, riding to hounds and writing to friends. Every day she wrote to her relatives in the ruling families of Europe, filling her letters with titbits of family news and tittle-tattle of court conversation. On 10 October 1711, when she informed her aunt Sophie, the Electress of Hanover, of the latest story she had heard, she had no idea that she was serving posterity:

> A man spent many years in the Bastille and died there wearing a mask. Two musketeers were at his side to kill him if he removed his mask. He ate and slept with the mask on. No doubt this treatment was unavoidable because he was otherwise very well treated, well lodged and given everything he desired. He received communion in his mask. He was very devout and read continuously. No one could ever learn who he was.

Where Madame got her story from she did not say. However, since her contacts were restricted to the inner circles of the court, one may

'Two musketeers were at his side to kill him if he removed his mask.' A romantic nineteenth-century interpretation by Neuville. (*Photograph Viollet*)

assume that her information originated with someone highly placed and presumably well informed.

At least one of Voltaire's informants, the second Maréchal de La Feuillade, had the same credentials, although he had been dead for all of twenty-seven years when Voltaire presented his testimony. For him, apparently, the existence of the Man in the Iron Mask was not in question: it had been admitted by his father-in-law, Michel de Chamillart, who had been a government minister under Louis XIV from 1699 until 1709. Chamillart had claimed to know the prisoner's identity, and on his death-bed in 1721 had acknowledged that it was a state secret.

Voltaire gave the names of two more of his informants, one a physician named Marsolan, the other an army officer named Riouffe. Their testimony, which like that of La Feuillade was at best second-hand, was at least third-hand by the time it reached Voltaire: Marsolan's story by way of Maréchal de Richelieu and Riouffe's story by way of the Marquis d'Argens.[1] Marsolan claimed to be passing on information given him by his father-in-law, who professed to have been the physician who treated the Iron Mask in the Bastille. Riouffe claimed that once in his youth he had seen the Iron Mask in Cannes, but he offered no information on that experience; his contribution was based upon local traditions which had grown up around the mysterious prisoner during his stay on Sainte-Marguerite. Who Voltaire's remaining sources were is not known. He dropped other names to suggest that his information was reliable, but was never specific about them.

The account he gave in 1751 was nonetheless particular and precise. In the excerpt already quoted he alleged that at the time of his arrest the Iron Mask was tall and young, handsome and noble, was made to wear a mask with a movable jaw and threatened with death if he tried to take it off, that he stayed on Sainte-Marguerite from 1661 until 1690 and was then transferred by Saint-Mars to the Bastille where he died in 1703. In the rest of the passage he makes even more detailed assertions:

> The Marquis de Louvois,[2] (who was the Minister of War at the time,) went to see him on the island, before he was moved, and remained standing while he talked with him, showing great respect. The unknown man was conducted to the Bastille where he was lodged as well as one could be in that castle. He was refused nothing that he asked for. His greatest pleasure was in lace and linen of exquisite fineness. He used to play the guitar. He was fed sumptuously and the governor rarely sat down in his presence. An old physician of the Bastille, who had often treated this extraordinary man when he was sick, said that he had never seen

his face, although he had often examined his tongue and the rest of his body. That physician said that he was admirably well built, that his skin was rather brown, that he held one's attention by the mere sound of his voice and that he never complained of his fate nor gave any hint of who he might be.

In the 1752 account, a story told by Riouffe and supposedly well known in the region of Cannes, was added. It was a story which later caught the imaginations of numerous writers including both Alfred de Vigny and Alexandre Dumas.

The governor himself used to serve him at table and then withdraw, locking him in. One day the prisoner wrote with a knife on a silver plate and threw it out of the window towards a boat which was near the shore, almost at the foot of the tower. The fisherman, whose boat it was, picked up the plate and took it to the governor. He in astonishment asked the fisherman: 'Have you read what is written on this plate and has anyone seen it in your hand?' 'I cannot read,' replied the fisherman. 'I have just found it and no one else has seen it.' The peasant was detained until the governor was sure that he could not read and that the plate had not been seen by anyone else. 'Off you go,' he said to him then, 'and count yourself lucky that you cannot read.'

In 1758, an old man of eighty-two, living in Périgueux, read Voltaire's book, found his account of the Iron Mask inaccurate and wrote off to an editor in Paris to set the record straight. The old man was Joseph de Lagrange-Chancel, a poet and playwright, who in the time of Louis XIV had been something of a prodigy at court, writing verse with ease when still a child and having his first tragedy performed when only eighteen. With the support of Racine[3] and the protection of the Princesse de Conti,[4] his reputation and fortune seemed well assured, but in 1717 he fell out of favour and in 1720 he took revenge by publishing an invective in verse against the Regent. He was arrested soon after and imprisoned on Sainte-Marguerite. Escaping after three years, he published another invective in Holland, but was pardoned after the Regent's death and allowed to return to France. However, he was received coldly by his former friends and retired to live out his life on his estate in Périgueux. The letter he wrote was addressed to Elie Fréron, the editor of a periodical called *L'Année Littéraire*, a man detested by Voltaire as someone who sought to build a reputation for himself by contriving to demolish the reputations of others. Lagrange-Chancel wrote his letter on 4 June 1758 and died that same year without seeing it in print. Fréron loaned it to someone soon after he received it and was unable to get it back and publish it until May 1759.

According to Lagrange-Chancel, Voltaire was misinformed on two important points: the Iron Mask had been arrested in 1669 not 1661, and Saint-Mars had been the governor of Sainte-Marguerite and in charge of the Iron Mask before taking him to the Bastille. Three witnesses supplied Lagrange-Chancel with further evidence and all three claimed to have got their information at first hand. The first was Charles de Lamotte-Guérin, the governor of Sainte-Marguerite, who had succeeded Saint-Mars in that post and had been a lieutenant on the prison staff of the island for at least six years before that. The second was Louis de Formanoir, a lieutenant commanding the prison guard, who was the nephew of Saint-Mars and had been a member of the garrison in the time the Iron Mask was there. The third was a certain Dubuisson, who had been an employee of the great financier Samuel Bernard[5] and had been imprisoned in the Bastille at the same time as the Iron Mask.

M. de Lamotte-Guérin, who had the command of those islands in the time that I was detained there, assured me . . . that M. de Saint-Mars, who obtained the governorship of these islands after that of Pignerol, showed great respect for this prisoner, that he always served him himself on dishes of silver and often provided him with clothes as rich as he might desire; that when he was ill or had need of a physician or surgeon he was obliged on pain of death not to appear in their presence except in his mask of iron, and when he was alone he could amuse himself by pulling out the hairs of his beard with tweezers of brilliantly polished steel. I saw a pair which he had used in this way in the hands of M. de Formanoir, nephew of Saint-Mars and lieutenant of a Free Company assigned to the guard of the prisoners. Several people told me that when Saint-Mars was leaving with his prisoner to take up the governorship of the Bastille the prisoner, who was wearing his iron mask, was heard to say to him, 'Does the King want my life?' 'No, my prince,' Saint-Mars replied, 'your life is safe. You have only to allow yourself to be led.' I learned more from a man named Dubuisson, cash-clerk of the famous Samuel Bernard, who after spending some years in the Bastille was transferred to Sainte-Marguerite. He was in a room with some other prisoners directly above the room occupied by this unknown man and by means of the chimney-flue they were able to communicate and exchange information. When they asked him why he refused to reveal his name and fortune, he replied that such a confession would cost him his life and the lives of those to whom he disclosed his secret.

In 1763 Voltaire came back to the subject in the sequel to his *Essai sur l'Histoire Générale*. He had received a letter from a certain Guillaume-Louis de Formanoir de Palteau of the Château de Palteau near Sens in Burgundy, claiming that the mysterious prisoner 'stayed in this château, that several people saw him get down from a litter, that he was wearing a black mask and that the event is still remembered in the district.' The credentials of this new informant were exceptional: he was the son and heir of the nephew and heir of Saint-Mars himself. When Saint-Mars died in 1708, his children were already dead. The property he had acquired during his lifetime went to the three sons of his sister, the youngest of whom, Louis de Formanoir, had been a lieutenant on Sainte-Marguerite when Lagrange-Chancel was there. The great house and estate of Palteau was inherited by the eldest of these nephews, Guillaume de Formanoir de Corbé, who like Louis had been a member of the prison staff serving under Saint-Mars. He had accompanied his uncle to the Bastille and had served as his lieutenant there, hoping to succeed him as governor. When on the death of Saint-Mars he was passed over in favour of someone else, he retired to Burgundy, married although already turned sixty, and left a son, born in 1712, to inherit the estate of Palteau along with its name. This son was Voltaire's informant. The letter itself Voltaire did not publish, but five years later, on 19 June 1768, Guillaume-Louis de Palteau wrote another letter on the same subject to Fréron, who published it immediately in his *L'Année Literaire*. In this letter Palteau made frequent mention of another member of the family who had served under Saint-Mars: an officer named Zachée de Blainvilliers, who was a cousin of Saint-Mars and by upbringing more like a younger brother. Saint-Mars, whose parents had both died when he was a child, had been raised by the father of Blainvilliers.

Since it appears that the Man in the Iron Mask continues to exercise the imaginations of our writers, I am going to inform you of what I know about this prisoner. On Sainte-Marguerite and at the Bastille he was known only by the name of 'Tower'. The governor and the other officers showed him the greatest respect: he was accorded all that a prisoner could be. He often took walks and always with a mask on his face. It is only since the publication of M. de Voltaire's *Siècle de Louis XIV* that I heard it said that the mask was made of iron and fitted with a spring mechanism: this circumstance was perhaps forgotten in the accounts I was told; but he only wore this mask when he went out to take the air or when he was obliged to appear before some stranger. M. de Blainvilliers, an infantry officer, who was a family friend of M. de

Saint-Mars, the governor of Sainte-Marguerite and afterwards of the Bastille, told me on several occasions that to satisfy his curiosity, which had been greatly aroused by the lot of 'Tower', he had taken the uniform and arms of a soldier on sentry duty in a gallery under the window of the room which the prisoner occupied while on Sainte-Marguerite and from there he had spied on him all through the night and had seen him very clearly. He said that he was not wearing his mask, that he was white-faced, tall and well-built, though somewhat thick in the lower part of the leg, and white-haired although he was still in the prime of life. He spent almost the whole of that night pacing about his room. Blainvilliers added that he was always dressed in brown, that he was given fine linen and books, that the governor and officers remained standing with their hats off in his presence until he allowed them to put their hats back on and sit down, and that they often went to keep him company and to eat with him.

In 1698, M. de Saint-Mars moved from the governorship of the island of Sainte-Marguerite to that of the Bastille. On his way to take up his new post, he stopped off with his prisoner at his estate of Palteau. The man with the mask arrived in a litter which preceded that of M. de Saint-Mars and they were accompanied by several men on horseback. The peasants went to greet their master. M. de Saint-Mars ate with his prisoner, whose back was turned to the dining-room windows which gave onto the courtyard. The peasants I have questioned could not see if he ate with his mask on, but they saw very well that M. de Saint-Mars, who was facing him at the table, had two pistols beside his plate. They had only one man-servant to wait on them, and the dishes were brought to an ante-chamber where he went to get them, being careful to close the door of the dining-room behind him. Whenever the prisoner crossed the courtyard he had the black mask on his face; the peasants noticed that his teeth and lips were visible and that he was tall with white hair. M. de Saint-Mars slept in a bed put up for him beside the bed of the man with the mask. M. de Blainvilliers told me that when he died, which was in 1704, he was buried secretly at Saint-Pauls and drugs were put into the coffin to consume the body. I never heard it said that he had any trace of a foreign accent.

This last remark was in reference to a story in the same connection which had been published earlier that year in the same periodical.

An English surgeon named Nelaton who used to go regularly to the Procope Coffee House, recounted on numerous occasions that during the time he was chief apprentice in a surgeon's shop at the Saint-Antoine gate, he was sent to bleed a prisoner in the Bastille. The governor took him into a room where there was a man who complained a great deal of pain in his head which was enveloped in a towel knotted behind his neck. He recognized from the man's accent that he was English.

The man responsible for this story was Poullain de Saint-Foix, a former cavalry officer who had established a literary reputation for himself with a string of fashionable plays. He was a much better duellist than he was a writer, but since he threatened to cut off the ears of anyone who criticized his work, his reputation was equally good in both.

Much later, in his *Essais Historiques sur Paris*, Saint-Foix offered two more pieces of information about the Iron Mask not previously published. The first referred to Palteau's report that, when the mysterious prisoner died, drugs were put into the coffin. 'These drugs were unnecessary,' Saint-Foix remarked, 'if the story is true that the day after the burial someone got the gravedigger to disinter the body so he could see it, and in place of the head they found a large stone.' Where he got this story from he didn't say, and no one dared to ask. Nor did he feel obliged to give the origin of his second revelation:

It is quite certain that Madame Le Bret, mother of the late M. Le Bret, the First President and Intendant of Provence, used to choose the finest linen and the most beautiful lace in Paris at the request of Madame de Saint-Mars, her close friend, and send it to her on Îsle Sainte-Marguerite for this prisoner, which confirms the account given by M. de Voltaire.

Still in 1769, however, the year Fréron published Palteau's letter, a book appeared in Liège which established beyond reasonable doubt the foundation in fact of all the wild rumours and reports. The book was *Traité des différentes sortes de preuves qui servent à établir la verité de l'histoire* and the author was Henri Griffet, a Jesuit who had been chaplain of the Bastille from 1745 until the Jesuit Order was banned from France in 1764. He was a man of impressive intelligence and learning even for a Jesuit, a teacher of humanities at the top Jesuit school in Paris when only seventeen and for some time Preacher in Ordinary to the King. He had already published a number of works on theology and history before his treatise appeared. The evidence he brought to light was documentary, drawn from a manuscript record of unquestionable validity which still exists and may be consulted today in the Bibliothèque de l'Arsenal in Paris: a personal journal of prison business kept by

Etienne Du Junca, King's Lieutenant and second in command at the Bastille from 1690 to 1706.

'Of all that has been said or written about this man in the mask,' Griffet wrote, 'nothing can be compared for certitude to the authority of this journal. It is an authentic piece of evidence; a man on the spot, an eye-witness, who reports what he has seen in a journal written entirely in his own hand where he noted down each day what was happening under his own eyes.' Du Junca dated all his entries and in the course of 1698 included the following memorandum:

> On Thursday 18 September at three o'clock in the afternoon M. de Saint-Mars, governor of the Château de la Bastille, arrived to take up his appointment coming from his governorship of the islands of Sainte-Marguerite and Honorat, having with him in his litter a longtime prisoner of his he had with him in Pignerol, whom he always keeps masked and whose name is not spoken. As soon as he got down from the litter, the prisoner was put into the First Room of the Basinière Tower to await nightfall, then at 9 p.m. he was moved by myself and M. de Rosarges, one of the sergeants brought by the governor, to the Third Room of the Bertaudière Tower which I had furnished some days before his arrival following instructions received from M. de Saint-Mars. The prisoner will be served and looked after by M. de Rosarges. The governor has charge of his upkeep.

No further news of the prisoner was given by Du Junca until five years later when he made the following entry:

> On the same day, Monday 19 November 1703, the unknown prisoner in the mask of black velvet who was brought here by the governor, M. de Saint-Mars, when he came from the island of Sainte-Marguerite, and has been in his charge for a long time, died at ten o'clock in the evening without suffering any serious illness, having felt just a little sick after mass the day before. Surprised by death he did not receive the sacraments, but M. Giraut, the chaplain, had heard his confession the day before and exhorted him a little before he died. This prisoner unknown, who had been in prison for such a long time, was buried on Tuesday 20 November at 4 p.m. in the cemetery of the parish church of Saint-Paul. On the mortuary register he was given a name of as little account as the names of M. de Rosarges, major, and M. Reil, surgeon, who witnessed the register.

In the margin of this note, Du Junca then added a postscriptum: 'I have since learned that on the register he was called M. de Marchiel and that 40 livres were paid for his burial.'

Griffet produced corroboration for Du Junca's account by quoting another document: the prisoner's burial certificate. 'On the 19th, Marchioly, aged forty-five years or thereabouts, died in the Bastille and his body was buried in the cemetery of the parish church of Saint-Paul on the 20th of this month in the presence of M. Rosage, major of the Bastille, and M. Reghle, surgeon-major of the Bastille, whose signatures follow. Rosarges. Reilhe.' Prison staff and parish priests were evidently not chosen for their prowess in orthography – 'Rosage, Rosarges; Reil, Reghle, Reilhe; Marchiel, Marchioly' – but, as Griffet pointed out, the name given to the prisoner for the burial register was pure invention anyway. It was standard practice to conceal the identity of even well-known prisoners in public records, so one may be quite sure that a false name and age were given for a prisoner so secret as to be a mystery even to the governor's second in command.

Du Junca never saw the prisoner's face, but he saw the mask he wore well enough to know that it was made not of iron but of black velvet. Nor did he notice anything exceptional in the form of the mask; no spring mechanism to move the jaw, presumably no jaw-piece at all, just a normal loo-mask which covered the brow, cheeks and nose. 'It is unlikely,' Griffet concluded, 'that he had to keep on his mask when he ate alone in his room, in the presence of Rosarges or the governor, who knew him perfectly. He was therefore obliged to wear it only when he crossed the courtyard of the Bastille to go to mass, so that he was not recognized by the guards, or when some official, who was not a party to the secret, had to be allowed into the room.'

Finally Griffet offered testimony gathered while he was himself employed in the Bastille. In 1745, when he was appointed prison chaplain, the governor was René de Launey, who had been a member of the prison staff since 1710. From him Griffet passed on more information, not previously published.

Memory of the masked prisoner was still strong among the officers, soldiers and servants of the Bastille when M. de Launey, who has long been governor, arrived there to take up a post on the general staff of the garrison, and those who had seen him in his mask, when he went by in the courtyard to go to mass, said that there had been an order after his death to burn everything that had been in his personal use, like linen, clothes, mattress, blankets, etc., that even the walls of the room where he had lodged were scraped and white-washed and that the floor-tiles were pulled up and new ones laid, so much was it feared that he might have found a means to hide some note or sign, the discovery of which could have revealed his name.

After Griffet's authoritative contribution nothing new, except the snippets of hearsay offered by Saint-Foix, was added to the evidence until 1780 when Jean-Pierre Papon published his *Voyage Littéraire de Provence*. Papon was a member of the Oratorian order and for many years the director of their library in Marseilles. His book was part of a much larger work, his *Histoire Générale de Provence*, which was published over a period of almost a decade with the last volume in 1786. In the course of his travels through Provence it was only natural that he should visit the island of Sainte-Marguerite in the Bay of Cannes and ask questions about 'the famous prisoner in the iron mask whose name perhaps will never be known.'

'On 2 February 1778, I had the curiosity to enter the room of this unfortunate prisoner. It was lit by only one window on the northern side, piercing a very thick wall and closed by three iron grilles placed at an equal distance apart. This window gives onto the sea.' Though Papon did not make the point himself, it was clearly impossible for Blainvilliers to have spied on the prisoner through this window, as Palteau had claimed. Apart from Lagrange-Chancel, Papon was the first investigator ever to visit the island, and the rest of his contribution came from people he met who claimed to have got their information from witnesses who were living when the mysterious prisoner was there. From them he learned how strict the security precautions surrounding the prisoner had been.

> One day as M. de Saint-Mars was in conversation with him, keeping outside the room in a kind of corridor so that he could see at a distance anyone who approached, the son of one his friends arrived and headed towards the place where he heard the noise. When the governor saw the young man, he closed the door of the room immediately, ran quickly to meet him and in a state of agitation asked him if he had overheard anything. As soon as he was assured that he had not, he sent him off that same day and wrote to his friend to say that this adventure had come so close to costing his son dearly that he was sending him home to avoid any further accident.

No one interviewed by Papon knew the story of the fisherman and the silver plate related by Voltaire. He was told that 'two sentries were posted at the two extremities of the fort facing the sea and they had orders to shoot on boats which approached within a certain distance,' which made Voltaire's story unlikely. There was, however, a new story to tell in place of the old.

I found in the citadel an officer of the Free Company who was seventy-nine years old. He told me that his father, who had served in the same company, had told him several times that one day a 'frater' – that is to say a barber – saw something white floating on the water under the window of the prisoner. He went to get it and took it to M. de Saint-Mars. It was a very fine shirt, carelessly rumpled up, and the prisoner had written upon it from one end to the other. When M. de Saint-Mars had smoothed it out and read a few lines, he asked the 'frater' in great consternation if he had been curious enough to read what it said. The 'frater' protested that he had read nothing, but two days later he was found dead in his bed. It was a story that the officer had heard told so many times by his father and by the chaplain of the fort at that time that he regarded it as incontestable.

Papon had one more tale to tell.

The following story seems to me equally certain, after all the evidence which I collected on the spot and in the monastery of Lérins[6] where the tradition is preserved. Someone of the opposite sex was sought to serve the prisoner and a woman of the village of Mougins[7] came to offer herself in the belief that this would be a way to make the fortune of her children. But she was told that she would have to renounce seeing them and anyone else in the world and she refused to be locked up with a prisoner, the knowledge of whom cost so dearly . . . The person who served the prisoner died on Sainte-Marguerite. The father of the officer of whom I was just speaking, who had been used as a trusted agent by Saint-Mars for certain matters, often told his son that he had gone to the prison at midnight to get the corpse and had carried it on his shoulders to the burial spot. He thought it was the prisoner himself who was dead; it was, as I have just said, the person who served him, and that was why a woman was sought to replace him.

Nine years after the publication of Papon's book, the Bastille fell to the people and from those who had read the various accounts of the masked prisoner published to that date, including the extracts from Du Junca's journal reproduced by Griffet, the sensational stories of finding a skeleton in an iron mask abandoned in some forgotten dungeon drew not the slightest attention. Their interest was riveted on the story that something else had *not* been found. In the great prison register, two hundred and fifty folio-sized pages in a locked portfolio of morocco leather, page 120 was missing, and that was the very page on which, according to the date recorded by Du Junca, the registration of the prisoner should have appeared. An official committee, set up to collect and examine all the papers of the Bastille, published their findings in instalments during 1789 and 1790. The best they were able to produce for the missing page was a separate record made in 1775 by the then major of the Bastille, a man called Godillon Chevalier, whose information could have been taken entirely from Griffet's book. Chevalier was quoted as saying that the original page had not been removed in any attempted cover-up. On the contrary, the page was missing precisely because of a government attempt to elucidate the affair. It had been in the prison files until 1775 when an official inquiry had been ordered into the existence and identity of the mysterious prisoner. The page had then become part of a special government dossier in which all records relative to the prisoner were gathered together. What had become of the dossier, however, no one knew, nor unfortunately could anyone find out.

1. *Marquis d'Argens*: Jean Baptiste de Boyer, 1704–1771. French writer who had a position of influence at the Prussian Court where Voltaire stayed from 1750 to 1753 while writing his *Siècle de Louis XIV*.
2. *François-Michel Le Tellier, Marquis de Louvois*, 1639–1691. Minister of War under Louis XIV from 1662 to 1691.
3. *Racine*: Jean, poet and dramatist, 1639–1699.
4. *Conti*: junior branch of the House of Condé which was itself a branch of the Royal House of Bourbon.
5. *Samuel Bernard*: Comte de Courbet, 1651–1739. French banker and financier through whom and from whom Louis XIV raised enormous loans.
6. *Monastery of Lérins*: on the island of Saint-Honorat.
7. *Mougins*: village close to Cannes.

CHAPTER THREE

FACES BEHIND THE MASK

The reasoning used by Voltaire to help his readers solve for themselves the mystery of the Iron Mask's identity consisted of two simple syllogisms. The first was that in 1661, when the mysterious prisoner was arrested, no one well-known disappeared and so therefore the prisoner was a man unknown. The second was that though he was unknown no one was allowed to see his face, and so therefore he looked like someone who was well-known. Voltaire carried his argument no further, but on the basis of this intelligence the reader was expected to have no difficulty in deducing the rest for himself. Since the prisoner's face was concealed with a mask, ordinary differences in styles of appearance and conditions of life were inadequate to counteract the resemblance, therefore he must have been the very double of the person he resembled. The only person sufficiently well-known to make such an absolute measure necessary was Louis XIV, and the only explanation for such a complete resemblance was that the prisoner and the King were identical twins. Amazing, but elementary.

The logic is impeccable, but the argument is specious. The first syllogism takes for both its premises suppositions which are unwarranted, and the second employs for one of its premises the conclusion of the first. It is untrue to say that in 1661 no one well-known disappeared. In fact someone very well-known was arrested in that year and not only disappeared from public life, but became soon after a prisoner of Saint-Mars at Pignerol.[1] However, and in any case, there are simply no grounds for the belief that the mysterious prisoner was arrested in 1661. Lagrange-Chancel gives at least some reason to believe that the arrest took place in 1669, and as it happens a veritable celebrity did actually and literally disappear at that time.[2] Voltaire's swift logic is without foundation; nor is that the only reason to suspect that he has misrepresented the facts. His argument leads to a theory which makes sense only if he was guilty of inventing his description of the prisoner to suit a public misconception about the appearance of the King.

To anyone reading contemporary descriptions of Louis XIV, the description of the Iron Mask, as being above average height with a good figure and a noble bearing, might seem to support Voltaire's hypothesis. All those who saw Louis XIV described him in those very terms, as for instance did the Venetian ambassador, Aloïse Grimani, who reported that he was of a 'tall build and majestic appearance.' The impression of tallness, however, was contrived: Louis XIV was a little man, very much below average height. He wore shoes with four-inch heels, a periwig, which added another six inches to the top of his head, and wherever he went, indoors or out, a high-crowned hat. His apparent height was something over six feet, but his actual height was only five feet two inches. The prisoner, we may presume, wore neither periwig nor high-heels and so if he looked tall the fact is that, unlike the King, he was tall. Identical twins, we may conclude, were never so unlike.

None of Voltaire's readers seemed to appreciate the significance of this, but most of those who were tempted to play armchair detective were in any event satisfied with a logic less than elementary. In their haste to give the prisoner a princely identity they did not even pause to appreciate the necessity to Voltaire's theory of a near-perfect resemblance. For them the mask could be explained by a much less striking resemblance, a likeness which was not even a full family-likeness, a similarity of feature due to the prisoner and the King being half-brothers by the same mother, Louis XIII's wife, Anne of Austria. In the second edition of *Questions sur l'Encyclopédie*, published in 1771, Voltaire's reference to the Iron Mask was developed along these lines in a long and laborious note inserted by the publisher:

> From the manner in which M. de Voltaire has recounted the matter, the publisher conjectures that this famous historian is just as convinced as he is of the suspicion he now intends to reveal, but that M. de Voltaire, as a Frenchman, did not wish to say it openly, especially since he had said enough to ensure that the clue to the puzzle would not be difficult to find. Here then is my interpretation: the Iron Mask was doubtless a brother, and an elder brother, of Louis XIV, whose mother had that taste for fine linen referred to by M. de Voltaire. While reading contemporary memoirs which record this characteristic of the Queen, I remembered that the Iron Mask had the same taste and became convinced that he was her son, something which already seemed

likely in the light of all the other circumstances.

It is well known that for a long time Louis XIII had not lived with the Queen, and that the birth of Louis XIV was due to a happy chance cleverly exploited, a chance which compelled the King to sleep in the same bed as the Queen. Here then is how I believe things took place. The Queen imagined that it was her fault that an heir to Louis XIII had not been born. The birth of the Iron Mask undeceived her. The Cardinal, to whom she confided the secret, knew more than one way of profiting from it. He contrived to turn the event to his own benefit and the advantage of the State. Convinced from what had happened that the Queen could bear children to the King, he arranged the situation which produced the chance of a single bed for the King and the Queen.

The Queen and the Cardinal, equally aware of the necessity of hiding from Louis XIII the existence of the Iron Mask, had him raised in secret. It was a secret from Louis XIV until the death of Cardinal Mazarin and then he learned that he had a brother, an elder brother whom his mother could not disown and who more-over bore features which in a noticeable way declared his origin. Reflecting then that this child, born in wedlock, could not without embarrassment and scandal be declared illegitimate after the death of Louis XIII, Louis XIV judged that he could not use a wiser and more just method to assure his own security and the tranquillity of the State than the one which he employed. It was a method which spared him from committing a cruelty which a monarch less principled and magnanimous than Louis XIV would have con-sidered a political necessity.

It has often been suggested that Voltaire himself is the real author of this note, that he used the publisher as a front to print his own final and conclusive revelation, but the note is so blurred and confused, so padded out with banality and repetition, that it is difficult to imagine how anyone could take such a suggestion seriously. Cleared of coyness and claptrap, the theory is simple enough: Louis XIV's mother, unable to conceive a child by her husband, imagined herself to be sterile. When she and her husband stopped living together she took a lover and one day to her surprise and alarm she found herself to be pregnant. This child, born and raised in secret, became the Iron Mask. Louis XIV was born later, after the Queen arranged to have the King spend one night in her bed.

The publisher's vague references to 'the Cardinal' appear to be a deliberate equivocation designed to cover confusion and uncertainty as to who the Cardinal in question was. At first sight it seems that

Rex.   *Ludovicus.*

Louis XIV's apparent height was something over 6ft, but his actual height was only 5ft 2in. Cartoon by W. M. Thackeray in *Notes sur Paris* reproduced in *Marly-le-roi* by Piton. (*Photograph Bibliothèque Nationale*)

Ludovicus rex.

Cardinal Mazarin is referred to since he is the only one mentioned by name. Mazarin was Prime Minister from 1642 to 1661 and the Queen's devoted ally; there is even reason to believe that sometime after the death of Louis XIII in 1643 he became the Queen's husband by morganatic marriage. That he would have protected her if she had turned to him for help is credible, but he was not at that time in a position to do so. If the Iron Mask was older than Louis XIV, then his birth was prior to 1638 and the Cardinal trusted by the Queen would then have to be Cardinal de Richelieu, who was Prime Minister before Mazarin from 1624 until 1642. Richelieu, however, was the Queen's implacable enemy and exploited every opportunity possible to set the King against her. It is difficult to imagine that the Queen would have confided to him so perilous a secret.

To give the publisher his due, however, the basic theory he proposes is not altogether without interest. It is perfectly true that when Louis XIV's parents brought him into the world they had been married for twenty-three years without producing a child, that for many years they had been living separately in mutual distrust, and that this conception had been the consequence of a deliberate plan to have the King spend just one night in the same bed as the Queen. In August 1637, she had been found guilty of treasonable correspondence with Spain and had been placed under house arrest at the Louvre. By that time she had already been estranged from her husband for more than ten years and the King certainly had no wish to share her bed ever again. On the night of 5 December 1637, so the story goes, the King was caught in a storm in the centre of Paris and was unable to reach his own bed, which had been prepared for him at the Condé estate of Saint-Maur, south-east of Vincennes. According to the custom of the time, his household staff, along with his bed and furniture, food and kitchen, went ahead of him each day to prepare his supper and lodging wherever it was that he planned to spend the night. Cut off from them, he literally had no bed to sleep in, and so was persuaded by Guitaut, the Captain of the Queen's Guard, to spend the night at the Louvre. As a consequence, the King and Queen ate together and, since there was no other royal bed available except the Queen's, slept together as well.

News of the event spread quickly through the city and the following morning, after the King's departure, the Queen was informed by the Superior of the Franciscan Order in Paris that one of his fellow friars had received word from heaven that a Dauphin had been conceived. He was right: nine months later to the very day, the Queen bore a son, the future Louis XIV. The newborn baby was wonderfully large and well-developed, with two teeth already fully grown, and were it not for the fact that everyone knew the Queen had just given birth to him, one would have thought he was at least three months old. Such being the marvel of Louis XIV's conception and birth, there is clearly room for conjecture on more than one score.

Louis XIII was not happy with women; he feared and distrusted them and his Queen, Anne of Austria, was not the kind of woman to help him overcome his difficulty. He was cold by nature and unsure of himself, a neurotic and chronic invalid, suspicious, prudish, repressed and morose. She, by contrast, was hot-blooded and self-possessed, coquettish and wilful. She was, moreover, Spanish and his lifelong fear and detestation of the Spanish bordered on paranoia. When they were married in 1615, they were both only fourteen years of age. The Queen Mother put them to bed together on the wedding-night, but thereafter no amount of persuasion could induce the young King to share his wife's bed again until four years later when against his will and in spite of his tears, he was literally picked up and carried to her bedroom. Despite their incompatibility they then managed to live as man and wife, but the King only out of a sense of duty to beget a son and heir. In March 1622, the Queen was said to have had a miscarriage when she was six weeks pregnant, but not everyone was prepared to believe it, and the King's obedient submission to the functions of procreator was otherwise without fruit. For many it was not without significance that the King continued into his middle twenties with no sign of a beard, being given his first shave, and that for form rather than necessity, only on 1 August 1624 when he was twenty-three years old. Hope for a son and heir grew dim and the relationship, such as it was, disintegrated gradually until in 1625 whatever sense of conjugal obligation remained in the King was shattered by his wife's scandalous behaviour with the Duke of Buckingham.

Buckingham had been sent by Charles I of England to escort his future queen, Henrietta of France, the sister of Louis XIII, to London. Darling of fortune, favourite of kings, idol of society, Buckingham outshone all the most brilliant stars of the courts of Europe. He had youth, beauty and charm along with fame, wealth and power, an irresistible combination which at first sight dazzled eyes to his arrogance and flippancy, his aggressiveness and conceit. He was an accomplished courtier, an exciting and romantic personality, but as a statesman, diplomat and commander he was brash, self-seeking and incompetent. He arrived in Paris on 24 May 1625 with a retinue worthy of a king and overwhelmed the French nobility with the kind of splendour and refinement they admired as characteristic of themselves: provocative, extravagant, exquisite. His appearances at court were a sensation, his clothes dripping with pearls and diamonds which broke off and fell as he moved, scattering beneath the feet of his admirers.

Anne of Austria, twenty-three years old and her marriage already cold, was as fascinated by him as were her ladies-in-waiting, and Buckingham, sensing a personal triumph, played gallant to her with a total disregard for propriety.

On 2 June, Henrietta of France, escorted by Buckingham and his party, left Paris for Boulogne, and the Court, including Anne of Austria and the Queen Mother[3] but not the King, accompanied them as far as Amiens. There one evening while walking in the garden of the house where Anne was staying, Buckingham lured her away from the company and seized her in his arms. At what stage her cry brought their companions rushing to the scene is not certain. However, her servants and attendants maintained that she could not have been held in Buckingham's passionate embrace long enough to substantiate the story, told later by Cardinal de Retz, that the next morning she commissioned her friend the Duchesse de Chevreuse 'to ask Buckingham if he was quite sure she was not in danger of being pregnant.'

Two days later, Henrietta's party continued their journey to Boulogne alone, with farewells at the gates of Amiens. Buckingham, with his head in Anne's carriage, screened by the curtains, wept disconsolately and she was deeply affected. At Boulogne, contrary winds delayed Henrietta's departure and under the pretext of carrying a letter to the Queen Mother, Buckingham dashed back to Amiens to see Anne again. She had been so upset by the leave-taking that she was unwell and in bed surrounded by her ladies. Buckingham burst into her bedroom and threw himself down at her bedside, kissing the sheets and proclaiming his love in loud and reckless abandon. The Queen was flattered, the Court stupefied, the King outraged, and Buckingham was warned never to set foot in France again.

Whatever doubts Louis XIII might have had about his wife's disloyalty, they were reinforced the following year when the 'Chalais Conspiracy' was uncovered. The ringleader was Anne's closest friend the Duchesse de Chevreuse. She had persuaded the Comte de Chalais, who was her lover, to join in a plot to assassinate Cardinal de Richelieu. The King's brother, Gaston, was found to have played a leading rôle in the conspiracy too. The accusation was made that with Richelieu out of the way the King was to be deposed and his marriage annulled so that Gaston could take his place on the throne and Anne could become Gaston's wife. When questioned about this by Richelieu in front of the King and the Queen Mother, Anne denied any knowledge of the plan and sought to argue her innocence with the remark that 'she would have had too little to gain in the exchange.'

The coup was to have been carried through on the wave of a French

Protestant uprising backed by English troops promised by Buckingham and when in the following year French government troops were sent against the Protestant stronghold of La Rochelle, Buckingham sailed to its defence with a force of 8,000 men. His expedition was a disaster but, though forced to withdraw, he planned to return. In England, however, his star had waned. An attempt by Parliament to impeach him had been blocked by Charles I, but he was universally detested for his perpetual profiteering and endless bungling. On 23 August 1628, while with the fleet in Portsmouth supervising preparations for a second expedition, he was assassinated by one of his own officers. When the news reached Anne of Austria, she was stunned and incredulous. 'It's a lie,' she is reported to have exclaimed. 'I've only just received a letter from him.'

With Anne of Austria's honour called so evidently into question, the number of Iron Masks proliferating from her sullied reputation, whether as illegitimate progeny or as illicit progenitors, is legion. For those who claim that the Iron Mask was an illegitimate brother of Louis XIV, Buckingham is the favourite candidate for father and, since the only direct contact he ever had with the Queen was limited to the last week of May and the first week of June 1625, the birth date of this Iron Mask is established as the beginning of March 1626.[4] A popular alternative to Buckingham is Mazarin: 'You will like him Madame,' Richelieu is supposed to have said when presenting Mazarin to the Queen. 'He looks like Buckingham.' The champions of these theories do not explain how it was possible for the Queen to conceal a pregnancy throughout its full course and bear a child in secret, but it is a fact that at one time she did manage, for a while at least, to keep a pregnancy hidden.

At the beginning of 1631, she was taken ill with what has since been established was a miscarriage. The fact that she kept that pregnancy secret has allowed the conjecture that it was not her husband's child and that after some hesitation she underwent an abortion. If in fact the King was the father of this child he gave no sign of being so either by mark of tenderness before the pregnancy or show of disappointment after the miscarriage. Those who propose that the King was not the father place the date of this conception to a time in September 1630, known later as the Day of the Dupes, when the King was so ill that everyone assumed he would die. Since at that date he had no son and heir, the crown would have passed to his brother Gaston, and in anticipation of this the Queen Mother made the mistake of ordering Richelieu's arrest. At that same time, so the theory goes, the Queen also did some anticipating: she sought to preserve her position as Queen by becoming pregnant. Who it was she employed to impregnate her on command is not specified, but whoever he was he too has won a place among the candidates for the Iron Mask.

Another variation on the same theme makes the Iron Mask the father of Louis XIV himself. Already in the seventeenth century it was rumoured that Louis XIII was impotent and that to furnish him with an heir his wife had to resort to a lover. Louis XIV, to his enemies, was always 'the Great Bastard'. An example of this belief is the anonymous libel entitled *Les Amours d'Anne d'Autriche avec C.D.R.*, published at Cologne in 1692. That version goes as follows: since Louis XIII is unable to have children, his brother Gaston, who is a widower with just one daughter for heir, is sure to succeed to the throne. Cardinal Richelieu, with an eye to the main chance, proposes his niece to Gaston in marriage, hoping thus to provide Gaston with a son and himself with a grand-nephew who would one day be king. Gaston rejects the offer and in the resulting quarrel strikes him. Richelieu, angry, humiliated and afraid, looks about for an alternative. Anne of Austria meanwhile has fallen in love with a young foreigner, whose name is given only as C.D.R., and Richelieu has the clever idea of arranging to get this young man into her bed so that she will conceive a child and cut Gaston out of the succession. His plan works perfectly and the fruit of this union is Louis XIV. The book sold well and, to the fury of the French government, was published again in 1693 and 1696. A sequel was promised in which the author was to relate the 'fatal catastrophe' which overtook C.D.R. in consequence, but it never appeared. Fifty years later it was suggested that this 'fatal catastrophe' was an iron mask and life-imprisonment.

As recently as 1934 this same ground was reworked by Pierre Vernadeau in his book *Le Médecin de la Reyne*, and made to yield yet another candidate for the Iron Mask. The account he gives is derived from two separate sources in the Limousin region of France: one a tale passed on by generations of the medical profession in Limoges, the other a local tradition relating to the village of Saint-Léonard, fourteen miles east of Limoges. The church of this village, also called Saint-Léonard, was the centre of an ancient fertility cult still popular in the seventeenth century: pregnant women prayed to the relics of Saint Léonard for a safe and easy delivery, while women who wished to be pregnant addressed their prayers to a curious object known as 'the bolt of Saint Léonard'.

It is known for certain that in May 1638 the relics of Saint Léonard were taken to the Queen in Paris to assure the birth of her child, but the people of Limousin claim that the bolt of the saint was also taken to her some months before that to ensure the child's conception. The saint's aid in the act of fecundation was not officially acknowledged because the miraculous nature of the operation might have been questioned. Though people of faith would have attributed the longed-for conception to the power of Saint Léonard, there were sceptics who might have entertained the view that the success of the bolt was due to the potency of a not dissimilar object belonging to the young man who invariably accompanied it, in this instance a certain Nicard, known to his fellow countrymen as 'Beautiful Legs'.

Apparently Beautiful Legs also accompanied the relics of the saint to Paris in May and presumably went there again to collect them sometime after the Queen was delivered of her child in September. That he had the wonder-working bolt with him then as well and remained in Paris at the Queen's disposal until early the following year is thought more than likely since miraculously, just three months after the birth of her first child, the Queen conceived a second. Beautiful Legs was not, however, the Iron Mask, at least the people of Limousin do not make that claim. According to a Docteur Boulland of Limoges, who got his information from a Docteur Mazard, founder of the Limoges School of Medecine, the Iron Mask was nonetheless a man from Limousin, imprisoned for possessing the forbidden knowledge that Louis XIV was not the son of Louis XIII.

The Queen's physician referred to in the title of Vernadeau's book was a certain Pardoux Gondinet who was born and raised in the village of Saint-Yrieix twenty-five miles south of Limoges, studied medecine at Bordeaux University and took up practice in Paris. He was appointed physician to Anne of Austria on 5 November 1644 and after her death in 1666 returned to Saint-Yrieix, where he continued to practice with the title of 'physician to the late Queen' until his own death in 1679. In the following year, on 14 December 1680, his son-in-law Marc de Jarrigue de La Morelhie also died, or at least that is what the official records show; in fact tradition has it that he was kidnapped by the French secret police, was imprisoned in the fortress of Pignerol, and died in the Bastille twenty-three years later, masked and anonymous. While sorting through the private papers of his late father-in-law, Morelhie had come across the report of an autopsy carried out upon the body of Louis XIII, in which appeared clear proof that the King had been incapable of reproduction: the corpse had been found to have the testicles of a child. Unable to keep the evidence to himself, Morelhie foolishly confided the secret to his fellow-countryman, Nicolas de La Reynie who though his friend was also the King's Lieutenant-General of Police. La Reynie informed Louvois, the Minister of War, who informed the King, and the result was that both Morelhie and the autopsy report were made to disappear in double quick time. How it had been possible for Gondinet to come into

Louis XIV, who ordered the arrest and imprisonment of the Iron Mask. Artist unknown. (*Photograph Bibliothèque Nationale*)

possession of this fateful report is not very clear. As Vernadeau heard the story, Gondinet had actually participated in the autopsy, but that is hardly likely. He was after all physician to the Queen, not the King, and in any event was not appointed to that position until the year after Louis XIII's death.[5]

One other theory which relates directly to Louis XIV's own birth was a claim put about at the end of the eighteenth century as propaganda for the House of Orléans, the junior branch of the Royal House of Bourbon. According to this, the Iron Mask was a woman. Inspiration for the idea probably came from one of Voltaire's informants, a certain Madame Cathérine Cessis of Cannes, who in 1759, when she 'was close on one hundred years old', maintained that she had been allowed to meet the Iron Mask just before his departure for the Bastille. She claimed that he had removed a glove to take her hand and that she had recognized at once from the smoothness and softness of his skin that in fact he was a woman. Las Cases gives an account of the theory in his report of the conversation with Napoleon already mentioned. 'It was supposed that Anne of Austria, pregnant after twenty-three years of sterility, gave birth to a daughter, and the fear that she might not have another child led Louis XIII to remove this daughter and fraudently substitute for her a boy who later became Louis XIV.' Thus the Iron Mask was revealed to be a tender maiden disguised as a man and the mask became a necessity to hide the napless delicacy of her cheek and chin. There were convents aplenty where this hypothetical daughter could have been safely hidden away, but her parents, the King and Queen, preferred to hand her over to prison guards and turnkeys. The point of the story as put about in Paris was political, however, not romantic, as Las Cases went on to explain. 'The year after, the Queen gave birth again, this time to a boy, Philippe,[6] the head of the House of Orléans. Thus he and his offspring were the legitimate heirs, while Louis XIV and his offspring were nothing more than intruders and usurpers.' In the events which led up to the Revolution, the then Duc d'Orléans[7] sided with the people against the old regime and voted for the execution of Louis XVI, but his popularity, while it lasted, had nothing to do with any claim he might have had to the throne. 'A pamphlet on the subject,' Las Cases concluded, 'was circulating in the provinces at the time of the fall of the Bastille, but the story was not successful and died out without ever catching on in the capital.' Nevertheless the story was still going the rounds as late as 1895, when it was reported in the press that a former mayor of Cannes by the name of Mero had disclosed to a friend that one of his ancestors of the same name had served as doctor to the Iron Mask during his imprisonment on Sainte-Marguerite; he too had claimed that the prisoner was a woman.

The fall of the Bastille led to innumerable revelations and disclosures relevant to the Iron Mask. Soon after the supposed discovery of a mouldering skeleton in a rusted vizor, a journalist published a story about the discovery of a document hidden in a wall. He claimed that in late July 1789, when the Bastille was given over to sightseers and demolition workers, a Venetian tourist hunting for souvenirs was approached by a mason who wanted to sell an old piece of paper covered in writing. He had found it, he said, hidden in the wall of the Third Chamber of the Bertaudière Tower, the very room where the Iron Mask had been lodged on his arrival at the Bastille in September 1698. The mason wanted 3 livres for the paper, but the message it contained made it cheap at the price. The prisoner who had written it was one of Louis XIV's own sons, the Comte de Vermandois, who by all accounts had never been a prisoner at any time, and he had written it in 1701 when officially he had been dead for eighteen years. The journalist made no attempt to produce the tourist or the document, but the supposed text he reproduced in full:

> In the name of the Holy Virgin, protecting Saint of all the French, in my despair. May God concede, at her intercession, that one day all mankind is made to know the dreadful fate, kept secret from the world, to which the orders of a barbarous father have unjustly condemned me. I am Louis de Bourbon, Comte de Vermandois, Grand Admiral of France. As punishment for a rash and foolish act I was imprisoned in Pignerol Castle and after that on the island of Sainte-Marguerite and finally in the Bastille, where I will probably finish the course of my sad life. I have already tried several times to make it known that I am still alive but always in vain and so I write this note and hide it in a hole in the wall of my chamber hoping that some turn of fate will make it known to men. I have written and hidden this paper on my birthday, 2 October 1701, at six o'clock in the evening. They are going to make me move rooms and thus may Heaven grant that my prayers will be answered. Signed: Louis de Bourbon, Comte de Vermandois, the most miserable and the most innocent of men.

As candidate for the Iron Mask, Vermandois was not new. On the contrary he had been one of the first contenders, proposed by an anonymous writer as early as 1745, six years before Voltaire's first published reference, and his case had been championed thereafter by Henri Griffet, the man who brought Du Junca's journal to light. The tragically short life of Vermandois, as it is officially recorded, is quickly told.

He was born on 2 October 1667, the natural son of Louis XIV and

Louise de La Vallière, their fifth love-child and their last. The love in which he was conceived died before he was born, and while he was still a small child his parents turned away from each other and from him, his father drawn to another woman and the children of her love, his mother to God and the isolation of a Carmelite convent. He and a sister, the only ones of the five children to survive infancy, were well provided for nonetheless. Acknowledged and proclaimed legitimate by their father, they were raised in the home of Colbert, the Controller of Finance, and given status and position at court: at the age of two, Vermandois was named Grand Admiral of France and at the age of thirteen, his sister was married to the Prince de Conti. They were, by all reliable accounts, as good-looking and good-hearted as their mother, and they were well-liked at court in spite of the active hostility of the new favourite, Athénais de Montespan,[8] who saw them as rivals to the fortunes of her own children.

At the beginning of November 1683, soon after his sixteenth birthday, Vermandois was sent to join the army in Flanders and took part in the opening skirmishes of the siege of Courtrai. Only after he had distinguished himself in the battle line was it realized that he had been hiding a fever and was in fact very ill. On 4 November the King was informed of his son's condition and sent orders that he be brought home immediately. The boy, however, was too ill to move. On 8 November he was bled and seemed to recover, but on 12 November his condition worsened and on 16 November he received the last sacraments. Throughout his illness the King received daily reports from the commanding officer, who was present on the night of 18 November when the young man died. The body was transferred in solemn procession to Arras on 24 November and on 27 November was interred with doleful pomp in the cathedral choir. The King then made an endowment of 10,000 livres to the cathedral chapter so that a requiem mass would be said every day for a year and a mass of remembrance on 18 November each year in perpetuity.

The unofficial version, offered by the anonymous writer in 1745, appeared in a book entitled *Mémoires secrets pour servir à l'Histoire de Perse*, which presented events at the French Court under the guise of Persian history. A simple key to the fictitious Persian names, published with the third edition in 1759, left no doubt as to the real significance of what was described. The Persian king, 'Cha-Abas', was Louis XIV; the 'Indian maiden' was Louise de La Vallière; their son, 'Giafer', was Vermandois; the King's son and heir, 'Sephir Mirza', was the Dauphin;[9] the place named 'Feldran' was Flanders; the 'Island of Ormuz' was the island of Sainte-Marguerite; and the citadel of 'Ispahan' was the Bastille.

This prince was passionately fond of women and had several favourites, one of the first of whom was an Indian who though plain was tall and shapely and blessed with a heart and mind to compensate for her lack of beauty. Her heart was full of that delicate tenderness which constitutes the magic of love and is perhaps the most important quality in a woman. Cha-Abas loved her beyond all measure and had a son by her whom he called Giafer. This young prince was raised with the greatest possible care; he was handsome, well-built and quick-witted, but arrogant and hot-tempered. To Sephir Mirza, the heir to the crown and the only son recognized by Cha-Abas, Giafer could not bring himself to show the respect due to a prince born to be his king.

These two princes, who were about the same age, had very different characters. Sephir Mirza had all the agreeable qualities Giafer had, but by the gentleness, affability and generosity of his disposition altogether surpassed him. It was these virtues, as admirable as they are rare in a prince born to succeed to the throne, which made Sephir Mirza the object of Giafer's enmity, and the reason why he lost no opportunity to declare how much he pitied the Persians, destined as they were to be ruled one day by a prince who lacked character and the strength to command. Cha-Abas was aware of Giafer's conduct and conscious of the impropriety of it, but his royal authority yielded to his paternal love and, absolute monarch though he was, he could not assert his will upon this son who abused his love.

At last one day Giafer forgot himself so far as to strike Prince Sephir Mirza. Cha-Abas, informed at once, feared for the guilty young man, but, whatever desire he might have had to pretend ignorance of the offence, the respect he owed to himself and to his crown and the commotion caused by the affair at court made it impossible for him to heed the promptings of his heart. With great reluctance he summoned his closest counsellors, explained to them his painful problem and asked their advice. All agreed, considering the enormity of the crime and conforming to the laws of the state, that the penalty was death. What a blow for a doting father!

One of the ministers, more aware than the others of the suffering of Cha-Abas, told him that there was a way of punishing Giafer without taking his life: that he should be sent at once to the army, which at that time was on the frontiers of Feldran, and soon after his arrival it should be put about that he had contracted plague, thus to frighten and keep away anyone who might otherwise wish to see him; that after a few days of his pretended illness he should be said to be dead and then while the whole army witnessed his burial, with funeral honours worthy of his birth, he should be moved by night with the utmost secrecy to the citadel on the Island of Ormuz, there to live out his days. This proposal was well-received by everyone and especially by the unhappy Cha-Abas.

People of loyalty and discretion were chosen to carry out the scheme and Giafer left for the army with a magnificent retinue. Everything went off as planned; while the death of the unfortunate prince was mourned throughout the camp, he was taken by unfrequented roads to the Island of Ormuz and handed over to the governor there, who had received prior orders from Cha-Abas not to let his prisoner be seen by anyone.

One sole servant, who was party to the secret, was taken along with the prince, but he died on the journey. The officers in charge disfigured his face with knife-slashes to stop him being recognized and, having stripped him as a further precaution, left him stretched out beside the road and continued on their way.

The governor of the citadel of Ormuz treated his prisoner with the greatest respect: he personally served him at table, carrying the dishes from the door of the apartment where they were brought by the cooks, none of whom ever saw Giafer's face. One day the prince contrived to scratch his name with the point of a knife on the back of a plate. A slave who found the plate thought to curry favour by taking it to the governor, imagining that he would be rewarded for his trouble, but the poor man was mistaken: he lost his life on the spot and the secret which was of such great importance was buried with him. A useless precaution since, as is demonstrated by this account, the secret was badly kept . . .

Giafer stayed several years in the citadel of Ormuz and was only made to leave it to go to Ispahan, when Cha-Abas, in recognition of the governor's faithful service, gave him the then vacant governorship of that citadel. It was in effect a prudent measure to make Giafer follow the destiny of the man to whom he had first been confided. It would have been acting against the laws of good sense to enlist a new confidant who might have proved less loyal and less conscientious.

Both at Ormuz and Ispahan the precaution was taken to put a mask on the prince whenever, because of sickness or some other circumstance, it was necessary to let him be seen. Several reliable witnesses maintained that they saw this masked prisoner more than once, and they reported that he addressed the governor with easy familiarity, although he by contrast was always most respectful.

If one wonders why, having outlived Cha-Abas and Sephir Mirza by so many years, Giafer was not set free as would have been proper, one should remember that it was not possible to re-establish him in his original condition, rank and dignity. His tomb existed and there were not only witnesses but written records of his burial, the authenticity of which could not be destroyed in the minds of the people, who to this day are still persuaded that Giafer died of plague in the army camp of Feldran.

It should be noted at once that as an account of what happened to Vermandois, this story rests upon a number of important misrepresentations of fact. Never was it said that Vermandois had contracted plague and at no time was it even suggested that his illness was contagious. Nor was there ever any commotion at court over a quarrel of any kind involving Vermandois and the Dauphin. Had there been so much as a rumour that Vermandois had struck the Dauphin it would have been mentioned by someone at the time, but nowhere in all the recorded gossip of the period is there any trace of such an incident. In a letter written on 6 June 1700, the Princess Palatine referred to a story published in German that a son of James II of England had once given the Dauphin a box on the ear and about that she declared: 'There is not a word of truth in it.' If anyone else had ever boxed the Dauphin's ear she would surely have known and would certainly have said so. There is moreover no evidence for the belief that Vermandois disliked the Dauphin or lacked proper respect for him, and the fact that the sister of Vermandois was always one of the Dauphin's closest friends makes it unlikely that there was ever any enmity between them. One might add furthermore that the Dauphin was a less agreeable person and Vermandois a more agreeable person than their respective representations in Persian dress, that the Dauphin was six years older than Vermandois and that so far as Vermandois was concerned Louis XIV was never a doting father.

Henri Griffet was nonetheless convinced that the tale of Giafer was the true story of Vermandois and the solution to the mystery of the Iron Mask. To support his opinion he had little real evidence to offer, but a passage he found in the *Mémoires* of the Grande Mademoiselle,[10] who was first cousin to Louis XIV, did at least establish as fact the claim that Vermandois had done something serious enough to be in disgrace shortly before his departure for the army:

Some days previously, news came that the army, which so far that year had done nothing, had laid siege to Courtrai. M. de

VERMANDOIS

Vermandois, first proposed as candidate for the Iron Mask in 1745. After a painting by Mignard. (*Photograph Bibliothèque Nationale*)

Vermandois left to go there and M. de Lauzun[11] left Paris for the same destination. M. de Vermandois had only recently returned to court. The King had not been pleased with his conduct – he had taken part in orgies – and had banished him from his sight. He stayed on at Versailles but without seeing anyone, only going to the academy and in the morning to mass. The King did not like the company he had been keeping. One did not know the details and one did not wish to know. It caused Madame de La Vallière a great deal of pain. He was given a good talking to and he made a full confession, so it was supposed he would behave himself.

Unquestionably, Vermandois had been in disgrace, but the punishment described is perfectly consistent with the kind of discipline any sensible parent might decide necessary for an adolescent in danger of being led astray by bad company. There is certainly no suggestion of a crime serious enough to merit the fate of the Iron Mask, and one can be sure that the young man's disgrace was represented in the worst possible light by the Grande Mademoiselle. Besides being a frustrated old maid and a malicious gossip, she was a fervent supporter of the Montespan faction, and Vermandois was the pet aversion of Madame de Montespan. As the older half-brother of her sons, the Duc de Maine and the Comte de Toulouse, she considered him to be their chief rival in the affection and favour of the King, and so missed no opportunity to defame him. What the Grande Mademoiselle had to say about the tragic death of Vermandois makes it clear that, if he had ever been guilty of anything more serious than ordinary adolescent misbehaviour, she would have recorded it: 'Madame de Montespan sent me a letter. She said that M. de Vermandois was dead and that the King had given his charge of admiral to the Comte de Toulouse. He had fallen sick at the siege of Courtrai after drinking too much brandy. People said that he showed great courage and they talked about his character and conduct as people do about someone they like. As for me I was not at all upset. I was only too pleased that M. de Maine no longer had a brother to take precedence over him.'

What Griffet lacked in evidence for his advocacy of Vermandois as the Iron Mask, he made up for in ingenuity. He proposed that 'Marchioli', the name used on the Iron Mask's burial certificate, which he read as 'Marchiali', was an anagram of 'hic amiral' (i.e. 'in this space the admiral') and thus denoted Vermandois as Grand Admiral of France. Of all the Iron Mask theories of the eighteenth century, Griffet's was the most popular, and the conviction that Vermandois had died wearing a mask in the Bastille became so entrenched and widespread that in 1786, just three years before the pretended discovery of the letter hidden in the wall, Louis XVI ordered the opening of the tomb in Arras Cathedral. This was done in the presence of the Bishop of Arras and the Attorney-General who together signed an official report testifying to the discovery of 'a body complete and well-formed'. Arguably, of course, it was not the body of Vermandois, but an extra body posed unlimited problems for the argument.[12]

1. Nicolas Fouquet was arrested and imprisoned 5 September 1661.
2. The Duc de Beaufort disappeared at the seige of Candy 25 June 1669.
3. *Queen Mother*: Marie de'Medici, 1574–1642, wife of Henri IV and mother of Louis XIII.
4. In a book entitled *Les Grandes Heures des Iles de Lérins* published in 1975, Jean-Jacques Antier reproduced in a French translation the text of a letter supposedly written by Benjamin Franklin to Sir James Jay on 28 November 1782. In this Franklin reported how he had talked with the Duc de Richelieu the day before on the subject of the Iron Mask and Richelieu had told him that the Iron Mask was the illegitimate child of Anne of Austria and the Duke of Buckingham. According to Monsieur Antier, this letter was found in a collection of previously unpublished letters printed in Baltimore in 1863. When asked about this letter, the librarians of the Benjamin Franklin Collection at the Yale University Library could find no record in their archives of any such letter written to Sir James Jay on the date given, nor of such a letter written to anyone on any date, and no trace of a book containing any kind of letter by Franklin published in Baltimore or elsewhere in 1863. Significantly enough, however, they did find a letter written by Franklin to Sir James Jay on 28 November 1782 though in that he spoke about some matter involving a certain Captain Francis Dundas and made absolutely no mention of Richelieu or the Iron Mask. When Monsieur Antier himself was asked about the letter which he had reproduced in his book, he could not remember where he had found it, neither the text nor the references he had given for it. While it seems unlikely that Franklin would have written two letters to Sir James Jay on the same day without making some reference to the first, however brief, in the second, it is nonetheless perfectly possible that a man like the Duc de Richelieu would have been capable of telling such a story about the Iron Mask. However, there would be no more reason to believe his story true than there is to believe Monsieur Antier's letter real.
5. Curiously enough Saint Léonard was the patron saint of prisoners as well as of hopeful and expectant mothers. It was believed that all prisoners who invoked his name were delivered from their chains and enabled to go free while their guards stood by powerless to stop them. His churches were often hung with broken chains left by escaped prisoners as proof of his miraculous intervention. There is however no tradition that he intervened in the case of Morelhie.
6. *Philippe*: 1640–1701. Only brother of Louis XIV. Inherited the title of Duc d'Orléans from his uncle Gaston and passed it on to his own son and descendants.
7. *Duc d'Orléans*: Louis Philippe Joseph, 1747–1793. Assumed the name 'Egalité' as proof of his revolutionary spirit.
8. *Athénais de Montespan*: 1641–1707. She replaced Louise de La Vallière as Louis XIV's mistress in 1667.
9. *Dauphin*: Louis de France, 1661–1711, only legitimate son of Louis XIV.
10. *Grande Mademoiselle*: Duchesse de Montpensier, 1627–1693; daughter of Gaston.

11. *Lauzun*: Antonin Nompar de Caumont, Duc de Lauzun, 1632–1723. As will emerge in later chapters, he was himself a prisoner of Saint-Mars at Pignerol from 1671 to 1681.
12. The Cathedral of Arras was entirely destroyed during the Revolution.

CHAPTER FOUR

MORE FACES

If the name 'Marchiali' is an anagram of 'hic amiral', it could be applied equally well to another candidate: the predecessor of Vermandois as Grand Admiral of France, François de Vendôme, Duc de Beaufort. His candidature was first canvassed by Lagrange-Chancel in his letter to Fréron in 1758 and though at the time few people were prepared to take the proposition seriously, it has been argued again as recently as 1960.

Beaufort had the same royal grandfather as Louis XIV, his father Cesar de Bourbon, Duc de Vendôme, being the eldest son of Henri IV.[1] Vendôme was older than Louis XIII by seven years, but illegitimate, being one of three royal children, two boys and a girl, born to Gabrielle d'Estrées, Duchesse de Beaufort. Vendôme also had three children, two boys and a girl, of whom Beaufort was the youngest. Big and brawny with long blond hair, Beaufort looked like a Viking and his looks did not belie him. Having been raised in the country with an education limited to the arts of combat and the hunt, he was a true barbarian: a superb athlete and a prodigious fighter, uncouth and almost illiterate, simpleminded, thick-skinned and self-assertive. He saw himself as acting a central rôle in the affairs of the state and played to the gallery for all it was worth, propelling himself into the spotlight whenever the opportunity offered. His oafish lack of manners and his naive lack of discernment made him a figure of ridicule at court; but it was this very absence of education and refinement, this honest muddle-headed blundering in search of a hero's rôle, which drew the ordinary people to him, while his genuine courage and energy in war and adversity earned him the admiration of all.

In 1636, at the age of twenty, he had already won honour and favour by distinguishing himself in action against the Spanish, but in the intrigues of court he took the side of the disgraced Queen, Anne of Austria, and the enemies of Louis XIII's minister, Cardinal Richelieu. His father had always been prominent in the factions hostile to Richelieu and from 1626 to 1630 had been imprisoned at Vincennes for involvement in the Chalais Conspiracy. In 1642, he himself was implicated in another conspiracy against Richelieu, having to take refuge in England, but later that same year Richelieu died and so he was able to return. The Queen had absolute confidence in him. In her own words he was 'the most honest man in France' and, on the eve of the King's death in May 1643, she entrusted her children to his safekeeping, afraid that the King's brother, Gaston, or the Prince de Condé, who was commander-in-chief of the army, might attempt to kidnap the future King.

In the power struggle which followed, however, the Queen as Regent found her true champion not in the plain he-man Beaufort but in the wily con-man Mazarin. Opposition to Mazarin rallied behind Beaufort, but in September 1643 the Queen had him arrested and imprisoned at Vincennes. There he remained, rejected and ignored, until in May 1648 he managed to slip past his guards and escape. By that time the political situation had degenerated into an open squabble between Mazarin and the Parlement of Paris, the first of a confused series of violent conflicts, known later under the general name of the Fronde. Mazarin had the backing of the Queen, but the people of Paris gave their support to the Parlement with such vigour that she and her children fled the city and appealed to Condé for protection. The only other great military commander in France at that time, Maréchal Turenne, was sympathetic to the Parlement, but he failed to win over the troops under his command and so took refuge with the Spanish. Beaufort then offered his services to the Parlement and with a group of other nobles was given command of a newly raised army of 12,000 men.

These troops, untrained, undisciplined and ill-equipped, were so ignominiously routed by the forces of the Queen led by Condé that their generals were ridiculed and their efforts turned to laughter. Condé himself called the conflict 'the war of the chamber-pots' and said it should only be recorded in comic verse. For Beaufort however the experience turned out to be a personal triumph. The common people of Paris were captivated by him and their adulation was not diminished by his defeat. In the time the conflict lasted he lived in the heart of the city and mixed with his raggle-taggle neighbours on equal terms, drinking and joking with them, gossiping and arguing, brawling and womanising. His enemies called him the 'King of the Market' but at a time when the King of England had just been executed by his people[2] and the King of France was in hiding from his, it was not a title to be scoffed at.

In the course of 1649 everyone changed partners. Condé and the generals who had been opposed to him joined forces against the rest and in January 1650 the rest collaborated to have three of the generals, including Condé, arrested. Condé's supporters in the country threatened insurrection, and in February 1651 the Queen banished Mazarin

Beaufort, one of the first Iron Mask candidates ever proposed. He was thought to be the mysterious prisoner as early as 1687. After a painting by Nocroit. (*Photograph Bibliothèque Nationale*)

and had the three generals released. Beaufort at this time kept guard on the Palais Royal to be sure that the Queen did not try to take the young King to join Mazarin. For all his supposed stupidity, Beaufort demonstrated more consistency than most of his fellow disputants. Throughout the length of this burlesque and bloody war, his actions were motivated only by his opposition to Mazarin, and this in spite of the fact that his father had aligned himself with Mazarin from the first and, in that very month of February, his elder brother had taken one of Mazarin's nieces in marriage.

Condé, meanwhile, impatient for a showdown, left Paris to raise an army and in January 1652 Mazarin returned from exile, also with an army. Then in a final comic-book change-about, Condé who had won all his glory as a general in victories over the Spanish army turned to Spain for help, while Mazarin gave the command of his forces to Turenne, who just three years before had tried to get his troops to turn against Mazarin and had since been fighting with the Spanish against the French. Beaufort and his sister's husband, the Duc de Nemours, shared the command under Condé. Their victories were brilliant, their defeats honourable, but for Beaufort the experience was a personal disaster. He quarrelled with his brother-in-law and in July 1652 fought and killed him in a duel. Twelve days later Mazarin was dismissed from office and his enemies, with the exception of Condé, were finally persuaded to submit to the will of the young King. Beaufort was banished from Paris and the court and was not restored to favour until six years later. Mazarin, by contrast, was recalled to office after only six months.

In 1663, two years after the death of Mazarin, Beaufort succeeded his father as Grand Admiral of France, a post which included control over trade as well as war, his full title being 'Grand Master, Chief and Superintendent-General of the Navigation and Commerce of France'. As it was, however, the ships and men which constituted the French Fleet at the time were a beggarly assortment not even capable of protecting the French coast from pirate raids. Louis XIV's ministers were aware of the need to build a new fleet and Colbert especially was convinced of the enormous political and economic advantages to be had from a major investment in sea-power; but none of the ministers, Colbert in particular, was prepared to see Beaufort at the head of such an enterprise. Both the Ministry of Finance and the Ministry of War sought to supervise and control the new admiral. His authority was questioned, restricted, undermined, and yet he went to work with such dash and drive to transform the little he had into a fighting force that in the following year he was able to begin a series of expeditions against the Barbary pirates along the coast of the Maghreb. As always his personal valour in the fighting was spectacular and his popularity with the lower ranks resounding, but as in any campaign he ever led the endeavour itself, though not an outright failure, was far from being a success.

In 1669, Louis XIV was persuaded by the Vatican to send an expedition to Crete, at that time known as Candy, to help the Venetians against the Turks. For twenty-four years the island had been under siege and only the chief city, which is today Iraklion, had not surrendered. The reasons which motivated Louis XIV to make such a gesture were political not religious, but in appearance at least it was a crusade against the infidel. The expeditionary force was 7,000 strong and was led by the Duc de Navailles with Beaufort in overall command. The Duc de Vivonne, who was the brother of the King's new mistress, Athénais de Montespan, was commander of the galleys and among the other officers was Colbert's brother, Colbert de Maulevrier, and Beaufort's nephew, the young Duc de Vendôme. From the Pope, Beaufort received the title 'Captain-General of the Naval Army of the Church' and from the King the order that under no circumstances was he personally to set foot on Crete or engage in any fighting.

The fleet reached Crete on 19 June and found the city in a worse plight than had been anticipated; one of the two bastions already fallen, the streets burning and blocked with debris, the population decimated and in despair, the garrison reduced to half its number, sick and demoralized. Beaufort joined Navailles in a council of war with the Venetian commanders, Morosini and Montbrun, at which it was decided to disembark the troops by night on the 24th for a sortie at first light on the 25th. Against the express orders of the King and the earnest advice of everyone else, Beaufort refused to be left on board. He went ashore with the troops and took command of the left wing with Colbert's brother.

When the attack began, the Turks, taken by surprise, ran for their lives and the French went after them deep into their camp. In the midst of the charging ranks, however, an ammunition dump, hit by a chance bullet, blew up; a battalion of French Guards was suddenly and completely annihilated. Shock and confusion at the tremendous explosion, horror and incomprehension at the appalling carnage, stopped the French army in its tracks; then, convinced that the ground ahead was mined, the front line turned back upon the rest. The French troops who stood firm were trampled by the troops who fled, or took them for Turks in the dark and cut them down. The Turks finding themselves at an advantage launched a counter-attack and what was left of the French army broke up. Beaufort, trying to rally his troops, was abandoned on the field and only when the beaten army had taken refuge inside the city was it realized that he was missing.

Two days later, the Intendant of the Fleet, whose name was Brodart, wrote to Colbert to report that Beaufort was still missing and that whether he was 'dead or captive' no one could say. All that was known for certain was that he had been 'left among the enemy'. Spies had been sent into the Turkish camp to find out what had happened. Sometime later one such spy was said to have reported that Beaufort was dead, that he had been killed in the fighting and his body, like the bodies of all the other French dead, had been beheaded and stripped; that his head had been thrown in a heap with the rest in front of the Grand Vizier's tent and his armour had been sold. An officer named Flacourt, who was despatched under a flag of truce to the Turkish camp, could not find Beaufort among the prisoners and yet a prisoner named Montigny, who was allowed to examine the heads, could not find Beaufort's amongst them. Morosini thought he had seen Beaufort's headless body in golden armour on the field and Montbrun later maintained that the Grand Vizier had sent Beaufort's head to Constantinople where for three days it had been carried through the streets on the end of a pole as a sign that the Christians had been defeated.

Proof of Beaufort's fate could not be established, but under the circumstances it seemed reasonable to suppose that he was dead. It was presumed that the reason no trace of him could be found was due to the fact that among all those hundreds of dead men, the piles of bodies beheaded and stripped, the heaps of heads battered and mutilated, it would have been difficult to identify anyone. A solemn memorial service was held at Notre-Dame in Paris and all the courts of Europe went into mourning. Not that everyone had reason to mourn. Colbert, one may be sure, was not saddened by the loss. Since Beaufort had no children, the office of Grand Admiral was left open to anyone the King wished to choose and his choice fell upon the Comte de Vermandois, who was at that time a child of two living under the care and protection of Colbert himself. Athénais de Montespan had no reason to be unhappy either: the post of acting-commander of the fleet was given to her brother, the Duc de Vivonne.

There were, however, a great many people who refused to believe that Beaufort was dead. On 31 August, Navailles withdrew from the island, abandoning it to the Turks, and when his troops disembarked at Marseilles nine days later they brought with them the story that Beaufort had been captured alive and taken to Constantinople. Meanwhile the English had received word from Athens, and the Vatican from the islands of Milos and Corfu, that Beaufort had been seen on a Turkish ship in the Aegean. Before the end of the month there were people in Paris prepared to wager that Beaufort was still alive. Just how wild these rumours were was difficult at that juncture to say, but it was evident that, if the Turks really did have the cousin of Louis XIV captive, they would do something to exploit the situation before very long. As time elapsed and the Turks continued to make no move at all, it seemed more and more certain that he was indeed dead. Nonetheless the people of Paris ten years later were still clinging to the belief that he was a prisoner in Constantinople and one day would escape and return. No doubt this faith was nourished by many more rumours, because as late as summer 1682 one such story was going the rounds at court. It was said that a dragoon, who after being captured at Candy had escaped from prison and returned to France, had seen Beaufort alive and well and apart from a big blond beard, unchanged, in the prison of the Seven Towers in Constantinople.

According to Lagrange-Chancel, Beaufort's prison was not in Turkey but in France. At the siege of Candy he was kidnapped by the French secret service, smuggled back to France and clapped behind bars in Pignerol with his head encased in an iron mask. In his letter to Fréron, Lagrange-Chancel had this to say: 'M. de Lamotte-Guérin, who had the command of those islands in the time that I was detained there, assured me that this prisoner was the Duc de Beaufort who was said to have been killed at the seige of Candy but whose body according to the commentaries of the time could never be found . . . If one considers the Duc de Beaufort's turbulent spirit and the part he played in the disturbances in Paris at the time of the Fronde, one will not perhaps be surprised at the violent course of action employed to secure him, especially since the post of admiral, which he had received in reversion, put him every day in a position to cross the great designs of M. Colbert who was in charge of the Admiralty. This admiral, who in the eyes of the minister, seemed so dangerous, was replaced, according to that minister's wishes, by the son of the King and the Duchess de La Vallière, the Duc de Vermandois, who was only two years old.' One might add here, in support of Lagrange-Chancel's theory, that Colbert's brother, with whom Beaufort shared command during the battle, was certainly well placed to arrange such a kidnapping.

For most of Lagrange-Chancel's readers, Beaufort was not sufficiently dangerous to Colbert or the King to warrant arrest and imprisonment in such an extraordinary fashion. For all his rebellious deeds of the past and dreams of future glory, his continuing popularity and increasing influence, the limitations of his personality made him a serious threat to no one except assailants in pitched battle. Some more important reason had to be found if he was to be seriously considered as a candidate for the Iron Mask. It was not until the twentieth century that anyone came up with such a reason, and in the meantime the issue was further complicated in 1868 by Augustin Jal, the scholar-historian and keeper of the Admiralty archives. He had reason to believe, he said, that Beaufort had entered a monastery in Crete. Neither killed, captured nor kidnapped at the siege of Candy, Beaufort the vanquished crusader had turned his back on war and become a monk in the Orthodox Church. What vision transformed his character on the battlefield and what angel led him from it alive remained a mystery; but those who nevertheless saw sense in the hagiography found supporting evidence for his sudden transformation in the passionate remorse he had shown after killing his own brother-in-law seventeen years before. Apparently at that time he had talked of entering a Carthusian Monastery to expiate his crime.

Beaufort as monk and Iron Mask was the final shape of the argument reached in 1960 by Dominique de La Barre de Raillicourt. According to his scenario, French secret service agents kidnapped Beaufort from the monastery in Crete two years after his disappearance. They had planned and even attempted to kidnap him during the expedition to Candy, but he had escaped and gone into hiding. What motivated the decision to have him live out the rest of his life in prison was the realization that he possessed a secret dangerous to Louis XIV and could not be relied upon to keep it. Presumably Louis XIV had only discovered the secret himself on or after his mother's death in 1666. His father, he had been thunderstruck to learn, was not Louis XIII but Beaufort. One may easily imagine his horror and alarm at the news, but, unhappily for the hypothesis, imagination is not enough. That Anne of Austria had tender feelings for Beaufort and that he was passionately devoted to her is a fact recorded in numerous contemporary memoirs, but never was it said by anyone that they were lovers. Moreover, at the time of Louis XIV's conception, Anne of Austria was under house-arrest at the Louvre and Beaufort like all her favourites and admirers was not allowed to visit her.

To give the hypothesis its due, however, Beaufort's face was so well known to the common soldier and the ordinary man, both of Paris and of Provence where his family had estates, that if he had been secretly held a prisoner on Sainte-Marguerite and in the Bastille a mask would have been necessary to hide his identity. Also, for what it is worth, there are points of similarity between the description of the Iron Mask as given by Voltaire and the known behaviour of Beaufort during his imprisonment at Vincennes: his pleasure in fine clothes and good food and the fact that he played the guitar. Beaufort, like Voltaire's Iron Mask, was 'admirably well-built' and being the grandson of Henri IV he would have been treated by his gaolers with the greatest respect.

However, at the time of the Iron Mask's death in 1703, Beaufort would have been 87 years old and though such longevity was possible in a man of such robust health, it seems hardly likely when his last thirty years and more had been spent cooped up in prison.

The most serious single argument against the whole hypothesis is provided by a letter written on 8 January 1688 by Saint-Mars, the Governor of Sainte-Marguerite, to Louvois, the Minister of War, in which he declared: 'Throughout the province some say that my prisoner is M. de Beaufort and others that he is the son of the late Cromwell.' Both names were clearly meant by Saint-Mars to be amusing examples of error and ignorance. The mysterious prisoner, one must therefore assume, was not the Duc de Beaufort, and Lamotte-Guérin was not revealing inside information confided to him as a prison officer, but merely repeating a false rumour which anyone could have picked up anywhere in the region.

As a footnote to the facts and figments of Beaufort should be mentioned the 'timid conjecture' made by François Ravaisson in the preface of his *Archives de la Bastille* published in 1879. For him there seemed a possibility that the Iron Mask was Beaufort's aide-de-camp, the Comte de Kéroualle. He offered the conjecture that Kéroualle was captured with Beaufort at Candy and was then sent by the Turks to France to negotiate Beaufort's ransom. Louis XIV, only too pleased to be rid of Beaufort, had Kéroualle masked and imprisoned. Why masked, Ravaisson does not explain, nor how in 1671 the Admiralty records were able to list Kéroualle as killed in action aboard the flag-ship *Monarch*.

Yet another princely candidate for the Iron Mask, picked from yet another illegitimate branch of the same tangled tree, was Monmouth: one of the love-children of Louis XIV's cousin Charles II[3] of England. He was born in Rotterdam in 1649, two months after the execution of his grandfather, Charles I, and was called to London in 1661, two years after the restoration of the crown to his father. Until recognized by his father, the boy lived in Paris with his mother, a Welsh girl by the name of Lucy Walters, who had met Charles in Holland when as a young man of eighteen he had been in refuge there from the Roundheads. On his arrival in England the boy was married, though only thirteen, to Anne Scott, the Countess of Buccleuch, heiress to one of the richest estates in the kingdom, and in the following year was made a Knight of the Garter and Duke of Monmouth.

In the absence of a legitimate son, Charles heaped Monmouth with honours and distinctions normally reserved for a Prince of Wales. In the presence of his father, when others were obliged to remove their hats, he was allowed to keep his on, and during official mourning he was

MONMOUTH

Monmouth, first proposed as candidate for the Iron Mask in 1768. After a painting by Kneller. (*Photograph Bibliothèque Nationale*)

permitted to wear the royal purple as though he were a prince. At the age of nineteen he was made Captain of the King's Guard and at the age of twenty-one he was admitted to the Privy Council. Such marks of favour were not everywhere approved, but so pleasant a person was he that no one resented his good fortune. He was the most charming of men, handsome and sweet tempered, gracious and generous, a brilliant courtier and a fine soldier, as popular in city, camp and Parliament as he was in his father's palace. In 1673 he was given command of an English auxiliary force sent to assist the French in their invasion of Holland, and when he returned was given a hero's welcome by the people of London. At that stage his popularity appeared to have little or no political significance, but five years later it was obvious that it had, and he was obliged by his father to leave London for exile in Holland because his presence had become an incitement to rebellion.

The factor which had transformed the political situation so much in that interval was the problem of the King's successor. A few years after the royal marriage in 1662, and with increasing certainty as more time elapsed, it was realized that the Queen was unable to bear children and that therefore, on the King's death, the succession would pass to his brother James. This was a prospect which Parliament and the people came to regard with growing dismay. Since the King of England was titular head and sworn defender of the Church of England, it was unthinkable that he should owe allegiance to any other faith. In 1669 however James had secretly become a Roman Catholic and though he had been persuaded by the King to keep up a pretence of Anglicanism, the truth was suspected, and after four years of equivocation came out when he resigned all public office rather than take an anti-Catholic oath.

The King was only three years older than his brother and his health was to all appearances excellent, so there was no strong reason to suppose that James would ever succeed to the throne, but whether he did or not it was certain that one of his children would. In April 1673, when it became generally known that the heir-presumptive was a Catholic, fears for the future were only calmed by the knowledge that he was a widower and that his two daughters, the only children he had, were both staunch Protestants. In November of that same year, however, he married again, this time a Catholic. Clearly any son born of this second union would take precedence over the daughters of the first, and such a son would certainly be raised in his father's new faith. Unless something were done to alter the line of succession, it was wellnigh certain that, by the ordinary processes of devolution, the future Kings of England would be Roman Catholic.

As opposition to James gathered momentum Charles, himself a

would-be Catholic, temporized. While keeping up the appearances of Protestantism, he had in 1670 signed the secret Treaty of Dover with Louis XIV, promising to proclaim himself a Catholic and reclaim his kingdom for the Church of Rome. When the time came he was to have the backing of French troops to put down any resistance from his people, and in the meantime he was receiving large sums of money from France. No one except his brother and three ministers were privy to this agreement, but his equivocal attitude on political and religious issues gave rise to serious doubts and suspicions.

Though it was not until 1678 that any plot for a Catholic take-over came to light, and though it came in a version so sensationalized and from a witness so untrustworthy that it was not even credible, the nation was ready to believe the worst. The plot, it was claimed, was the work of the Pope, the King of France and the General of the Jesuits, in league with five Catholic peers and with the connivance of James and the Queen. All the shipping in the Thames was to be set on fire, the French army was to land in Ireland, Catholics were to massacre their Protestant neighbours and all the nation's leaders, including the King, were to be assassinated. Incited more by rumour than report, the populace was soon carried away on a wave of anti-Catholic hysteria. In April 1679, when Charles convened a new Parliament, the Commons insisted on debating a bill to exclude James from the throne, and the confused political situation crystallized into a conflict between two factions: the pro-James party, which came to be called Tories, and the anti-James party which came to be called Whigs.

In the search for an alternative heir to the throne, one group of Whigs picked upon Monmouth. His widespread popularity, his plain uncomplicated Anglicanism and his amenable character made him the perfect choice. He was the very antithesis of his rival, as open, trusting, indulgent and affable as James was secretive, suspicious, authoritarian and cold. With a little flattery and good fellowship he could moreover be easily influenced and controlled. The story was put about that Monmouth was not illegitimate after all, that Charles had been married to Lucy Walters and that their contract of marriage still existed, locked up for safe keeping in a certain black box. Charles denied this categorically in a public declaration, but Monmouth took to wearing the royal coat-of-arms without the bar-sinister which until then had indicated his illegitimacy. It was at that juncture in September 1679 that Charles deprived him of all public office and banished him to Holland.

When the new Parliament met in October 1680, the Exclusion Bill was passed by the Commons but rejected by the Lords. Charles dissolved Parliament and called a new one for March 1681, but again the Commons demanded the Exclusion Bill and again Charles dismissed them. Tension mounted and at the instigation of the Whigs, Monmouth returned in defiance of his father and went on a tour of the country to win popular support. In November 1682, Charles had him arrested for disturbing the peace but could not bring himself to punish him and even allowed him to stay on in England. Monmouth, unrepentant, undeterred, continued to keep company with his Whig friends, and when in June 1683 a conspiracy to raise an open rebellion was disclosed, he was implicated. A group of extremists had planned to assassinate Charles and James at Rye House near Hoddesdon on their way back from the horse-races at Newmarket. Because the races that year had ended earlier than expected and Charles had returned to London ahead of schedule, the plot had failed, but during an interrogation of the suspects it emerged that Monmouth and certain Whig lords were in the process of planning an uprising in London, Bristol and Newcastle. The conspirators were rounded up and the leaders put on trial for their lives. One committed suicide in prison, and two were executed. Monmouth was not even arrested; his father merely sent him off again to Holland.

Having professed himself contrite, Monmouth had little doubt that he would soon be recalled; Charles was too fond a father to keep his favourite son in exile for long. In February 1685, however, the prospect was abruptly and drastically changed: Charles died and was succeeded by James. Not only did this mean that Monmouth could no longer hope to go home to England; he would have difficulty finding a home anywhere else. No foreign court could be expected to risk bad feeling with the new King by showing hospitality to his onetime rival. Monmouth's host in Holland, William of Orange,[4] asked him to leave, offering the advice that if he went to Hungary to fight against the Turks he would be well-received by the Emperor[5] and well thought of by all of Europe. Unsure what to do, he moved to Brussels and there he encountered exiles like himself who had a very different proposition to make. According to them, if he were to land in England and claim the crown, the Whig lords, the city of London and all the surrounding counties would immediately rally behind him. The Earl of Argyll, paramount chief of the clan Campbell, was in Amsterdam, preparing an invasion of Scotland. Monmouth had only to time his landing in England to coincide with that and his success was assured. Persuaded that he would be swept to the throne on a popular uprising which no military, political or religious leader would dare to withstand, Monmouth threw in his lot with the rebels.

Argyll set sail for Western Scotland with 300 men at the beginning of May and Monmouth for Western England with 80 men at the end of the same month. On 11 June he landed at Lyme Regis in Dorset to an enthusiastic welcome and there in the market-place published a manifesto in which James was denounced as a tyrant, a murderer and a usurper, accused among other things of poisoning his own brother, the late King. The declaration also pronounced Monmouth legitimate and the rightful successor to the throne, but announced that he was putting his claim to one side until it could be judged by a free Parliament. Peasants, artisans and traders, day-labourers and apprentices rushed to the standard and in twenty-four hours the rebel army numbered 1,500 men. Three days later, when the assembled horde marched inland, their mere appearance put to flight an army of 4,000 militia drawn up to stop them at Axminster. New recruits flocked in from every side as the march north continued, and Monmouth was everywhere hailed with adulation. On 18 June he reached Taunton in Somerset and was received with such acclaim that on 20 June he forgot his original declaration and proclaimed himself King. His followers were only too delighted, but since he bore the same Christian name as his hated uncle and another King James would have caused confusion, everyone called him 'King Monmouth'.

From Taunton the army, now numbering 6,000, marched on through Bridgwater, Glastonbury and the Mendip Hills towards Bristol, but on 25 June was driven off by a force of regular troops when trying to cross the River Avon at Keynsham. Monmouth, who had expected to enter Bristol without meeting serious resistance, wavered irresolutely and then drew back. Most of his infantry were barefoot rustics, armed with mattocks and scythes, and what few cavalry he had were mounted on young horses bred for coach or cart and not yet trained to the bridle. Matched against regular soldiers, the rustics were little better than a mob, while the horses were likely to take flight at the first sound of a musket. With such an army he was unwilling to risk a major battle, and yet he had little or no hope of finding reinforcements which would render it more effective. After two whole weeks he had the support of no one except the common people of the towns and villages he had marched through. London had not stirred, nowhere had there been a spontaneous uprising, and not a single member of the aristocracy or gentry, the Commons or the Church, had taken his side. Parliament had put a price on his head and an army of regular troops had been despatched from London to destroy him. On 28 June with the advance guard of those troops already on him, he received news that Argyll had been routed, made captive and executed. Knowing then that his venture had failed, he wanted to give up, but his lieutenants, who still had hope of success, argued that he could not abandon the thousands of simple people who had put their lives at risk by following him.

On 2 July the rebel army returned to Bridgwater and on 5 July the government forces pitched camp just three miles away at Weston on the plain of Sedgemoor: 2,500 troops, cavalry, infantry and artillery, backed up by 1,500 militia. A battle was unavoidable, and its outcome appeared to be a foregone conclusion. Sedgemoor was reclaimed marshland, flat and bare, criss-crossed by wide, deep trenches, and on such terrain the superiority of the government troops, both in fire-power and manouverability, presaged a massacre. Government officers and men, confident and careless, got drunk on local cider.

Monmouth, seizing the only advantage left to him, decided upon an immediate night attack. In moonlight, obscured by banks of thick fog, he moved his valiant peasants out onto the moor. So far as he knew, there were two trenches to be crossed before the enemy could be reached, and he had guides to lead the way across them. At the second trench, however, a guide missed his way and though the column got across, the noise of their confusion alerted the enemy guard who quickly raised the alarm. Monmouth unflustered drew up his battle-line and moved to the attack only to discover his way barred by a third trench which he had not expected. The two armies, facing each other across this trench, opened fire in the darkness and the horses of the rebel cavalry took fright and stampeded. Their headlong retreat caused panic in the rear, and the supply carts, waiting with what ammunition there was, drove off with the rest. When the government cavalry charged the flanks they were repulsed, but Monmouth knew that with day about to break and ammunition almost spent the situation was hopeless. Treacherously then he took horse and fled, leaving his followers to fight on until the government artillery was brought up and their ranks were broken by heavy shelling. At dawn the routed army poured back into Bridgwater, and the cavalry swept after them, cutting them down in the streets.

Monmouth, riding for his life, fled north to the Bristol Channel with the intention of hiding in Wales, then changed his mind and with two companions rode south-east through Wiltshire, heading for the New Forest and the southern coast. By the time the three men reached Cranborne Chase their horses were dying on their feet and had to be abandoned. Disguised as peasants they continued on foot, but the local militia had been alerted in the meantime and early the following morning one of the two companions was captured. The area was sealed off and the search intensified. At dawn the next day the other companion was taken, and some hours later Monmouth himself was found, wearing the ragged clothes of a shepherd and crouching in a ditch. According to the government account, the soldiers who made the capture did not at first recognize him. His hair had turned white and he cringed in half-witted terror before them, unable to speak or to stand. However, in his pockets, which were crammed with raw pease, were a purse full of gold, his watch, his rings and even his medals, including the Order of the Garter.

Later that day under guard at Ringwood, he was permitted at his own request to write to the King and degraded himself ignominiously in a letter of abject supplication, pleading that he had been misled by others, imploring forgiveness and begging to be allowed to speak to the King in person. On the following day he wrote to the Queen Dowager, entreating her to intercede for him, and on the three-day journey to London shocked all observers by his craven behaviour. On 13 July, with his arms bound behind his back, he was allowed into the royal presence and there he begged for his life at any price. Grovelling and weeping at the King's feet, he swore that he was wrong but not to blame, that he was sorry and understood the errors of his ways, that as proof of his new-found virtue he was even ready to renounce the Anglican faith and become a Roman Catholic. In the Tower later that day he was informed that he would be executed in two days' time and in an access of renewed terror prayed for a respite, beseeching the King's mercy and the help of anyone he thought the King might listen to.

After such ignoble behaviour it is astonishing to find that he went to his death on Tower Hill with the courage and dignity of a true hero. A huge crowd, silent and mournful, saw him salute the guard with a smile and mount the scaffold with a firm tread, heard him speak with tenderness of the woman he loved and with sorrow for the bloodshed he had caused, watched him pray with serenity and prepare himself for the axe with composure. The priests and bishops who were there exhorted him to address the people on the necessity of obedience to the government, but he refused. To the executioner he gave six guineas and the promise of more if he did his job well, then knelt down and stretched his neck across the block. The first stroke was badly delivered, and lifting his wounded head he looked reproachfully at the executioner. The second stroke was no better, nor yet the third. With the head half-severed the body continued to move, and still two more blows were needed to stop it. The head was then separated from the shoulders with a knife. Angry and tearful, the spectators rushed forward and, while the guard struggled to protect the executioner from them, they dipped their handkerchiefs in the dead hero's blood.

One explanation for this extraordinary transformation from shameless cowardice to noble heroism was that the government had told lies about Monmouth's behaviour in captivity in the hope of discrediting him with his followers and sympathisers. Another explanation was that the hero who died on the scaffold was not Monmouth at all, but a devoted friend who looked like him and chose to die in his place. In the West Country the common people, who for decades afterwards kept as relics odd buttons and ribbons he once had worn, found truth in both explanations: King Monmouth was for them a hero without blemish and he was not dead; one day, they confidently believed, he would return to avenge their suffering. Over a thousand of them had died at Sedgemoor and for a week after that the army had crippled and slaughtered hundreds more in an orgy of looting, rape and torture. The prisons of Somerset and Dorset were packed with prisoners and, in the notorious Bloody Assizes which followed, Judge Jeffreys filled the villages with executions and floggings, with bodies rotting in irons and severed heads on poles. Hundreds who had been able to bribe their way out of prison before the trials began escaped on ships to New Zealand, and Jeffreys had nine hundred more transported as slaves to the plantations of the West Indies. In such devastation, the broken dream of those simple people was transmuted to a messianic faith which found expression in local ballads:

> Then shall Monmouth in his glories
> Unto his English friends appear,
> And will stifle all such stories
> As are vended everywhere.

The strength of the people's belief in Monmouth's second coming was so great that in Wiltshire just one year after the rebellion and in Sussex more than ten years later, imposters managed to pass themselves off as Monmouth on the common people and, until they were arrested and exposed as cheats, received help and shelter, money and protection.

The theory that the Iron Mask was Monmouth was first proposed by Saint-Foix in 1768. His argument was founded upon the persistence into the early eighteenth century of the rumour that Monmouth was still living, and to that tradition he added two stories of his own. He claimed that a certain Abbé Tournemine had told him that he had overheard Fr Francis Sanders, who was the confessor of King James in exile,[6] tell the Duchess of Portsmouth that Monmouth was not the man who had been executed. He also claimed that soon after the execution a certain noblewoman, having heard the rumour that someone had taken Monmouth's place at the block, bribed the guards to open the coffin and realized from an examination of the body's right arm that in fact the dead man was not Monmouth.

Having established the tradition as fact in his own eyes, Saint-Foix then came up with a third story culled from a sensational and scurrilous pamphlet published anonymously in Holland under the title *Amours de*

Charles II et de Jacques II, rois d'Angleterre. In this a man referred to as 'Colonel Skelton' and described as 'a former commander of the Tower', was made to say: 'The night after the pretended execution of the Duke of Monmouth, the King, accompanied by three men, came himself to take him from the Tower. His head was covered with a kind of hood and he got into a coach with the King and the three men.' Where Monmouth was taken, the anonymous author did not have his Skelton divulge, but Saint-Foix was quite sure that he was put aboard ship for France that very night, and the hood which hid his face was replaced by a mask of iron, if indeed it was not already covering one. Perhaps it is worth noting, as a point of information, that a certain Beril Skelton was indeed Commander of the Tower during the reign of James II, but for one month only, and that in 1688 just before James fled into exile. At the time of Monmouth's imprisonment, this same Skelton was the King's envoy in Holland.

For the rest of his theory Saint-Foix leaned heavily on the supposition that though James was notoriously cold-blooded, he was not so monstrous as to take the life of his own brother's son. He argued that Monmouth's death was pretended in order to remove the popular hope he embodied, and that he was smuggled to a prison in France to reduce the risk of his discovery or escape. According to Saint-Foix it was altogether in the interest of Louis XIV to assist James in this way, since their religious and political views were so similar and were threatened by the kind of popular opposition which Monmouth had come to represent.

It was in support of Monmouth's candidature that Saint-Foix offered the story about an apprentice surgeon named Nelaton being called to the Bastille to bleed a prisoner whose head and face were kept covered with a towel and who spoke French with a strong English accent. The purpose of the towel, Saint-Foix thought it reasonable to suppose, was not to hide this prisoner's identity but to hide the fact that his identity was already hidden by an iron mask. Reasonable or not, Nelaton's story could, however, be used to support theories other than the one Saint-Foix proposed. Monmouth was not the only English-speaking candidate. One of the very first explanations of the mystery identified the Iron Mask as 'an English milord' who had been made to disappear by the French secret service thirteen years after Monmouth's execution. Saint-Foix and his contemporaries, including Voltaire, Griffet and Lagrange-Chancel, were unaware of this version, but it was the explanation accepted within the French royal family during Louis XIV's own lifetime.

Just three years after Monmouth's failed rebellion came the Glorious Revolution in which James was driven from the throne by his nephew and son-in-law, the Dutch prince, William of Orange. In December 1688, James was allowed to escape to France where Louis XIV gave him refuge and support. He had loyal defenders in Scotland and Ireland, but his attempts to re-establish himself the following year with a French-backed army came to nothing. In England William ruled jointly with his wife Mary,[7] while James set up a court-in-exile within the court of Louis XIV, his hopes of future restoration bolstered by his host and protector, who persisted in the view that William and Mary were usurpers. Jacobite officers, driven from Britain, flocked to their King in France and served him by serving in the French army against William and his allies.

Sooner or later, the Jacobites believed, the English would reject William as a foreigner, and when Mary died in December 1694 they imagined that William on his own was too unpopular to resist a concerted effort against him. By the following spring agents sent from France were in London to sound out the situation, and in the summer James was informed that to be sure of success the uprising would have to be preceded by the abduction or assassination of William and followed up by his own appearance in England at the head of a large army. As things really were, William had no need to fear the mood of the people. In October he returned from a victorious military campaign against the French in the Spanish Netherlands[8] and on the strength of the popularity this gave him, he called an election and established his parliamentary backing more firmly than ever. Nonetheless James decided to go ahead with his plan and in January despatched two of his top officers to London: one to prepare a nationwide insurrection, the other to organize William's elimination.

The first of these was the Duke of Berwick, an illegitimate son of James, born and raised in France. He was twenty-five years of age but already a soldier for ten years and a field commander of proven ability, holding the rank of lieutenant-general in the French army. The second was Sir George Barclay, about whom little is known beyond the fact that he was a Scotsman in his early sixties who had distinguished himself at the head of Jacobite Highlanders fighting William's troops in Scotland and Ireland. The two men travelled separately but by the same route, embarking on a privateer from France and slipping ashore in England at a smuggler's hideout on the deserted flats of Romney Marsh. Berwick did not stay long. A masked ball was arranged for him at which he was able to meet members of the aristocracy sympathetic to James; however, he achieved little beyond the promise that they would take up arms against William when James was himself in England with an army at his back. When Berwick returned to France, it was clear that everything hinged on Barclay.

In London Barclay made contact with a Catholic priest who was a secret agent and through him passed the word to a group of Jacobite terrorists whose names he had been given before he left. To avoid arousing curiosity he was obliged to change lodgings frequently, but always after nightfall on Mondays and Thursdays he walked under the lamps of Covent Garden with a white handkerchief hanging from his coat-pocket. It was in this way that his future accomplices were able to recognize and approach him. At least twenty men sent from France, in twos and threes by way of Romney Marsh, arrived to join him, while from London and the surrounding countryside he gradually enlisted twenty more. Arms and horses were acquired, the pattern of William's day-to-day movements was established, and a plan was formed. From the very outset, it seems, the aim of the operation was not to kidnap William but to kill him.

William went hunting in Richmond Park every Saturday. He left his palace in Kensington in the early morning and travelled by coach, with an escort of twenty-five guards, through Turnham Green to Chiswick. There he left his coach and took a boat across the Thames. His escort waited with the coach at the landing-stage and brought him back to Kensington by the same route when he returned in the late afternoon. The road between the landing-stage and Turnham Green was narrow and winding, with one section so deep in mud that the coach had difficulty getting through. Here, it was decided, the assault should be made. The commandos were to turn up individually at Turnham Green in the early afternoon and when William was seen to be on his way back across the river, they were to take up their positions on the road in four groups, ready to rush out simultaneously while the coach and guards were labouring through the quagmire. Any guards who survived the opening hail of bullets would be so encumbered by the morass of mud and fallen bodies that they could be despatched without difficulty at close quarters and so, as well as pistols and eight-ball muskets, the commandos were issued with stabbing swords. By February, everything was decided including the date of the operation.

James, meanwhile, was camped at Calais with a French army ready to put to sea. There would be no insurrection, Berwick had told him, unless he was first prepared to invade England for its throne. England would be invaded, he had decided, but first that throne had to be vacated. Barclay had prepared fuel for bonfires on the cliffs of Kent and would light them when his mission was accomplished. It was for that signal that James was waiting.

Among Barclay's forty men, however, three were traitors, and unknown to the rest of the group or to each other they gave warning of the plan to the Earl of Portland, William's friend and confidant.

Portland was not prepared to take the first of the informers seriously, but when a second arrived and repeated what the first had said, he thought it wise to play safe. That day was Friday and the ambuscade was fixed for the next day. At Portland's insistence, William cancelled his trip to Richmond and since the weather was cold and stormy gave that as his excuse. Barclay had no reason to suspect treachery and so simply postponed his plan to the following Saturday.

In the course of the week that followed the third informer gave his warning and when Friday came around again, the second informer returned to reiterate his. This time he met William as well as Portland and was persuaded to give more details of the plan, including the names of the ringleaders. The following day William again cancelled his trip to Richmond. This time the reason was that he had some slight illness, but Barclay's suspicions were aroused. When he discovered that the guards at the palace had been doubled and the troops in London put on the alert, he called off the plan and made his escape. Three of the leading conspirators were arrested before dawn and seventeen others before noon the next day. The gates of London were by that time closed and road-blocks had been set up. Within a few days all the conspirators except Barclay had been caught, and the local militia had been called to arms for fear of a French invasion.

The failure of Barclay's mission had far-reaching consequences for James, and they were all bad. William's position was strengthened by a renewed wave of anti-Jacobite, anti-Catholic, anti-French feeling, and this at a time when his handling of affairs at home and abroad was beginning to prove effective. With the prospect of genuine political and economic stability ahead, even Jacobite sympathizers saw James as a divisive rather than an alternative force, too unpredictable and reactionary to be trusted. The Jacobite cause, for the moment at least, was lost, and though James himself did not recognize it his protector, Louis XIV, did. In spring 1697, just one year after the failed insurrection, Louis XIV sued for peace with the English and their allies, offering among other concessions to recognize William as lawful king. The treaty was signed that autumn and in the following year Portland was received at Versailles as the English Ambassador to France.

The marks of dignity and honour shown to Portland by the French were manifest and unstinted, but the difficulties of the new relationship were every day apparent in the problems posed by the presence in the French court of James and his followers. That Louis XIV would continue to treat James as king in name while recognizing William as king in deed was something the English had expected, but they had hoped that the banished king and his court would have been prevented from showing their faces under the nose of William's ambassador.

What particularly incensed Portland was the sight of Berwick and Barclay parading with brazen nonchalance before him. In a private audience with Louis XIV, he accused them of being arch-conspirators in the recent plot to assassinate his king and demanded their extradition. Louis denied categorically that Berwick had ever been a party to such a crime, and though for Barclay he could make no such denial, he protested that he did not know what had become of the man. Not only was Portland unable to lay hands on Berwick, he was thereafter unable to lay eyes on Barclay, and in the absence of further provocation from him was obliged to let the matter drop. What happened to Berwick is now recorded history: he became a naturalized Frenchman and a Marshal of France, celebrated as the victor of the battle of Almansa. What happened to Barclay, no one knows – unless, as some imagined, he became the Man in the Iron Mask.

It was just thirteen years after Barclay's disappearance that the Princess Palatine heard tell of a mysterious prisoner and wrote to her aunt the Electress of Hanover to tell her about it. The man had died in the Bastille after many years of imprisonment, during all of which time he had been forced to wear a mask even when he lay down to sleep. There had been guards beside him day and night with orders to kill him if he tried to take the mask off, and yet he was otherwise very well looked after, well-lodged, well-fed and given everything he desired. Who he was and why he was treated in this strange way, no one could ever find out. The letter containing this information was written on 10 October 1711 and twelve days later was followed by another explaining that in the interval the Princess had been allowed into the secret.

'I've just learned the identity of the masked man who died in the Bastille. It was not out of cruelty that he was made to wear a mask. He was an English milord who had been mixed up in the Duke of Berwick affair against King William. He died like this so that the King could never learn what had become of him.' Which King it was who could not be allowed to know about the prisoner is not at once evident. In a letter from Versailles, reference to 'the King' ought to mean Louis XIV, but it seems hardly possible that he is meant. Presumably it is William who is referred to, and the explanation appears to be that Louis XIV had Barclay imprisoned and his identity kept secret in prison to avoid him being kidnapped by William's agents. The need for the mask could then be explained by the fact that an anti-Jacobite spy would have recognized Barclay if ever he saw his face, and that many of the prisoners in the Bastille were there precisely because they were suspected of being British or Dutch agents. Since prisoners usually lived two or three to the same cell, short-term and long-term prisoners together, and were moreover obliged to change cells or cell-mates frequently, messages were easily passed from one prisoner to another and from inside the prison to the outside world. If by chance another prisoner had seen and recognised Barclay in the Bastille, William would have been told.

1. *Henri IV*: King of France, b. 1553, reigned 1589–1610.
2. Charles I was executed on 30 January 1649.
3. *Charles II*: King of England, b. 1630, reigned 1660–1685.
4. *William of Orange*: b. 1650, Stadtholder of Holland 1672–1689, became William III, King of England, 1689–1702.
5. *Emperor*: Leopold I, Archduke of Austria and Holy Roman Emperor, b. 1640, reigned 1658–1705.
6. *James in exile*: having reigned as James II from 1685 to 1688, he lived in exile in France until his death in 1701.
7. *Mary II*: Queen of England, b. 1662, reigned 1689–1694. Daughter of James II.
8. *Spanish Netherlands*: modern Belgium.

CHAPTER FIVE

AND EVEN MORE

Barclay was not the only man to become a candidate for the Iron Mask because of attempted regicide. Twenty-three years before his attempted assassination of William, there was an abortive bid on the life of Louis XIV and, according to Theodore Jung, whose book *La Verité sur le Masque de fer* appeared in 1873, the Iron Mask was the ringleader of that conspiracy. At the time of his arrest, this man gave his name as Louis Oldendorf and claimed to be a Dutch national from Nijmegen but, when the French secret service first discovered him, he was in Brussels and was using at least two other names as well: Kiffenbach and Harmoises. Nothing more is known of his background, but Jung argues that he was a young nobleman from Lorraine who had previously been a cavalry officer in the service of the Empire, and whose true name might well have been 'Marchiel', as the Iron Mask's name at burial was once transcribed.

The plan, so far as it can be made out, was to ambush the King's carriage on the open road when he travelled north in April 1673 to follow his army in the spring offensive against Holland. Oldendorf was in contact with government agents from Holland, Spain and Austria and had with him in Brussels a band of ten men from Holland, Ireland and Lorraine. In Jung's view, however, Oldendorf was no ordinary terrorist: he was one of the masterminds of an international organization which for more than a decade conspired to overthrow Louis XIV and his regime. Their sinister stratagems lay behind the attempted insurrections of Roux de Marcilly in 1669 and of La Tréaumont and Rohan in 1674, and behind the secret infiltration of the French court by the most vicious and degraded criminals of the underworld. Jung also held them responsible for a wave of assassinations which included the deaths of Monsieur's first wife, Henrietta of England, in 1670, of Foreign Minister Lionne in 1671 and of the Duke of Savoy in 1675.[1] The organization, Jung would have us believe, had cells in all the capitals of western Europe and numbered among its leaders and supporters Catholics as well as Protestants, royalists as well as republicans, statesmen and bankers as well as exiles, gangsters and adventurers.

Louvois got wind of a plot against the person of the King sometime in 1672, and by October of that year his agents had the suspects under surveillance in Brussels. In March 1673, Versailles was put under heavy guard, the governors of the cities where the King was expected to pass on his journey north were ordered to tighten security, and police traps were set up on all the main arteries. The suspects vanished from Brussels on 27 March, but on the night of 28 March four horsemen crossing a ford over the River Somme near Péronne were ambushed. Only one was captured, the man who called himself Louis Oldendorf. He was moved to the Bastille on 1 April and there he was interrogated by Louvois himself. French agents in Brussels seized a box of papers belonging to the suspects and sent it to Paris. More travellers were arrested on the roads from the Spanish Netherlands and some of these like Oldendorf were taken to the Bastille. There was no attempt upon the King's life, but no trial either. What happened to the arrested men, including Oldendorf, is not known.

Jung would have us believe that Louvois had all the evidence he needed to execute the conspirators but preferred to keep them alive as secret prisoners because Oldendorf possessed information which compromised a number of important people within the French court. Louvois later used this information as a means of insinuating his agents into the international organization and of blackmailing his personal enemies and political opponents. According to Jung, Oldendorf was kept in the Bastille for a year and then transferred to Pignerol where he arrived on 7 April 1674. It is true that a prisoner was moved from the Bastille to Pignerol at that time, but it was not Oldendorf.[2] Jung's book is one of the best-informed of all the books on the Iron Mask: his search for the truth 'still buried in the dust of contemporary records' was a major contribution to the subject; but ironically, paradoxically, the conclusion he drew from his discoveries is totally lacking in any supportive evidence.

That the Iron Mask was at the centre of an international conspiracy against Louis XIV was also proposed by Camille Bartoli, whose book *J'ai découvert l'inconcevable secret du Masque de fer* was published as recently as 1978. According to him, the conspirators were members of the Secret Order of the Temple, a clandestine organization which, he says, replaced the Order of the Knights Templar when it was destroyed by Philippe IV[3] of France at the beginning of the fourteenth century. Bartoli gives a dramatic description of how he learned the 'inconceivable secret' from a mysterious stranger who in 1976 was staying at the Hotel Negresco in Nice, an elderly and distinguished-looking man who claimed to be himself a member of the Secret Order and who revealed the 'inconceivable secret' to him on condition that he publish it.

His revelation was that the Secret Templars of the seventeenth century were seeking, as were the Templar Knights before them, to impose their 'Great Design' upon the world, a political and religious system to unify all nations and sects; and as a first step towards this, they believed it was necessary to restore the throne of France to the legitimate Frankish Kings. The original rulers of the Franks were the Merovingians who were kings by right of birth, and the Carolingians who followed them were descended from a junior branch of the same family. However, the rulers of France thereafter, the Kings of the Capetian, Valois and Bourbon dynasties, were all descended from a usurper, Hugues Capet,[4] and so were not legitimate. The crown of France belonged by divine right to the descendants of Charles de Lorraine,[5] who was the true heir when Capet usurped the throne at the end of the tenth century.

One of these descendants, the crusader Godefroi de Bouillon,[6] was the first King of Jerusalem, and it was in Jerusalem soon after his death that the Order of the Knights Templar was founded by a group of French knights. Sanctioned and supported by the Papacy, the Templars gradually developed into an international organization of great political and economic significance and two hundred years later were powerful enough to attempt to impose their Great Design. With ruthless and unprincipled cunning, however, the incumbent false King, Philippe IV, outmanoeuvered them. He installed a French pope at Avignon and got him to suppress the Order as heretical and immoral. Through the persecutions which followed, the organization lived on undercover, Bartoli claims, and by the beginning of the seventeenth century had regained sufficient strength, albeit secret, to attempt the Great Design again. The assassination of Louis XIV's grandfather, Henri IV, the repeated conspiracies against Louis XIII, and the wars of the Fronde which raged during Louis XIV's minority, were all the work of the Secret Order of the Templars.

Finally in 1661, Bartoli explains, when Louis XIV took the reins of government into his own hands, he came to realize the conspiracy which menaced him and in 1664 managed to discover the identity of the 'Great Monarch' who was to replace him on the throne. The man in question, descended from Charlemagne and heir to the Merovingian kings, was Henri de Lorraine, Duc de Guise: one of the leading figures at court, former Archbishop of Reims, fifty years old and without heir. Though it would not have been difficult for Louis XIV to eliminate the man, it was altogether impossible for him to eliminate the threat he represented. Were he to have killed him, the divine inheritance would have passed to another member of the Lorraine family and the Secret Templars, believing Louis XIV guilty of regicide, would have had no qualms about assassinating him. The only way out of the danger for Louis XIV was to neutralize the Secret Templars by making the Great Monarch his

GUISE

Guise, first proposed as candidate for the Iron Mask in 1978. After a painting by Citermans. (*Photograph Bibliothèque Nationale*)

prisoner and holding him hostage. It was certain that so long as the Duc de Guise was alive, the Secret Templars would give their allegiance to no one else, and so long as he was a prisoner they would do nothing to endanger his life. In that same year therefore, the Duc de Guise was kidnapped and, while it was given out that he had died, the Secret Templars were allowed to know that he was imprisoned in Pignerol and would be killed the moment any attempt was made to release him.

This, according to Bartoli, was how it was that the Duc de Guise became the prisoner known later as the Iron Mask. He was not, however, the masked prisoner who died in the Bastille in 1703. In fact, he died in 1694 at the age of eighty while he was on Sainte-Marguerite and another prisoner, a simple valet, was then made to wear the mask in his stead so that the Great Monarch should appear to be still alive and the Secret Templars would continue to remain in check. Since the masked valet was not replaced by another prisoner when he died in 1703, one must assume that the danger posed by the Secret Templars was at that time less acute, but a couple of years later Louis XIV was informed that his crime against the Great Monarch had been published for all posterity, written in some esoteric form and incorporated into one of the buildings of Nice. His advisers were of the opinion that the building was the castle, and so in 1706 French troops stormed into Nice and, against the counsel of all military experts, reduced the castle to rubble.

The information given to Louis XIV about the existence of such a message was correct, Bartoli tells us, but the advice as to its whereabouts was wrong. Thus it was that the 'inconceivable secret' of the Iron Mask escaped destruction, and hence it is that it may be seen in Nice today, represented in arcane emblematic form on the medallions which decorate the vaulting of the sacristy and oratory of the monastery of Cimiez, unchanged since they were painted in 1686: a winged dragon and the moon; a bee in the flame of a candle; a pearl in a scallop-shell; a hand holding a lance; a mirror leaning against a tree; a snake touching its head with its tail; etc. – although you would need to read Bartoli's book and be enlightened on the appropriate meanings of these enigmas, as conceived by the mysterious stranger from the Negresco Hotel, in order to appreciate the secret in all its inconceivability.

Not only has the mystery of the Iron Mask been revealed by adepts of the secret art, it has also been solved by addicts of the art of secrecy. In 1893 Etienne Bazeries, in collaboration with Emile Burgaud, brought out a book entitled *Le Masque de fer. Révélation de la correspondence chiffrée de Louis XIV* in which he employed his talents as a cryptographer to establish yet another theory. His book was the consequence of a discovery he had made two years previously when he had been asked to decipher eight coded letters printed at the end of the *Mémoires* of

Nicholas Catinat, a Marshal of France in the time of Louis XIV. One of these letters led him to the conclusion that the Iron Mask was a certain general by the name of Vivien de Bulonde.

In the summer of 1691, when the French were at war with the Savoyards in Piedmont, Catinat assigned to Bulonde the task of capturing the town of Cuneo. Bulonde made his assault on 23 June and, being repulsed, laid siege. He had been told to expect reinforcements, but when news came in of the approach of an Austrian army, he panicked and fled, abandoning his artillery, munitions and wounded. This action compromised the whole campaign; when report of it reached Paris, Louvois is said to have run 'weeping and in desperation' to the King. In July, Bulonde was arrested and sent to Pignerol. It was in a coded letter from Louvois to Catinat, where Bulonde's arrest was ordered, that Bazeries made his discovery: 'It is not necessary for me to tell you with what displeasure His Majesty has learned of M. de Bulonde's gross negligence in deciding, against your orders and for no good reason, to lift the siege of Cuneo. Knowing the consequences better than anyone, His Majesty is aware how great a set-back it will be for us not to have taken this stronghold, which will now have to be taken during the winter. It is His Majesty's wish that M. de Bulonde be arrested, conducted to the citadel of Pignerol and held there under guard, that at night he be kept locked up in a room of that same citadel and in the day be given liberty to walk upon the ramparts with . . .'

The next word, represented by the number *330*, Bazeries for some reason could not decipher. The interpretation most likely to occur would be 'with a soldier' or 'with a guard', but after consideration Bazeries decided it must mean 'with a mask': Bulonde was to be allowed to walk along the walls of the citadel wearing a mask. In fact the French language makes this interpretation unlikely because the usual meaning of the word 'masque' in the context of such a sentence would produce an altogether different meaning: not 'with a mask' but 'accompanied by a masked man'. Bazeries, however, had made up his mind and set to work to find corroboration.

This he turned up eventually in a second letter, written six years after the first, not in code this time, and from the Minister of War to the Iron Mask's gaoler on Sainte-Marguerite. There the following injunction appeared: 'You have no other conduct to follow with regard to those who are confided to your charge than to continue to watch over their surety without saying anything to anyone about the past acts of your longtime prisoner.' Bazeries, examining the original manuscript of this letter, noticed an error crossed out after the words 'about the' and claimed that he could distinguish the word 'gal' under the crossing-out. Since 'gal' was the commonly accepted abbreviation for 'general', it seemed to Bazeries very evident that the minister had forgotten himself for a moment and had referred to the mysterious prisoner by his true title. Bulonde was the only general to have been imprisoned at Pignerol, and all the prisoners at Pignerol were moved to Sainte-Marguerite in 1694. Conclusion: the Iron Mask was Bulonde.

From an unintelligible cipher and an illegible crossing-out, Bazeries felt confident that he had unlocked the state secret kept hidden for more than two hundred years. What he did not seem to appreciate was the fact that Bulonde's disgrace and arrest had never been a secret from anyone. The affair was reported in *La Gazette* on 2 September 1691, and one did not need to be a cryptographer to read that. In fact Bulonde was never a prisoner in the state prison of Pignerol; he was merely confined within the citadel under the guard of the garrison commander, and indeed was only kept there for a few months, the order for his release being issued in November of that same year. Though further evidence against Bulonde's candidature is unnecessary, it has been produced nonetheless: his signature on business receipts dated 1699 and 1705, and a record of his death in 1709.

One of the most remarkable theories ever proposed for the Iron Mask's identity was one which first appeared in a pamphlet published in 1883 by a writer who, as though lacking the strength of his convictions, sought to hide his own identity under the pseudonym 'Ubalde'. It was his belief that the Iron Mask was Jean Baptiste Poquelin, the master spirit of French theatre, known to the world as Molière. Unhappily for Ubalde, most people who read the pamphlet decided he was a crackpot, were more interested in identifying him than in his identification of the Iron Mask, and lost interest when they discovered that he was just an obscure music teacher by the name of Anatole Loquin. Nonetheless he persisted with further variations on his original theme in 1893 and 1898, culminating with a book in 1900 which contained the definitive version and bore the title *Un secret d'état sous Louis XIV, le Prisonnier Masqué de la Bastille, son histoire authentique*. Though he published the book under his own name, he sought to cover himself again, spending the entire first half of the volume reproducing material from Jung and refuting propositions by other writers. As it is, the theory itself, when finally he worked up the courage to launch himself upon it, is a good deal less wild and woolly than he was ever given credit for.

For a proper appreciation of the theory, some knowledge of Molière's life is necessary, but this can be quickly given. He was born in Paris in 1622, the eldest son of a wealthy merchant-upholsterer, was educated by the Jesuits at the college of Clermont, the best secondary school of the day, and went on to study law, it being his father's intention that he would one day succeed him in the family business. At the age of twenty-one, however, he abandoned his studies for the theatre, took the stage name Molière, and with an actress-friend called Madeleine Béjart formed an acting troupe. For two years the young couple struggled to establish their troupe in Paris, but unsuccessfully, and when Molière had been imprisoned for debt and obliged to beg help from his father, they gave up and moved to the provinces. There they lived as itinerant players, performing in market-towns and country mansions mainly in the south, and did not return to Paris until thirteen years later. By that time their repertory included plays of their own, farces and sketches written by Molière, and these won them the attention and protection of Monsieur, the King's brother, who had them perform for the King.

Royal approbation paved the way for success and largely because of the popularity of Molière's own pieces the troupe was soon well established. In 1661, Fouquet commissioned Molière to produce a spectacular entertainment as part of his grandiose house-warming party at Vaux-le-Vicomte and for that he turned his hand to something new, the first of his highly successful comedy-ballets. In 1662, he went on to sound another new note in his comedy *School for Wives*, which proved highly controversial and a great success at the box-office. With *Tartuffe* in 1664 he took this new comedy form even further, 'to castigate vice and folly' in an attack upon religious hypocrisy, but the play was banned and his next play *Dom Juan*, though showing to full houses, was stopped after only fifteen performances. In that same year, however, his troupe was granted the title of 'The King's Troupe' and he continued undeterred to write and produce his plays for the court and the town until his death in 1673: comedies like *The Misanthropist* in 1666 and *The Miser* in 1668, comedy-ballets like *The Would-Be Gentleman* in 1670 and *The Imaginary Invalid* in 1673. In 1667, a revised version of *Tartuffe* was banned again, but in 1669 a third version was authorized and became an immediate and immense success. It was at the age of fifty and the height of his career that he died, a victim of the consumption from which he had suffered for several years.

In the view of Anatole Loquin, this death was a pretence and Molière lived on for another thirty years, a secret prisoner, masked to hide his identity. For all of ten years, and particularly for the last three years before his supposed death, powerful enemies had conspired to destroy him. A smear campaign had been mounted to convince the King that he was a criminal degenerate who if brought to trial for the monstrous crime he had committed would certainly be sent to the stake. Eventually in 1672 the King had come to realize that whether Molière was guilty or not, the case against him was too strong to be ignored. The pretended death was therefore arranged at the King's command, with or without Molière's collusion, or the connivance of his wife, or the realization of

Molière, first proposed as candidate for the Iron Mask in 1883. After a painting by Mignard. (*Photograph Bibliothèque Nationale*)

his enemies, and the horror of public trial and execution was thus avoided.

Hostility to Molière first manifested itself at the beginning of 1663 in the controversy over his comedy *School for Wives*. Rival playwrights and acting troupes objected to it on artistic grounds, but an important section of the public was scandalized by what was seen to be a lack of proper reverence and respect for things holy and established. Among these critics were members of a secret organization called the Company of the Holy Sacrament, the avowed aim of which, since its foundation more than thirty years before, was to guard the religious orthodoxy and moral probity of French society. Made up, as it was, of leading figures from the Church, the nobility and the magistrature, with cells in all the provincial capitals of France, it had enormous influence. Louis XIII had granted the organization legal status, and Anne of Austria gave continual support until her death in 1666. Vincent de Paul had been closely associated with its members in his work for orphans and the sick, galley-slaves and the victims of war, but more typical of the Company as a whole was its crusade 'to stop all scandals and profanities', by which was understood the theatre in general and artists like Molière in particular, along with a whole range of activities and attitudes thought depraved, from immodesty in dress to Protestantism.

To what extent Molière knew of the Company's existence, the identity of its members and their animosity towards him, one cannot say. In 1663 he might not have known that the parish priest of Saint-Sulpice, who had made life difficult for him and his newly-formed troupe in 1643, was a member of the Company of the Holy Sacrament or that the reason his patron in the Languedoc, the Prince de Conti, withdrew his protection in 1655 was because he had been persuaded to join the same organization. No doubt he had heard that in Normandy and Bordeaux in 1658 and in Paris in 1660 a number of cases had come to light of apparently devout and saintly men making themselves rich by the appropriation and sequestration of other people's property, but he might not have known that these were also members of the Company. Presumably he realized that the religious bigots who disapproved so strongly of his plays disapproved also of the King's private life; but he might not have known that Mazarin and, after him, Colbert, alarmed by the political ambitions of these people, had tried to suppress the secret organization to which they belonged, and for all their ministerial powers had failed.

Though it is impossible to say whether Molière deliberately wrote his *Tartuffe* as an attack upon the Company, his subject was without question drawn from those scandals involving the Company men which first entered the news in 1658, and that being so, the Company certainly saw it as an attack. In April 1664, when word got out concerning the kind of play he was preparing, the Company called a secret meeting to discuss a means of having it banned. The play was performed in spite of their opposition on 12 May, but only for the court, and though the King liked it he gave way to Company pressure and declared it unsuitable for public performance. While Molière appealed for support to friends in high places and even persuaded the papal legate to speak favourably of his play, the Company went to work on the public with a pamphlet written by the parish priest of Saint-Barthélemy. According to this, Molière was 'a demon rigged out in flesh and the clothes of a man, the most notorious free-thinker and blasphemer who ever was,' and his play was 'a profane and sacrilegious act' for which he deserved 'to be publicly executed, and given a foretaste of the fires of hell by being burned to death.' In a petition to the King, Molière pleaded that his play had been 'judged diabolical without even being seen', but apart from private performances for Monsieur and the Prince de Condé, he was unable to show it again. The play was banned because his picture of false religious devotion presented too close a resemblance to the Company-man and so was falsified by the Company into an attack upon religious devotion itself. When for his next play he chose as a subject the impious reprobate Don Juan, it was only too easy for the Company to denounce that as further evidence of his irreligion and to have that banned as well.

Twice in less than a year the Company had forced Molière from the stage, but privately the King was sympathetic and publicly he gave his support by granting Molière's troupe his name. Encouraged by this evidence of royal approval, Molière set to work on a revised version of his *Tartuffe*, changing the title to *Panulfe*, and on 5 August 1667, while the King was absent from the capital, went ahead and staged it. The first night sold out and the play seemed set for a successful run, but the next day the following notice reached Molière from the President of the Parlement: 'I know that you are not only an excellent actor, but also a very able man who does honour to his profession and to France. Nevertheless with all the good will that I have for you, I cannot allow you to perform your comedy. In my opinion it is very fine and instructive; but it is not the job of actors to instruct men on matters of Christian morality and religion.' Molière closed his theatre and on 8 August prepared a petition to be delivered to the King. Just three days after that, however, before the King had time to intervene, the Archbishop of Paris issued a proscription on the play, forbidding anyone in his diocese to perform, watch, print or read it in public or private 'under pain of excommunication'. The President of the Parlement, Guillaume de Lamoignon, and the Archbishop of Paris, Hardouin de Péréfixe, were both members of the Company.

The doors of Molière's theatre stayed closed for more than seven weeks, as though finally in the face of such powerful opposition he had been demoralized, but eighteen months later he came back with a third version of the play. This time he was armed in advance with a written authorization from the King to perform it in public. It was first shown on 5 February 1669, and was presented fifty-five times before the end of that year. In March it appeared in print and by June had reached a second edition. The Company had after all failed to silence him, and the play they had contrived to ban for almost five years proved so popular that of all his plays it was, as it still is, the most frequently performed. Neither the first nor the second version of the play survives, but so far as one can gather the differences from one version to another were minor and served only to diminish those ambiguities which had allowed the Company to get away with their original condemnation of the play. In the person of Tartuffe, religious fraud was pilloried and with him, in so far as he resembled him, the Company-man was exposed as a cheat and made to look ridiculous.

From the first scene of the play, Tartuffe is presented as a sanctimonious bigot and a self-righteous prude who with an ingratiating show of moral rectitude and spiritual devotion has wheedled his way into the confidence and home of a man called Orgon. Thereafter he is proved to be a hypocrite and a crook whose display of virtue and piety is as false as it is excessive, designed to win from Orgon the material and social advantages he pretends to reject. That Tartuffe is an impostor is evident to everyone in Orgon's family, but their combined efforts to undeceive Orgon only push him further into Tartuffe's control; eventually he even decides to break off his daughter's engagement to the man she loves in order to give her in marriage to Tartuffe. Orgon's wife speaks to Tartuffe on his own, hoping to persuade him against the plan, but he takes advantage of the occasion to try to seduce her. He yearns to possess the beauty of God, he tells her, and that divine loveliness he sees manifest in her. She need not fear for her honour, he tells her, because he is a man of discretion and will keep her favours a secret. Orgon's son, having overheard these declarations, denounces him to his father, who refuses to believe the accusation. When his son persists in it, Orgon drives him from the house, disowned and cursed. Tartuffe, he decides, will be his sole heir and will marry his daughter that very evening. In proof of his trust he wants to go even further and make a deed of gift to Tartuffe of all his property. Tartuffe accepts but only, as he says, to ensure that Orgon's wealth will be used for the glory of God and not given to someone who might employ it for evil purposes.

In a last desperate bid to open Orgon's eyes, his wife has him hide under the table while she talks to Tartuffe again, deliberately leading the scoundrel on to repeat his earlier attempt at seduction. This time he makes the additional assertions that a sin kept secret is no sin at all and that Orgon is fool enough to believe anything Tartuffe wants him to believe. Orgon, at last disabused, orders Tartuffe from his house, but the deed of gift has already been made and, soon after Tartuffe's departure, a bailiff arrives to expel the family; legally Orgon's house and all his possessions now belong to Tartuffe. There is worse in store. Orgon had in his keeping a box of letters belonging to a friend in disgrace. Tartuffe has taken these letters to the King and, before Orgon can flee, an officer arrives with a warrant for arrest. For a moment it seems that Tartuffe has perverted the judgement of the King just as he has perverted the teachings of God, but the officer's warrant turns out to be for the arrest of Tartuffe, not Orgon. The King, who can read the hearts of men and knows the false man from the true, has not been deceived by the impostor. Tartuffe is taken off to prison, Orgon's daughter is married to the man she loves, and everyone lives happily ever after.

For his victory over the Company of the Holy Sacrament, Molière was to pay dearly; at least, that was the belief of Anatole Loquin. According to his theory, the success of *Tartuffe* only made the Company more determined to stifle Molière, and this time permanently, by destroying him in the eyes of his friends and especially in the good opinion of the King. The ground had already been prepared by scandalmongers and little was needed to set their work of character assassination in motion. The matter in question was Molière's marriage in 1662 to Armande Béjart, the younger sister of Madeleine. There had been gossip at the time because of sympathy for Madeleine. She had shared so much of her life with Molière, had been his mistress once, his partner always, and had raised Armande as if she were her own daughter. Among Molière's enemies the tittle-tattle had taken on an offensive tone and, in November 1663, during the slanging match which followed his play *School for Wives*, Racine reported to a friend that an actor from a rival company, Zacharie de Montfleury, had been using the story to make trouble for him: 'Montfleury has made a suit against Molière and has given it to the King. He accuses him of marrying the daughter after sleeping with the mother. But Montfleury is not listened to at court.' In 1663, the King had no time for such back-biting and in 1664, when Molière's first child was born, he was pleased to be the godfather.

In January 1670, however, just less than a year after Molière won the right to perform his *Tartuffe*, the gossip turned openly vicious as the result of a verse-comedy called *Elomire* which was published in pamphlet form. The play was obviously satirical and, since the title was an evident anagram of 'Molière', no one had any doubt about the author's true meaning. Who the author was is not known, but in Loquin's view the play was written to order for the Company. Everyone knew that Molière was old enough to be his wife's father and that she was young enough to be the daughter of his one-time mistress; the allegation made in the play went just one step further. In Act I Scene iii, Elomire is made to declare that his wife is his own daughter. No doubt the slander was not in itself new, but until then it had never been made public. The accusation was serious. If Molière's marriage was incestuous, the penalty demanded by law was death at the stake.

One may be sure that Molière's friends, including the King, were eager to dismiss the charge as absurd, but presumably the facts of Armande's birth were as uncertain then as they are today. No birth certificate exists and what documents remain are imprecise and contradictory. According to her contract of marriage she was 'about twenty years of age' in 1662, which would place her birth in about 1642, but according to her burial certificate she was fifty-five years old in 1700, which would fix her birth in 1645. This doubt about the year of her birth is enough to raise the possibility that she was indeed the daughter of Madeleine, and not her sister, because it is known that Joseph Béjart, the father of Madeleine, died in 1642. Nothing can be proved either way of course, but if Molière's wife was the daughter of Madeleine and was born after 1643, when Madeleine had become Molière's mistress, then Molière might very well have been the father of his own wife. It has been suggested that Armande's own uncertainty about the situation, when exposed to whispered accusations of incest, was the chief reason for her infidelity to Molière and the breakdown of their marriage in 1664, but whatever her own feelings and beliefs, the allegation of incest followed her throughout her life. In 1676 she was openly traduced in a court of law as 'the daughter of her husband, the wife of her father' and in 1688 was slandered in the same way in a pamphlet called *La Fameuse Comédienne*.

As Loquin sees it, *Elomire* was the beginning of the end for Molière. The seeds of doubt were sown and, with careful tending, grew to fruit. For a year or so he continued to enjoy popularity and patronage, but all the time his reputation was gradually being eroded by his inability to check the rumours about his marriage. In February 1672 Madeleine Béjart died, and it was in the course of the following months that Molière lost favour at court. Lully, the Master of the King's Music, refused to work with him any more and so he was obliged to find someone else to write the music for his new play, *The Imaginary Invalid*. Lully made difficulties for him even then, demanding that the score be reworked repeatedly, and finally, when the play with its music was ready, the King did not wish to see it. According to Loquin, Lully's hostility was not, as is often claimed, the cause of Molière's fall from grace, but only an effect. Lully, feeling the King grow cool towards Molière, abandoned him in order to keep his own favoured position.

The King's change of attitude towards Molière was, in Loquin's opinion, directly related to Madeleine Béjart's death. Since she was buried in Saint-Paul cemetery, it is certain that on her death-bed she renounced the acting profession and received the last sacraments because, without that, actors and actresses were denied burial in holy ground. Loquin speculates that the Company managed to convince the King that in her final confession she had acknowledged herself to be the mother, and Molière to be the father, of the girl who had become Molière's wife, denouncing him as the guilty architect and the girl as the blameless victim of that heinous relationship. The King then determined to separate the incestuous couple and punish Molière but, to avoid any possible slur upon himself, he chose to do so without public scandal. The day chosen for Molière's pretended death was one year to the day that Madeleine Béjart had died, a coincidence too striking in Loquin's view to be the work of chance, though why the King should have wished that anniversary to be observed, he does not say.

The only contemporary description of the circumstances of Molière's death was made by a fellow-actor and member of the troupe called Charles Varlet de La Grange. He kept a diary of the troupe's activities, and for Friday 17 February 1673 he made the following entry: 'This same day after the comedy, at ten o'clock at night, M. de Molière died in his house in the rue de Richelieu, having played the rôle of the Imaginary Invalid, greatly discomforted by a cold and inflammation of the chest which caused him to cough, and that so badly that in the strenuous efforts he made to clear his lungs he ruptured a vein.' His death though sudden should not have been a surprise if it is true that he had been suffering from consumption for seven or eight years; but, in the preface to the collected works of Molière published nine years after his death, La Grange maintained that though for some years Molière had some chronic lung problem which caused him to cough, 'his constitution was otherwise excellent and had it not been for the unhappy chance that his sickness was not treated, he would have had the strength to overcome it.' La Grange considered that the ruptured vein was an accident, due to the violence of the coughing fit, and claimed that it 'shortened his life by more than twenty years'. This point of view is of central importance to Loquin's theory, for he would have us recognize that La Grange had seen and worked with Molière almost every day for ten years, had been with him at the theatre just a few hours before his death and yet, though fully aware of how ill he had been that day, was surprised to learn of his death. La Grange was not a doctor, it is true, but he was not a fool either. The seriousness of Molière's illness, Loquin concludes, was an invention put about later to make his sudden death seem plausible.

It was not until 1704 that a biography of Molière appeared. Thirty-one years had elapsed since his supposed death and by that time most of the people who had known him intimately, including his wife and La Grange, were dead. Loquin finds some dark significance in this, as he does in the fact that only one year had elapsed since the death of the Iron Mask. The biography was written by Jean Léonor de Grimarest who had not known Molière but had got most of his information, including the circumstances of his death, from someone who had: the actor Michel Baron. Molière had adopted Baron at the age of twelve, taking him into his troupe and making him one of his own family. At the time of Molière's death Baron was twenty and their relationship was closer than it had ever been. According to Baron, on the morning of that fateful day Molière confided to him that he knew he was going to die and, after the evening performance, sought him out in his dressing-room. Baron, realizing how ill he was, called a sedan-chair and had him carried home. There he got him into bed and stayed with him until he saw that he had begun to spit blood. At that he went to find Molière's wife, but by the time he returned with her to the bedroom Molière was dead. Later that same night he personally went to the palace to inform the King.

Baron's account of Molière's death, as recorded by Grimarest, is today the generally accepted version. It includes the kind of inconsequential detail that makes for credibility: Molière in bed not wanting to eat a bowl of his wife's broth and asking for a piece of parmesan cheese instead. 'I thought I should go into detail about Molière's death,' Grimarest declared, 'in order to disabuse the public on the various stories that have been invented about it.' What these stories were, he did not say, but one such story current at the time was that Molière had died on the stage, his real sickness not realized because he was acting the part of a man who imagined himself to be sick. That story, providing as it did a theatre full of imaginary witnesses, was in Loquin's opinion deliberately concocted as part of the official cover-up for the imaginary corpse, though as Loquin saw it, Grimarest's own account of Molière's death was just as much a fabrication: Baron, fully aware that he was the sole survivor of Molière's troupe and so could not be contradicted, took advantage of the situation to embroider the original story and give himself a star rôle in history. Loquin argues that for thirty-one years, until Grimarest gave Baron's version of what happened, there was uncertainty about the circumstances of Molière's death and the only good reason for this was that there were in fact no witnesses at all.

When it came to the circumstances of Molière's burial, Grimarest did such a sketchy job that his book was sharply criticized by the writer of an anonymous letter published in 1706. If he had given all the information he should and could have given, his critic said, 'he would have had enough material to fill a volume as big again as the book he wrote and it would have been packed with the very strangest things.' Grimarest wrote a letter of his own in reply, acknowledging the truth of this assertion, and in the next printing of his book included both letters as an annex. 'I found the material of that subject so delicate and difficult to deal with,' he explained in his letter, 'that I frankly admit I did not dare to undertake it.' Fear of the authorities had stopped him publishing the full story of Molière's burial, but as a responsible writer he considered the omission too important to pass over it in silence. If the claim is true, and it is a claim which his son is supposed to have made, that he himself was the writer of the anonymous letter criticizing the book, then that importance was considerable in his eyes. What little he does say about the burial is peculiar enough. That day 'an incredible mass of people' gathered in the street outside Molière's house. What kind of people they were and why they were there is not clear, but Molière's wife was terrified by them, and they only dispersed after she had thrown them money. The burial itself took place at night by the light of 'nearly a hundred torches'.

Some details are known of those 'delicate and difficult' matters which Grimarest was afraid to mention and Loquin produces them as further support for his theory. Molière's body was refused burial in holy ground because, it was said, he had died without renouncing his profession of actor. When his widow appealed to the King, the burial was allowed, but only at night and without requiem mass. The body was taken directly from the house to the cemetery of Saint-Joseph and, since it was normal procedure for witnesses to sign the burial certificate in the church register while they were at the church, the entry certifying Molière's burial remained unsigned. The widow had a monument erected on the grave, but a story circulated that the grave was empty. Soon after the burial, it was said, the body had been secretly moved to a common grave in unconsecrated ground 'close to the chaplain's house'. Such irregularities and uncertainties, Loquin argues, are perfectly consistent with the 'delicate and difficult' business of burying an empty coffin. Today Molière's supposed remains are honoured in the cemetery of Père-Lachaise where they were placed in 1817. They were removed from Saint-Joseph in 1792 during the Revolution, not from Molière's grave but from the common grave 'close to the chaplain's house'. Since under such circumstances no proper identification would have been possible, there is no good reason to believe that they are in fact the remains of Molière. That aside, however, the point for consideration is that presumably the remains were first looked for and not found under the tombstone erected by Molière's widow.

Loquin's investigation of the suspicious circumstances surrounding Molière's death and burial does not end there. It was not just the body which disappeared. Apparently all Molière's original manuscripts, his rough drafts, notes and fragments, his personal memos and private letters, vanished too. How is it possible, Loquin asks, that a writer, who wrote so much, left nothing in his own handwriting except 'a couple of receipts and a few signatures?' For Loquin there is only one possible explanation: his collected papers were deliberately destroyed by the organization which had destroyed him, the Company of the Holy Sacrament. To eliminate Molière and to restrict to *Tartuffe* the damage he had done was after all a minor achievement when compared to the full-scale anti-Protestant campaign undertaken by the Company which led eventually to the suppression of Jansenism[7] and the revocation of the Edict of Nantes.[8]

However preposterous Loquin's theory may seem, the most commonly voiced arguments against it are invalid. If Molière was the Iron Mask, it is said, then he lived for thirty years in prison from the age of fifty to the age of eighty, and that would have been impossible for a man suffering from consumption. According to Loquin, however, the seriousness of Molière's illness was invented as part of the cover-up: he was not consumptive at all. Molière's wife remarried in 1677 and if Molière had still been alive, it is said, then the authorities would not have allowed her to do so. According to Loquin, however, Molière was believed to be the father of his wife and so their marriage was null and void.

Perhaps the most delightful feature of Loquin's theory is the fact that the descriptions of the Iron Mask given by Voltaire and Palteau add up to what might very well be a portrait of Molière as an old man: white-haired, tall and well-built with a dark complexion and the voice of an actor which 'held one's attention by the mere sound'. But the most interesting feature is the fact that it answers a central question which most other theories evade or ignore: the reason for the mask. Molière's face was not only known to the general public but familiar to them; and he would have been recognized in the South of France, where he had led his troupe for thirteen years, as well as in Paris.

Molière was not the only Iron Mask to be incarcerated by religious bigots. Another theory professed the masked prisoner to be Archbishop Avedik of the Armenian Orthodox Church, Patriarch of Constantinople and Jerusalem, a man of simple birth and honest faith, loved by his spiritual flock and respected by his temporal masters, who was hounded into exile from Turkey and smuggled into prison in France by Jesuit missionaries and the agents of Louis XIV. It has been asserted that Avedik's first name was Michael, that the Armenian community actually called him saint during his lifetime and that the name 'Marchioly' in the Armenian language means 'Saint Michael': 'Mar' being the word for saint and 'Kioly' the diminutive for 'Michael'. That much of the story is an invention – 'Mar Kioly' has no meaning in the Armenian language and the first name of the patriarch was quite simply and precisely Avedik – but the truth of Avedik's secret abduction and imprisonment in the Bastille is incontrovertible.

Avedik Yevtokiatsi was born at Tokat in Armenia in 1657, the son of a weaver who was himself the son of an Orthodox priest. Though prepared from childhood for the weaver's trade, the influence of his grandfather, who taught him to read and write, led him into the priesthood. At the age of eighteen he became a deacon and, though he did not become a priest until the age of thirty-two, he so distinguished himself in defence of the Armenian community during an outbreak of brutal and bloody persecution by the Turkish population that just three years after his ordination he was nominated Bishop of Erzinkan and Erzurum. His reputation as a man of energy and discretion in his dealings not only with the Turkish and Moslem authorities but also with the Dominican and Jesuit missionaries in Armenia reached beyond his diocese and eventually prompted the Orthodox Churches of Constantinople to turn to him for help.

In the time of Louis XIV, as today, the Christians of Constantinople were members of the Greek or Armenian Churches, their faith being as much an expression of national origin and cultural identity as of religious belief. Missionaries from western Europe were received by them with cordiality and allowed to preach in their churches, but in their zeal to make converts to Catholicism the Jesuits went beyond the limits of good faith and plain sense, openly attacking Orthodox doctrine and secretly fomenting pastoral discord. By 1699 the situation was out of hand. The leaders of the Greek and Armenian communities appealed to the Sultan for protection and the Jesuit missionaries appealed to their embassies for support.

The French ambassador, though a priest himself, was not prepared to condone the excesses of the Jesuit campaign and so found himself accused in Versailles of sympathy to Islam. He was recalled and replaced by a man of more forceful temper, the Comte de Fériol. The new ambassador had distinguished himself in nothing except brawling over women and cards, and came to the post with nothing to recommend him except a sister-in-law who was the mistress of a government minister in Paris and a spell of service as a mercenary in the pay of the Turks in Hungary. Soon after his arrival in Constantinople he demonstrated his mastery of the situation by securing the exile of Avedik, the staunchest defender of the Armenian Church, on the charge that he had been heard to make some disrespectful remarks about Louis XIV. The Jesuit missionaries were delighted to have such a champion in their midst and direct contact between Fériol and Rome was quickly established.

Avedik, however, was not himself without influence. The Great Mufti, head of the Moslem religion in Turkey, was a personal friend of his and in February 1702 not only managed to have him released from exile but also to have him nominated Archbishop of Constantinople. Some retaliation against Fériol might have been expected, but Avedik showed no resentment. He insisted that the Jesuits should refrain from attacking Orthodox doctrine when preaching inside Orthodox churches but was otherwise conciliatory and exhorted the Armenians to tolerance and peace. Fériol, belligerent but powerless, bided his time and, when in July 1703 the Great Mufti was assassinated and the Sultan overthrown, rushed to persuade the new regime that Avedik should be deposed and imprisoned. The fortress of the Seven Towers in Constantinople, grim as it was, seemed to Fériol too pleasant a place for someone like Avedik. At his insistence the patriarch was moved to the island-prison of Ruad off the coast of Syria and kept, as Fériol himself reported with no small delight, 'in a cell full of water from which he could see no daylight.'

The Armenian community, loyal and resolute, refused to recognize any patriarch but Avedik and in December 1704, having put together a large sum of money, bribed the Grand Vizier to release and restore him. Again Fériol and the Jesuits feared retaliation, but again Avedik was conciliatory. There seemed every reason for him to be as rabidly anti-French and anti-Catholic as Fériol claimed he was, but in fact he gave no sign of being so. His attitude from the outset and throughout was never other than defensive: unyielding but forbearing. In December 1705, a deputation of three hundred well-to-do Armenians, led by Avedik, appealed to Fériol in person for his support towards a peaceful settlement with the Jesuits, but in February 1706 Fériol went to the Grand Vizier with a bribe of his own to have Avedik sent back to Syria. This time the French Government was prepared to ensure that he would not return.

The boat carrying Avedik stopped on its way at the island of Chios and it was there that he was abducted. His guard, bribed before setting out, handed him over to the French vice-consul who put him aboard a French merchant ship bound for Marseilles. The story told by the guards afterwards was that Avedik had been carried off by pirates. As it was, bad weather forced the French ship to put in at Genoa and there Avedik managed to smuggle two letters into the hands of a Greek who was on his way to Constantinople. One was addressed to the chief interpreter of the Turkish government, the other to a leading figure in the Armenian community. The letters reached Constantinople within a matter of days, but it was Fériol who received them. The Greek had broken his journey at Smyrna and there had confided in friends who had persuaded him to sell the letters to the French consul. Avedik meanwhile had been brought to Marseilles and locked up in the prison of the Arsenal.

Whatever it was the French government and the Jesuit Society had hoped to achieve by their abduction of Avedik, it was certainly not what happened, although what did happen was perhaps only to be expected. The cover-up story of a pirate attack was not believed and eventually under torture the guard confessed the truth. The French Embassy was notified that, if Avedik was not returned, the Catholic community would be held responsible. Fériol replied that he knew nothing at all about the matter, but if Avedik had left Turkey he had no doubt done so by his own design to escape going back to prison. The Turkish authorities were not deceived and the threat of reprisals was carried out. The Jesuits were banned and their printing-press destroyed. All Turks who professed the Catholic faith were rounded up, and those who did not apostasise were executed.

About Avedik's fate, however, nothing could be established. There were rumours that he had been seen in Malta and Messina, but people who went to hunt for him there could find no trace. The Vatican was greatly concerned that the truth should not get out, and warned Versailles repeatedly of the need to take every precaution. In February 1707, Louis XIV informed the Sultan that the French for their part had done their utmost to find the missing patriarch and after extensive investigations made in Italy and Spain had reason to believe that the poor man was dead. The Armenians knew the French were lying, and in 1708 a group of them even carried the search to Marseilles, but left without learning anything.

In the opinion of Pierre de Taulès, whose book *L'Homme au Masque de fer* was published in 1825, the story of Avedik, after his arrival in France, is the story of the Iron Mask. He was moved from Marseilles to the island of Sainte-Marguerite and from there some time later to the Bastille where, masked and anonymous, he died. Taulès was well aware that according to the journal of Du Junca the Iron Mask was brought to the Bastille on 19 September 1698 and died on 18 November 1703, the latter date being all of three years before Avedik's abduction, but as Taulès pointed out, the man responsible for finding and publishing that journal was Henri Griffet and he was a Jesuit. Du Junca's journal was a forgery, Taulès declared, invented by Griffet to cover up the fact that the Iron Mask had been a victim of the Jesuits, abducted and imprisoned at their instigation, against all code and conscience, all law and sense.

In fact, what happened to Avedik after his arrival in France is not now a secret and, though certainly an indictment of Jesuits and the Catholic Church, of Louis XIV and his government, bears little resemblance to anything ever said about the Iron Mask. In November 1706, he was moved from Marseilles and the Mediterranean Sea across France to the Atlantic coast and a monk's cell in the Benedictine abbey of Mont-Saint-Michel. The orders given to the abbot were that he was to be kept in secret and allowed contact with no one. As it was, he could not speak French and so was unable to communicate at all. Only in July 1707 did the authorities decide that a monk who had some knowledge of the Armenian language could be sent from Rome to act as interpreter. The first communication made by Avedik through this interpreter was an appeal for justice: 'Judge me', he is reported to have said, 'and condemn me to the punishment I deserve. Or else, if I am innocent, say so and set me free.' He would only go free, he was told, when he confessed his crimes against God and the true Church, abjured the Orthodox faith and became a Catholic. In December 1709 he was transferred to the Bastille, and in September 1710 he made his abjuration. Some days later he was ordained a Catholic priest and went to live with his interpreter in the parish of Saint-Sulpice, where unknown and unnoticed he said mass everyday until his death in July 1711.

This is not the only theory in which Jesuit machinations were held responsible for the Iron Mask's fate. The first version ever published of the mysterious prisoner's identity made him out to be a victim of the Jesuits. It was reported by someone who had been a prisoner in the Bastille during the nine months Avedik was there, as well as being there earlier during the last year and a half of the Iron Mask's life. On 16 May 1702, when according to Du Junca the masked prisoner had been in the Bastille for more than three and a half years, a certain René-Augustin Constantin de Renneville was arrested and imprisoned there. He had been working for the French secret service in Holland, but was a Protestant and suspected of being a double agent. No charge was ever made against him, but he was kept in the Bastille for eleven years and then exiled. From 1715 to 1719 he published his prison memoirs in four volumes under the title *L'Inquisition Française ou l'Histoire de la Bastille* and in the preface to the first volume he spoke about the prisoner who had come to the Bastille with Saint-Mars. It was a story he had got from two members of the prison staff, a turnkey called Antoine Ru, who had accompanied the prisoner from Sainte-Marguerite, and the prison surgeon, Abraham Reilhe, whose signature appears on the prisoner's burial certificate.

One day, when for some reason Renneville was taken out of his cell to some other part of the prison, he was led into a room where another prisoner happened to be and was quickly bundled out again. On the way back to his cell, he asked his guards who this prisoner was, and Ru replied 'that he had been a prisoner for thirty-one years and that M. de

Saint-Mars had brought him with him from the island of Sainte-Marguerite.' Renneville's curiosity was aroused and, when he persisted with his questions, Ru at length explained that the prisoner 'had been condemned to perpetual imprisonment for having written two lines of verse against the Jesuits when he was a schoolboy of twelve or thirteen.' Ru was unable or unwilling to say more, but Renneville remembered that a great uproar had been caused about thirty years before by someone writing a couplet against the Jesuits and posting it on the gate of their college in Paris. The name of that college had been Clermont College of the Society of Jesus and those words had been emblazoned in large golden letters above the gate. The couplet made its appearance when that name was taken down and replaced by another. The story, as told by Renneville, is this:

> The Jesuits invited the King and his court to honour with their presence a tragedy which they had staged to the glory of His Majesty and they had it performed by their very best students . . . The King was very pleased with it and as the rector of the college was escorting His Majesty away, one of the King's favourites praised the Reverend Fathers of the Society on the great success of the play, at which the King exclaimed. 'Is it so surprising? It's my own college!' The rector was too clever a courtier not to profit from this favourable remark. That very instant he sent for workers and ordered them to engrave 'College of Louis the Great' in large golden letters on black marble, insisting that it should be ready by the following morning . . . A schoolboy who witnessed the zeal of those Reverend Fathers wrote the following two lines of verse which he posted that night on the gate of the college and in various other places in Paris:-

> They have erased JESUS from here and put up the name of the
>   King.
> Impious people! No other God do they worship.

> The Society did not fail to clamour sacrilege and apparently the author was discovered. Though one of their youngest students, he was, if it was him whom I saw, condemned to perpetual imprisonment at the request of the Reverend Fathers and transferred to the Islands of Sainte Marguerite in Provence for that effect.

That however was not the end of Renneville's story. Some time later he was told by Reilhe that the prisoner had been freed two or three months after he had seen him. His liberation, moreover, had been secured by the Jesuits themselves through the intervention of a certain

Abbé Riquelet, who was attached to the Bastille as a confessor and was himself a Jesuit. 'During the time of his imprisonment, he had become the sole heir of his family, which possessed great wealth. He was notified of this by the charitable Riquelet, his confessor. The shower of gold which opened the Tower of Danaë had the same effect upon that of the Bastille. The zeal of the Abbé Riquelet made apparent to the Fathers of the Society, very disinterested people as everyone knows, the useful necessity of liberating his penitent, and the Society begged the King to pardon a lord whose family without him would have been extinguished. The King, who had only consented to the imprisonment of this child out of consideration for the Reverend Fathers, willingly signed his liberation at their request.'

Since Saint-Mars brought only one prisoner with him from Sainte-Marguerite and since Ru had accompanied him and was therefore well aware which prisoner that was, it seems safe to assume that when Ru told his story to Renneville he believed that he was giving genuine information about the masked prisoner. But since the Iron Mask died in the Bastille and Reilhe signed his burial certificate, it seems equally safe to assume that when Reilhe told his story to Renneville he knew that he was giving false information about the masked prisoner. Renneville in any case was more interested in seeing the Jesuits unmasked than in lifting the mask from a prisoner. His accidental meeting with the prisoner had been so brief that he had not even noticed a mask. Where Ru got his information and why Reilhe gave his, are for us dimensions to a mystery of which Renneville was not even aware.

1. These 'assassinations' are usually regarded as natural deaths, though there was talk of assassination at the time.
2. It was a Dominican monk, as will emerge later.
3. *Philippe IV*: King of France, b. 1268, reigned 1285–1314.
4. *Hugues Capet*: King of France, b. 939, reigned 987–996.
5. *Charles, Duc de Lorraine*: d. 995 ?, was the son of Louis IV, King of France, who died in 954; the brother of Lothaire, King of France, who reigned 954–986; and the uncle of Louis V, King of France, who reigned 986–987.
6. *Godefroi de Bouillon*: 1061–1100, became Duc de Lorraine in 1089 and King of Jerusalem in 1099.
7. *Jansenism*: a Roman Catholic religious movement of unorthodox tendencies condemned by the Pope and suppressed by Louis XIV.
8. *Edict of Nantes*: promulgated in 1598 by Henri IV, granting religious freedom to Protestants; revoked by Louis XIV in 1685.

CHAPTER SIX

THE MAN IN THE VELVET MASK

'M. de Saint-Mars has taken up the post of governor of the Bastille, bringing with him a prisoner and leaving another at Pierre-Encise on his way through Lyon': thus reported *La Gazette d'Amsterdam* on 3 October 1698. In the Bastille itself, Etienne Du Junca, the King's Lieutenant, recorded in his prison journal that the new governor arrived on 18 September direct from Sainte-Marguerite and that the prisoner who accompanied him was 'a longtime prisoner of his he had with him in Pignerol, whom he always keeps masked and whose name is never spoken.' According to Du Junca, it was three o'clock in the afternoon when the governor's party arrived and the prisoner was put into the First Chamber of the Basinière Tower until nine o'clock that night, at which time he was moved by Du Junca and a sergeant called Rosarges to the Third Chamber of the Bertaudière Tower. Rosarges, who was one of the men Saint-Mars had brought with him from Sainte-Marguerite, was given charge of the mysterious prisoner, and Du Junca had nothing more to say about him, and possibly nothing more to do with him, until he recorded his death five years later. He referred to him then as 'the unknown prisoner in the mask of black velvet' and noted that his burial certificate had been signed by Rosarges, promoted in the meantime to major, and by a surgeon called Reilhe, who also held the rank of major. The actual burial certificate, destroyed in a fire in 1871 but preserved in a facsimile copy published the year before, verifies the information given by Du Junca, albeit with orthographical differences. No other official record referring to the prisoner while he was in the Bastille is known to exist, except a short despatch from the Comte de Pontchartrain,[1] Controller of Finance, to Saint-Mars on 3 November 1698, just six and a half weeks after the prisoner's arrival, which says: 'The King vouchsafes that your prisoner from Provence makes his confession and takes communion whenever you judge proper.'

According to later information, based it was claimed on the evidence of eye-witnesses, the masked prisoner used to go back and forth through the courtyard on his way to and from mass, but other than that nothing is known about his life in the Bastille. By all accounts, the Third Chamber of the Bertaudière Tower was large and well-lit, one of the best rooms in the prison, but the prisoner did not stay there until his death. One year after his arrival, it was given to a man called Falaiseau; a year and a half after that it was occupied by a woman called Anne Randon; and a year and a half after that, it was shared by three prisoners: a French count, an English banker and an Italian priest. All that can be said for certain is that, since the masked prisoner had to pass through the courtyard to go to mass, he was not kept in the Liberty Tower where the chapel was at that time, but in one of the seven other towers of the prison. So far as one can make out, all these towers were constructed in more or less the same way, with prison rooms one on top of the other: one or two basement dungeons, three or four large chambers numbered upwards, the upper ones being the best, and a small vaulted room at the top. The towers were round and the rooms octagonal, varying in size according to the thickness of the wall, but up to seven yards across in the largest chambers. The lowest dungeons were cold, wet and black, with air-vents but no windows, and always liable to flooding from the moat. The upper chambers in contrast had large fireplaces and windows six feet high giving panoramic views across the rooftops of Paris.

All eight towers were a hundred feet high, linked by curtain-walls of the same height, and they were disposed in a simple rectangular form, except for the two central towers of the eastern side which were slightly advanced to form a bay. Originally the castle had served as a city gate and the archway of this, still crowned with statues on the outer face, could be seen in outline in the structure of the wall between the two projecting towers. The castle was surrounded by a moat, forty yards across, and beyond that by an outer wall, sixty feet high. One entered from the rue Saint-Antoine through a gate with a guardhouse; thence by a drawbridge and another gate to the governor's residence; thence by another drawbridge, gate and guardhouse to a barrier in the entrance of the castle proper; and thence into the main courtyard which was about forty yards long by twenty-five wide, shut in by six of the towers: the County Tower, Treasure Tower and Chapel Tower in line on the right; the Basinière Tower, Bertaudière Tower and Liberty Tower on the left. Warrens of lean-to shacks stretched along the foot of the walls between the towers, those on the right serving as barrack-rooms for the soldiers and those on the left as dormitories for the prison staff. A row of buildings filled the open space between Chapel Tower and Liberty Tower, closing off the yard from the remaining two towers. In these buildings were the kitchens, storerooms and offices, the living-quarters of the King's Lieutenant and the interrogation room. Steps and an alley-way led through them to a small courtyard full of chickens and garbage with the Corner Tower on the right, the Well Tower on the left and a line of hovels, where the servants lived, along the wall between them.

Knowledge of the particular people who were employed as prison staff at any given time is fragmentary at best, but for the men who guarded the Iron Mask when he was there, including those who came with him from Sainte-Marguerite, a fund of information is provided by Renneville's account of his own imprisonment. Most of his portraits are grotesque and derisive, filled with hatred and condemnation, but there are enough precisions in his accounts, enough exceptions and qualifications in his judgements, to argue that the pictures though harsh are not altogether unfair, as is demonstrated by the description he gives of his arrival at the Bastille:

At last we reached the dreadful place and, as we entered, the sentinels put their hats in front of their faces the moment they saw us. I learned afterwards that they practice this strange custom because they are forbidden to look any prisoner in the face. When we arrived at the courtyard of the governor's quarters and got down, we were met at the foot of the steps by an agreeable-looking man, who I learned later was the King's Lieutenant, M. Du Junca, and another little figure of a man, very unpleasant-looking and very shabbily dressed, who was the nephew of the governor and called Corbé. They conducted us, the officer and myself, into the apartment of M. de Saint-Mars. The two guards had begun to climb the steps to follow us in, but M. Du Junca turned and made them go back, saying haughtily: 'You have surrendered this gentleman to us and we are quite equal to the responsibility. Wait at the bottom of the steps.' We entered a chamber draped in yellow damask fringed with silver which seemed to me appropriate enough, as did the governor who was in front of a big fire. He was a little old man of very meagre appearance, whose head and hands and whole body kept shaking all the time. He received us very politely, reached out his trembling hand and put it into mine. It was as cold as a lump of ice and I said to myself: 'There's a bad sign. Death or his deputy is making a bond with me.'
The officer gave him the King's letter or the order of arrest and

took him into a corner of the room so that he could whisper something in his ear, but since the governor was too deaf to hear he had to repeat what he said in a louder voice and I heard these words distinctly: 'M. Chamillart ordered me to recommend this gentleman to you and to bid you treat him more favourably than the other prisoners . . .' The governor offered everyone breakfast, but the officer thanked him saying that I had already taken care of that and had given them an excellent burgundy to drink. He then took leave of the governor and his companions and left me with them. The governor ordered his nephew to go and prepare the Second Chamber of the Chapel Tower for me, at which that little man replied with astonishment 'The Second Chapel?' 'Yes,' replied his uncle, swearing by the holy name of God and shooting terrible glances through him for all that his eyes were cloudy and dull. 'Do what I say and don't answer back.' His nephew went off at the double, and when I was alone with him and M. Du Junca, the governor asked me if I had been long at court. I told him that I had arrived there from Holland just four months before, and he began then to puff himself up and boast of his exploits, which under the circumstances was not in the least appropriate.

He told me that he had left Holland the day after the birth of King William, formerly the Prince of Orange, because the day before, when everyone was celebrating, he had picked a quarrel with seven Dutchmen, had killed four and disarmed the other three. I looked at this paladin who made himself out to be Hercules and he seemed to me little better than excrement. From there he had embarked for Lisbon where he had carried off the prize in a famous tourney. After that he had moved to the court of Madrid where he had won acclaim in a bullfight, carrying off the prize for that too and the admiration of all the ladies, who had well-nigh drowned him in a deluge of perfume-eggs filled with scented water. Every fourth word he uttered was an oath to assert this big talk which was so at odds with his puny size. Apparently he was going to take me to India to carry off some princess there when his nephew came to say that I could leave because everything was ready. My new host protested at great length that he would have every possible consideration for me, that I would be well treated and that he would visit me often.

Eight days later, Renneville was taken to see Saint-Mars for a routine interrogation and that was the only other time that he ever saw him. Apart from Saint-Mars, Du Junca was the only prison officer commissioned and nominated by the King and he had already been adjutant at the Bastille for eight years when Saint-Mars arrived. 'It is true', Renneville says, 'that it was M. Du Junca who was the first to put double doors on the rooms and also extra grilles on many windows to deprive prisoners of the view over the streets of Paris. Moreover, in almost all the rooms, he blocked up all but one of the windows, something which was extremely detrimental to the health of the occupants. Furthermore, he would not permit any communication at all between the prisoners. In his eyes, a hole made in a fireplace or a floor to effect contact between neighbours was a serious offence and he punished it severely.' Nevertheless, Renneville says he was 'obliging, affable, mild, honest', and declares: 'So far as I am concerned, he never did anything but good to me personally, and I must report my feelings sincerely: the good qualities he had far outweighed the bad.'

The prison physician, whose name was Fresquier, and the Abbé Riquelet, the Jesuit priest who was attached to the prison as confessor, were nominated respectively by the King's own physician and the King's own confessor, but for all the rest of the prison staff, the hiring and firing was done by the governor. Saint-Mars brought five members of his previous team with him when he moved to the Bastille, and of these Jacques Rosarges was the one chosen to take special charge of the masked prisoner. Renneville calls Rosarges 'the monster' and describes him as a short-built, slack-limbed, gargoyle-headed figure in a coarse cloth coat of rags and patches, ignorant, stupid, brutal and drunk. His face was bloated and discoloured with drink, his eyes were bleary red, his lips, which were thick, were blue and covered in pustules, while his nose was like a squashed fruit 'charged with twenty or thirty other little noses of different colours'. Whenever he made an appearance he was reeling drunk, bowing low and flourishing his hat in a ludicrous imitation of what he thought to be good manners. From what he told Renneville, he had been in service with Saint-Mars ever since Pignerol and had risen through the ranks, starting out as a simple soldier with a musket. For a bribe he would promise anything and, to keep himself in brandy, he was ready to plunder anything of value the prisoners might have, including even the clothes on their backs.

The prison chaplain, the Abbé Giraut, had also been brought by Saint-Mars from Sainte-Marguerite. There, presumably, he had been the sole spiritual guide and confessor of the masked prisoner and certainly it was he who, according to Du Junca, heard his confession the day before he died and exhorted him on his death-bed. His hold over the governor, Renneville tells us, was very strong: 'The priest was the pet of Saint-Mars and Saint-Mars was the puppet of the priest'. It was on Giraut's recommendation that Saint-Mars chose the extra members of staff he needed once he arrived at the Bastille. Renneville describes him as a man of average height, neat and dapper in dress, with hollow eyes, protruding mouth and a nose 'like the beak of a parrot'. His complexion was unhealthily pale and he was coughing and spitting continuously, but his lungs, Renneville would have us believe, were less corrupt than his soul. The man was a whited sepulchre, 'an execrable goat' who debauched the women under his spiritual care, including even the nuns of nearby convents. Along with Corbé, he made the woman prisoners, willing or not, his jades. Those who abandoned themselves to his lechery received favoured treatment, while those who resisted were punished and threatened until they surrendered, or were simply brutalized and raped.

Corbé's full name was Guillaume de Formanoir de Corbé. As the nephew of Saint-Mars, he later inherited the Château de Palteau and it was his son, born in 1712, who supplied information on the masked prisoner in letters to Voltaire in 1763 and Fréron in 1768. Renneville says he was about fifty years old when he first saw him, and at that time he had been in the service of his uncle for about eighteen years. 'From his appearance', Renneville declares, 'it never occurred to me that it was the nephew of the governor I was speaking to.' Dressed as he was in a poor grey coat of short-napped cloth worn threadbare, a pair of shabby blue breeches frayed and patched at the knee, a rusty outmoded wig and a dilapidated hat stuck with an old black half-bare feather, he looked 'more like a bumbailiff than an officer'. He was dirty and unshaven with a mouthful of rotten teeth and 'at least two thirds of his face was mouth'. His forehead was narrow, his eyes small and black and his sharp- pointed nose looked 'like a suppository'. That Renneville detested the man is obvious, but he claims that everyone detested him, his fellow gaolers as much as the prisoners. 'He walked bent double with knock-kneed legs as contorted as those of a basset, but his spirit was even more deformed and crooked than his body'. Seconded by an illegitimate son called Jacques La France, who acted as his lackey, 'one of the most vicious and villainous characters' in the Bastille, Corbé altogether surpassed his worst colleagues in the maltreatment and exploitation of the prisoners, more brazen in his thievery than Rosarges, more savage in his lechery than Giraut.

The chief turnkey, a man called L'Ecuyer, had also come to the Bastille from Sainte-Marguerite. He told Renneville that he had been with Saint-Mars for thirty-two years, a year longer than Rosarges, but had been passed over for promotion because he could not read or write. He was a heavily built, hump-backed, round- shouldered man whose head appeared to grow out of the middle of his chest. Apart from a few strands of greasy hair around the ears, this misplaced head was bald and had a dark red face 'like the mask of a devil in an opera'. Dreadful though he appeared, however, 'he still had some kind of fear of God', Renneville thought, and found him 'the least vicious . . . and the most conscientious of the officers'.

Under L'Ecuyer there were three turnkeys, Boutonnier, Bourgouin and Ru, all of whom, Renneville says, were better than their masters. Boutonnier was a Jew from Paris and had been a button-maker before working at the Bastille. Renneville saw little of him but found him compassionate. Bourgouin was from Burgundy and had been a dragoon until Giraut, who knew his uncle, had got him the job of turnkey. He was, Renneville says, an honest man, friendly and kind: all the prisoners liked him, but he did not fit in such a place and did not keep his job for long. Antoine Ru was the least benign of the three, but, though he stole the prisoners' food and would do little for them unless he was bribed, he laughed a great deal and was far from being a wicked man. He had been with Saint-Mars on Sainte-Marguerite and was about fifty years old when Renneville first saw him. His head and face were a mass of tangled red hair, stiff with dirt, and he went around in nothing but a dirty shirt and drawers, stinking 'worse than the filthiest goat'.

Both Ru and L'Ecuyer must have known something about the masked prisoner but probably little more than the fact of his existence, along with some general idea of the duration of his imprisonment. Normally the prisoners' meals were brought to the cells by the turnkeys, but from what Du Junca had to say about the masked prisoner it seems that in his case Rosarges was personally responsible. Presumably it was also Rosarges, and not Ru or L'Ecuyer, who had served at table for Saint-Mars and the masked prisoner during their stop-over at the Château de Palteau, reported by Corbé's son in his letter to Fréron.

One more member of the prison staff remains to be mentioned, a man who was not previously with Saint-Mars on Sainte-Marguerite, but who nonetheless must have had contact of some kind with the masked prisoner for it was he, with Rosarges, who signed the burial certificate. This was Abraham Reilhe, the surgeon of the Bastille. The title 'surgeon' is today misleading. At that time, when the common treatment for most illnesses was to bleed the patient, the surgeon was simply the man called to do it. Usually he was a barber by profession, though he might also administer purges on demand, pull teeth, lance boils or sear wounds, and if he had some knowledge of the butcher's trade might very well offer to perform amputations as well. Reilhe had been a barber in an infantry company prior to his job at the Bastille and Saint-Mars had hired him on the recommendation of Giraut shortly before Renneville's arrival. As a surgeon he was, according to Renneville, so ignorant and incompetent that he was responsible for the death of more than one prisoner. He was a little man, quick-witted and adaptable, acquisitive and ambitious, a sycophant and an opportunist. When he first came to the Bastille he had nothing to wear but an old army uniform and he was deferential to an extreme with everyone, but once he had settled in and established himself in the good opinion of his superiors, he took to wearing the governor's cast-off clothes, his old jerkins and wigs, and treating the prisoners with insolence and contempt.

Not only did Renneville give us a full portrait gallery of the men who guarded the masked prisoner, but also what is almost certainly a brief glimpse of the prisoner himself. When he entered the room where the prisoner from Sainte-Marguerite happened to be, he was bundled straight out again so he did not have time to see much at all. He did not notice that the prisoner's face was covered by a mask, but he did not see the prisoner's face anyway. 'As soon as the officers saw me coming in,' he explains, 'they made him turn his back towards me which stopped me seeing his face.' The prisoner turned so quickly that he glimpsed nothing more than the back of his head. 'He was a man of average height,' he says, 'but well built and his hair which he wore in a very thick pony-tail was black with not a single strand of white in it.' Jet black hair, thick and strong, is not what one would have expected. According to Palteau, who got his information from eye-witnesses, the prisoner's hair at this time was white. If Palteau's information was correct, Ru's identification was wrong; but it is unlikely that Ru could have been mistaken or deliberately untruthful about the prisoner Renneville saw, and the fact that the prisoner was made to turn around as soon as Renneville walked in does seem to bear him out.

The contradiction between Palteau and Renneville defies all resolution unless, as might easily have happened in that sudden and rapid glimpse, Renneville himself made a mistake. What he took to be a pony-tail of black hair might very well have been the knot and tail of two broad bands of black velvet which wrapped the prisoner's head and held his mask in place. If the prisoner was really the man Ru said he was, then he was certainly wearing a mask because, according to Du Junca, the prisoner from Provence was always kept masked. Renneville, however, had no reason to suppose that he had seen the back of a mask. In all the record of his eleven years in the Bastille, he never once mentions seeing or hearing of prisoners wearing masks. Presumably therefore it did not occur to him that the prisoner he glimpsed was wearing one.

Unfortunately Renneville's picture of the mysterious prisoner, obscure as it is amidst the vivid portraits of his gaolers, is blurred by yet another error. The date he gives for the encounter was sometime in 1705 and we know from Du Junca that the prisoner died in 1703. The mistake this time is certainly Renneville's. If his date is correct, then his informants were wrong and that is out of the question. Although it is only unlikely that Ru would have mistaken another man for the prisoner he travelled with from Sainte-Marguerite, it is altogether impossible that Reilhe could have mistaken another inmate for the man whose burial certificate he had signed. The only possible explanation is that Renneville, writing twelve years or more after the event, made a mistake in the date, or alternatively that '1705' was a printer's error, overlooked in the reading of the proofs. The first edition of Renneville's book has so many printer's errors that two and a half pages of major corrections had to be included at the end. Three words were accidentally omitted from the text just six lines before the mention of 1705 and there is yet another error in the catchword at the foot of the same page. So far as one can learn from Renneville's account, there were only two occasions between the time of his arrival in May 1702 and the death of the masked prisoner in November 1703 when he was taken from his cell to any room other than another cell. The first was 24 May 1702 when he had to be questioned by Saint-Mars, and the second was 13 May 1703 when he had to be questioned by Du Junca. It was on one or other of these two occasions that, by accident and without knowing it, he met the prisoner who was later known as the Man in the Iron Mask.

The lack of official records and communications referring to the masked prisoner in the time he was in the Bastille is no doubt due to the fact that, in matters of security, the minister responsible could deal with the governor in person without needing to put anything on paper. The Comte de Pontchartrain, who was the minister in charge, rarely visited the prison, but his deputy, M. Desgranges, did so regularly. As the father-in-law of the youngest son of Saint-Mars, he made social as well as official calls. In prisons far from Paris, however, even secret communications could only be made by correspondence, and before being at the Bastille Saint-Mars had always received directions from his superiors in writing, and had sent regular written reports to them. Most of these dispatches have not survived, but there is a good deal of information to be had from those that remain. By way of clarification it should be noted that the Bastille came under the control of the Ministry of Finance, but all the other state prisons in France were the concern of the Ministry of War. The last Minister of War with whom Saint-Mars had to deal was the Marquis de Barbezieux.[2] On 19 July 1698 the governor received from him the following dispatch: 'The King sees fit that you leave the islands of Sainte-Marguerite and come to the Bastille with your long-time prisoner, taking care to avoid him being seen or known to anyone. You can write in advance to His Majesty's Lieutenant of the Bastille to keep a room ready to accommodate this prisoner on your arrival.'

As governor of Sainte-Marguerite, Saint-Mars had charge of a number of prisoners but only the masked prisoner, called his 'long-time prisoner' by the minister and Du Junca, accompanied him to the Bastille. Earlier references by Barbezieux or Saint-Mars to his 'long-time prisoner' clearly concern the same man and so it is the masked prisoner who is referred to in an angry letter addressed to the prison governor by the minister on 17 November 1697. 'With your letter of the 10th, I received the copy of the letter M. de Pontchartrain wrote to you concerning the prisoners who are in the islands of Sainte-Marguerite under orders from the King, signed by him or the late M. de Seignelay.[3] You have no other conduct to follow with regard to those who are confided to your charge than to continue to watch over their surety without saying anything to anyone about the past acts of your longtime prisoner.' This letter was written less than a year before the prisoner moved to the Bastille and came under the authority of Pontchartrain's ministry, but the post of governor of the Bastille was not vacant until the following month, when François de Besmaux, the then governor, died, and at that stage there had been no talk of moving Saint-Mars. Barbezieux resented the Controller of Finance meddling in the affairs of the Ministry of War.

Saint-Mars was governor of the Île Sainte-Marguerite for eleven and a half years, from April 1687 until September 1698, and the fortress he commanded, incuding the prisons he built, still stands. It is not an impressive building, more like a fortified village than a castle, but facing the town of Cannes on the French Riviera, its situation is spectacular. It rises from an outcrop of rock on a long low island, thick with pines and eucalyptus trees, less than half a mile from the tip of Pointe-de-la-Croisette, the bay of la Napoule and the distant red-rock mountains of the Esterel on one side, the bay called Golfe Juan and the far off white-ice peaks of the Alps on the other. Six rectangular windows, identical, in line and evenly spaced, mark the eastern end of the wall which faces across the sea to Cannes. These are the only windows in that wall and they are always in darkness because their orientation is due north. They are the windows of the prison cells.

The coast has been altogether transformed in the three hundred years since Saint-Mars was there. Seen from the terrace of the fortress today, the bays either side are a continuous stretch of hotels, public buildings and apartment blocks, shops, restaurants, gardens and villas, the shoreline a chain of yacht harbours, beaches, parks and promenades; in his day the land was bare and deserted. Cannes was that section of modern Cannes which is called Le Suquet, just a small fishing village built on a hill a couple of miles west of Pointe-de-la-Croisette and surrounded by marshland. The village had no harbour and the fishing

View of the fort on Isle Ste.-
Marguerite, which has
changed little since the Iron
Mask was imprisoned there.
Engraving by Bourgnin.

Inset, left: The recently-renovated prison–cell, traditionally said to be that of the Iron Mask. *Inset, right:* A present–day view of the fort. The windows of the six prisons are in line overlooking the sea. The second from the left is said to be that of the Iron Mask.

boats were beached among reeds at the foot of the hill. On Pointe-de-la-Croisette itself, where today the Palm Beach Casino stands, there was nothing but a bastion and the hills behind were wastes of scrub and moorland. It was a lost corner of France reached only from the north by hard travelling across the harsh and desolate mountains of the Pre-Alps or by sea along the coast from Marseilles, a perilous voyage since even the coastal waters were infested with pirates from North Africa. The Esterel, which was bandit country too dangerous to cross, blocked access from the west, and the border with Savoy was less than fifteen miles along the coast to the east.

South of Sainte-Marguerite, across a narrow strait, is the smaller island of Saint-Honorat, famous for its old monastery with its fortified tower. People today who wish to visit the tower and the fortress, to picnic in the woods and swim in the protected waters between the islands, have a choice of several boat services from various points along the coast. The fortress has become a student holiday centre, combining language classes with courses in sailing and skin-diving. The original garrison area has been taken over for that, but the prison building remains unchanged.

To reach the prison cells today one must pass, as one did three hundred years ago, by way of the adjoining building where Saint-Mars and his family used to live and which serves today as a small marine museum. The museum foyer was formerly the guardroom and access to the prison building can only be made from there. Through a narrow doorway one enters a high-vaulted passageway which leads to the right, a distance of forty feet or so, dimly lit by a single oval-shaped window high up in the arch of the wall on one's left. There are two doors of heavy wood reinforced with iron in the facing wall, and it is the nearest of these doors, so tradition has it, which gives on to the prison of the Iron Mask. In the time of Saint-Mars, the passage, which is narrow, was severely cramped by the presence of two bulky screens built in front of the doors and by a simple altar which stood in front of the end wall on one's right. The screens were of timber braced with iron and had solid doors bolted and padlocked. Under the oval window another larger doorway gives on to a second passageway, longer and less dim, which continues the first and contains the doors of four more cells. These doors too were once enclosed by screens.

The door to the Iron Mask's prison cell is no different from the others. It is of massive wood studded and strapped with iron and has rings for a bolt. It pulls backwards into the passageway, giving access through the thickness of the wall, a depth of three feet, to another door of the same construction which pushes forward into the cell. When this inner door is open at right angles to the jamb, it lies flat against the wall of the cell, allowing an unimpeded view from the doorway of the entire room: twenty feet to the wall facing the door, fifteen feet to the wall on the left. The walls either side curve overhead in a smooth arc like the sides of a tunnel and in the wall at the end, four feet from the ground, is a large barred window, seven feet high by four feet wide. Beyond the window, the prison wall drops sheer, flush with the cliff, to rocks and waves more than a hundred feet below. However, the window affords no view of this; the wall it pierces is six feet thick and the opening is closed by three iron grilles set one behind the other, restricting the view to a narrow section of the distant mainland. On the left of the window is a fireplace and on the right a privy. The wall is roughly plastered and the floor is paved with brick.

Some idea of the security measures which surrounded the life of the masked prisoner in this room is provided by a report addressed to Barbezieux by Saint-Mars on 6 January 1696. Here also, nearly three years before the move to the Bastille, he was referred to as the 'longtime prisoner':

You ask me to tell you what arrangements are made when I am absent or sick for the day to day visits and precautions regarding the prisoners who are in my charge. My two lieutenants give the meals at set times in the way they have seen me give them and as I still very often do when I am feeling well. This is how it is done. The senior lieutenant takes the keys to the prison of my long-time prisoner with whom we begin. He opens the three doors and enters the room of the prisoner who duly hands him the dishes and plates which he himself has piled together. The lieutenant has only to go out of two doors to give them to one of my sergeants who puts them on a table two steps away, where the other lieutenant inspects everything going in or out of the prison and sees that there is nothing written on the dishes. Once he has been given all that is necessary, an inspection is made inside and under the bed, from there to the bars of the window and to the privy. A complete search of the room is made and very often a body-search as well. Then when he has been asked in a civil fashion if he needs anything else the doors are closed and the same thing is repeated with the other prisoners.

Their table-linen is changed twice a week, along with their shirts and the other linen they use, it being counted and carefully inspected both when it is collected and when it is returned. One can be badly caught out in the coming and going of laundry for the prisoners of consequence, some of whom I know have attempted to bribe the washerwomen. They, however, swore to me that they were unable to do what was asked of them because I had the linen soaked as soon as it came out of the rooms and because when it was clean and half-dry the washerwomen came to my apartment to iron and fold it in the presence of one of my lieutenants, who locked up the laundry baskets in a strong-box until they were to be handed over to the prisoners' valets. One must be on one's guard about the candles too. I have known some which, when broken or employed, were found to have paper in them in place of the wick. I used to send for them to Turin, to shops which were not suspect. Ribbons leaving the prisoners' cells are also dangerous, because they may write on them as they do on their linen, without one realizing it. The late M. Fouquet used to make fine paper and I would let him write on it, then I would go at night and take it from a little pocket which he had sewn into the seat of his breeches and I would send it to your late father.

At this point the report has been so badly torn that the next five lines are impossible to read, but from what few legible words remain it seems that Saint-Mars is explaining how he ensures that the prisoners are unable to speak or shout to anyone. He then concludes:

> As a final precaution, the prisoners are given surprise visits from time to time at irregular hours of the day and night and it is frequently discovered then that they have been writing messages on their dirty laundry. No one else could possibly read what they write, however, as you know from the pieces I have sent you.

One of the lieutenants referred to by Saint-Mars, the officer who stood at a table in the passageway inspecting everything that went in or out of the cell, was no doubt Palteau's father Corbé; and to bring the scene to life one has only to remember Renneville's description of him, crooked and unkempt, sly and malevolent. The other lieutenant was Lamotte-Guérin who later, as the successor of Saint-Mars, was governor of the island during the imprisonment of Lagrange-Chancel. Saint-Mars had arrived on Sainte-Marguerite with two other lieutenants, Laprade and Boisjoly, but the former had been transferred in May 1692 and the latter had been retired in December 1693. Lamotte-Guérin replaced Laprade as King's Lieutenant in the islands, being described as such in an entry for 22 January 1693 in the parish register of Cannes where the birth and baptism of his son was recorded. Corbé replaced Boisjoly, receiving his promotion in January 1694. Among the sergeants referred to in the report, one was certainly the drunken Rosarges, brutal and slovenly with his bloated purple face, and another was possibly the huge hump-backed L'Ecuyer.

Voltaire's story of the silver plate found by the fisherman and Papon's story of the shirt found by the barber come to mind when one reads that Saint-Mars was afraid his prisoners might try to get messages past the guard by writing on their plates and their linen. As it is, however, no actual report of these stories survives as proof. All that does exist is a mention, made earlier by Saint-Mars, that another prisoner, a Protestant minister named Pierre Salves, had been writing on his dishes, made of pewter not silver, and on his dirty laundry, but so far as one can make out he never threw any of these things out of the window. His intention was to communicate with the other prisoners if he could, and with the outside world, but only by means of the washerwomen. Saint-Mars had reason to be on his guard but not, so far as we know, because of anything attempted by his 'longtime prisoner'.

In a letter to Saint-Mars on 13 August 1691, Barbezieux, who at that time had just succeeded to the Ministry of War following the death of his father, Louvois, gave instructions which clearly concern the same 'longtime prisoner': 'Whenever you have something to tell me about the prisoner who has been in your charge for twenty years, I beg you to employ the same precautions that you used when you wrote to M. de Louvois.' In 1691 Saint-Mars had been governor of Sainte-Marguerite for four years; before that he had been governor of Exiles for six years; and before that he had been at Pignerol for sixteen years. Barbezieux may have used the number twenty as a round figure to cover anything from eighteen to twenty-two years, but whatever year it was that the prisoner first came into the custody of Saint-Mars, the minister's statement is in perfect accord with Du Junca's note that the masked prisoner had been with Saint-Mars ever since Pignerol. Moreover, since Saint-Mars brought only one prisoner with him when he arrived from Exiles to take up his post at Sainte-Marguerite, the prisoner he brought was evidently that same 'longtime prisoner'.

News of his appointment to Sainte-Marguerite reached Saint-Mars in the remote snow-covered mountains of Exiles in January 1687. In the six years that he had been there he had sought every possible opportunity to get away from the place, asking the minister for leave of absence to visit Turin or to take the waters at Aix-en-Savoie, and begging for a change of post. His prisoner and prison staff were to go with him to the island and all were no doubt as relieved as he was to know that it was the last winter they would have to spend in those bleak and desolate mountains. When Louvois wrote to tell Saint-Mars of his new appointment he wanted to be sure that the prisoner would be transported safely and that there would be a secure prison waiting for him on the island when he got there. He decided that before Saint-Mars moved his prisoner he should go to the island and make arrangements for his reception, but he was also concerned that proper precautions should be taken for the safeguard of the prisoner while Saint-Mars was away.

Eager to reassure the minister that he appreciated the importance of his prisoner's security, Saint-Mars wrote back on 20 January:

> The orders I will give for the surveillance of my prisoner will be strict even to the point of preventing as always any communication with my lieutenant, whom I have forbidden ever to speak to him and who obeys me to the letter, so I can answer to you, sir, for his complete surety. I think the most secure mode of transport for conducting him to the islands would be a sedan-chair covered in oil-cloth so that he will have sufficient air without anyone being able to see him or speak to him during the journey, not even the soldiers whom I will pick to be close to the sedan. It will be less troublesome than a litter which can often get broken.

Saint-Mars set off to make his tour of inspection at the end of January, and by the beginning of March had sent his report and recommendations to Louvois. There was only one prison cell in the island-fortress and for security reasons it was inadequate. A new prison had to be built and Saint-Mars proposed two separate cells sealed off from the rest of the fortress by an access through his own home. The other four cells were a later addition, commenced only after the original plan for two had been completed. On 16 March Louvois told him to go ahead: 'Along with your letter of the 2nd of this month I received the enclosed memo and plan of what needs to be done to build the prison and lodging you require to ensure the security of your prisoner on the island of Sainte-Marguerite, amounting to 5,024 livres.[4] I have instructed this to be paid to you from emergency funds so you can construct this building yourself in the way you want it done.' The cost, which actually reached 6 926 livres before it was finished, might be thought considerable if undertaken solely for the accommodation of one prisoner and the fact that there were two cells, not one, may have led to the later assumption, demonstrated by Papon's story of the woman from Mougins, that the prisoner had a servant living in the prison with him.

Saint-Mars put the builders to work and on 26 March set off back to Exiles, his only anxiety being that he would not be allowed to make the transfer to the island until the new prison building was finished. He had, however, assured the minister that he could manage to make the existing prison cell secure enough to accommodate the prisoner temporarily and soon after his return to Exiles he received the necessary authorisation for this. The existing prison cell was in fact occupied by a young delinquent who had tried to take money from his own father at pistol-point, but he was of no consequence to anyone except his family and Louvois said he could be moved out to make room for the prisoner from Exiles. On 18 April Saint-Mars set out for the island with his prisoner and on 3 May he wrote to Louvois to report his arrival:

> I arrived here on 30th of last month having spent only twelve days on the road because my prisoner was ill, due he claimed to not having as much air as he would have wished. I can assure you, my lord, that no one in the world saw him and that the way in which I guarded and conducted him throughout the journey left everyone guessing as to who my prisoner could be . . . The prisoner's bed was so old and dilapidated, as was everything he had, the table-linen as much as the furniture, that it was not worth the trouble of bringing it here . . . and I got only thirteen écus[5] for the lot . . . I was charged two hundred and three livres for eight porters to bring a sedan-chair from Turin and carry my prisoner here in it, the cost including the price of the chair, and I have paid.

The arrival of Saint-Mars and his mysterious prisoner caused quite a stir in the region. Rumours that a prisoner of great importance was to be brought to the island had been circulating for some time. A letter written on 3 May by a certain Abbé Mauvans to a certain M. de Seguiran in Aix-en-Provence gives some idea of the local talk. Mauvans' letter is an account of a voyage he had made with some friends along the coast to Genoa. On 18 April, four days out from Saint Tropez, they had made a stop-over at Sainte-Marguerite:

> In the afternoon the wind was not favourable and that decided us to put in at the islands which we had intended to see only on the voyage back. We made a landing on Sainte-Marguerite at five o'clock and M. de Mazauges and I climbed to the fortress to get permission to enter the Tower of Saint-Honorat. We obtained that from the first captain and then we made a tour of the island. They intend to make new fortifications there: we saw the preparations: work will begin as soon as M. de Saint-Marc (sic) arrives. He had left some time before to go and get that unknown prisoner who is being transported with such great precaution, and who has been made to understand that when he is sick of living he has only to speak out his name, because the order is to give him a pistol-ball in the head if he does that. We were told that the lodging to be built for this prisoner would be connected to the governor's lodging, that only the governor would see him, that he would serve his meals and be almost his only gaoler and guard . . . I've

CROMWELL

Richard Cromwell, who in 1687 was thought to be the mysterious prisoner known later as the Iron Mask. From a painting by Robert Walker. (*Photograph Trewin Copplestone*)

just this minute learned from the military commissioner, himself newly arrived on the islands, that the state prisoner got there three days ago . . . Before I close my letter, I could give you particulars of the journey of this man and the guise under which he was seen in Grasse, but it is time to rejoin the company and continue our journey.

The new prison took all of eight months to complete, and stories of what had been seen and heard by visitors to the island and workers on the building site soon dispelled what reservations remained among the local people about the importance of the mysterious prisoner. On 8 January 1688 Saint-Mars was finally able to report to Louvois that the work was finished and the prisoner installed.

I am proud to inform you that my prisoner, who continues in his usual poor health, has been put into one of the two new prisons which you instructed me to have built. They are large, handsome and well-lit, and as for their excellence as prisons I do not think there could be any safer and sounder in Europe. This is especially so with regard to the danger of prisoners communicating orally with someone nearby or far off, and that could never be said for any of the places where I had charge of M. Fouquet after his arrest. With relatively few precautions one can even have prisoners taking walks about the island without fear that they might escape or pass messages. I take the liberty, my lord, to inform you in detail of the excellence of this place in the eventuality that you may have prisoners you wish to keep in complete security but with a reasonable degree of freedom. Throughout the province, some say that my prisoner is M. de Beaufort and others that he is the son of the late Cromwell.[6] Here attached is a short note of expenses incurred on his account for last year. I do not give any details so that those who deal with it will not be able to probe into things they are not supposed to know.

The year before this, when Saint-Mars received notification of his appointment to Sainte-Marguerite, the order was that he should take more than one prisoner with him. At that time Louvois wrote:

It gives me great pleasure to inform you that the King sees fit to grant you the governorship of the islands of Sainte-Marguerite. Prepare yourself to make the transfer as soon as you are ordered to do so. It is His Majesty's intention that as soon as you receive your warrant you make a tour of inspection of those islands to see what needs to be done for the safe and proper accommodation of the prisoners in your charge.

However this letter, dated 8 January 1687, was crossed by a letter from Saint-Mars, dated 5 January, in which he informed the minister of the death of one of his prisoners. The letter itself no longer exists, but a letter from Louvois, dated 13 January, in which he acknowledges its receipt, does. The correspondence thereafter, as we have seen, makes mention of only one prisoner.

At Exiles, therefore, Saint-Mars had two prisoners: the masked prisoner, who went on from there to Sainte-Marguerite and the Bastille, and another who died a few days before he received news of his transfer. The death of this second prisoner had been expected. On 3 November 1686, Louvois wrote to Saint-Mars: 'It is all right to let one of your two prisoners, the one who has dropsy, make his confession, but only when you are sure that death is imminent.' That these two were the only prisoners Saint-Mars had at Exiles is apparent in the way the minister frames his instructions. It is also made evident by a letter from Saint-Mars to Louvois on 11 March 1682. 'You advise me, my lord, how important it is that my two prisoners have contact with no one. Ever since you gave me that command, I have guarded the two prisoners in my charge as severely and strictly as formerly I guarded MM Fouquet and Lauzun.'

Exiles today is an abandoned frontier fortress, built on a spur of rock in the middle of a mountain-valley which was French when the fortress was built, but is now Italian. With a river on one side and a road on the other, it rises in ramps and ramparts through tier upon tier of salient wall and buttress, irregular in shape, but geometric in line, monolithic, bare and solid. In the time of Saint-Mars it was a very different construction: an assortment of separate buildings walled in under a crumbling old castle, not much bigger than a large house, which had been built, battered by war and rebuilt in bits and pieces through the centuries, around a single round tower thought to date from Roman times. Some years after the departure of Saint-Mars it was pulled down and replaced by the present fortress, which was the 'latest word' in French fortification design. The valley it commands, narrow between steep slopes of fir trees and bare stone, is the main link between Briançon and Turin. The frontier with France is only four miles away to the north, but there the mountains are impassable, with peaks more than ten thousand feet high. The road crosses the border to the south-west, sixteen miles up the valley, and not until Susa, nine miles down the valley, is it joined by a road which crosses the border from the north. There is a railway line today as well as the road, but it is buried in a tunnel along the side of the valley and, without a map, one would not know that it was there. The valley has changed little since the time Saint-Mars and his prisoner were there, except that the snowstorms, which made the winters so long and dreadful for them, have established the fame of nearby ski-stations like Sestrière and Serre Chevalier.

Plans of the vanished castle show that it was rectangular in shape with round towers at its corners, each of different height and girth. The two largest towers were at the western end with the biggest of these, the Roman Tower, overlooking the river; the other dominated the drawbridge at the entrance to the castle itself. The road from here passed through the outbuildings and led to the main gate which pierced the wall above the less precipitous northern slope overlooking the main road. The full width of the western end of the castle, including the towers, was taken up by the castellan's quarters and separated from the rest of the building by open stepways and landings which led down to the door and the drawbridge. East of the entrance-hall along the northern wall were the kitchens, store-rooms and servants' quarters, giving onto a long open courtyard under the southern wall. In the time of Saint-Mars, the prison guard as well as the household servants lived here and the prisoners were kept in the old Roman Tower, sealed off behind the castellan's private quarters, which were occupied by Saint-Mars and his family.

The shape of the prison cells was semicircular, half the available area of each floor of the tower being taken up by a spiral staircase and landings. The radius of this semicircle was only about ten feet and the cramped space was further reduced by a thickening of the wall around the window embrasure which, though a good six feet square, was closed off from the room by a line of bars. The actual windows were three feet wide armed with another row of bars. In the masked prisoner's room the window looked south across the river to the valley's gloomy north-facing slope, to evergreens on all-grey rock or featureless unmelting snow. The turbulent, twisting, white-water river was too far below to be visible or even audible to the prisoner; and the only sign of life to reach him at his window was the sight of an occasional traveller on the distant mountain track which led to Pragelas in the next valley, or the sound of an occasional passer-by below on the castle road which skirted the foot of the tower.

'The prisoners can hear people talking as they go by on the road below their tower,' Saint-Mars informed Louvois, 'but they themselves could not make themselves heard if they wanted to. They can see people on the mountainside in front of their windows but they cannot themselves be seen because of the gratings which seal off their rooms. Night and day I keep two sentries of my company posted at a reasonable distance on either side of the tower where they can see the prisoners' windows. They are commissioned to watch that no one

Left: View of the Fortress of Exiles as it was in 1681, the year the Iron Mask was moved there from Pignerol. Engraving by Breton. *Below:* Artist's reconstruction of the Bastille as it must have been in 1700. (*Photograph Bibliothèque Nationale*)

speaks to the prisoners, that they do not shout through the windows and that passers-by who linger on the road and the slopes of the mountain are made to move on. Since my room is connected to the tower and has no other view than on to the road, I hear and see everything, including the sentries, who are consequently kept on the alert.

'As for the interior of the tower, I have arranged it in such a way that the priest who says mass for them cannot see them because of a screen which I have erected to cover their double doors. The servants who bring the food leave what is necessary for the prisoners on a table, and my lieutenant carries it into them from there. No one talks to them except me and, when I am there, my officer, their confessor, the Abbé Vignon, and a physician who is from Pragelas, fifteen miles away. As for their linen and other necessities, I take the same precautions as I did for my prisoners in the past.'

Louvois made it clear to Saint-Mars that he did not want more than one of the prison officers to have any contact with the prisoners and it seems safe to assume that the man so entrusted was Laprade. This senior lieutenant, who had been with Saint-Mars for eight years at Pignerol, was to stay with him, as second-in-command, all through the time at Exiles and for the first five years at Sainte-Marguerite, before being transferred to a command of his own. As an extra security measure, it seems he was given a room in the Roman Tower above the prisoners. The other lieutenant was Boisjoly, who had been with Saint-Mars only since his departure from Pignerol. Corbé and his younger brother, as well as Rosarges, L'Ecuyer and possibly Ru, were also members of the prison guard and garrison, which amounted all told to forty-five men. The Abbé Vignon said mass for the prisoners on one of the landings outside their rooms and heard their confessions when they were allowed to make them, which was only once a year. Both prisoners were often in poor health and the physician from Pragelas must have visited them many times, especially when the one with dropsy became so gravely ill. However, nothing about that physician, not even his name, is known.

In all the time he was governor of Exiles, Saint-Mars had only two prisoners and these were the same two that he had brought with him from Pignerol. At Exiles they needed no name to designate them because they were the only ones confined there, but at Pignerol, where there were several prisoners, they had to have a name of some sort to differentiate them from the rest. In official dispatches exchanged during the short period before and after their transfer to Exiles, they were referred to by a special code-name. It is interesting to note that, according to Palteau, the masked prisoner was known to the prison staff of Sainte-Marguerite as 'Tower', and that might well have been a shortened form of this original code-name which appears in the following letters from Louvois.

2 March 1682. Since it is important that the prisoners at Exiles, who at Pignerol were called 'the prisoners of the Lower Tower', have no contact with anyone, the King has ordered me to command you to have them guarded with such strictness and care that you can answer to His Majesty for their being unable to speak with anyone, not only from outside but even from among the garrison of Exiles.

9 June 1681. At the King's behest I am sending you the letters confirming your appointment to the governorship of Exiles. It is His Majesty's intention that you have the two prisoners of the Lower Tower leave the citadel of Pignerol in a litter as soon as the place at Exiles, which you consider suitable for their safe confinement, is ready to receive them, and that you have them conducted there under the escort of your company, whose marching orders are attached. And immediately following the departure of the said prisoners, the intention of His Majesty is that you go to the said Exiles to take up the governorship and make your future residence there.

12 May 1681. I am asking M. de Chaunoy to go with you to Exiles to inspect the buildings and report on the rearrangements necessary to accommodate the two prisoners of the Lower Tower who are, I believe, the only ones His Majesty intends to transfer to Exiles. Send me a memo of all the prisoners in your charge noting beside each name what you know of the reasons for their arrest. With regard to the two of the Lower Tower, you have only to write that name without adding anything else.

Tracing back through what evidence there is from the death of the masked prisoner in 1703 to this letter of 1681, the ground is firm. Official documents and reliable witnesses establish beyond question that the mysterious prisoner, popularly known as the Man in the Iron Mask, did exist. From 1698 to 1703 he was in the Bastille, where he certainly wore a mask, albeit a mask of black velvet and not of iron. Before that from 1687 to 1698 he was on Sainte-Marguerite, where he was referred to as the 'longtime prisoner'. Before that from 1681 to 1687 he was at Exiles, where he had a fellow detainee, and before that he was at Pignerol, where in 1681 he and his companion were referred to as 'the prisoners of the Lower Tower'. Now as it happens the prisoners who were at Pignerol in 1681 are all known. There were six of them, though in fact only four were officially declared to be prisoners. To all appearances the two undeclared prisoners had been liberated in 1680. Who these two secret prisoners were is known. One of them was the Iron Mask.

1. *Comte de Pontchartrain*: 1643–1727, was Minister of State from 1689 to 1714.
2. *Marquis de Barbezieux*: 1668–1701, was the son of Louvois.
3. *Marquis de Seignelay*: 1651–1690, Secretary of State, 1669–1690, was the son of Colbert.
4. *livre*: French money of account which subdivided into 20 sous. At this period the official rate for the louis, a coin of fine gold weighing 6.69 grams, was 10 livres, and for the écu, a coin of fine silver weighing 27.14 grams, was 3 livres. These figures are taken from an article by Jean Belaubre in the catalogue to the exhibition devoted to Colbert at the Hôtel de la Monnaie in Paris in 1983.
5. *écu*: French silver coin; 13 écus were equivalent to 39 livres.
6. *son of the late Cromwell*: Richard who succeeded Oliver as lord protector. After his abdication in 1659 he lived in France under an assumed name, then after 1680 in seclusion in England until his death in 1712.

CHAPTER SEVEN

TWO PRISONERS OF CONSEQUENCE

When Saint-Mars was given command of the state prison in the citadel of Pignerol in January 1665 he had only one prisoner: Nicolas Fouquet. Then aged fifty, the former Superintendent General of Finance had been arrested and imprisoned in September 1661, tried for embezzlement of state funds and conspiracy to rebellion, found guilty and sentenced in December 1664 to imprisonment for life. The troop of musketeers which made the arrest was led by d'Artagnan, more famous from fiction than in fact, and his second-in-command was Saint-Mars who stayed with Fouquet thereafter until the trial was over as permanent escort in his successive prisons, Angers, Vincennes, Moret and the Bastille. The fate of Fouquet shaped the fortune of Saint-Mars: he became the prison-governor of Pignerol because, after more than three years under his guard, Fouquet had become his prisoner.

The actual sentence delivered by Fouquet's judges, in a majority vote of fourteen to ten, had been for his banishment and the confiscation of all his property. The ten out-voted judges would have condemned him to death by strangulation and there is little doubt that the King would have preferred that. As it was, he decided that the sentence given was too mild and he changed it immediately to perpetual imprisonment. Fouquet was certainly guilty of embezzlement, but in the general corruption of the times that made him no different from anyone else in government or finance. His crime was rather a matter of style; he invented the Louis XIV style before Louis XIV had any style at all. He was everything the young King wished to be and the jealousy and resentment this engendered in the monarch could be appeased by nothing less than the superintendent's complete destruction.

Fouquet came to power in the minority of Louis XIV when the Queen Mother was Regent and Cardinal Mazarin ruled France as her

FOUQUET

Fouquet, first proposed as candidate for the Iron Mask in 1837. Painting by Bourdon. Château de Versailles. (*Photograph Lauros-Giraudon*)

Prime Minister. Under His Eminence, the superintendent became super-eminent. Mazarin, the Italian peasant, was disliked by everyone except the Queen. Fouquet, French to his fingertips, was popular to the point of adulation. Mazarin envied and distrusted him but, knowing next to nothing about state finance himself, could not survive without him. Fouquet was a financial wizard, a master of improvisation, who created wealth around him with dazzling facility and breathtaking negligence. He was the supreme provider: preserver of the crown, protector of the court, patron of the arts. His friends were scholars, lawyers, doctors, writers and artists. His intellectual and artistic discrimination was masterful; his social and material sense majestic. When he built a house for himself at Vaux-le-Vicomte he created a work of art which set the style in Europe for over a hundred years. He was charming and generous, gifted and accomplished, civilized and worldly, but like many brilliant men he lacked deep passion and did not understand its power in others; he lacked psychological insight and judgement; he lacked the seriousness and caution of good minds less sure of themselves, and did not appreciate the danger he ran by alienating them.

On 17 August 1661, he invited the King and six thousand guests to a party at Vaux. By that time his downfall was already planned, but the King was so mortified to find himself the guest of a subject so much more of a king than himself that he very nearly had him arrested on the spot. The guests were overwhelmed by the magnificence of their host, the splendour of the house, the marvel of the garden, the prodigality and refinement of the entertainment: curtains of water from a thousand jets; cascades, canals and cataracts of water in carved stone; chamber music among flowers and trees; realistically sculpted statues and geometrically sculpted shrubbery; forests of round-topped orange trees in tubs; pavilions of striped silk; gondolas with gilded prows; a lottery with horses and jewels for prizes; dancing, gaming and water jousts; a ballet by Molière; fireworks by Torelli; and the house a mirage of light, its gold encrusted rooms ablaze with candelabra like burning trees, with coloured marble and mirrors, with Savoyard carpets and Genoan velvet, with lacquer, rock-crystal and brocade, procelain, paintings and tapestries. There were a hundred tables laid with silver and Venetian lace and the King's own table was set with massive gold. In the grand salon the King received a portrait of himself painted by Le Brun and saw on the dome above his head work in progress for a painting which depicted Fouquet's apotheosis in the symbol of the sun, also by Le Brun. The squirrel, Fouquet's emblem, was emblazoned everywhere, and with it his motto *Quo non ascendet*: 'Wither might one not ascend'. Mazarin, on his death-bed just five months before, had warned the

King to get rid of Fouquet and had recommended Colbert to him as the best man to help him do it. Colbert's emblem was a snake.

On 5 September 1661 the King was twenty-three, and as a birthday present to himself he had Fouquet arrested. The snake arranged the rest: fixed the judges and faked the evidence. If Fouquet had been condemned to death, the King was heard to say later to his mistress Louise de La Vallière, he would have let him die. At one time Fouquet had even tried to seduce Madame de La Vallière with a large sum of money; the maids-of-honour at court were always prepared to give information and favours for the money he offered, but Madame de La Vallière had remained faithful to the King. 'I only want justice,' the King told his ministers, 'and I am careful about what I say because, when it is a question of a man's life, I don't want to say too much.'

Fouquet's life was spared, but by that time the King had taken everything else. Versailles was begun with the spoils of Vaux. The King took its treasures and appropriated its makers. The tapestry factory, set up near Vaux, was moved to Paris and became the Gobelins. Paintings, sculptures, a thousand orange trees, porcelain, glass and plate, all went to Versailles and with them Le Vau, the architect, Le Nôtre, the gardener, and Le Brun, the decorator. The King's own library was begun with thirteen thousand volumes which he took from Fouquet, who in prison and on trial for his life was refused all books and counsel, was refused even paper and pen, and yet contrived to write five volumes of defence, using chicken bones and soot, upon his own shirts. When years later the Sun King finally emerged, tricked out in all his glory, the gross affectation of his posturing was saved from the ridiculous only by the subtle glimmer that still remained of that light which he had stolen from the Superintendent Sun.

When the Bastille was taken on 14 July 1789, and rumours were put about of bones and messages found mouldering in abandoned dungeons, the first published report that the remains of the Iron Mask had been discovered gave it out that he was Fouquet. One week after the Bastille fell, a broadsheet appeared with the banner headlines: 'The Skeleton of the Iron Mask found by the Nation this 22 July 1789'. The dramatic discovery was depicted as it happened and described by someone who had been on the spot. 'It was necessary to gain possession of this fortress to know at last the identity of that famous person whom we found as a skeleton, eight days after the capture, with chains on his neck, feet and hands and an iron mask at his side. We made the round of the cell and there we found an inscription which said that he was called Superintendent Fouquet and that he had been taken from the islands of Sainte-Marguerite and brought with an iron mask to the fort of the

Broadsheet published in Paris in 1789 reporting the supposed discovery of the skeleton of the Iron Mask in the Bastille. (*Photograph Bibliothèque Nationale*)

Bastille during the reign of Louis XIV. He died in the reign of Louis XV and was found in the reign of Louis XVI, on 22 July 1789'.

Further proof should have been unneccessary but three weeks later was forthcoming anyway. On 13 August, an article in the magazine *Loisirs d'un patriote français* revealed yet another remarkable discovery. 'Here is a fact which, to tell the truth, is only supported by a simple card which a man curious to see the Bastille picked up by chance with some other papers; but this card, giving as it does the complete answer to problems which up until now could never be solved, is a major piece of evidence. The card bears the number 64 389 000 – a figure which is unintelligible – and the following note: "Fouquet arriving from the islands of Sainte-Marguerite with an iron mask." After which three Xs. And underneath "Kersadion".' Who Kersadion was, no one has ever been able to find out. Nor is it known what became of the card. Like the skeleton and the inscription found earlier, it seems to have disappeared as miraculously as it appeared.

It is of course unlikely that anyone was at all surprised to learn that these sensational claims were totally without foundation. The official version of Fouquet's death had been ignored by sensation-mongers before, but the facts of the matter could easily be established. On 6 April 1680, *La Gazette* had carried the following announcement: 'We are informed from Pignerol that M. Fouquet has died of apoplexy.' This brief notice apart, the great man's death in the prison where he had been sent fifteen years before passed almost unremarked. His family, it was said, received the body and some time in the following year decided to move it to Paris so that it could be buried in the family vault. If the Nation had any doubts about that, the mortuary register of the Church of the Visitation in the Convent of the Dames de Sainte Marie in the rue Sainte-Antoine in Paris could always be consulted: 'On 23 March 1681 was buried in our church, in the chapel of Saint Francis de Sales, M. Nicolas Fouquet, who was elevated to all the degrees of honour in the magistrature, councillor of Parlement, rapporteur of the Council of State, Procurer General, Superintendent of Finance and Minister of State.'

Dead and buried, as Fouquet demonstrably was, more than twenty years before the masked prisoner was known to have died, no one proposing the superintendent's name for the Iron Mask could hope to be taken seriously. In 1836, however, forty-seven years after the pretence that Fouquet's skeleton had been discovered in the Bastille, it was revealed that the official record certifying where his remains really were was also a pretence. In that year a search was made in the burial vaults of the same convent for the body of a former Archbishop of Bourges. His coffin proved difficult to locate and was eventually discovered in the vault of the Fouquet family. An inventory of all the coffins was then made and their epitaphs carefully recorded. No sign of any coffin for Nicolas Fouquet could be found. The entry in the mortuary register of the convent was evidently incorrect, but there was no known record of Fouquet's burial in any other place. Paul Lacroix, in his book *L'Homme au Masque de fer* published in 1837, was the first to point out the full significance of this: that the obvious reason for a pretended burial was to give credibility to a pretended death. Investigation had shown him that in fact Fouquet's death was far from certain; apart from anything else, there was no death certificate.

Doubts about Fouquet's death had been raised before, but only with regard to the circumstances. It was Voltaire, in his *Siècle de Louis XIV* published in 1751, who had first focused attention on the uncertainty: 'Fouquet was imprisoned in the fortress of Pignerol and all historians are in agreement that he died there in 1680, but Gourville asserts in his *Mémoires* that he was liberated from prison sometime before his death. The Comtesse de Vaux, his daughter-in-law, had already given me endorsement of this fact, although his family believe the contrary. Thus while his least act, when he was in power, attracted attention, no one really knows where this unfortunate man died.' Hérauld de Gourville, who had been a colleague and close friend of Fouquet at the time of his arrest, made only a glancing reference to his release from prison, as though he assumed it was common knowledge. He offered no details on the matter, but Robert Challes, another contemporary, not mentioned by Voltaire, went much further.

Challes, who was one of Colbert's secretaries, maintained in his *Mémoires* that Fouquet was pardoned at the intercession of the Dauphin's wife and left prison as soon as the news of his release arrived, refusing to stay there a moment longer. 'He set off that very evening, but by some strange turn of fate he met his death at Chalon-sur-Saône. For supper that evening he had eaten a veal-breast stew. Indeed he had eaten a good deal of it and either his stomach could not digest it all or the joy of his recall, which until then he had kept pent up inside, could no longer contain itself without bursting. At two o'clock in the morning he called out and an hour later in great tranquillity he died. The astonishing thing is that there was no post-mortem examination and so it is still not known whether he died of natural causes or was poisoned.'

Chalon-sur-Saône was all of three hundred miles away from Pignerol by difficult mountain roads, but according to Challes, Fouquet was not at Pignerol at all, he was at Lyon. There is not a grain of evidence to support this version of things, but for Paul Lacroix the fact that Fouquet was reported to have died both as a prisoner at Pignerol and as a free man somewhere else confirmed suspicions raised by the false burial registration. The contradictory reports, it seemed to him, were a consequence of some inconsistency or inadequacy in the official explanation of Fouquet's death in 1680. There had been no burial in 1681, he decided, because there had been no death in 1680. Fouquet had lived on as a secret prisoner, masked to hide his identity, and had been the mysterious prisoner in the mask who had gone with Saint-Mars to the Bastille and had died there in 1703. Certainly what descriptions there are of the Iron Mask's appearance and behaviour could all be applied to Fouquet, including even the swollen legs described by Blainvilliers. One might be disposed to argue that Fouquet was too old to be the Iron Mask, since in 1703 he would have been eighty-nine years old, but it is a fact that his family made old bones; his own mother lived to be ninety-one.

'You know, I suppose, of M. Fouquet's death from apoplexy just when he had received permission to go and take the waters at Bourbon.' So Bussy-Rabutin wrote in a letter to a friend, echoing the general belief that Fouquet was about to be liberated when he died. The authorities had been planning his release for some time and the suggestion that they had suddenly changed their minds and faked his death in order to keep him secretly in prison, sealed off from the world for ever, is not on the face of it very likely. Lacroix, however, saw a connection between the mysterious origins of the Iron Mask as a secret prisoner at Pignerol and the first cautious steps of Madame de Maintenon[1] as the King's favourite at Versailles. It was the discovery of Fouquet's attempt upon the virtue of Madame de La Vallière which had earned him imprisonment instead of banishment in 1664, Lacroix suggests, and it was the revelation of his attempt upon the virtue of Madame de Maintenon which made him the Man in the Iron Mask in 1680.

The King's mistress in 1680 was Madame de Montespan in name, Madame de Fontanges in bed and Madame de Maintenon in everything else. Madame de Montespan, it is said, sought to clear the field for herself by poisoning Madame de Fontanges and slandering Madame de Maintenon. For twenty years Madame de Maintenon had been a widow and for eight years before that she had been married to a man who was paralysed. In 1680 her reputation was pure beyond reproach, but only, so Madame de Montespan said, because she had successfully covered up her scandalous goings-on as a frustrated young wife and a merry young widow. Her husband had been an impoverished poet, and both before and after his death she had received gifts of money from powerful friends, among whom had been Fouquet.

When Fouquet was arrested in 1661, a box of love-letters was discovered among his papers and a great many ladies at court were embarrassed to find themselves in print, exposed as his one-time mistresses, payed for services rendered as concubines, agents or spies. The actual letters no longer exist, but the alleged texts were published. Two of them, which in the original publication were thought to be by Madame de La Baulme, were later attributed to Madame de Maintenon. It was Jean Louis Carra who was responsible for this attribution in a book he wrote on the Bastille in 1789. The texts he gave are as follows:

> Letter One: 'I do not know you well enough to love you and perhaps when I get to know you I will like you less. I have always fled from vice and naturally I flee from sin, but I assure you that I hate poverty more. I have received your 10,000 écus and, if you wish to bring me 10,000 more in the next two days, I will see what I must do.'

> Letter Two: 'Until now I was so convinced of my strength that I would have defied the whole world. But I assure you that the last meeting I had with you left me spellbound. I found in your conversation a thousand enchantments which I had not expected, indeed, if I ever see you alone, I do not know what will happen.'

Whether or not these two letters were written by Madame de Maintenon, and indeed Carra had no grounds for his attribution, Lacroix would have us believe that her past relationship with Fouquet was a source of embarrassment for her and of humiliation for the King. It was moreover a repetition of the same painful experience which the King had suffered twenty years before with Madame de La Vallière. Whatever he saw as gold had been touched by the Superintendent Sun: such was his neurosis. The repetition of the nightmare took him by surprise. With Madame de La Vallière forgotten behind the walls of a convent, he had been prepared to forgive Fouquet, but when his plans for Fouquet's release were already under way, he heard the gossip about Madame de Maintenon, as told by Madame de Montespan, and his old anguish, with all his fear and hatred of Fouquet, returned. Thus the death of Fouquet was invented to avoid the necessity of liberating him, and the mask became a necessity to hide the deception.

On 2 May 1679, less than a year before Fouquet's supposed death and less than two and a half years before Saint-Mars moved to Exiles with two prisoners, one of whom was the Iron Mask, the state prison at Pignerol received a new prisoner who, to judge from one contemporary report, was actually wearing a mask when he was brought in. According to this account, which was published in July 1687, just eight years after the prisoner's arrest, the man in question was 'the secretary of the Duke of Mantua' and he had been kidnapped in Savoy. The French ambassador in Turin had invited him out for a day's hunting and had led him into a trap. A couple of miles outside the city he had been 'surrounded by ten or twelve horsemen who siezed him, disguised him, masked him and took him off to Pignerol'. The information was given in a letter from Italy which appeared in a periodical of history and current affairs printed in Leyden. At the time of its publication, Saint-Mars had just moved the Iron Mask from Exiles to Sainte-Marguerite and the author of the letter, showing himself to be remarkably well-informed, went on to give the very latest developments. 'At Pignerol he was too close to Italy and, although he was carefully guarded, it was feared that the walls might talk. He was therefore taken from there and sent to the islands of Sainte-Marguerite where he is at present under the guard of M. de Saint-Marc (sic) who is the governor there.'

In Spring 1687, when Saint-Mars and his mysterious prisoner moved to Sainte-Marguerite, everyone in the region was talking about it. On 3 May, the Abbé Mauvans, who had visited the island before their arrival and had heard eye-witness accounts of their journey through Grasse, wrote to tell a friend in Aix-en-Provence all about it. M. de Mazauges, who had visited the island with him, wrote the same news to a friend in Paris, a certain M. de Villermont, who replied on 20 August: 'I have been assured that the prisoner, whom you told me about recently as being taken to the islands of Sainte-Marguerite in such an extraordinary manner, is an Italian named Count Matthioli, formerly the secretary of the Duke of Mantua, whom he betrayed by disclosing secret information to the Spanish.'

Matthioli's name was variously spelt in official French correspondence, but most commonly appeared as 'Marthioly' which, when pronounced with a strong Southern French accent sounds more like 'Markhioly'. There seems little doubt that the name 'Marchioly', which appeared on the burial certificate of the Iron Mask in 1703, was a simple mis-spelling of the same name. Evidently the parish priest of Saint-Paul, who made the certificate, had been told by Rosarges, who was from the south of France, that the prisoner's name was 'Markhioly', by which he meant 'Matthioli'. To a man like Du Junca the name meant nothing, but to anyone acquainted with French interests and involvements in Northern Italy it would have been instantly recognizable as Count Ercole Antonio Matthioli, one-time secretary of state and supernumerary senator of the Duke of Mantua, who had disappeared from the city of Turin more than twenty-four years before.

After all, it seems, there is not, and never was, any real mystery about the identity of the famous masked prisoner. The information was always there in public records and popular publications for anyone to read, but not until 1770 was this realized. In that year a certain Baron de Heiss wrote to the authors of the *Journal Encyclopédique* quoting from the account published in Holland in 1687, and further evidence was quickly added. In 1788, Louis Dutens in his *Correspondence interceptée* reported that Louis XV was asked by his mistress, Madame de Pompadour, to reveal the identity of the Iron Mask and he replied 'that he believed it was a minister of an Italian prince'. In 1801 Pierre Roux de Fazillac produced government documents to support this belief and in 1822 it was confirmed with the publication of the *Mémoires* of Madame de Campan, who had been first lady-in-waiting to Queen Marie-Antoinette, the wife of Louis XVI.

Soon after Louis XVI came to the throne in 1774, Madame de Campan reports, he began to go through the papers of his grandfather, Louis XV. He promised to tell his wife anything he discovered relative to the Iron Mask, though it was his opinion 'from what he had heard said on the matter, that this Iron Mask had become a subject of such inexhaustible conjecture only because the work of a celebrated writer had excited interest in the detention of a state prisoner who had some peculiar tastes and habits'.[2] When eventually he had examined all the documents, he announced to his wife, in the presence of Madame de Campan, 'that he had found nothing in the secret papers analogous to the existence of this prisoner and that he had therefore questioned M. de Maurepas about it'. The Comte de Maurepas, who was seventy-three years old at that time, had come to office as Secretary of State under Louis XV, just fifteen years after the Iron Mask's death, and his reply was 'that the prisoner was a subject of the Duke of Mantua who because of his disposition to intrigue was a very dangerous character. He was lured to the frontier, arrested there and kept a prisoner first at Pignerol and then in the Bastille.' As for the mask, Madame de Campan concludes, it is altogether possible 'that the captive Italian sometimes showed himself on a terrace of his prison with his face so covered', since that was just one of 'the peculiar tastes and habits' of Italians in general; it was 'formerly the custom in Italy for men and women to wear a mask of black velvet when they exposed themselves to the sun.'

In December 1677, when the French first made contact with Matthioli, he was living quietly in Verona with his wife and two children, a brilliant and ambitious man thwarted just two years before in what had been a promising career. He was bitterly disappointed and disillusioned, but at the age of thirty-seven not altogether prepared to give up the hope of re-establishing himself. The Duke of Mantua was living in Venice, a profligate who at the age of twenty-five was addicted to the giddy masquerade of Venetian high society, his only interest apart from dissipation and depravity being his need to find enough money to pay his debts. Government of his subjects he had left to his mother who stayed on in the ducal palace at Mantua, sharing her power and her bed with a monk called Bulgarini.

As a young man lecturing in law at the University of Bologna, Matthioli had been picked out by the old Duke of Mantua to become his Secretary of State. The Duke had died soon after and, since at that time his son and heir had been only thirteen years of age, government control had passed into the hands of the dowager Duchess. Matthioli's influence over the young Duke had been strong and so he had been kept on as a supernumerary member of the senate, a position which carried with it the title of count, and his future rise to eminence had seemed assured. When the young Duke had come of age, however, he had proved himself a wastrel, ready to leave the reins of government in anybody's hands so long as he was supplied with money enough to finance his debauches. A struggle for power had ensued and Bulgarini, backed by the Duchess, had forced Matthioli out.

The French viewed this situation with interest. The Duke of Mantua was also the Marquis of Monferrato and the French had their eyes on Casale, the capital of Monferrato, which was a fortified town on the River Po to the east of Turin. They were as eager to acquire Casale as an outpost as they had been to acquire Pignerol as a frontier-post. Between these two citadels, Turin, the capital of Savoy, could be kept under virtual siege, and the south-east corner of France would project its defences deep into Italy with a bastion to threaten Milan and Genoa. The Duke of Mantua was kept so short of money by Bulgarini and was in consequence so harrassed by creditors that an offer to buy Casale for a large sum of ready cash was sure to tempt him. Secrecy was, however, essential if French occupation of the town was to be managed peacefully. There would be an uproar the moment the sale was realized; not only the Savoyards, but the Spanish, who controlled Lombardy, would be certain to object in the strongest terms. In the opinion of the French ambassador to Venice, the Abbé d'Estrades, the best way to approach the young Duke was to go through Bulgarini's rival, Matthioli, who was sure to be delighted to have an opportunity to reassert himself in Mantuan affairs.

A journalist, named Giuliani, who was a secret agent for the French, made contact with Matthioli in Verona and sounded him out. As expected he was interested, and a meeting was arranged with d'Estrades, who flattered and encouraged him. By the middle of January 1678, Matthioli was negotiating the French offer with the Duke of Mantua and had even exchanged polite letters with Louis XIV himself. The Duke wanted a million livres for Casale, but the French were only prepared to put up 300,000. Matthioli finally fixed a meeting between d'Estrades and the Duke at a masked ball in Venice during Carnival when, as d'Estrades informed the King, 'everyone, even the Doge, the oldest senators, the cardinals and the papal nuntio, must go about in masks.' They met in a small square and there, at midnight, masked amidst the masked crowd, they discussed the deal for over an hour. D'Estrades refused to raise the offer and the Duke, hard pressed for money, eventually accepted.

Matthioli, whose discretion, it was thought, could be relied upon, was commissioned to represent the Duke in drawing up a final agreement and for this he was invited to Paris. When the time came for him to leave he excused himself, saying that he was ill. The Duke, who wanted his money as quickly as possible, urged him to go and finally, with the promise that when the deal was done he would make him his prime minister, persuaded him to go. In October Matthioli and Giuliani left for Switzerland and from there slipped into France. On 8 December the contract was ready and Matthioli signed in the Duke's name. The money was to be paid in silver, half when the Duke gave his ratification and half when the French troops took possession. Matthioli's good offices were much appreciated by the French, and before returning to Italy he was invited to a secret audience with the King at which he received from the King's own hand two hundred golden louis for himself, a large diamond from the royal collection and promises of preferment for his family.

In January, secret preparations for the occupation of Casale were begun. Nicolas Catinat, who was then a brigadier-general, was appointed governor-to-be and, using the name Richemont as a cover, went to stay with Saint-Mars in Pignerol. The troops who were to serve as garrison were kept at Briançon until the end of February, then sent to Pignerol to join him. Meanwhile the Abbé d'Estrades had been transferred to Turin to be at the centre of things when Casale changed hands and a special envoy, Baron d'Asfeld, was sent to Venice for a meeting at which he was to receive from Matthioli the contract of sale ratified by the Duke. The French were, however, apprehensive. In mid-February Louis XIV had been informed by the Duchess-Regent of Savoy that she knew all about the secret agreement. He had chosen to go ahead with the plan anyway, but not without misgivings. On 9 March, the day before his rendezvous with Matthioli in Venice, Baron d'Asfeld, travelling through Lombardy, was arrested by order of the Spanish governor of Milan. The secret, it then emerged, was known to everyone.

Matthioli was suspected of treachery, but it was difficult to prove. Catinat was commissioned to take d'Asfeld's place and another meeting with Matthioli was arranged, this time in Casale itself. Catinat went there accompanied by Saint-Mars, both furnished with false identity papers, but Matthioli did not turn up and they too were arrested. Fortunately for them their true identities were not realized and, after interrogation by the governor of the town, they were released. By the beginning of April, d'Estrades was convinced of Matthioli's double-dealing, but it was not until the end of April that this was confirmed from Paris. Matthioli had shown the secret agreement to the Duchess of Savoy on 31 December, just three weeks after he had signed it in Paris. His intention had been to scuttle the sale before it could be ratified, and when he had seen that his disclosure had not produced the desired effect, he had gone to the Spanish in Milan. Meanwhile, alarmed by the sudden uproar, the Duke of Mantua had been embarrassed into a public denial of any plan to sell Casale and the Spanish had come up with an offer to buy the town for 600,000 francs.[3]

It makes little sense that, having committed himself to engineer the sale, Matthioli should have wished to sabotage it. What he hoped to gain out of the situation he created is not at all clear. It is, however, certain that the Duchess of Savoy reacted to the information he gave her in a way no one would have anticipated, and so the situation which resulted was not the one he had intended to create. Since the French occupation of Casale was directed primarily against Savoy, it did not occur to him that the Duchess would report her discovery back to France, and as it was he never imagined that she had done so. Perhaps what he expected was that the Duchess herself would make a bid for Casale with a better offer than France, as the Spanish eventually did; or that she would set up an alliance of powers against the sale, in which he would be able to play a key rôle and so establish himself as the strong man of Mantua. Whatever his original expectations and intentions might have been, his greatest mistake was his failure to appreciate that the French were fully informed of his duplicity. They pretended ignorance and he believed them, telling them that the agreement had been ratified as promised. D'Estrades, ordered to get the signed agreement out of him with the least possible trouble, came quickly to the conclusion that kidnapping the man was the only sure way. On 2 May he lured Matthioli into a trap and had him smuggled into Pignerol prison that same day.

The signed agreement, as things turned out, could not be found and so the occupation of Casale could not be made, but the plan was postponed, not abandoned. Two years later, on 8 July 1681, the Duke of Mantua signed the necessary papers and on 30 September the French troops took possession. What had happened to Matthioli in the meantime was something about which no one with any power or influence seemed to care. Shortly before his disappearance he had been in hiding from the Duke of Mantua, who had hired assassins to hunt him down. When d'Estrades had contacted him in Turin, he had been carrying 'two pistols in his pockets and two more, with a dagger as well, in his belt.' Presumably his family and friends supposed that he had been assassinated and did not dare to enquire further. In April 1679 Louis XIV had specified 'that no one should know what becomes of this man' and in August 1681 he had reassured the Duke of Mantua that Matthioli would never be released without his consent.

Matthioli's fate was not a secret for long, however. In 1682 the full story was published in a fifty-eight page pamphlet entitled *La Prudenza trionfante di Casale*, written in Italian and printed in Cologne. The account was accurate and named everyone involved, even Giuliani. About Matthioli's disappearance there was moreover no mystery. The writer of the pamphlet was as well-informed on that as he was on everything else: Matthioli had been kidnapped by the French, he said, and imprisoned in Pignerol. Just three years after Matthioli's disappearance, therefore, everyone knew what had happened to him and why. Five years after that, when Saint-Mars was transferred to Sainte-Marguerite, it was assumed that the secret prisoner he brought with him was Matthioli. Saint-Mars denied it, of course, with jokes that the mystery-man was the Duc de Beaufort or Richard Cromwell, but no one of any sense believed him.

Two of the most celebrated writers on the Iron Mask, Marius Topin, whose book appeared in 1869, and Franz Funck-Brentano, writing in 1894, were altogether convinced that Matthioli was the prisoner in the mask who died in the Bastille in 1703. In their interpretations they sought to debunk the old mystifications, but overreached themselves in their determination to explain away all the mysteries. Like other Matthiolists, the best explanation they could find for the mask was the one first offered by Madame de Campan. Matthioli wore a mask not because he was made to but because he chose to. No one knew him in France, of course, and so there was no question of anyone recognizing his face, but to conceal his identity was not the purpose of the mask. His baggage had been seized by the French when they kidnapped him and it is known from official correspondence that Saint-Mars took these bags with him when he left Pignerol for Exiles. A mask, Topin declares, 'would certainly have formed part of his personal effects'. There was nothing mysterious about it. He had one because he was an Italian and he wore it because for him it was the natural thing to do. It would be difficult to better the comment made on this by Theodore

Jung writing four years after Topin: 'It is altogether as if one were to say "Since this gentleman is Spanish, he must be carrying castanets".'

For all Matthiolists, the single most striking piece of evidence in the case lies in the fact that the Iron Mask was buried under Matthioli's name. Topin established that, at the time of the masked prisoner's death, the Duke of Mantua happened to be visiting Paris as a guest of Louis XIV; he then argued that Louis XIV authorized the use of the prisoner's true name on the burial register in order to let the Duke know that the man, whose reappearance he feared, was dead. One wonders why the Duke would have trusted a record in which false names were always used, when a word in private from the King himself would have sufficed. 'Far from corroborating the system which sees in Matthioli the man in the mask', Jules Loiseleur wrote two years before Topin's book appeared, 'the entry on a public register of a name so close to his is, on the contrary, one of the most decisive arguments against that system.'

Though at the end of the last century most investigators were prepared to accept that the Iron Mask was Matthioli, and though that is the most common explanation of the mystery given in works of general reference even today, no investigator of the twentieth century has ever found the case convincing. On the contrary, it is now argued that public knowledge of Matthioli's imprisonment in Pignerol was deliberately used by the French authorities to provide a cover for the identity of the real secret prisoner. In this way the curiosity of people who were intelligent and informed could be satisfied before their investigations brought them too close to the truth. Without pressing that argument, however, it is worth remarking that the sedan-chair in which the prisoner was boxed up for the journey to Sainte-Margeurite was carried by eight porters brought especially from Turin, and it is hardly likely that Saint-Mars would have chosen Italian porters if his secret prisoner had been an Italian.

1. *Madame de Maintenon*: Françoise d'Aubigné, Marquise de Maintenon, 1635–1712. Displaced Madame de Montespan in the affections of Louis XIV in the late 1670s and became Louis XIV's wife by morganatic marriage in 1684.
2. A reference to Voltaire.
3. *francs*: at the beginning of the seventeenth century the franc was a coin of fine silver weighing 23 grams. Under Louis XIII it became a money of account.

CHAPTER EIGHT

THE PRISONERS OF PIGNEROL

What was in the seventeenth century the French Pignerol is today the Italian Pinerolo, a pleasant little town of 40,000 inhabitants situated on a hill in Piedmont twenty-three miles south-west of Turin. Here the valleys of the Chisone from the west, the Lemina from the north and the Pellice from the south emerge from the Alps on to the wide open plain of the Po. When the French army was in occupation, the town was girded all around by bastions and ravelins and guarded from the north by a citadel built in the style of the time like a three-tiered mountain of terraced masonry. On the topmost platform of the citadel stood the keep, a many-towered rectangular block which, though high, was dwarfed by one enormous tower more than twice the height of the rest. Of all these buildings and fortifications, however, nothing now remains. In 1696 the French destroyed them when they were obliged to abandon the town to the Savoyards. The prisons were in the keep and so vanished with the rest, just fifteen years after the Iron Mask's departure.

Plans and descriptions of the time make it clear that the long northern face of the keep was only a curtain-wall, and that a fortified gate gave access through this to an interior courtyard which was enclosed by buildings on its other three sides. Six towers, all different in size and structure, were incorporated into the exterior face of these buildings, one at each corner and two mid-façade on the south and west walls. All the buildings at the western end of the keep, including the great tower and two others, were occupied by the commander of the citadel and his officers. Some of the buildings on the south side were used as store-rooms and all the rest of the structure, including the remaining three towers, was taken up by the state prison. The tower at the north-east corner housed the prison chapel and the other two towers contained the prison cells. The prison guard were lodged in the interior section of the southern buildings, their rooms facing across the courtyard to the northern curtain-wall, while the prison governor had all the eastern end, excluding the towers, for himself. Both prison-towers had three floors with a prison room on each. The tower at the south-east corner, which was known as the Angle Tower, was reserved for prisoners of rank; the rooms were spacious and well-furnished with floors of wood and large windows which looked out at the mountains and on to the town. The other prison-tower, which was placed midway along the southern façade of the keep, was known as the Lower Tower and, so far as one can make out, the rooms there were much smaller than in the Angle Tower, with bare stone floors and small windows high up in the wall. Between the two prison-towers were the store-rooms of the citadel, and these included the main powder-magazine.

Fouquet left Paris under d'Artagnan's guard a couple of days before Christmas 1664 and after a hard journey by frozen roads through snow-bound mountains reached Pignerol three weeks later. Saint-Mars, already there, had found a valet to serve him and had prepared rooms on the third floor of the Angle Tower, the best in the prison, to accommodate him. From Vaux to Pignerol: zenith to nadir. The prison regime was strict, but he was not ill-treated. He could not leave his prison apartment, was denied pen and ink and forbidden all contact with the outside world; however, he lived in spacious rooms with a view upon the mountains, had the attention and companionship of a servant, received good food and wine, wood for the fire, clean clothes and linen, was allowed to hear mass on Sundays and Holy Days, to confess five times a year and to have one book at a time to read. So much more than a bare necessity for the life of his body and soul, so much less than the bleak minimum for the survival of his spirit.

One night six months after Fouquet's installation, the powder-magazine of the citadel was hit by lightning in a storm and blew up, destroying the surrounding buildings and causing a large part of the prison to collapse including the roof and floors of the Angle Tower. By a miracle he and his valet had been standing in the window-recess at the moment of the explosion, watching the mountains in the storm, and they were left perched in the thickness of the wall altogether unharmed when the ceiling came down under the weight of the roof and the floor gave way. Until the damage could be repaired they were moved to the fortress of La Pérouse nearby, and when workers began to clear the rubble, Saint-Mars discovered among the broken furniture a bunch of pens made from chicken bones, a bottle of ink made from soot and a bundle of white linen strips cut from shirts and covered in writing; all were hidden in the back of a chair. Fouquet's valet was taken from him and soon afterwards was reported dead. The cause of death is not now known, but it is not inconceivable that he would have lived longer if he had informed Saint-Mars of Fouquet's secret writings. Security precautions around Fouquet were increased, and when he returned to the Angle Tower a year later, all his white shirts and ribbons had been changed for black and instead of one valet he had two, presumably intended as spies as well as servants, to inform upon each other as much as upon their master.

The names of these two valets were Champagne and La Rivière. About their backgrounds nothing is known, but there is reason to believe that they were originally servants of Saint-Mars and they were young enough for Fouquet, then aged fifty-one, to think of them as boys. Whatever it was Saint-Mars offered in order to persuade them to take the job, they were almost certainly deceived, since in effect they became prisoners too, locked up with their master and never allowed out. One of them, probably Champagne, was sufficiently intelligent and amiable for Fouquet to start teaching him Latin and pharmacy. La Rivière was melancholy by nature and a chronic hypochondriac; he had a depressing effect upon Fouquet who, though fond of him, preferred the diligent and affectionate disposition of Champagne.

For the first four and a half years at Pignerol, Fouquet was the only prisoner Saint-Mars had; then on 19 July 1669 Louvois wrote telling him to prepare a cell for someone by the name of Eustache Dauger or Danger[1]. Nine days after that the King wrote a letter under his private seal to Captain Alexandre de Vauroy, the garrison commander of Dunkirk, ordering him to arrest on sight a man named Eustache Dauger and take him immediately to Pignerol. Dauger's arrest was top secret: even the governor of Dunkirk was not allowed to know about it. To explain Vauroy's absence from Dunkirk, the governor was shown a cover-up dispatch from Louvois ordering Vauroy to hunt down officers of the Spanish army who supposedly had crossed the border from the Spanish Netherlands in pursuit of deserters.

'I am giving you notification in advance,' Louvois wrote to Saint-Mars on 19 July, 'so that you can prepare a cell where you can safely put him. You must make sure that the windows are so placed that they do not give on to anywhere accessible to anyone and that there are enough doors closing one upon the other that the sentries will not be able to hear anything. You personally must take the wretch whatever he needs for the day once a day and you must never listen to anything he tries to tell you, no matter what the pretext might be. You must threaten to kill him if he ever opens his mouth to speak to you about anything except the bare necessities of his life. I am informing M. Poupart to start forthwith whatever work it is you will require done, and you will prepare the furniture necessary, taking note of the fact that, since the prisoner is only a valet, he will need nothing of any significance.' Dauger arrived in Pignerol on 24 August and Saint-Mars informed Louvois immediately: 'M. de Vauroy has delivered Eustache Dauger into my custody and I have locked him up in a secure place until the cell I am having prepared for him is ready. In the presence of M. de Vauroy I warned him that if he ever spoke to me or anyone else about anything other than his simple needs I would run him through with my sword. Your orders will be carried out to the letter.'

For someone who was 'only a valet' the security precautions were extraordinary. People in the citadel were curious about the new prisoner and, in the absence of any information at all, rumours began to circulate before the month was out that he was at least a marshal of France or a president of the Parlement. In September both he and Fouquet were ill. Louvois gave permission for Dauger to be bled whenever it was judged necessary for his health and, for his salvation, permission to receive books of piety, to make his confession four times a year and to hear the mass which was said for Fouquet on Sundays and Holy Days, so long as his attendance could be managed without him being in the same room. And so Saint-Mars and his two prisoners, Fouquet with his two valets and Dauger, who was only a valet, lived on through the autumn of 1669, cut off from the world of the living behind the walls of their prison, locked within the walls of the citadel, lost within the mountains of Piedmont. At least to all appearances cut off.

In December Saint-Mars made a shattering discovery. A plan had been mounted under his very nose to break Fouquet out of prison. Two of Fouquet's friends had managed to get themselves inside the citadel and make contact with him. Messages and letters had been exchanged, prison guards had been bribed and an escape organized. One of the friends was Fouquet's devoted servant La Forêt, the other was a gentleman named Valcroissant. Saint-Mars moved quickly, but before he could have them arrested, they escaped over the border to Turin. He demanded their extradition and the Savoyard authorities complied. A scaffold was erected in the prison yard in full view of Fouquet's window and, when his two friends were brought in, La Forêt was hanged. Valcroissant was held over for trial in which, six months later, he was found guilty of carrying a letter from Fouquet to his wife, and condemned to five years in the galleys.

Meanwhile the guards were interrogated and those involved summarily executed, Champagne and La Rivière were isolated for questioning and the windows of Fouquet's prison rooms were fitted with projecting grilles, the lower sections of which were closed so that he could see nothing out of them except the sky. Though Champagne and La Rivière were certainly implicated in the escape plan, they were not punished. Possibly they had been the ones to inform Saint-Mars, but since they were not rewarded either that seems unlikely. What is more probable is that Saint-Mars would have punished them if he could have found replacements, but since no one else could be persuaded to take such a job they were spared and allowed back into Fouquet's service.

Louvois was very concerned about the breach of security, not only as it affected Fouquet, but also with regard to Dauger. In March he learned that, during the time Fouquet's two friends had been working under cover in the citadel, someone had managed to speak to Dauger. So far as the minister knew, it could have been Valcroissant or La Fôret or Champagne or La Rivière. They had asked Dauger if there was something of importance he wanted to tell them but he, suspecting that they had been sent by Saint-Mars to test him, had told them to leave him alone.

Clearly the cell Saint-Mars had chosen for Dauger, until the special cell could be got ready, was not secure enough and the minister was annoyed. On 12 April, however, the special cell was finished and Dauger was safely sealed off inside. The eight months' work needed to prepare this cell had added fuel to the rumours about Dauger's identity and, as Saint-Mars explained to Louvois, he had felt it necessary to add some outlandish stories of his own in order 'to make fun of them' and render the speculation ridiculous. Finally, in August, Louvois himself came to Pignerol with the King's chief military engineer, Vauban, to inspect the city's fortifications and while he was there was able to make his own assessment of security measures within the prison. As a result of his visit, though for what precise reason it is not known, the entire garrison of the citadel, with the exception of Saint-Mars and his close staff, was changed.

More than a year elapsed before Saint-Mars received a third prisoner. This was Antonin-Nompar de Caumont, Comte de Lauzun, aged thirty-eight, soldier and courtier, Colonel-General of the Dragoons and Captain of the King's Bodyguard, longtime favourite and confidant of the King, arrested and imprisoned by special order under the King's private seal. By all accounts he was an unattractive man: sharp-faced, stocky and aggressive, being feared and disliked at court for his constant intrigues and tantrums, his envious spirit, impudent manner and savage wit. What appealed to the King was his courage and daring but, though this appeared as valour undaunted on the field and madcap nonchalence at home, it often showed as brazen insolence in high council or full court. The King was delighted and infuriated with him in turn, covering him in honours one minute and throwing him into prison the next. In 1665 he spent six months in the Bastille for quarrelling openly with the King and in 1669 he was there again, though only for a few days. That the King did not keep him there longer the second time was due only to the King's great affection for him. Anyone else would have been locked up for good. The story of what led to his arrest in 1669, as recorded by Saint-Simon, gives a vivid picture of the man and an idea of the trouble he was to give Saint-Mars.

Lauzun had decided that he wanted the post of Grand Master of Artillery, which in 1669 came up for sale, and pestered the King to buy it for him. The King more or less promised to do so, but did nothing about it. After a time Lauzun became impatient and asked the King's new mistress, Madame de Montespan, to put in a good word for him. She said she would, and he had every reason to believe her. Just the year before, he and Madame de Montespan had pretended to be lovers in order to cover up her affair with the King and that very year, when she had borne a child to the King, he had been the one to smuggle the baby out of the palace. Nevertheless he was suspicious and, to find out what if anything she was going to say, he hid himself under her bed that afternoon when the King came to see her. Only Lauzun would have had the nerve and affrontery to do such a thing. There, while the couple made love and talked upon the pillow, he listened and heard Madame de Montespan broach the subject, as he had asked, but only to slander and deride him. That night in the midst of the court he asked her if she had remembered to speak in his favour, and when she replied with a show of friendly concern that she had, he bent to her ear and told her she was 'a liar, a bitch and a whore'. Word for word then he recounted what in fact she had said and she, horrified by the realization that she had been spied upon that afternoon, fainted.

The King, informed by his outraged mistress of the whole affair, chose to do nothing about it, but Lauzun was not finished. He faced the King directly, also in full court, and reminded him of his promise. The King wished to avoid the subject and was clearly trying to get out of his obligation but Lauzun, angry and defiant, was not going to let him get away with it. He drew his sword, broke it over his knee and, throwing the pieces at the King's feet, declared that he would never devote himself to the service of a king who broke his word for a whore. The King, trembling with rage, raised his cane and then, as if holding himself in check, turned away. He would be angry with himself if he struck a gentleman, he said, and pulling open a window he flung his cane outside. High drama! Lauzun was arrested the next day, but after a couple of weeks in the Bastille was returned to favour. The King did not give him the post he wanted so much, but he gave him another by way of compensation and, in spite of Madame de Montespan's dissatisfaction, they were soon good friends again.

Lauzun's imprisonment in Pignerol in 1671 was the consequence of yet another piece of scandalous impropriety. In December 1670, the Grande Mademoiselle, Duchesse de Montpensier, proposed marriage to him and he accepted. She was the daughter of Gaston d'Orléans, Louis XIII's brother, and so first cousin to the King himself. Why she was still unmarried at the age of forty-three was because of a shortage of marriageable kings. The reason she wanted to marry Lauzun was, in her own words, 'to taste the sweetness, once in my life, of being loved by someone worth the trouble of loving'. And the reason Lauzun accepted her proposal was the prospect of marrying someone worth more than any other heiress in Europe, who in proof of her love was prepared to make over all her wealth to him: a principality, a province and four duchies.

At first the King did not object and plans for the act and contract of marriage went ahead; then, after listening to the concerted objections of his family, ministers and mistress, he forbade it. The Duchess was inconsolable, but Lauzun, it was thought, could be consoled; the King offered to make him a duke, a peer of the realm and a marshal of France. Lauzun refused. 'Sire,' he said, 'you have created so many dukes that it is no longer an honour to be one, and as for the baton of marshal, Your Majesty may give that to me when I have properly earned it.' What greater sign could the poor rich Duchess have that her hero was worth the trouble of loving. She seemed to blossom in spite of her loss, to be giddily happy in spite of her sadness. In May 1671, one of the Dutch gazettes reported that she and Lauzun had married in secret. The story was preposterous but, as everyone at the French court knew, Lauzun was certainly capable of such a thing. The story was not denied. No official statement of any kind was delivered, but in November 1671 Lauzun was arrested and, with an escort of musketeers led by d'Artagnan, was packed off to Pignerol. No question this time of a room in the Bastille to cool his heels for a few days or weeks. He was going to the prison of a frontier fort at the furthest possible distance from Paris and Versailles. The King had cast him off, to be ignored and forgotten.

Lauzun arrived in Pignerol on 16 December 1671 and was given rooms directly below Fouquet in the Angle Tower. Louvois, knowing Lauzun would stick at nothing to get free, advised full-time surveillance and suggested spy-holes. Saint-Mars found this impossible because of the design of the building, but was confident that with the valet he had hired to serve and spy on Lauzun he would be able to keep his prisoner firmly under control. He was wrong. 'I thought

P

View of the city and citadel of Pignerol in the time the Iron Mask was imprisoned there. (*Photograph Bibliothèque Nationale*). *Inset:* Lauzun, who met the Iron Mask and learned his secret in the prison of Pignerol. Painting by Lely. Saumur Museum. (*Photograph Lauros-Giraudon*)

M. Fouquet the most difficult of prisoners to guard,' he told Louvois, 'until I got M. de Lauzun. Now I tell you he is a lamb compared to this one.' Lauzun overwhelmed him from the start with a lunatic onslaught of questions and protests, pleas and complaints, nagging, whining, bullying and sulking; pious and submissive one day, rebellious and demented the next; always unpredictable, contradictory, exasperating. By the middle of January, the valet-spy had to be withdrawn; Lauzun, hysterical, was refusing to eat the food he served. In March, Saint-Mars found him another valet, but not one he could trust to be a spy. Lauzun let his beard grow and neglected himself entirely; he refused to change his clothes, refused to even make his Easter duties, and allowed his rooms to become a shambles with clothes, linen, furniture and dishes scattered about in such disorder that proper security inspections were impossible. At the height of winter he ripped up the floor-boards and set the room on fire. At the height of summer he claimed to be freezing and had such great fires burning in his room that he set the place on fire again.

There was method in Lauzun's madness, that was evident, and after ten years as Fouquet's gaoler, Saint-Mars realized that he was up to something. Going through his clothes one night in July 1672, he discovered a large nail in one of the pockets and, since it was far from obvious why or how Lauzun had got hold of such a thing, he decided to investigate. From the tight security controls he personally kept on Lauzun, he knew that the nail had not been in the cell to start with and could not have been smuggled in later with food or laundry. The only possible explanation was that it had arrived in the cell by way of the window. All the guards who in the previous couple of days had been on sentry-duty outside the Angle Tower were interrogated, and under threat of torture one of them confessed that he had been bribed to get a letter to Lauzun, and had done this by wrapping the letter around a nail and throwing it through the window. The man who had given him the letter was a certain Heurtaut, who had recently arrived in Pignerol from Paris with another man named Plassot. Saint-Mars sent troops to arrest the two men and Heurtaut was caught at the town gates on his way to Turin. Plassot had already gone to Turin in the company of a certain Madame Carrière, who had herself just returned from a trip to Paris with one of the officers of the citadel, a man named Mathonnet. In Heurtaut's possession was found a letter in code from Paris written by Madame de Lamotte d'Argencourt, one of the Queen's lady-companions and one of Lauzun's lady-friends. Saint-Mars, it seemed, had uncovered a conspiracy.

Heurtaut refused to talk and, before he could be persuaded to do so, committed suicide, but the Savoyard authorities agreed to extradite

Plassot and Madame Carrière. A search set in motion for Mathonnet traced him to Lyon where he was arrested. By the beginning of September, Plassot, Mathonnet and Madame Carrière were all in prison at Pignerol undergoing interrogation. Heurtaut had been a valet in Lauzun's household and it appeared that he had been financed by Madame d'Argencourt to set up Lauzun's escape. With Plassot, his cousin, he had come to Pignerol to organize it. He used the seductive charms of Madame Carrière to enlist the aid of Mathonnet, who had then gone to Paris to deal directly with Madame d'Argencourt. That at least was the way things seemed to have transpired, but none of the prisoners admitted to an involvement in any plan to liberate Lauzun; since no actual evidence could be found to prove them guilty of any crime, Mathonnet and Madame Carrière were released in October. Plassot was detained for further interrogation, but was always too ill for this to be possible and eventually, in July 1673, when it seemed he was about to die, he too was allowed to go free. Only after he had been gone for some time was it realized that he had left a bag in the inn where he had been living before his arrest, and that this bag was full of assorted poisons, presumably meant in Heurtaut's original plan for the elimination, if necessary, of Saint-Mars and his staff.

Lauzun in the meantime continued to act like a madman, but it seemed he was only playing for attention, hoping to win consideration. With Louvois, for instance, who wanted him to resign and sell his various positions at court, he was doing his utmost to establish some sort of special relationship, dragging the negotiations out for as long as possible. But with Saint-Mars the game was more a method of diverting attention. Almost certainly within the first few months he had made contact with Fouquet on the floor above, exchanged messages or even talked with him, and he was already at work on two secret passages. One was an enlargement of the chimney which would allow him to visit Fouquet, the other by way of a hole under the floor-boards to the empty rooms below and the possibility of escape. How long it took him to open a passage into Fouquet's rooms is not known, but to manage it alone without being discovered must have occupied many months. To set up an escape route took him years. Once he had opened a way to the floor below, he had to loosen bars on a window, find means to climb down the outside wall to the bottom of the dry moat below, then dig a tunnel through the side of the moat under the surrounding walls into the outer precinct of the citadel. All this under the alert eyes of his gaolers and guards without causing the slightest suspicion.

Saint-Mars continued to report that all was well and, since he believed it himself, his superiors had no reason to doubt it. Life as a prison commander had its compensations. Well paid as he was, with high-cost prisoners in his charge, he was soon rich enough to start acquiring property and so qualify for letters of nobility. Moreover, though Fouquet was always difficult to manage and Lauzun almost impossible, Dauger, apart from an occasional sickness, gave no trouble at all. In December 1673, he could write to Louvois: 'As for the prisoner of the tower brought by M. de Vauroy, he says nothing and lives content, like a man altogether resigned to the will of God and the King.'

Heurtaut and company had not been state prisoners even though they had been held in the prison of Saint-Mars. Until 1674, Saint-Mars had only three state prisoners: Fouquet, Dauger and Lauzun. On 7 April of that year, his fourth prisoner arrived, brought from police custody in Lyon by Saint-Martin, an officer of Pignerol sent to fetch him. The name of this prisoner is not known, and Jung claimed that he was Oldendorf. However, in later correspondence between Saint-Mars and Louvois he is referred to as 'the monk' or 'the Dominican' and from this it is possible to shed some light on his immediate background. In January 1673, a Dominican monk was arrested and imprisoned at the castle of Pierre-Encise in Lyon. His crime was not political. He was at the centre of a scandal involving the ignoble behaviour of a number of noble ladies. It was his claim to have discovered the philosopher's stone which drew the ladies to him, but his knowledge of the 'great work' embraced secrets of the bedroom not proper to the disciplines of alchemist or monk and, whatever the mysteries he was adept in, they had little to do with philosophy. The Princess of Würtemberg was one of his devotees and, since the King had devoted time to her, she was expected to be devoted to no one else. The Comtesse d'Armagnac was another, but she was the daughter of the governor of Lyon and the niece of the Archbishop of Lyon. It was the Comte d'Armagnac himself who was responsible for conducting the monk to prison.

From Lyon he was moved to the Bastille and from there a year later he was transferred to Pignerol. A police officer took him back to Lyon, where Saint-Mars had him collected. On 18 April 1674, Louvois wrote to Saint-Mars: 'I was relieved to hear of the arrival of the prisoner brought by M. de Saint-Martin. Since it is the King's intention that he should be treated with great severity, it will not be necessary for you to provide a fire in his room, at least until the coldness of winter or an actual illness obliges you to do so, and you will give him no other nourishment but bread, wine and water. He is an out and out scoundrel who could never be treated badly enough nor made to suffer the kind of punishment he deserves. However, you may allow him to hear mass, so long as you are careful to avoid him being seen or having contact with anyone, and His Majesty sees fit that you furnish him with a breviary and books of prayer.'

In the following September, Fouquet's valet Champagne became ill and died. He remained in Fouquet's rooms until the end and Fouquet, watching him die, was stricken with grief and despair. For eight years of prison life his only solace and support had been that young man's energy and optimism. Alone with La Rivière his health and spirits, low as they were, declined even more. A letter he was allowed to write to his wife five months later reveals to what dark state the Superintendent Sun had been reduced after fourteen years of imprisonment. Defeated, unwanted, forgotten in the grey limbo of the world's indifference, he pined for human comfort and concern, for someone kind and good to care for his soul, for someone strong and sensible to care for his health. He yearned to see his wife and children. He longed to receive the sacraments more than just five times a year. His physical ailments, real and imaginary, were endless: colds and inflammations, stomach and liver troubles, gallstones, haemorrhoids, sciatica, swollen legs, failing sight, rotten teeth, headaches and buzzing in the ears. At sixty years of age, broken in health and spirit, he looked for nothing but peace of mind.

In autumn 1674, therefore, Saint-Mars was seeking another valet to replace Champagne. Two valets were in his opinion better than one because, as he had explained to Louvois earlier, 'one alone gets too depressed, and also if either becomes sick the other one can do the nursing.' To find another, however, was difficult. He had had the same problem trying to find valets for Lauzun. 'None of my servants would go in there for a million,' he had told Louvois then. 'They have seen that those I put with M. Fouquet have never come out again.' For Lauzun he had managed to find two, but the second only as a replacement for the first. As a result Lauzun, like Fouquet, had only one valet, so in fact two more servants were needed. On 20 February 1672, when Lauzun's first valet had been withdrawn and the second was proving difficult to find, Saint-Mars had proposed to Louvois that he have Dauger do the job, since after all he was 'only a valet'. 'It is so difficult here to find valets who are prepared to be locked up with my prisoners that I would like to take the liberty of proposing an alternative. That prisoner who is in the tower, the one you sent me with the officer from Dunkirk, would it seems to me make a fine valet. I don't think he would tell M. de Lauzun where he comes from once I warned him not to. I'm sure he would give him no information at all. And he wouldn't just tell me to leave him alone as all the others do.' The reasons Louvois gave for refusing this proposal are not known, but after the death of Champagne the subject was raised again.

On 30 January 1675 Louvois wrote to Saint-Mars: 'His Majesty gives his permission for the prisoner brought by M. de Vauroy to serve as valet to M. Fouquet, but whatever happens you must refrain from putting him with M. de Lauzun, or with anyone other than M. Fouquet. That is to say, you can give the said prisoner to M. Fouquet when he does not have his valet and not otherwise.' Six weeks later when Saint-Mars was still unable to find servants, Louvois returned to the same subject, reiterating the same concern: 'You can give M. de Lauzun a valet if you can find one suitable, but no matter what the reason you must not give him the prisoner brought by M. de Vauroy who, as I have informed you, should serve M. Fouquet alone and only when it is necessary.'

Thus one may clarify the state of affairs in the prison of Pignerol in 1675, ten years after Saint-Mars had received his appointment: Fouquet, worn out with sadness and old age, living with his valet, La Rivière, on the third floor of the Angle Tower; Lauzun, bearded and wild, living with his servant in jumbled disorder on the floor below, planning his escape and visiting Fouquet in secret by a passage he had made in the chimney; Dauger in the Lower Tower, sealed off alone in some specially constructed cell and resigned to the will of God and the King, but visiting Fouquet by special permission whenever La Rivière was indisposed; and the monk, also in the Lower Tower, isolated in some other cell, without fire or comfort of any kind, living on bread and books of prayer, his mind disintegrating as the months went by, all but ignored by Saint-Mars, already forgotten by Louvois.

In February 1676, Lauzun finished digging the underground passage that would take him clear of the prison into the outer precinct of the citadel, but when he came to make his escape he had the misfortune to reach freedom under the startled eyes of a servant-girl. Seeing the bearded phantom rise up from the ground in the dark, she gave a scream of terror which alerted the guard. Lauzun was taken immediately and all his years of patient labour were cancelled at a stroke. The news of his escape attempt spread quickly, however, and made a sensation at Versailles. He was the hero of the hour and, by his honourable failure, won more voices for himself with the King, more generous feelings and open support than any successful escape could have achieved. Saint-Mars was reprimanded, but neither Lauzun nor his valet were punished.

In May 1676, Saint-Mars received a fifth prisoner: Dubreuil, alias Samson, resident of the free city of Basel, private agent specializing in military espionage. He had been hired by the French to spy on Austrian troop movements in Germany, but was discovered to be in the pay of the Austrian and Spanish governments as well as the French. He was kidnapped by the French secret service in Switzerland or Swabia and smuggled over the border into Alsace. Louvois ordered the kidnapping on 25 February, but Dubreuil was a slippery character and was not caught until 24 April. He was taken first to Brisach, thence to Besançon and from there to Lyon. On 2 May Louvois notified Saint-Mars of his imminent arrival: 'In the next day or so you will receive a prisoner named Dubreuil, arrested in Alsace, who will be brought to you by fifteen guards of Monsignor the Archbishop of Lyon. It is important to have him well guarded, and the King desires you to take custody of him in the dungeon of the citadel of Pignerol. Put him with the last prisoner who was sent to you and keep me informed about him.'

The 'last prisoner' was the Dominican monk, who after two and a half years of isolation and callous treatment had become deranged; his cell was foul, and he was violent. Dubreuil, horrified, begged to be moved, but Saint-Mars had his orders and Louvois was not interested. 'I must warn you not to let yourself be deceived by his fine talk,' Louvois wrote in June. 'You must regard him as one of the biggest scoundrels in the world and the most difficult to keep under guard.' Nonetheless Dubreuil managed to persuade Saint-Mars that he had information of such importance to communicate that on 28 July he was allowed to write directly to the minister. In this letter he made the claim that there was a plot afoot to assassinate Louvois, with Fouquet's brother, the Bishop of Agde, as ringleader; then, having proved his concern for the minister, he expressed the hope that the minister would show some concern for him and allow him to move cells. 'I am here,' he wrote, 'with a man who is completely insane and unbearable to live with. He has polluted the room so badly that one can scarcely breathe. I have not been able to eat or drink for a week and left in this wretched place I will surely die.' From Louvois no response at all, until Saint-Mars himself confirmed that the monk was insane.

In a letter to Saint-Mars dated 3 November, Louvois showed himself baffled. 'Who is this prisoner with M. Dubreuil whom you say has gone mad? Note down his name for me and the name of whoever it was who brought him to you and send me a copy of the order for his imprisonment so that I might better understand what the situation is.' Louvois himself had written the order consigning the monk to Pignerol and two and a half years later he had forgotten everything about him. Not that the monk's harsh treatment would have been ameliorated had Louvois not forgotten. Once his memory was refreshed, he recommended the bastinado as the most appropriate treatment for madness in prisoners and was delighted to learn from Saint-Mars later that the mere threat of it had rendered the monk more reasonable. 'That man is one of the biggest scoundrels there is in the world,' he remarked, employing his favourite expression, 'and all the signs are that he is just pretending to be mad.' But Saint-Mars had scruples about beating a priest and needed to be reassured. 'It is true,' Louvois explained, 'that those who beat priests out of contempt for their holy office are excommunicated, but it is permissible to chastise a priest when he is malicious and you are responsible for his conduct.' Saint-Mars had proposed moving the monk into a cell with Lauzun's valet. Louvois did not oppose the idea, but suggested an alternative: leave the monk and Dubreuil together, but chain the monk to the wall. 'Remember to be on your guard with M. Dubreuil,' the Minister concluded in characteristic fashion. 'He is one of the wiliest scoundrels one could ever meet.'

If one reviews the five prisoners of Pignerol in 1677, one can distinguish three distinct categories: two prisoners of rank, Fouquet and Lauzun, who occupied spacious rooms and had servants; two 'scoundrels', Dubreuil and the monk, who shared the same cell; and one top-security prisoner, Dauger, who lived alone in a cell especially constructed for him. When a prisoner of rank played the mad-man, it was tolerated, and even though he might attempt to escape he would not be punished; but a 'scoundrel', driven insane by years of cruel treatment, was thrashed and kept on a leash when he misbehaved. The top-security prisoner had contact with no one; he was forbidden to speak of his past even to Saint-Mars, and yet he was allowed out of his cell to act valet to one of the prisoners of rank when he was alone. He was not himself a prisoner of rank, he was 'only a valet', but he was not a 'scoundrel', he was a 'wretch'. How he was treated when he gave trouble is not known. It seems he lived 'altogether resigned to the will of God and the King'.

Towards the end of 1677, Lauzun received special authorization to have his brother and sister come to Pignerol to see him. His signature was needed to ratify formalities of succession following two deaths in the family, that of his eldest brother and that of a great-uncle. Meetings with a notary were held each afternoon for four days from 27 November to 1 December. They took place in the apartment of Saint-Mars, who was there in person to ensure that nothing but legal matters was discussed. Lauzun made the most of it, playing the haggard prisoner with dazed look and tangled beard, debilitated by prison fever and blinded by the light of day, smiling bravely through his tears. His sister's heart-strings were so violently plucked by the four-day show that when on the last day he assigned to her full powers of attorney to divest him, if she wished, of all that he had inherited, she fell at his feet in an excess of emotion and had to be restrained by the guards. Lauzun blessed her, asked only for her prayers, and told her to put her trust 'in the mercy and benevolence of God and the King'.

Kings, like God, may work in unexpected ways, for it was on that very day that Louvois wrote to Saint-Mars informing him of a special favour granted by the King to the prisoners of rank: a public and well-publicized demonstration of royal benevolence and mercy. Fouquet and Lauzun were to be allowed to walk together in the prison compound for two hours every day. To be sure, they were to be closely guarded, forbidden to speak of anything related to their lives in prison or the reasons they were there, and would be obliged to hold their conversations in high clear voices across the head of Saint-Mars, but it was a dispensation of considerable significance. From such a sign the prisoners might hope for more important concessions, and a year later these materialized.

On 23 November 1678, Louvois took the unusual step of addressing himself directly to Fouquet and asking him to make a confidential report on what if anything Dauger had revealed of himself to La Rivière. Though Louvois' original intention had been to allow Dauger to serve Fouquet only in the absence of La Rivière, the two valets had evidently met. 'Sir,' Louvois wrote, 'it is with great pleasure that I carry out the instructions which it has pleased the King to give me, in advising you that His Majesty is disposed to grant considerable ameliorations of your life in prison in the near future. However, as he desires to be informed beforehand if the man named Eustache, given to you as a servant, has not spoken in front of your other valet of how he was employed before coming to Pignerol, His Majesty has commanded me to raise that question with you and to tell you that he is waiting for you to notify me of the truth of the matter without qualification so that he might take appropriate measures regarding what Eustache may have said of his past life to his colleague. The intention of His Majesty is that you should reply in a personal manner to this letter without divulging its contents to M. de Saint-Mars.' A letter from Louvois to Saint-Mars, written on 27 December 1678, makes it clear that Saint-Mars was also asked to make a special report on Dauger's contact with La Rivière, but neither his nor Fouquet's reply survives.

In January 1679, the promised ameliorations came into effect. Fouquet and Lauzun were allowed to walk together in the precincts of the citadel, to visit each other in their rooms and to have visitors. Saint-Mars and his guards were in attendance all the time and there were orders to shoot the prisoners if they tried to escape, but with such signs of increasing clemency the prisoners and their families could cherish the hope that eventually there might even be a pardon. With these new concessions, however, came a warning to Saint-Mars about the importance of security arrangements surrounding Dauger, who it seems was now allowed to see La Rivière as well as Fouquet. 'Every time M. Fouquet goes down to M. de Lauzun's room, or M. de Lauzun or any visitor goes up to M. Fouquet's room, M. de Saint-Mars should take care to remove the man named Eustache, and not allow him back into M. Fouquet's room until only M. Fouquet and his longtime valet are there. The same thing applies when M. Fouquet takes his walk in the citadel. The said Eustache must be made to stay in M. Fouquet's room and only allowed to accompany M. Fouquet when he walks alone with his longtime valet in the place where for some time His Majesty has seen fit for M. de Saint-Mars to let him take the air.'

On 20 January Louvois wrote to Fouquet again: 'You will learn from M. de Saint-Mars the precautions which the King wishes to be taken to prevent Eustache Dauger from communicating with anyone except yourself. His Majesty expects you to give your closest attention to the matter because you know how important it is that no one has knowledge of what he knows'. To Saint-Mars Louvois wrote on 15 February: 'His Majesty leaves it to you to work out with M. Fouquet whatever you think best for the security of the man named Eustache Dauger, I merely remind you to ensure above all else that he does not talk to anyone in private.'

On 2 May 1679 Saint-Mars received his sixth prisoner, Count Matthioli, who was arrested in circumstances not exactly the same as those published in 1687. What in fact happened was that the Abbé d'Estrades contacted him in Turin towards the end of April and persuaded him that Catinat had been authorized by the King to pay whatever was necessary to speed along ratification of the sale of Casale. A meeting was arranged for 2 May, at six in the morning in a church on the southern outskirts of Turin. It was raining heavily, rain which had continued non-stop for three days. Matthioli joined d'Estrades in his coach and they drove through the flooded countryside to meet Catinat, who was waiting in a country house close to the border. The roads were swamped, the bridges broken, the fords too full to cross. Three miles from the house they were obliged to leave the coach and continue on foot through the pouring rain. Matthioli had every reason to turn back, but he did not; he even worked for an hour to repair a bridge with planks so that he and d'Estrades could cross a swollen river. When they reached the house, Catinat was waiting there with a squad of troops led by Villebois, one of the lieutenants of Pignerol prison. Matthioli was siezed and, without more ado, was bundled over the border into France. By two o'clock that same day he was in the custody of Saint-Mars.

Two days later, on 4 May, Saint-Mars received his seventh prisoner, Matthioli's valet. This unfortunate man had received a note, brought to him by Catinat's agents, to the effect that his master was staying with friends in the country for a few days and would send a coach to collect his belongings. The valet, suspecting nothing, prepared the baggage and went with it in the coach to join his master. The coach was driven to Pignerol, the valet was thrown into a cell and Matthioli's belongings were ransacked. To the great annoyance of Catinat, however, neither the documents of sale nor any papers of significance were found. Under interrogation, Matthioli explained that he had confided all the papers to his wife, who had deposited them for safekeeping in a convent in Bologna; then he claimed that they were hidden with other papers in his father's home in Padua; finally he maintained that he had given them all to the Duke of Mantua. Agents were despatched to Bologna, Padua and Venice to acquire by any means necessary whatever papers Matthioli had hidden in each place. However, though an abundance of documents was found, the actual ratification of sale was not amongst them.

Catinat did not, so far as one can ascertain, accompany the cross-examination with torture, but Louvois had informed Saint-Mars that he wanted Matthioli treated in such a way that he would 'have cause to repent his wrong behaviour'. Throughout the month of May, he emphasized the point repeatedly. Apart from the bare necessities of life, Matthioli was to receive nothing. Even the attentions of doctor and priest were to be denied him. As a security precaution the name Matthioli was not mentioned, and in correspondence between Pignerol and Versailles he was referred to as 'Lestang'. This, however, was only for the first year. In that time also he was kept in solitary confinement. When eventually he was allowed to regain his name and made to share a cell with another prisoner, he had lost his sanity and the prisoner he was put with was the lunatic monk. What was happening to his valet meanwhile is not known, except that his fate in prison, though just as real as his master's, was even less significant in the eyes of the authorities.

In the very month that Matthioli and his valet lost their freedom behind the walls of Pignerol, Fouquet received yet another dispensation which, for him, rendered those walls less terrible. On 10 May 1679, Louvois made the following announcement to Saint-Mars: 'Being pleased to allow Madame Fouquet, her children and M. Fouquet de Mézières to go to Pignerol to see M. Fouquet and visit him freely, His Majesty has commanded me to tell you that it is his intention that you permit Madame Fouquet to see M. Fouquet at any time she might desire, to stay in his room and even to spend the night there as often as she might wish. As for his children and his brother, His Majesty sees fit that they be allowed to talk with him and keep him company without your officers being present.' And so at the age of sixty-four, after eighteen years of imprisonment, Fouquet had the comfort of his family around him and the almost certain prospect of eventual freedom. He was permitted to take charge of family affairs once again, and it was rumoured that as a first step to liberation he was to be allowed to take the waters at Bourbon. Lauzun, meanwhile, had shaved off his beard and was looking dapper and debonair in uniform. He had the use of four horses within the citadel and exercised them every day. Surrounded by the officers and ladies of the citadel, his wily and resourceful spirit had greater scope and manoeuvrability to further his return to favour and advantage. The Grande Mademoiselle had been given to understand that she could save him from prison if she were to surrender some of her many titles and estates to the children of Madame de Montespan and the King. That she should start bargaining in earnest was all that Lauzun desired.

In autumn Fouquet's wife returned to Paris, but his youngest daughter, Marie-Madeleine, stayed behind and as winter approached sought permission to live with her aged father in prison so that she might look after him all the time. On 18 December, Saint-Mars was authorized to prepare a room for her on the floor above Fouquet's apartment and to install a connecting staircase for her. It was only a week or so after this that Fouquet came to a proper appreciation of the feelings which motivated his daughter to such an act of love and devotion. She was having an affair with Lauzun who, by means of the secret passageway he had effected to Fouquet's room and the private staircase Saint-Mars had effected to her bedroom, was prepared to exploit the situation to its best advantage. Fouquet, angry and hurt, sent his daughter away and broke off his relations with Lauzun, who for his part was not in the least put out. He could be sure that the Grande Mademoiselle would hear of the romance, and the fear that she might be replaced in his affections would spur her to more urgent action on his behalf. Compromising Fouquet's daughter was after all just one of the many cards he had in play.

On 27 January 1680, he played what he thought was a trump, sending a letter to Louvois to say that he had something of great personal significance to tell him:

> I protest that my impatience to leave prison is no greater than my impatience to have you informed of what I have to tell you, but it is altogether essential that it should be by word of mouth and that you alone should be informed without anyone else being able to know about it. It is in your interest that it should happen in this way, and I would like to tell you once again how I am quite sure that you have not found a servant who has proved himself to you personally and to all your family in terms so important, tangible,

practical and agreeable, so suited to your taste and the state of your fortune . . . I ask only that I might inform you by someone in whom I have entire confidence without anyone else being able to find out. I would have entrusted my sister, de Nogent, and my brother, the Chevalier, but for this particular matter I need Barrail. He alone can do it properly. It is important for you that it should be him, and I beg you, sir, to be amicably disposed and send him to me, because in any case it is of an importance for you above anything you could imagine.

Louvois was diffident, but gave his permission anyway and Barrail arrived in Pignerol on 17 March. What the secret information was is not known for certain, but in all likelihood it was the proposal, which Lauzun certainly made through Barrail at about this time, that a marriage should be arranged between the daughter of his sister, the Comtesse de Nogent, and Barbezieux, Louvois' son. The couple were as yet young (Barbezieux was only twelve years old) but marriages of power and position were made early, and there were immense possibilities for Louvois in such a marriage. If Lauzun were to make his niece his heir, then Barbezieux would benefit directly from Lauzun's marriage with Mademoiselle. With a fat bait like that, Lauzun hoped to win everything: the Minister's support, his own freedom and Mademoiselle's hand and fortune.

What Eustache Dauger was doing through all this is not known, but presumably his visits to Fouquet, restricted as they were to times when he was alone, had become few and far between. As for the other prisoners, a letter from Saint-Mars to Louvois on 6 January 1680 reveals that the harsh treatment they had been subjected to had resulted in the same sad fate for all: 'I should tell you, my lord, that M. de Lestang is become like the monk I have charge of, that is to say mad to the point of extravagance, from which M. Dubreuil is not exempt either.' A fuller explanation followed on 24 February: 'M. de Lestang, who has been in my custody for almost a year, complains that he is not treated as a man of his quality and the minister of a great prince should be. Nevertheless I follow your lordship's commands to the letter on this matter as in everything else. I think his wits have turned from the things he tells me: that he talks every day with God and his angels, that they have informed him of the death of the Duke of Mantua and the Duc de Lorraine; and as clear proof of his madness, that he has the honour to be a close relative of the King, to whom he wishes to write and complain of the treatment he gets from me. Seeing that he is not in his right senses, I have no wish to give him paper and ink for that.' On 23 March 1680, Saint-Mars sent off a dispatch to Louvois informing him that one of his seven prisoners had died. Two days later Barrail left Pignerol and would have reached Paris with the same news a day or so after the official report from Saint-Mars reached Versailles. On 6 April, *La Gazette* announced the death: 'We are informed from Pignerol that M. Fouquet has died of apoplexy.' The letter in which Saint-Mars reported the death to Louvois no longer exists and so there is no actual description of Fouquet's last moments. However, a reply from Louvois to Saint-Mars, dated 8 April, suggests that Fouquet's eldest son, Louis-Nicolas, the Comte de Vaux, was present at the time. Also on 8 April, Louvois replied to a letter he had received from the Comte de Vaux: 'Sir, I have received the letter which you took the trouble to write to me on the twenty-ninth of last month and I have spoken to the King about Madame your mother's request that she be allowed to take the body of M. Fouquet away from Pignerol. You can rest assured that His Majesty has given orders for that and she will have no difficulty.' On the following day Louvois wrote to Saint-Mars authorizing him 'to deliver the body of Fouquet to his family so that they might have it conveyed wherever they think best.'

In his letter of 8 April to Saint-Mars, Louvois showed himself concerned, but not because Fouquet had died. Saint-Mars had allowed the Comte de Vaux to take away some of his father's papers and Louvois was annoyed about that; but what occupied him most was the fact, just discovered by Saint-Mars, that Lauzun had been using a secret passageway to visit Fouquet. All the precautions taken to avoid a meeting between Dauger and Lauzun had therefore been in vain. It was almost certain that they had seen each other, and no doubt talked together.

> From the letter you wrote me on the twenty-third of last month, the King has learned of the death of M. Fouquet and of your judgement that M. de Lauzun knows most of the important things M. Fouquet was acquainted with and that the man named La Rivière knows them too, on which point His Majesty has commanded me to inform you that after you have sealed up the hole through which without your knowledge MM Fouquet and de Lauzun communicated with each other, and rebuilt it so solidly that no one could tamper in that area again, and after you have dismantled the staircase which leads from the room of the late M. Fouquet to the room you would have arranged for Mademoiselle his daughter, it is His Majesty's intention that you lodge M. de Lauzun in the room of the late M. Fouquet . . . that you persuade M. de Lauzun that the man named Eustache Dauger and the said La Rivière have been set free and that you say the

same thing to all those who ask you for news of them; that nevertheless you shut them both up in a room where you can assure His Majesty that they will not be able to communicate with anyone by word of mouth or by writing, and that M. de Lauzun will not be able to perceive that they are locked up there.

Officially therefore at this time, Saint-Mars lost two prisoners: Fouquet who died and Dauger who was released along with Fouquet's valet La Rivière, who though living in prison had not been listed as a prisoner. Thus he was left with five acknowledged prisoners: Lauzun, the monk, Dubreuil, Matthioli and Matthioli's former valet. Actually, however, he still had seven prisoners because though Fouquet was dead, his valet, La Rivière, had become a secret prisoner like Dauger and was locked up with him. After this letter the names of the two secret prisoners were suppressed, except for one more reference to Dauger made by Louvois in the postscript to a letter dated 10 July. The minister had just received a packet containing something which Saint-Mars had found in Fouquet's clothes. 'Tell me,' he wrote, 'how the man named Eustache was able to do what you sent me, and where he was able to get the drugs he needed to do it. I hardly believe that you provided him with them.' It is usually assumed that the drugs referred to were those necessary for making invisible ink, something which Fouquet had been known to make and use in the past, and that the packet in question contained an object of some kind written upon by Dauger, something personal belonging to Fouquet by which Dauger had hoped to pass a message to the outside world. Be that as it may, in the text of the same letter appeared the first recorded use of the code name given to the Iron Mask and his companion: 'It will be enough,' Louvois wrote, 'to let the prisoners of the Lower Tower make their confessions once a year.' The only prisoners for whom at that time Saint-Mars needed a new directive were the two whose security status had just changed: Dauger and La Rivière.

In June Lauzun's valet was liberated. Like La Rivière he had entered the prison not as a prisoner but as a valet to serve someone who was a prisoner. Unlike La Rivière, however, he had not got himself mixed up with state secrets. Once the security precautions surrounding Lauzun were relaxed, he could be paid off and sent away with the warning that if he ever came within twenty-five miles of Pignerol again, he would end his days in the galleys. In August, Matthioli ceased to be a top-security prisoner and was moved into a cell with the Dominican monk. This cell was in the Lower Tower, but these poor crazed creatures were clearly not 'the prisoners of the Lower Tower.' Matthioli had recovered his name, but was still as mad as a hatter and his bedlam antics with the lunatic monk were a source of amusement for Saint-Mars and his men, as witness a letter of 7 September: 'For four or five days after your Lordship allowed me to put Matthioli with the Dominican in the Lower Tower, Matthioli thought the Dominican was a man I had put with him to keep an eye on what he did. Matthioli, who is almost as mad as the Dominican, strode up and down with his cloak over his nose, saying that he was not being fooled by me and that he knew more than he would like to say. The Dominican just sat on his bed with his elbows on his knees and watched him gravely without listening. Signor Matthioli, who remained convinced that he was a spy we had planted on him, was disabused when one day the Dominican got out of bed, stark naked, and began to preach a sermon, if you could call it that, altogether without rhyme or reason. My lieutenants and I saw all their antics through a hole above the door.'

Locked up with a man whose mind had shattered, Matthioli's own mind disintegrated even further and his gaolers were able to exploit the situation for something they valued even more than idle entertainment. When he arrived in Pignerol the Italian was wearing a ring set with the diamond which Louis XIV had given him. Saint-Mars with his usual rapacity soon managed to pocket it and then, realizing that it had been a gift to Matthioli from the King, decided to play safe. He informed Louvois that Matthioli had given a ring to Blainvilliers and that he was looking after it until further notice. He mentioned it only in passing and omitted to say that the ring was set with a diamond. Louvois however knew his man and asked for a full report. On 26 October Saint-Mars told his tale:

> To give you, my lord, a fuller explanation than I have done so far of this diamond ring which M. Matthioli gave to Blainvilliers, I will take the liberty of saying that I believe it was as much out of fear as anything that he gave it to him. The prisoner had insulted him to his face and had even written malicious things about him in charcoal on the walls of his cell, which obliged the officer to threaten him with severe discipline unless he was more polite and better behaved in the future. When he was put into the tower with the monk, I ordered Blainvilliers to show him a cudgel and warn him that with such a thing bedlamites were transformed into reasonable men and we would know how to make him sensible if he did not become so. This warning was duly given and some days after, when Blainvilliers took him his dinner, he said to him. 'Sir, here is a little ring which I want you to have and which I beg you to accept'. Blainvilliers told him in answer that he took nothing from prisoners and would take it only to hand it over to me. I do believe it is worth as much as fifty or sixty pistoles.

Louvois played the game. 'You must keep the ring which M. Matthioli gave to M. Blainvilliers,' he replied on 2 November, 'so that you can give it back to him if ever the King orders his release.'

On 22 April 1681, Lauzun was freed, reducing the number of prisoners to six: four official and two secret. Then on 12 May Saint-Mars was promised the governorship of Exiles with instructions to take only the two secret prisoners with him. The documents confirming his appointment were dispatched from Versailles on 9 June and with them Louvois sent a letter explaining, among other things, the precautions to be taken for the transportation of the two prisoners. At the end of this letter he added: 'With regard to the bags which you have belonging to M. Matthioli, you should take them with you to Exiles so that you can return them to him if ever His Majesty decides to set him at liberty.' This letter was dictated to a scribe, as was the usual practice in the ministries, and Louvois added his signature at the end. For the scribe, who could put two and two together as well as the next man, it was obvious therefore that one of the two prisoners going to Exiles was Matthioli. Also to anyone at Pignerol, who knew Matthioli's bags and saw them loaded up with the rest of the baggage for Exiles, it would have been evident that Matthioli was being transferred. In fact we know that Louvois was being cunning; he was pleasing Saint-Mars by giving him all Matthioli's belongings, including one might add the diamond ring, and at the same time amusing himself by giving everyone the impression that Matthioli was one of the two secret prisoners.

Since the existence of the two prisoners of the Lower Tower was not acknowledged, the existence of two new prisoners had to be invented before they could be moved. To do this, Catinat, who was still waiting in Pignerol for orders to occupy Casale, was recalled to Paris; then at the beginning of September he was sent back in secret and in disguise to take up residence with his valet in the Angle Tower. Saint-Mars pretended that they were prisoners newly arrived, and thus the number of official detainees was raised to six. On 8 September 1681, Catinat wrote to Louvois: 'I arrived here on the third of the month, and would have got here on the second were it not for the precautions I took with M. de Saint-Mars so that I might enter in secret. I call myself Guibert and I am some sort of engineer committed by order of the King. Guibert is from Nice, and I had myself arrested beyond Pignerol on the road from Pancarlier. To all appearances M. de Saint-Mars holds me prisoner here, even though with a profusion of figs of an admirable plumpness and excellence.' In the weeks that followed, the contract with the Duke of Mantua was finalized. Catinat left his prison and appeared in the citadel as though just arrived, then on 28 September left at the head of his troops to take possession of Casale. At the same time Saint-Mars left Pignerol for Exiles with his two secret prisoners.

There is little room for doubt that the two prisoners taken to Exiles were Dauger and La Rivière. Of the four prisoners left by Saint-Mars to Lieutenant Villebois, his successor at Pignerol, the identity of three is certain. On 25 September 1681, Saint-Mars wrote to inform the Abbé d'Estrades in Turin that he had just received his warrant for the governorship of Exiles, and since d'Estrades had been responsible for the kidnapping of Matthioli he gave news of him. 'I will have in my charge two blackbirds I have here who have no other name than the gentlemen of the Lower Tower. Matthioli will stay here with two other prisoners.' Matthioli's valet was considered of such little account that, though a prisoner, he was not even counted. That he was still confined is certain because of later references to him. On 1 May 1684, for instance, Louvois wrote that he was delighted to hear Villebois had punished the valet for bad behaviour, and in a letter of 27 December 1693 we find that he and Matthioli, still at Pignerol, had been caught hiding messages in the linings of their clothes. As for the 'two other prisoners' who stayed behind, one was certainly Dubreuil. Louvois referred to him in a letter he wrote to Villebois on 24 May 1682, displeased to learn that he had been giving Villebois trouble and recommending a sound thrashing as the best means to cure his insubordination. No specific reference to the Dominican monk exists to prove that he stayed on at Pignerol, but presumably he did: demented as he was, he certainly was not one of the two prisoners who went to Exiles. They were often described as sick, but never as mad. 'The gentlemen of the Lower Tower' were evidently La Rivière and Eustache Dauger. Since we know that La Rivière was only a valet, we may assume that he was the prisoner who died at Exiles on 5 January 1687 and, though Eustache Dauger was described by Louvois as 'only a valet', we must conclude that he was the Man in the Iron Mask.

1. *Dauger or Danger*: traditionally the name has been read as Dauger and that is why, for the sake of convenience, I use that reading here.

CHAPTER NINE

DUNKIRK CONNECTIONS

It has been argued that the name 'Eustache Dauger' was not the mysterious prisoner's true name. Prison names were usually single, a surname or a nickname, as Matthioli at Pignerol was called 'Lestang' and Protestant ministers on Sainte-Marguerite were called 'Songster' and 'Scribbler'. According to Palteau, Dauger was known by the nickname 'Tower' among the prison staff, and in the course of his thirty-four years as a prisoner he had a number of code-names: 'the prisoner from Provence', 'the longtime prisoner', one of 'the prisoners of the Lower Tower' and 'the prisoner brought by Captain de Vauroy'. The fact that 'Eustache Dauger' is a complete name, both forename and surname together, does give the impression of authenticity, but arguably it was after all just an invention. Since the reason for the man's imprisonment was so secret and the security measures surrounding him so thorough, it is highly unlikely, so the argument runs, that those who imprisoned him would ever have risked using his true name. As one writer puts it: 'Whatever the man's real name may have been, we may be quite sure it had no resemblance to "Eustache Dauger".'

If 'Eustache Dauger' was a prison pseudonym, then the field of inquiry is open to any man of any name who might conceivably have disappeared in the region of Dunkirk in late July or early August 1669. The first candidate fulfilling those conditions was offered in 1903 by Andrew Lang in a book entitled *The Valet's Tragedy and Other Studies*. Like investigators before him, he had followed a line of enquiry first suggested by Theodore Jung, but his contribution was altogether new. Jung had proposed various possible solutions to the mystery of Eustache Dauger's arrest, one of which was that it could be found 'in the records of the trial of Roux de Marcilly, and in the dispatches of the French Ambassador to England'. For the trial in question, no official record survives, but Lang pieced together what information he could find and, in his own words, 'pushed the inquiry into a source neglected by the French historians, namely the correspondence of the English ambassadors, agents and statesmen for the years 1668, 1669.' Today a more detailed account than his exists, published in 1969 by Aimé-Daniel Rabinel in a book entitled *La Tragique Aventure de Roux de Marcilly*. For a proper appreciation of the candidate discovered by Lang, the story of Roux as given by Rabinel should first be told.

In April 1668, a Frenchman calling himself Claude Roux de Marcilly, a Protestant from Nîmes in the Languedoc, arrived in London and took up lodging at a small hotel run by a Swiss wine-merchant in Chandos Street near Oxford Circus. The name of the hotel was 'The Loyal Subject', which ironically Claude Roux was not. France was at war with Spain for possession of the Franche Comté and the Spanish Netherlands, and Roux had just come from Brussels, the capital of the Spanish Netherlands, with a letter of introduction from the governor there to the Spanish ambassador in London. He was an unimpressive, unattractive man in his late forties, his hair black turning grey, his clothes soberly cut in greys and browns. Usually he kept to the hotel during the day and went out only in the evening. He called at government offices in Whitehall, or at the Spanish and Austrian embassies, and made regular visits to a French wine-merchant called Gerard, whose shop in Covent Garden he used as a mailing address for correspondence with Geneva and Paris. Occasionally he also met an Englishman named Samuel Morland who was a scientist and inventor, well-known for his experiments in hydrostatics and hydraulics and reputed to be one of the foremost engineers of the day.

It was not the cause of science with attracted Roux to the Englishman. Thirteen years before, Morland had taken part in a diplomatic mission sent by Cromwell to the Duke of Savoy to plead against the persecution of the Waldensian[1] population there and had distinguished himself enough in the Protestant cause to be kept on in the region afterwards as chargé d'affaires in Geneva. His turning to science had coincided with the return of the monarchy to England and the termination in consequence of his career in the diplomatic service, but his genius for survival was not restricted to scientific accomplishments. Among his many achievements was that fact that, after serving as a secret agent for Cromwell, he had managed to engineer himself a pardon from Charles II by providing a list of his fellow-spies. At the science of double-cross he was unusually inventive, and towards the end of May, having heard a little of what Roux had to say about his reasons for being in London, he invited the Frenchman to his home for dinner so that they could be alone together and talk freely.

Roux arrived in the late afternoon and stayed until the early morning. Morland was a generous host and a good listener. He put his guest at ease and got him to talk, showed understanding and admiration, made sympathetic remarks and asked questions. Roux, who enjoyed talking about himself, was delighted to have such an appreciative audience and spoke out with reckless confidence. His audience, however, was larger than he suspected. Henri de Ruvigny, the French ambassador, had also been invited. He had arrived shortly before Roux and was hidden in a curtained closet where he could watch and listen without being discovered, comfortably seated with pen and paper provided by his host to take notes of all that was said.

Roux gave him plenty to write about. He was, he explained, the special envoy of a secret political organization known as the Committee of Ten which had its headquarters in Geneva and was dedicated to the overthrow of Louis XIV and his government. A revolution in France was imminent; he personally had spent the last ten years working to achieve it. There were any number of Frenchmen ready to assassinate Louis XIV and countless numbers of French Protestants eager to revolt and set up a republic. The Languedoc, Provence, Dauphiné, Guyenne, Poitou, Brittany and Normandy: all were armed and prepared. However, to be sure of success they needed outside assistance. England, Holland and Sweden were already leagued in a defensive pact against France. What the Committee of Ten wanted was to extend this alliance to include Switzerland, Spain and Austria, with a military commitment to support such a revolution. The Swiss Cantons had shown themselves favourable to the idea, and Roux's mission for the last two months had been to persuade the Spanish and the English to participate. He was having frequent meetings with Lord Arlington,[2] the English minister, and with the Spanish and Austrian ambassadors. To them, however, he had made no mention of a future French republic. In return for their miltiary backing, they had been led to believe that all the territory lost by Spain to France since 1630 would be handed back and that the sovereignty of all the rebel provinces would be given to England, to be shared between Charles II and his brother James. The Spanish had already pledged their support and were assisting Roux with passports and money. The English for the moment were holding back, but if necessary the revolution would go ahead without them.

Morland seemed impressed and Roux, who liked to be impressive, pressed his advantage. He knew Louis XIV personally, he said, and had met him in private many times. He also knew Monsieur, the King's brother. In fact he was so well known that it was something of a disadvantage. In all the time he had been in London he had not dared to go out during the day for fear of meeting Ruvigny who would be sure to recognize him. Spying through his closet-curtain, Ruvigny did not recognize Roux as anyone he had ever seen before, but though these claims to personal significance and social grandeur were an obvious pretence or delusion, they did not discount the real importance of what the man had to say. Morland, primed beforehand, fished for Roux's secret contacts and extracted the names of two members of the Committee of Ten: Colonel Balthazar, a former officer in the French army, and Count Dohna, a former governor of Orange;[3] the names of his correspondants in Paris and Geneva; and the date and route of his return to Geneva – leaving 1 June by way of Brussels and the French border-towns of Charleville and Sedan.

Roux took his leave, altogether unaware that his host had betrayed him; and Ruvigny lost no time getting off a full report to Lionne, the Foreign Minister in Paris, so that the governors of Charleville and Sedan could be alerted in good time to expect Roux and arrest him. As it was, Roux delayed his departure until the beginning of July because the English were beginning to show an interest in opening negotiations with the Swiss, and because the Spanish governor in Brussels was being replaced; he wished to meet the new man before reporting back to Geneva. When finally he left, he was carrying a passport issued by the English authorities for a journey to Switzerland. He also held letters of introduction and credit from the Spanish and Austrian ambassadors to officials of the Franche Comté, including the Spanish governor in Besançon. On 1 August, while the French were still waiting for him to show up in Sedan or Charleville, he arrived in Switzerland with an imposing protector: Chief Justice Borrey of the Franche Comté, who accompanied him and paid his expenses.

As a first condition to an alliance with the Swiss, the English wanted them to extradite the English Parliamentarians who had voted the death-sentence on Charles I. At the time of the Restoration, these men had taken refuge in various European countries and all except those in the Swiss Cantons had since been extradited to face the charge of regicide. Roux, who to see Louis XIV executed was quite prepared to sacrifice the executioners of Charles I, went to Zurich, Berne and Geneva to argue for their extradition. Balthazar, as well as Borrey, went with him, and while he was in Switzerland he was Balthazar's guest at his home in Prangins near Nyon on Lake Geneva.

The French ambassador at Solothurn in Switzerland reported to Lionne on 10 August that a mysterious Frenchman from England was discussing an Anglo-Swiss alliance in Zurich and on 7 September that this same Frenchman had travelled through Switzerland with Borrey and was last heard of staying at Saint-Claude, forty miles from Geneva in the Franche Comté. That the man at Saint-Claude was the unsaintly

Claude Roux was established beyond question for Lionne by a description of the man furnished by the ambassador's informant in Zurich. On 23 September, a Guards officer named La Grange was despatched with a dozen men to hunt down and capture Roux wherever he might be, in or out of France, but by the time he crossed the frontier into the Franche Comté, his quarry had vanished without trace. By a strange coincidence, Roux had left Saint-Claude at the very moment the ambassador had got news that he was there.

The coincidence was no accident. The ambassador's information was supplied by two agents: one in Zurich who knew nothing about Roux and had difficulty learning anything, and one in Geneva who knew everything about Roux and would have had difficulty hiding it. The informant in Geneva was Roux's friend and host Balthazar: an intelligence agent for France as well as a member of the Committee of Ten, he was playing a double game like Morland, but in this case to the advantage of Roux. Balthazar was a wealthy Swiss national of German origin who had served in the Swedish, French and Palatinate armies before settling in Switzerland. People who did not like him said that his money had been made out of pillage and malversation. Probably he had been working for French intelligence since his retirement from the French army thirteen years before, and as recently as January he had served as ambassador-extraordinary for France on a mission to the Duchy of Brunswick-Lüneburg in northern Germany. Not until Ruvigny heard him named as a member of the Committee of Ten did the French have any reason to suspect that he was a double agent and whatever Lionne thought of Roux's disclosure he had not passed it on to the ambassador at Solothurn.

Balthazar, unaware that in Paris his double rôle was known, continued to put on a show. Sooner or later, he realized, the ambassador would learn something about Roux's visit to Geneva, and silence from him on such a matter would seem odd. Late in August, therefore, he supplied the ambassador with vague and misleading information about three strangers in the area, who he thought were envoys from Sweden, Holland and England, having meetings with the governor of the Franche Comté. He promised to investigate the matter further and make a full report. However, by 31 August the ambassador had still heard nothing more from him and wrote to Lionne to ask if perhaps Balthazar had sent his report directly to Paris. It was only after another week's delay that the report finally appeared, and in it Roux's name was not given. He was simply described as 'a Frenchman who changes his name often and claims to have been sent from England'. The other two men were identified as Borrey and the superintendant of finance at the Abbey of Saint-Claude. The Frenchman, Balthazar declared, was staying at Saint-Claude. In fact, Roux had just left.

It was two or three months before Roux was back in England. From the Franche Comté he went to Nancy in the Duchy of Lorraine for secret talks with the Duke,[4] whose enmity to Louis XIV was no secret, and from there to Brussels and possibly Holland. By the end of November he was certainly in London, staying once again at 'The Loyal Subject', and well-established with a secretary, a valet and two lackeys. The French, in the meantime, were still looking for him in Switzerland and the Franche Comté. If Morland knew he had returned, and presumably Roux contacted him soon after his arrival to let him know, then he tried his best to avoid him and made no attempt to inform the French embassy. Ruvigny had been recalled to Paris and Morland was refusing all contact with his successor, Croissy.[5] Morland lived in fear of his life. Ironically, one of his servants had turned out to be an English government agent and had reported his involvement with both Ruvigny and Roux. He had been questioned about them, his letters had been opened and he was being followed.

Roux, however, soon found another confidant, a dissident Frenchman who went by the name of Veyras and who like himself was a Protestant from the Languedoc. On a previous visit to England, this man had called himself Portail, but he had been deported then for subversive talk and was using a different name to avoid being recognized by the authorities. Both as Portail and as Veyras he had made debts and enemies enough to get himself rearrested, but he lived a charmed life, protected by Lord Orrery. Roux brought him into the ring with Balthazar and his fellow-conspirators; he brought Roux into the circle of Orrery and his fellow-intriguers. Orrery was popular at court as a writer of plays in the heroic French manner, and his work was admired by the Duke of Buckingham who also wrote for the stage, but his prowess in heroic verse was nothing compared to his valour in politics. Though he had been a confidential adviser to Cromwell, he had become a privy-councillor to Charles II. Buckingham, who was the son of Charles I's favourite and himself a favourite of Charles II, was a riotous, pleasure-loving character and Orrery had exploited this to make himself one of his closest friends. Buckingham's political views were vague and easily influenced; Orrery's were clear cut and convincingly expressed: in his view it was in the English interest to join forces with the Dutch in a war against Louis XIV.

Roux had meetings with the Dutch ambassador as well as the Spanish ambassador, with Buckingham as well as Arlington, and his tactics changed accordingly. Though still secretly financed by Catholic Spain, he now proposed a league of exclusively Protestant states to defend and protect the Protestants of France. On 26 December he had dinner with the Dutch ambassador and the next day drew up a report for Arlington. He argued that if he were to attend the General Diet of the Swiss Confederation on 25 January, armed with letters from Charles II and accompanied by Colonel Balthazar, he could bring the Swiss Cantons into the existing alliance between England, Holland and Sweden, on the new understanding that they would invade France to aid a Protestant insurrection. Buckingham and possibly Arlington were sympathetic in principle to the idea of a more forceful league against France, but Charles II certainly was not. He was already in secret contact with Louis XIV about the possibility of using French troops to restore Catholicism to England and, at a meeting held on the very day that the Swiss Diet met, he shared the secret with his brother, James, and three ministers, Arlington, Arundel and Clifford. Buckingham's absence from that meeting was a clear sign that the King did not fully trust him, and Arlington, whatever his proper feelings on the matter, was opportunist enough to give his support. Thus, while Roux was hoping to persuade the English to join a Protestant league against France, Charles II and his closest ministers, including Arlington, were secretly planning a Catholic alliance with her. Roux did not leave England for Switzerland again until the beginning of March, but he was wasting his time; his plans were no further forward when he left than they had been the year before.

The French, meanwhile, had lost track of Roux completely. After Balthazar's report in early September they had nothing to go on for six months, until on 6 March someone passed the word to Paris that he was in London. The informant, however, had played the same trick as Balthazar: Roux by a strange coincidence had just left for Brussels. Lionne, unaware of his informant's duplicity, wrote at once to Croissy in London to tell him what he had learned – that Roux was staying with Gerard in Covent Garden and was planning to return to Switzerland in the near future. Croissy soon discovered that Roux was not in Covent Garden, but it took him more than a month to find out that he had been staying in Chandos Street and had long since left. On 27 April, before his full report had reached Paris, Lionne got news from the Franche Comté that Roux had reappeared at Saint-Claude.

The informant this time was almost certainly a Catholic priest by the name of Ragny, who although French was a member of the religious community at the Abbey of Saint-Claude. Ragny had come to know Roux at the time of his first visit, when for his own reasons the priest had set out to win his confidence. For some years Roux had assumed the noble name of Marcilly and Ragny, whose father's mother had been a Marcilly, was curious to know by what right he made such a claim. Roux always pretended to have acquired the name with the purchase of one of the Marcilly estates near Orléans, but he was lying. Ragny resented the usurpation, particularly when he saw the kind of man Roux was. To get at the truth of the visitor's pretensions, he had played the convivial reprobate, which an anti-Catholic like Roux could despise and enjoy as a typical example of the age-old corruption of the Church (although the fact that Roux did not suspect Ragny's true hostility may suggest that the rôle of gourmandizing monk was sufficiently close to his actual character to make it easy for him to play). Roux in his usual fashion had wished to make an impression and Ragny soon heard enough of his hothead-talk to destroy him. Sometime towards the end of 1668 he was in touch with French intelligence, possibly with La Grange, and at the beginning of 1669 was contacted by a French agent named Mazel.

Captain in the light cavalry and equerry to Maréchal Turenne, Mazel had already proved his abilities as a special agent on a secret mission in 1667. His background made him a perfect choice to lead the commando squad assigned to kidnap Roux. He had been born and raised in Calvisson, Roux's own village near Nîmes, was the godson of Roux's own niece, and knew the man personally. He was moreover a Protestant, eager to demonstrate his loyalty to the regime by thwarting the subversive intentions of Protestants like Roux. A legal expert, barrister and doctor of law, he could also be counted upon to effect a kidnapping on foreign territory as discreetly as possible. The commando squad were all Protestants from the same cavalry regiment and included Mazel's elder brother. Their plan was to use Ragny to capture Roux the next time he appeared in the Franche Comté.

Soon after Roux arrived at Saint-Claude he realized that he was being followed, and at the beginning of May he moved to Balthazar's house at Prangins. Ragny wrote to him there inviting him to a party at the home of another priest at Les Rousses just north of Saint-Claude near the French border. Ragny's valet brought the letter and stayed to act as Roux's guide. Early on the morning of Sunday 12 May, Roux left Prangins on horseback with Ragny's valet and one of the two lackeys he had brought with him from England. At the Saint-Cergue pass, on the mountain road from Nyon, he was ambushed by Mazel and his men. Ragny's valet, thinking the attackers highwaymen, put up a fight and was shot. The lackey fled and Roux himself was taken. His captors tied his wrists to the pommel of his saddle, his ankles under the belly of his horse, and hurried him off at a gallop, leaving Ragny's valet for dead on the road. As the group passed under the walls of Bonmont Abbey, Roux began to shout for help and had to be gagged. The Swiss gave chase, but the frontier was crossed without incident; that night Roux was securely lodged in France, locked up in the fort at Ecluse, six miles from Bellegarde. Ragny's valet meanwhile had been found alive and taken back to Nyon, but died some days later. Ragny himself had made his escape from Saint-Claude just half an hour before troops arrived to arrest him. On 14 May, Roux was in prison in Lyon and on 17 May a general order was issued to assist his transfer to the Bastille.

Balthazar at first wished to pretend to the French that Roux had merely visited him on his way from somewhere else, but Roux told his captors that all his papers were at Balthazar's house. He persuaded Mazel to let him write a letter to Balthazar, asking him to send documents he had which proved that he was an envoy of the English. Mazel took the letter with Roux to Paris, but sent some of his men to Gex to prepare a raid on Prangins. Balthazar, warned of their intention, burned all the papers he had and went into hiding. Meanwhile the Council of Berne, in whose territory the abduction had taken place, was highly indignant. The kidnappers were cited before a tribunal and condemned to death by default. The significance of this was purely formal, but the judgement was posted on the door of Turenne's house in Paris, and he was sufficiently put out by it to send his secretary around the embassies to sound out the general feeling. The English ambassador also received a visit from the Spanish ambassador who insisted that he intercede for Roux but, knowing nothing of the man except what he had heard from the French, he refused. On 25 May, Louis XIV wrote to Croissy announcing Roux's capture and instructing him to deliver the news in person to Charles II and his ministers, starting with Arlington. He was to observe their faces carefully for any sign of discomfort or alarm, and to report back in detail. The English, however, were ready for Croissy. They intercepted the letter, deciphered it and summoned the ambassador to Whitehall to tell him the news, three days before they allowed the letter to reach him. Charles II met him in private. Having announced that a Frenchman named Roux, who claimed to be an envoy from England, had been arrested by the French in Switzerland, the king informed him that Roux had never been commissioned by the English to do anything whatsoever, not even to treat the question of the regicides in Switzerland; and that Arlington, who had met the man and listened to what he had to say, had considered him altogether untrustworthy and had merely given him a little money to be rid of him.

Roux persisted in the claim that he was employed by Charles II and professed to have things of such importance to say that he could reveal them to no one but Louis XIV. Lionne was sent to interrogate him in the Bastille, but days of questioning achieved nothing of relevance, except Lionne's private conviction that the man was mentally deranged. Rumours began to circulate that the French had nothing with which to charge Roux, and were going to put him on trial for some

The King and his Council, 1682. From left to right: Le Tellier, La Vrillière, Louvois, Croissy, Colbert, Condé, Louis XIV, Monsieur and the Dauphin. (*Photograph Bibliothèque Nationale*)

trumped-up crime of forgery or rape supposedly committed many years before in Nîmes. On 5 June the process of interrogation was handed over to magistrates of the criminal court and, after a week or so, Roux's spirit began to break. Meanwhile Lionne heard from Croissy that Roux's former valet in London, a Frenchman called Martin, might be useful as a witness; on 12 June, he replied that the man would be well-rewarded if he returned to France to give evidence. Mazel had been kept in Paris for that purpose, as had Ragny who, by way of recompense for the service he had rendered the King and compensation for the loss of his place at Saint-Claude, had already been given a pension of 3,000 livres.

On 14 June, Roux claimed to be ill, unable to urinate and in pain. The interrogation was suspended until a physician had examined him and decided that he was lying. On 17 June, he refused to eat, but the interrogation continued nevertheless, with a confrontation between him and Ruvigny and questions on information just received by Lionne from Croissy concerning his relationship with Veyras. On 20 June, he tried to commit suicide. Using a broken knife bought from one of the guards, he severed his genitals. His intention was to let himself bleed to death without the guards becoming aware, and as a pretext for any blood they might notice he also severed the little finger of his left hand. The guards did notice the blood and, finding a great deal of it, called the governor. Roux then pretended that he had passed a stone in his urine and some of the blood was a consequence of that. The prison governor had him stripped, saw the wound and called a surgeon to cauterize it. The bleeding was stopped, but loss of blood along with lack of food had left him so weak that there was a serious danger he might die before he could be judged. A hurried trial was held the next day, and judgement delivered the day after. Charged with high treason against State and King, Roux was found guilty and condemned to death. His execution took place that afternoon.

At 1 p.m. on Saturday 22 June 1669, he was brought haggard and fainting through the crowds which packed the square in front of the Grand Châtelet law courts and, on a scaffold there, was stripped and bound face-upwards across the executioner's wheel. Stretched out to be killed, he lay shivering and panting while a magistrate read his sentence and a priest urged him to repent; then he begged the comfort of a Protestant minister. This was forbidden by government edict, but when his request was refused he raised his voice in such a powerful outburst of vilification that a minister was sent for. He lay in silence then until the minister's arrival, at which he lifted his head and spoke out clearly, declaring that he was ready to die patiently like a good Christian. The minister pressed him to acknowledge his crimes, but

Roux swore that he had never contrived nor wished evil against the person of the King and that in all his dealings with foreign governments he had never sought anything but the welfare of his fellow-Protestants. The minister was allowed to pray with him a while, then made to withdraw and leave him to his executioners, who went to work immediately with iron bars, breaking the bones of his legs, arms and back. After eleven blows, they left him to die. The priest exhorted him in his final agony to abjure his religion, but he reviled the King for his cruelty instead and could be silenced only with a gag. He was two hours dying. At four o'clock his body was taken down from the wheel, dragged through the streets at the tail of a cart and thrown onto a refuse-dump.

Two days later Croissy, who did not learn of Roux's execution until 1 July, was still trying to persuade Roux's valet, Martin, to go to Paris to give evidence. He had his secretary talk to the man about it, but without success. Martin did not like Roux and for reasons of his own had left his service, but he professed to know nothing of Roux's political involvements. In Croissy's view, he knew more than he was prepared to say. His pretence at ignorance was due, Croissy thought, to the fact that he had a wife and family in London and did not want to take any risks. What seemed to frighten him was the possibility that the French authorities would assume he knew more than he did and once he was in their hands would keep him there. Croissy was sure that Martin could not be persuaded to go to France of his own accord and thought the best way to get him there was to have him deported. In a letter to Lionne, written on 1 July, just before he received the news from him of Roux's execution, he proposed asking Charles II to have both Martin and Veyras arrested and sent to Calais. In a postscript, acknowledging receipt of Lionne's news about Roux, he declared that he was nonetheless waiting for instructions concerning the arrest of Roux's accomplice, Veyras.

When at the beginning of the month there is top-level talk of having a valet in London extradited and handed over to the French police at Calais[6], and when at the end of that same month a valet is arrested on the highest government authority by the garrison commander of Dunkirk, then it is 'hardly conceivable', as Lang put it, that 'the two valets should be different men.' The valet Martin and the prisoner Eustache Dauger, who was 'only a valet', were in Lang's opinion one and the same. It is, of course, unlikely that Martin had anything of significance to contribute to what the French government already knew or suspected. His rôle in Roux's secret affairs, apart from carrying letters to and from people like Arlington's secretary, could not have been very important, and his knowledge of what was going on must have been limited to his assessment of the people he saw his master with and his interpretation of their overheard conversations. There, however, lay the tragedy described by Lang. The valet's worst fears were realized: the authorities assumed that he knew more than he did and 'he was locked up for not divulging what he did not know'. Once in prison he was 'caught in the toils of the system' and his 'long and mysterious captivity . . . was the mere automatic result of the red tape of the old French absolute monarchy.'

Lang closed the case at this point, confessing himself as baffled by the solution as by the mystery. He was apparently unable to admit that he might have been misled by a simple coincidence, and was presumably unaware that in the middle of that same July 1669, the ambassador in London got word from the minister in Paris that the valet Martin was no longer wanted. On 13 July Lionne replied to Croissy's letter of 1 July explaining that, since Roux had been found guilty and executed, Martin's presence was no longer necessary and Veyras was simply not important enough to bother with. For the sake of argument one could always imagine that the ambassador went ahead with his plan to have Martin extradited anyway, that the English refused to co-operate and that the French then assumed that Martin was concealing important information damaging to the English; the minister, believing that any letter he sent to the ambassador would be intercepted, deliberately sought to deceive the English by saying Martin was no longer wanted, but soon after that letter was sent an agent, possibly Vauroy himself, was dispatched to England to kidnap Martin in secret. Even with such an hypothesis to buoy it up, however, the theory is still too full of holes to stay afloat.

Why was the prisoner's name changed from Martin to Eustache Dauger? What difference could it have made to Saint-Mars or anyone else that his real name was Martin? Why was there such concern that he might have revealed the secret of how he had been employed before his imprisonment? What difference could it have made to the French government if La Rivière or anyone else had found out that he had once been the valet of Claude Roux? It is difficult, even for the sake of argument, to imagine answers to these questions, much less to the key question: why the mask? Lang gave the disgruntled reader no help at all, but in a footnote to his conclusion he produced the next best thing: a suggestion for an altogether different theory. 'One marvels', he wrote, 'that nobody has recognized in the mask James Stuart (James de La Cloche), eldest of the children of Charles II. He came to England in 1668, was sent to Rome, and "disappears from history".' Later in the same volume, Lang presented his version of this young man's story in an essay entitled *The Mystery of James de La Cloche* but, believing as he did that Eustache Dauger was 'undeniably' the valet Martin, he made out no case for him as the Iron Mask. That case was championed just one year later, however, by Edith Carey in a book entitled *The Channel Islands*, and again as recently as 1965 by Marcel Pagnol, who in his book, *Le Secret du Masque de fer*, amalgamated both of Lang's suggestions and came up with the claim that 'James de La Cloche . . . was Eustache Dauger after having been the valet Martin.' Clearly the story of James de La Cloche is rich in possibilities. The known facts and what must be the most reasonable interpretation of them are as follows.

On 11 April 1668, a strange young man turned up at the central Jesuit novitiate in Rome and asked to be admitted as a postulant. He had no money at all and, apart from a hairbrush and a few extra clothes, no personal belongings of any kind. He gave his name as James de La Cloche, his age as twenty-four and his nationality as English, though in fact he spoke nothing but French. Presumably the Jesuit authorities were not very enthusiastic about accepting him, but their reservations were quickly dispelled when he produced three extraordinary documents for their perusal: two in French, handwritten by Charles II of England, and one in Latin, handwritten by Queen Christina of Sweden, to all appearances authentic in style, signature and seal. The young man, it emerged from these papers, was an illegitimate son of Charles II, secretly recognized and protected by him. The Jesuits, realizing the immense possibilities of having such a remarkable young man in their midst, were now only too eager to welcome him into the Society. And remarkable he certainly was, though not for the reasons they supposed. The documents were forgeries.

The earliest in date was a certificate written by Charles at Whitehall on 27 September 1665, in which he recognized the young man to be his natural son, James Stuart; by the King's command, he had lived all his life under the name of James de La Cloche du Bourg de Jersey in France and other countries outside England and was to continue to live incognito, keeping the secret of his birth until his father's death. The second document in date was a bequest written by Charles at Whitehall on 7 February 1667 in which he willed that after his death the sum of £500 per annum should be paid to his son, James de La Cloche, on condition that he lived in London and remained an Anglican. The third was an attestation written by the ex-Queen of Sweden in Hamburg on 26 July 1667 in which she declared that James de La Cloche, whom she knew to be the natural son of Charles II, born in Jersey and raised in the Protestant religion, had renounced his Calvinistic faith and become a Roman Catholic.

The Jesuits, like the true writer of the letters, seemed unaware that Charles and his court were not in Whitehall in September 1665. In that month the population of London had been reduced to half its normal size by the ravages of the Great Plague. In June there were 590 deaths, in July 6,137, in August 17,036, and in September 26,230. No one stayed in the city unless he had to, and the King and his court were in fact in Oxford. Pepys, recording the desolation of London in September, observed that 'grass grows all up and down White Hall court'. Nor did the Jesuits seem to appreciate that in April 1668, when the young man gave his age as twenty-four, Charles himself was not yet thirty-eight; to have been the father it would have been necessary for him to conceive a child at the age of thirteen which, though not impossible, was nonetheless unlikely. In addition, the Jesuits did not find it suspicious that Charles should refuse public recognition to this illegitimate son, his supposed eldest, when for many years he had publicly recognized another. In 1668 the other illegitimate son had already been at court for six years and, at the age of nineteen, was Duke of Monmouth and Captain of the King's Bodyguard.

Who the young man really was is not known. That he was an impostor using false credentials is certain, but like all convincing liars his stories were constructed on a basis of truth. For example, the starting point for his hoax had its foundation in a real state of affairs in Jersey. There, just twelve years before his arrival in Rome, a certain Jean La Cloche had ennobled his name, at least in appearance, by changing it to Jean *de* La Cloche, following his marriage to Marguerite de Carteret, a daughter of the most noble family on the island. Ten years before this marriage, that is in 1646, it was this same Marguerite who, at twenty years of age, had first fired the heart of the then Prince Charles, visiting Jersey at the age of sixteen. By all accounts this youthful romance was altogether innocent, and certainly there exists no evidence or tradition that a child was born to Marguerite as a result. In any case the young man would have been two years old when Charles and Marguerite met. There is moreover no reason to believe that Marguerite had a child before she met Charles. The story told by the young man had evident links, however forged or forced, with the history of Jean La Cloche and his wife Marguerite, but in fact there exists no record nor rumour of anyone on Jersey called James de La Cloche.

The key piece of invention in the young man's confidence trick was also founded upon a circumstantial truth. He fabricated a major rôle for himself in a perfectly plausible story based upon a secret which Charles II had shared with only the highest authorities of the Roman Catholic Church. Any uncertainty the General of the Jesuits might have had would have been removed the moment the young man gave him to understand that he knew this secret. How the young man had got access to such knowledge one cannot say, but presumably he or someone helping him had managed to acquire inside information on a special mission sent by Charles to Rome in November 1662. The King's envoy had been Richard Bellings, the private secretary of the King's mother, Henrietta of France, and he had been commissioned to make two requests: one, known to the King's ministers, was to solicit a cardinal's hat for the chaplain of the Queen; the other, known to no one but the King, was to beg dispensations which would allow Charles to declare himself a Roman Catholic and bring his kingdom back within the Roman Catholic Church. The dispensations had not been granted and without them Charles had not dared to change his religious allegiance, but the fact that he had been frustrated in his wish to become Catholic at that time formed the basis of the story with which the Jesuits were to be swindled.

For four months, while the young man played the part of earnest postulant, there were no further developments, until in August two letters arrived by some secret means, both supposedly written by Charles II himself; one was addressed to the Father-General, the other to 'the Prince Stuart'. The writer of the letters did not realize that never under any circumstances would the illegitimate son of an English king receive the title of Prince, but fortunately for him the Father-General was not aware of this either. Both letters, moreover, spoke of the King's mother as being with him in London, whereas she had been living in France since 1665.

The letter to the Father-General was dated from Whitehall on 3 August and was written in French. In it, Charles confided that for a long time he had been a Roman Catholic by conviction, but as head of the Anglican Church he had been unable to embrace his faith openly and afraid to practice it secretly. The only priests at court were those in the service of his mother and his wife, and no matter how discreetly he might have arranged to see one of them, the suspicions of his anti-Catholic ministers and courtiers would have been aroused. How providential it therefore was that his own son should wish to become a Roman Catholic priest and might in the future join him at court to administer the sacraments to him in secret. His ordination, however, was not to take place in Rome. Charles himself could arrange for that to take place in London. Meanwhile, the Father-General was not to contact Charles directly for any reason nor to speak of his son's true identity to anyone, not even to the Queen of Sweden. As soon as possible, he was to send the young man to London so that Charles might talk with him, and if there was any way in which Charles could secretly help the Jesuit Society, he would be only too pleased to hear about it from his son when he arrived.

The second letter was also from Whitehall and dated the day after the first. Though addressed to the Prince Stuart, it was obviously meant like the other to be read by the Father-General. In it Charles declared that the Queen and the Queen Mother were both delighted at his son's decision to become a priest and eager to see him, but anxious about his weak constitution. He should visit London in autumn only if his health permitted, otherwise he should wait until spring. In the near future Charles planned to recognize him publicly and at that time, since his mother was noble, he could expect to receive precedence over the Duke of Monmouth. Indeed one day, if the kingdom were to return to the Roman Church and Charles and his brother were to die without issue, the crown of England would fall to him. Charles was well aware of his obligations to the Jesuits and it was his intention to recompense the Society in some important way. Meanwhile, the large sum of money which Charles had set aside for his upkeep and had given into the care of Queen Christina of Sweden had been borrowed by her for her own use. He was in the process of rearranging the matter, but in the meantime unfortunately there was no way that he could secretly send money to him in Rome.

Nothing then until the beginning of September, when unexpectedly the young man's plan hit a snag. News reached the novitiate that the Queen of Sweden was on her way to Rome. To save the situation the plan had to be advanced and so another letter suddenly arrived, supposedly sent from Whitehall on 29 August, in which Charles warned the Father-General not to let Queen Christina meet his son. He had written to her himself, he said, and told her that his son was leaving Rome for England so that Charles could arrange some financial settlement for him, a bank deposit of 40 or 50,000 écus. She was so badly in need of money that, if she saw his son, she might raise suspicions by trying to borrow money from him. Charles had told her that his son had not revealed his true identity to the Jesuits and that so far as they knew he had gone to Jersey to visit his mother, who had expressed the wish to become a Roman Catholic. His son was to leave Rome for London as soon as possible. Secrecy was of the utmost importance and the Father-General was to communicate with no one on the matter except Charles himself, through the intermediary of his son.

Preparations for the young man's departure were begun at once, but again there was a hitch. It being the custom in the Society, a Jesuit father was chosen to accompany him. Within a week another letter arrived from Charles to say that he had been advised by the Queen Mother and by Madame, his sister, that his son would probably be obliged to travel with a companion. It was however of the greatest importance that his son was not accompanied by an Italian. Suspicions would otherwise be aroused. His son should travel under the name of Henri de Rohan, as though he were a member of a noble French Protestant family well-known to the King, and under no circumstances was anyone to arrive in England with him. The Father-General would have to provide his son with money for the journey, but Charles would keep good account of all he owed.

The young man left Livorno on 14 October 1668 carrying a letter for Charles from the Father-General. He was accompanied by a Jesuit father, but the agreement was that he should leave him somewhere in France and collect him on his return. When he reappeared in Rome, sometime in mid-December, he was alone and was carrying two letters for the Father-General, both purporting to have been written by Charles at Whitehall on 18 November. In the first of these, Charles explained that his son had returned to Rome with a message of great importance for the Father-General, a request of some kind from Charles which he would deliver by word of mouth, and as soon as he had obtained what was asked he was to return to London. On his way back, he was to pick up the Jesuit father, who had accompanied him on his previous journey out and who was still waiting for him in France, and take him along to London.

Since the letter was false and involved the Jesuit companion in its fictions, it seems possible that the Jesuit companion was also false. If that were so, it would help to explain how a young man of twenty-four was able to arrive out of the blue to accomplish this kind of deception. Such a prodigy working on his own would surely have found himself easier and more rewarding victims to cheat than the Society of Jesus. All in all it seems reasonable to suppose that the young impostor was merely the front-man in someone else's stratagem, someone on the inside with sufficient access to secret files to know of Bellings' mission and sufficient knowledge of the Father-General to dupe him: a Jesuit to outsmart a Jesuit. Such a conjecture would fit the circumstances of what took place up to and after the end of 1668 with a fair degree of plausibility.

Since the forged letters were written in French, one might even assume that the accomplice was a French Jesuit and that he set up the hoax in the expectation that he would be given responsibility for supervising the studies of a postulant who spoke nothing but French. Thus he would have been confident that from the very start of the operation he would be able to control and direct developments at source. Also, as the young man's mentor, he would have considered himself the natural choice to accompany him on any journey he made. One might suppose that when arrangements were begun for the young man's departure to London another Jesuit, an Italian, was chosen to be his companion, and that it was for this reason that a letter arrived from Charles at the last minute to say that under no circumstances was his son to be accompanied by an Italian. Presumably the accomplice, being French, was then recognized to be the best choice and allowed to leave the novitiate with the young man as he had originally intended.

Be that as it may, the letters the young man was carrying make it clear that the chief reason for his return to Rome was to defraud the Father-General of a large sum of money. The first letter went on to say that Charles had heard from his son that the Jesuit house was badly in need of money and so he was going to assist them with a large donation before the year was out. In the meantime, however, he wanted the Father-General to provide for his son in any way he asked. He would keep an account of it all and settle with him later. The second letter was nothing less than an IOU, written by Charles, in which he promised to pay the Father General the sum of £20,000 within six months and, in a postscript, to pay an additional £800 to cover the travel expenses of his son, also within six months.

Exactly how much money the young man was able to extract from the Jesuits on the strength of these two letters we do not know. An extraordinary stroke of luck made that precise moment especially favourable for him, but it was then or never that the money had to be realized. By a strange coincidence, the events the swindlers had been pretending for the past few months were suddenly overtaken by similar events in reality. Soon after the young man returned to the novitiate with his two counterfeit letters from Charles, a genuine letter reached Rome from Charles's brother, James. It explained that he was a Roman Catholic by conviction and wished to know if it was permissible for him to practice the Roman faith in secret while continuing to practice the Anglican faith in public. That James should have been thinking along the same lines as the Jesuits believed Charles to be, must have had the immediate effect of strengthening the young man's position, but it was a position which in a short time was liable to collapse completely. There could be no question of continuing the hoax of a pretended contact with Charles once a real contact was made with his brother. The Jesuits at that time, however, with their confidence boosted, were as ready to be cheated as they ever would be. The swindlers had to get what they could, while they could, then vanish, and in fact so far as the Jesuits were concerned, James de La Cloche did disappear at this very moment.

On 27 December 1668, the day Claude Roux was drawing up his report for Arlington, hoping to persuade Charles II to send him as his envoy to the next Diet of the Swiss Confederation – the time also that

James de La Cloche was leaving Rome with a large sum of money borrowed in the King's name from the General of the Jesuit Society – Charles II wrote to his sister Henrietta of England, the wife of Louis XIV's brother, about some secret business known to no one in England but himself and 'one person more'. The secret business was his decision to become a Roman Catholic and to bring England back into the Roman Catholic Church. The 'one person more' might have been Bellings, who had been entrusted with Charles's mission to Rome six years before, or one of three ministers: Arlington, Arundel and Clifford.

Anti-Catholic sentiment in England was fierce and opposition within the government itself to such a move would have been so powerful that in retrospect it is difficult to imagine how Charles could have believed his plans had any hope of success. He realized of course that he would be putting his throne and possibly his life in jeopardy, that the strength of Protestant resistance might even unleash another civil war, but he believed that with outside help he could control the situation. For this financial and military backing, he turned to Louis XIV. In another letter to his sister on 20 January, he wrote: 'I am now thinking of the way how to proceede in this whole matter, which must be carried on with all secrecy imaginable, till the particulars are further agreed upon . . . I send you, heere enclosed, my letter to the king, my brother, desireing that this matter might passe through your handes, as the person in the world I have most confidence in.'

While he was actually writing this, Charles received a letter from his sister, conveyed to him by someone who, so far as one can gather, had been entrusted with it in spite of the fact that neither Charles nor his sister knew anything about him. 'I had written thus far,' Charles wrote, 'when I received yours by the Italian, whose name and capacity you do not know, and he delivered your letter to me in a passage, where it was so darke, as I do not know his face againe if I see him; so as the man is likely to succeede, when his recommendation and reception are so suitable to one another.' The passage in the letter is every bit as obscure as the passage in which the meeting took place, but the most reasonable explanation seems to be that the Italian had come from Rome carrying an answer to James's question and, having stopped off in Paris on his way, had been entrusted with a letter by Madame, on the recommendation of someone she could trust.

It was certainly at about this time that James received his answer from Rome, because what he learned from it obliged him to confide his problem to Charles and led to the secret meeting with Arlington, Arundel and Clifford on 25 January. Under no circumstances, he learned from Rome, was it permissible for a Roman Catholic to attend the services of any other religion. He could not continue to be an Anglican in public if he accepted the Roman Catholic faith. To Charles he declared that he was determined to become a Roman Catholic no matter what the consequences might be; to him Charles explained that he also intended to embrace the Roman faith, but only when he was sure that he could control the consequences well enough to take his kingdom into the Catholic Church with him. At that same secret meeting, Charles disclosed his plan for seeking the support of Louis XIV and chose Arundel to go to Paris to negotiate it.

Meanwhile, in Rome, the Father-General of the Society of Jesus fondly imagined that James de La Cloche was in London, engaged in secret confabulations with his father, Charles, about the promised donation towards the upkeep of the Jesuit house. And meanwhile, in Naples, sometime in that same January of 1669, two wealthy travellers turned up: one who though professing to be English spoke only French and later gave himself out to be the son of Charles II; and the other a Frenchman who claimed to be a Knight of the Order of Saint John of Jerusalem. The Frenchman took ship for Malta soon after and the Englishman, who was in poor health, was left alone in the kindly hands of a poor Neapolitan innkeeper and a simple parish priest.

At first he made no claim to be the Prince Stuart, though the parish priest later claimed that he had revealed this to him in secret and had produced two documents to prove it – a letter from the Queen of Sweden and another from the General of the Jesuits. Whatever the papers were which the parish priest saw, they were certainly not what the young man professed them to be. One must suppose that the parish priest was barely literate himself and pretended to read and recognize what it was the young man told him was there. In fact, as emerged later, he had no papers with him at all to back up his claim. At what stage he included the innkeeper and his family in the confidence is not known, but the fact that he was a rich foreigner, on his own and ready to be exploited, made him important enough in their eyes without the need for further claims; he had been in Naples for little more than a month when he was married to the innkeeper's daughter. Why there should have been such haste to the altar may be at least partly explained by the fact that a child was born just less than nine months later. Perhaps the young man was beguiled into the arms of the innkeeper's daughter at a time when the innkeeper was able to discover him there and oblige him to make an honest woman of her. The wedding took place in the cathedral of Naples on 19 February and the young man gave his name as Jacobo Enrico de Bovere Roano Stuardo: a compilation of James Stuart and Henri de Rohan. He paid the wedding bill, of course, and even provided a dowry for the bride. By March, the jubilant innkeeper was on a spending spree with his son-in-law's money, and local envy and suspicion bred rumours that the foreign young man was a coiner of false money. By order of the Spanish Viceroy of Naples, the inn was raided and the young man arrested.

Among his effects were found 200 doubloons[7] cash, a number of jewels and some letters in which he was addressed as 'Highness', but nothing incriminating. The authorities were nonetheless inquisitive and stupidly he tried to bluff his way through with the pretence that he was the Prince Stuart. Presumably because he was without the know-how and imagination of his accomplice, he was very soon out of his depth. The English consul was brought in to help clarify the situation, but found that the young man could speak no English and could produce no recognizable credentials. At his own request he was allowed to write to the General of the Jesuits in Rome, begging him to intercede. The Viceroy himself meanwhile wrote to Charles II for verification and, to play safe until he received an answer, he had the young man confined in the castle of Gaeta, well attended at a cost of 50 scudi[8] per month. Whether the Father-General ever received a letter or replied is not known, but at the beginning of June a reply from Charles arrived disclaiming all knowledge of the young man. The Viceroy had him brought back to Naples and thrown into the common prison. There was talk of having him whipped through the streets at the cart's tail as a common impostor but, at the supplication of his wife's family and the intercession of the Viceroy's wife, he was allowed to go free.

Not surprisingly he then left Naples, probably with the intention of never setting foot there again, but in August he was back, very ill and needing to be looked after. He now claimed to his wife's family that he had 50,000 pistoles and was going to take them all to Venice to live. His mother, the Lady Mary Henrietta Stuart of the Barons of Saint-Marzo, an altogether fictitious name, had died and left him an estate worth 80,000 scudi per annum. Before the end of August, however, he was dead himself, and found to be penniless. His father-in-law, who had supported him since his return and had even loaned him money to pay a notary to draw up his will, was also obliged to pay for his burial. The will, written in Italian, was an absurd piece of make-believe magnificence. To his unborn child he left his late mother's estate, and to his parents-in-law and their three other children, 50 scudi per annum each, assigning as security for the payment of this his personal estate, the purely fictitious Marquisate of Juvignis worth 300,000 scudi per annum. To his 'father', Charles II, he commended his unborn child and asked that if he were a boy he would grant him 'the ordinary principality either of Wales or Monmouth, or other province customary to be given to the natural sons of the Crown.' As his executor and the guardian of his child, he named his 'cousin', Louis XIV.

So ends the strange story of the odd young man who claimed to be the Prince Stuart, alias Jacobo Enrico de Bovere Roano Stuardo, alias Henri de Rohan, alias James de La Cloche du Bourg de Jersey. 'Hee was buried in the Church of San Francisco di Paolo out of the Porta Capuana,' wrote the British agent at Rome in his report to London on 7 September 1669, '. . . and this is the end of that Princely Cheate or whatever hee was.' As James de La Cloche he had swindled the Jesuits of Rome out of a large sum of money, but as Jacobo Stuardo he had deceived no one except an illiterate Neapolitan family who were altogether ready to be deceived. Since in Naples he had proved such a wretched clown, it seems certain that in Rome he had been master-minded by someone else. Of this accomplice nothing is known, but presumably he was the Frenchman who had been with the young man when he first arrived in Naples. No doubt it was there that they divided their ill-gotten gains and the accomplice, who had been the brain of the operation, took the lion's share before embarking on a ship for Malta. Whoever he was, he must have been an extraordinary character, and it is tempting to believe that he possessed the intelligence and wit to enjoy the hoax for its own sake as well as for the money it brought him. The family name of the innkeeper he chose to leave the young man with was 'Corona', and presumably he appreciated the aptness of this, just as he enjoyed giving the young man the name 'de La Cloche'. To call someone 'de la cloche' in French is to call him 'a beggar', while the word 'corona' in Italian means 'crown'.

As a footnote to the story of James de La Cloche, offered with no intention of proving or disproving, approving or disapproving any-thing, one might add that though in general the names used in the hoax were derived from some knowledge of the Stuart, Rohan and La Cloche families, two were not: the 'Marquisate of Juvignis' and the 'Barons of Saint-Marzo'. Apparently both were fictitious. What inspired the invention of the words 'Juvignis' and 'Saint-Marzo' is not known and presumably not important, but one of them presents a strange coincidence which, though no doubt lacking in any real significance, is nonetheless forcefully surreal: 'Marzo' in Italian is 'Mars' in French, and it is not a common name in either language.

1. *Waldensian*: proto-Protestant movement originating in the 12th century.
2. *Lord Arlington*: 1618–1685, served Charles II in exile, was his Secretary of State from 1662 and his chief minister from 1667.
3. *Orange*: independent non-French principality within France until confiscated by Louis XIV in 1673.
4. *Charles IV*, Duc de Lorraine, 1604–1675.
5. *Marquis de Croissy*: 1629–1696, brother of Colbert.

6. *Calais*: In Lang's day it was not possible to say where exactly Dauger was arrested. However in 1987, at the International Symposium on the Iron Mask held in Cannes, Stanislas Brugnon revealed the existence of a document establishing with near certainty that Dauger was indeed arrested in Calais. This document is an order for the reimbursement of expenses which was issued to Vauroy for his journey with Dauger in August 1669, and it specifies that Vauroy went from Dunkirk to Calais and from there to Pignerol.
7. *doubloon*: Spanish gold coin.
8. *scudo*: Italian silver coin.

CHAPTER TEN

AND
INTERCONNECTIONS

Edith Carey, like Andrew Lang, took the view that James de La Cloche was all that he purported to be, that his letters for all their inaccuracies and absurdities were genuine, and that the only deception practiced by him upon the Jesuits was a claim to be older than he actually was. She argued that in April 1668, when he asked to become a postulant, he was twenty-one, not twenty-four; he lied about his age because he thought the Jesuits would be more likely to accept him if he pretended to be older. That he was in fact twenty-one emerged later, she maintained, in the letter sent to the General of the Jesuits on 3 August 1668. There he was said to have been born when Charles was 'scarcely sixteen or seventeen years of age' and in the opinion of Carey that established the matter beyond reasonable doubt. He was the illegitimate son of Charles and Marguerite de Carteret, conceived in May or June 1646, when Charles made his first visit to Jersey, and therefore born in February or March 1647.

Marguerite de Carteret was the youngest daughter of the Seigneur of Trinity, and so presumably any child of hers would have been christened in that parish. Carey examined the Trinity parish register and uncovered possible evidence that some record of baptism made in late 1648 had been suppressed. She found that the original registrations of two baptisms had been cut out and two extra entries inserted on the opposite page as though they were copies of the ones which were missing. Apparently they were, but not necessarily. Arguably, one of the original entries had recorded the baptism of this child born to Marguerite de Carteret, and the disarrangement had been a cover-up ordered by Charles himself when he returned to Jersey in September 1649. Apart no doubt from this registration, the child's existence had been revealed to no one outside the walls of Trinity Manor and, since the secret continued to be well-kept, Charles probably took the child away with him when he left Jersey for France in February 1650. Marguerite herself remained on the island, because in Trinity Church in 1656 she was married to Jean la Cloche, the son of the rector of Saint Ouen.

The Carterets were the oldest and most distinguished family in Jersey. They had been lords of the island since the eleventh century when their ancestors accompanied William the Conqueror to England, and in the seventeenth century four of the five Seigneuries of Jersey were in their possession: Saint Ouen, Rozel, Melesches and Trinity. Though staunch Calvinists, they were dedicated Royalists. When Charles I was executed in February 1649 Sir George Carteret, Seigneur of Melesches and Lieutenant-Governor of Jersey, proclaimed Charles II king, and in October 1651 he and his fellow-Royalists abandoned their possessions in Jersey to follow their King into exile rather than accept Parliamentary rule. In 1660, when Charles was restored to the throne, he rewarded Sir George for his loyalty with the gift of 'a certain island and adjacent islets near Virginia in America' with a patent 'to build towns, churches and castles, and to establish suitable laws'. The name given to this new Carteret domain was New Jersey.

According to Carey, James de La Cloche was thirteen years old at the time of the Restoration and eighteen when he was called to England. In her version of things Charles privately acknowledged him to be his son, but would not do so publicly for fear that speculation about the boy's mother would lead to the truth which he had gone to such pains to hide. Since the boy was raised a Calvinist, the Carteret family were directly concerned in his upbringing, but the Carterets of Trinity and possibly Sir George Carteret were the only members of the family to know the secret. Marguerite was by that time the mother of six small children and her husband, who by all accounts was an ambitious and uncompromising man, knew nothing about the child she had borne nine years before he married her. If the truth had become public, the shame for the Carteret family, hard-line Calvinists as they were, would have been insupportable.

In his contact with the English court, James de La Cloche preferred the French-speaking company of the Queen Mother's household. She was a devout Catholic, and under the influence of her entourage he came to question the Calvinism in which he had been raised. Perhaps the disclosure, made to him in confidence, that his father was himself a Catholic by conviction helped in his conversion. In 1667 he left England for the Continent and while in Hamburg was received into the Catholic Church. His decision to join the Jesuits was made with the intention of one day helping his father to follow the dictates of his conscience and become a Catholic too.

Charles was at first delighted by the spiritual commitment and filial devotion manifested by his son. When the young man came to England in November 1668, he took him entirely into his confidence, revealing to him his plan for a secret alliance with Louis XIV and entrusting to him a message for the Vatican. No sooner had the young man left for Rome, however, than Charles had second thoughts. His son was too immature, too indiscreet, for such a confidence. Though sworn to silence regarding the truth of his own birth, he had revealed the secret to the Queen of Sweden and to the General of the Jesuits. He was too trusting of others to be trusted with information which, if betrayed, would cost Charles his throne and possibly his life. It was conceivable that the young man, in his naivity, would reveal the secret to the Protestant Carterets, who would not hesitate to denounce it openly as 'a foreign and Popish plot'. It was even possible that already before leaving London he had let enough of the secret slip to arouse the suspicions of Arlington, whom Charles suspected was in league with the fanatical Protestant, Claude Roux.

Needless to say, this account of James de La Cloche and his relationship with Charles and the Carterets, Arlington and the rest, has no demonstrable basis in fact. Carey was inventing a story to fit a theory, with nothing but plausibility to offer in its support, and as it was, the final link between her version of James de La Cloche and the facts of the Iron Mask proved difficult to forge. Her James de La Cloche returned to England in January 1669 and vanished into a secret prison prepared for him by Charles. The King, to cover the traces, arranged with the agreement of the Jesuits to have 'a red herring drawn across the scent': an impostor despatched to Naples 'to divert attention from the career and fate of the real James de La Cloche'. Holding the young man a secret prisoner in England was too risky a business to maintain for long, however; since it was as much in the interest of Louis XIV as of Charles II to ensure his 'perpetual silence and disappearance', he was taken to Dunkirk six months later and handed over to the French, who for security reasons changed his name to Eustache Dauger.

Pagnol, like Carey, wanted us to believe that James de La Cloche never set foot in Naples, and that when he left Rome in January 1669 he went to London. Unlike Carey, Pagnol was prepared to admit that the claims made by the young man to the Jesuits were false and that his letters were forgeries, but he argued that the young man really did believe himself to be the son of Charles II; he genuinely wished to be a priest so that he might help Charles become a Catholic. Though he was deceiving the Jesuits, Pagnol maintained, he had no intention of swindling them and he certainly was not masterminded by anybody else. His true identity was more noble than even he imagined, and his true story more romantic than even Dumas imagined. While Pagnol

The Man in the Velvet Mask, represented in the manner of a portrait as being a nobleman with an obvious resemblance to Louis XIV. Collection of the Comte de Lacour. (*Photograph Jean-Pierre Rhein*)

was quite sure 'that the mysterious prisoner, incarcerated under the name of Eustache Dauger, had been an important member of the conspiracy of Roux de Marcilly, under the name of the valet Martin,' he was also 'convinced that this man was neither valet, nor Martin, nor Dauger, . . . he was the twin brother of Louis XIV.' Back, with a cavalier flourish, to square one!

Some fast thinking was all it required, Pagnol believed, to bring the dead myth back to life. Brisk calculation had brought him to the view that, in thirty-four years of imprisonment, the Iron Mask had cost what in 1960 would have amounted to fifty million new francs. A secret which was worth that kind of money was not, Pagnol declared, 'the secret of a valet, who could have been hanged in five minutes with a rope for forty sous.' Moreover, rapid consideration had brought him to the view that a 'continual concern' had been shown for the prisoner's health, in spite of the fact that his 'death would have liberated Louvois – and perhaps the King – from a great anxiety.' This strange attitude on their part reminded Pagnol of the old belief that 'when one twin is ill, the other soon begins to sicken – and that if one of the two dies, the survivor in his turn dies soon after.' If after injecting the theory with ideas like that it was still cold, then Pagnol took the view that its revival could be effected by a heated attack upon Louis XIV. 'Today in the light of his acts which reveal his jealousy, his egoism, his cruelty, I am persuaded that if he had been born in a litter of quadruplets we would have had three Iron Masks.'

Energy and heat apart, however, Pagnol had nothing more to propose in his reanimation of the dead theory than the bogus document published by Soulavie. Even then, it was only for the description of the twin-birth that he wished to pass off this fabrication as authentic, since for the rest of the unfortunate prince's life he had a concoction of his own to offer. According to Soulavie, the rejected prince was taken to a remote house in Burgundy as soon as he reached boyhood and was kept there until the year 1660 when at the age of twenty-two he discovered the truth of his identity; he was in consequence masked and imprisoned. According to Pagnol, he was taken to England at the age of six and from there to Jersey, where he was passed off as the natural child of some French noble family and given into the safe keeping of the Carteret family. As a young man, the mystery of his birth along with a similarity to his cousin Charles, whose noticeable resemblance to Louis XIV may in Pagnol's view be verified from existing portraits, led him to believe that he was the son of Marguerite de Carteret by Charles. The Carteret family was aware that Charles secretly wished to become a Roman Catholic, and it was to win his father's recognition by helping him in this that, in 1668, the young man went to the Jesuits in Rome. In fact the young man was not so young. He was then twenty-nine, but thought the Jesuits would be more likely to accept him if he pretended to be younger.

The letters which so impressed the Father-General, though false, were a truthful representation of the dilemma in which Charles found himself and were forged by the young man for the sole purpose of establishing himself as a ready-made go-between for Charles and the Vatican in some eventual secret dialogue. When in December 1668 a genuine letter arrived from Charles's brother James, revealing that he too needed help, the young man decided that it was time to go to his father and explain himself; the Jesuits entrusted him with a reply for James as well as a letter to Charles. On his way to London, he stopped off in Paris to see Madame, the sister of Charles, and ask her advice. She recognized him immediately as the living image of Louis XIV, but said nothing to enlighten him and hurried him on his way with a letter of her own for Charles. The young man met the English King on 20 January 1669, and the obscure passage in the letter which Charles wrote that day about an Italian in a dark corridor whose face he would not recognize again, was a reference to that meeting. When Charles saw the young man and heard his story, he guessed that he must be the twin brother of Louis XIV and, realizing the political potential of this, shared the news with Arlington and Claude Roux.

Even in historical romances there is a limit to how much the reader's disbelief can be suspended, and when one recalls that on this very day, 20 January 1669, Charles wrote to Louis XIV proposing a secret alliance, it would seem that this limit has been reached. Nevertheless, for what it is worth, Pagnol thus continues his story. The young man, overwhelmed by the discovery of his true identity and frightened by the warnings of what would happen to him if ever his twin brother Louis XIV found out about him, allowed himself to be persuaded that his only hope lay in the success of the revolution planned by the Committee of Ten. Roux promised him the throne of France and in the meantime had him pose as his valet under the name Martin. Whether there was ever an actual valet called Martin, Pagnol does not make clear, but he does present us with another valet unnamed who takes advantage of the situation to make off with the Jesuit's money and escape to Naples. The marriage and death of the Prince Stuart recorded there was this man's story, and nothing to do with James de La Cloche. Roux left London in March and was arrested in May. He confessed under interrogation in June that the aim of his conspiracy was to oust Louis XIV in favour of his twin brother, who was at that moment living in London disguised as a valet. Lionne thought him mad but played safe anyway, and in July had James de La Cloche kidnapped and locked up in Pignerol under the name 'Eustache Dauger'. That Pagnol could seriously offer this rigmarole, as an elucidation of the mystery of the Iron Mask, is no small mystery in itself.

Lang, Carey and Pagnol were not the only Iron Mask hunters to carry the search into the undergrowth of political and religious intrigue in England in 1668 and 1669. The plots and counter-plots, deals and double-deals surrounding Charles II, along with the pretended involvement and unexpected entanglement of James de La Cloche, have all the makings of a secret worthy of the Iron Mask. Not surprisingly they have provided yet another theory and yet another candidate. In the view of Arthur Barnes, whose book *The Man of the Mask* was published in 1912, the secret of how the Iron Mask was employed before he was imprisoned was what Charles II called 'the great secret': his plan to use the financial and military support of Louis XIV to take his kingdom back into the Roman Catholic Church. In this respect, Barnes trod the same ground as Carey, but in his version of things the Iron Mask was a different man altogether: 'a mysterious priest-astrologer' by the name of Pregnani. It is known from reliable sources of the time that this man visited Charles from France in February 1669 and vanished on his return to France in July 1669, his disappearance thus coinciding perfectly with the arrest of Eustache Dauger. What follows is the generally accepted account of Pregnani's visit to England.

When, at the end of January 1669, Louis XIV received a secret letter from Charles II asking for his support, he was naturally very interested. An alliance with England was very much to Louis XIV's advantage. His ambitions for territorial expansion to the north and north-east had been checked less than a year before by the alliance between England, Holland and Sweden. In summer 1667 he had invaded and conquered large areas of the Spanish Netherlands, and in February 1668 had occupied the Franche Comté which also belonged to Spain. England and Holland, whose maritime and commercial rivalry had kept them at war with each other for two years, patched up their differences in July 1667 and entered a joint alliance against French expansion in January 1668. In the following April they brought Sweden into the alliance, and in May obliged the French to accept terms which limited their gains to Flanders. So far as Louis XIV was concerned, this peace was only a truce until the balance of power in Europe could be weighted his way and the frontiers of France could be extended to include the whole of the Spanish Netherlands, the Franche Comté and the Duchy of Lorraine. In return for supporting Charles against the Protestants in England, he therefore hoped to receive English support against the Dutch and Spanish in Europe. In his opinion, however, Charles was too devious and secretive, too frivolous and capricious to be relied upon, and so far as he could see the sympathies of his chief minister, Arlington, were not inclined to France. Arlington, it seemed, was strongly in favour of a pro-Dutch foreign policy and by all reports he had been in secret communication with Roux. Louis XIV was understandably cautious about the new relationship and glad when an opportunity presented itself to have someone worm his way into Charles's confidence to watch and influence him.

In February 1669, the Duke of Monmouth wrote to the Abbé Pregnani, an Italian priest resident in France, inviting him to England. Pregnani was a member of the Theatine Order, which was well-known in Italy and Spain but not elsewhere. The congregation was established in 1524 as part of the effort of the Roman Church to reform itself from within, the aim of its founders being to provide an example of poverty and spirituality to Roman Catholic clergy too often interested in wealth and worldly affairs. Monmouth, however, was not at all interested in the aims of the Theatine Order, nor to all appearances was Pregnani. The ladies of the French court, including Madame, the sister of Charles II, were Pregnani's chief concern and they took delight in his company because of his ability to tell fortunes from the stars. The Duke of Monmouth had met him on a recent visit to Madame in France, and Pregnani had revealed his past so accurately and foretold his future so favourably that they had become great friends. As well as being an expert in astrology, Pregnani was something of an adept in chemistry and, since Charles II had a passion for both of these sciences, Monmouth thought it would amuse his father to meet him. Louis XIV, informed of the invitation, had Pregnani briefed. Since Charles was as likely to be influenced by astrological suggestions as he was by logical proposals, Pregnani was to convince him by the movements of the stars that his only good and sure alliance was with France. He was to involve himself as much as possible in the King's amusements and the informal life of the court, and to give a daily account to Croissy of all that transpired.

Pregnani arrived in London on 26 February and took rooms in Covent Garden with Gerard, the French wine-merchant used by Roux as a postal agent. Roux himself was to slip out of England a few days later just as Lionne received information that he was in London. Pregnani visited the Duke of Monmouth that same day to pay his respects and at the same time sent a servant to Croissy with his letter of introduction from Lionne. On the following day he called upon Croissy to receive a more detailed briefing on the English court, and then he went to work. His début was a great success. There was a certain young lady at court whom Monmouth, Charles and James were all trying to seduce, and Monmouth asked Pregnani to tell him which one of them would be the first to succeed. Pregnani, without having seen this fortunate creature, was able to describe her character and appearance, her past life and current behaviour with such precision that everyone was impressed. The King, convinced by this that he had 'a great deale of witt' and was 'very ingenious in all things', asked him to draw up his horoscope and invited him to join the court at Newmarket the following week.

Pregnani was immediately popular, but not with everyone. Soon after his arrival, the Duke of Buckingham was informed by his sister, writing from the French court, that Madame had sent Pregnani to London for the express purpose of negotiating with Charles and Monmouth behind his back. Negotiating what, Buckingham did not know, but assumed that it must be something to his personal disadvantage, and his attitude to Pregnani was in consequence hostile and suspicious. As it was, Buckingham's attention was thus distracted from Arundel's visit to Paris and what was really happening behind his back.

The ingenious fortune-teller was not popular for long, however. At Newmarket he made a foolish and fateful blunder. Since he was supposed to be a prophet, some wag suggested he ought to be able to predict the winners. The challenge was made and accepted. Monmouth and James backed his forecasts heavily and lost a lot of money. For them it was amusing, but for their less wealthy friends and hangers-on, their servants and lackeys, who backed the same horses, it was a disaster. Pregnani's reputation as an astrologer collapsed. Buckingham's attitude to him was sweetened by the incident and Charles continued to enjoy his company, but no one took him seriously any more. He became at best a figure of fun, ridiculed mercilessly on all sides. Realizing that if he proved a failure in England he would lose all credit in France, the poor man delayed reporting his blunder to Croissy until the end of March, by which time he claimed he could still win the King's confidence and bring serious influence to bear through the horoscope he was preparing. Croissy believed him and Lionne gave him the benefit of the doubt, but the jokes made about him in the English court were soon being repeated in the French court. In May Lionne wrote to Croissy ordering him to arrange Pregnani's return.

Pregnani, desperate to salvage his prestige, begged for more time. 'If the Abbé Pregnani is not successful here, it will not be for lack of zeal or ability in the service of the King', Croissy told Lionne and argued for letting him stay in London a little longer. Pregnani, however, was more concerned to enlist a king in his own service and prevailed upon Charles to defend his name in Paris. 'I find the poore Abbé Pregnani very much troubled,' Charles wrote to Madame on 6 May, 'for feare that the railleries about foretelling the horsematches may have done him some prejudice with you, which I hope it has not done, for he was only trying new trickes, which he had read of in bookes, and gave as little creditt to them as we did. Pray continue to be his friend so much as to hinder all you can any prejudice that may come to him upon that score, for the man has witt enough, and is as much your servant as possible, which makes me love him.' Pregnani had certainly succeeded in winning Charles's serious attention and concern, but only in so far as he had proved himself such a serious failure that no one would be concerned to pay any attention to him ever again.

Lionne repeated his command that Pregnani be withdrawn, but again Croissy put him off. The post of ambassador had been given to Croissy because he was Colbert's brother, and in truth he was not up to it. Roux had been living under his nose in London, visiting Whitehall and the embassies of Holland, Spain and Austria for at least three months without him realizing it, and Charles thought him so obtuse that he refused to have him brought into the full secret of his dealings with France. Pregnani had no difficulty convincing him that with a little more time he could achieve his mission, and it was not until mid-June, after Lionne's third demand, that Croissy finally told Pregnani to leave. The departure was fixed for 25 June, but Pregnani managed to hang on still longer and left at last only on 5 July.

Between English dates and French dates at that time there was a difference of ten days, because France had adopted the revised calendar promulgated by Rome while England had kept to the old one. The 5 July in England was therefore the 15 July in France. When he left London, Pregnani was carrying a letter for Lionne from Croissy, but apparently he took his time along the way, and did not deliver it until after Lionne had received two subsequent letters from Croissy sent by normal post; at least that is what Lionne told Croissy in the reply he wrote on 27 July. The return of the astrologer was not noticed at the French court, but since his reputation there also had been destroyed by the disaster at Newmarket, the lack of interest is hardly surprising.

That Pregnani's story was as simple as that, Barnes refused to believe. Charles usually gave the appearance of being a fool only when he was being particularly clever and Pregnani, who made such a poor show as an astrologer, was after all a priest. It was evident that in his seemingly frivolous way Charles enjoyed Pregnani's company immensely, and since both were adepts in chemistry, no further excuse was necessary for the two of them to spend a lot of time together in private. Thus for four months, while Pregnani was at the English court, Charles had direct and easy access to the services of a priest. The timing for this extraordinary state of affairs was significant: it had come about, as though by chance, just one month after Charles had committed himself to a plan which if successful would make him and his kingdom Catholic. It was not, Barnes concluded, the work of chance. Charles himself had arranged the whole thing. After years of indecision, something had prompted him to act out his religious convictions, to seek the political support of Louis XIV and to have the spiritual support of this priest. And what had happened to arouse his conscience and courage in this way was nothing less than divine intervention, albeit through the impious workings of the impostor James de La Cloche.

Barnes took up the story of James de La Cloche on his arrival in Naples in January 1669. While he saw no reason to contest the generally accepted view that the young man was a fraud, he did not accept the idea that he had an accomplice. In his opinion the man who turned up with him in Naples was the Jesuit companion whom he abandoned in France, a genuinely loyal and trusted member of the Society of Jesus. La Cloche, having left him in France, had not expected to see him again. His story to the Father-General, about picking him up on his return through France and taking him on with him to England, had been a simple stratagem to get away without supervision of any kind when he left Rome the second time. Unhappily for that stratagem, however, the Jesuit companion had grown anxious waiting without news in France and had returned to Rome to ask for instructions. La Cloche had thus been caught in his own trickery. The companion had naturally expected to go with him again and this time all the way to London.

Before leaving Rome the two of them had been given a reply to the questions asked by James as well as a message for Charles, and they were in Naples to find a ship for England. La Cloche realized at this point that he could not keep up the game any longer and so he pretended to be ill. The Jesuit companion suspected nothing and, conscious of the importance and urgency of their mission, decided to continue the journey alone. Before going to Charles in London, he visited Madame in Paris; it was he who, on 20 January, met Charles in the dark passage, appearing unbidden like an emissary from heaven to remind Charles of his own most secret doubts and aspirations. From Charles, he returned to Madame, and from Madame, a month later, he returned to Charles, this time openly as Pregnani, an altogether false identity invented for him by Charles.

Having got thus far on a simple play of ingenuity and plausibility, Barnes chose to make unnecessary difficulties for himself, and ran his theory into dull and clumsy improbabilities. The priest's false identity was invented by Charles, but Louis XIV collaborated in setting it up. At the request of Charles, Louis had his minister Lionne write to his ambassador Croissy and deliberately deceive him into the belief not only that Pregnani was a celebrated astrologer from the French court, but also that he was a secret agent for the government. Why Louis XIV should have wished to mislead his own ambassador and jeopardize the security of his own secret service is difficult to imagine and the puzzle is made no easier by a further claim from Barnes that Louis XIV did not know who Pregnani really was or why Charles wanted to have him in England. Barnes did have Louis XIV realize the stupidity of this action, but not until three months had passed. Meanwhile, Croissy made the understandable assumption that Pregnani was as informed as he was on Louis XIV's secret intentions and so took him entirely into his confidence. The poor priest thus ended up knowing more than was good for him, which was the reason why Lionne demanded his return to France and why, when eventually Croissy got around to sending him there, he disappeared. Vauroy was waiting for him when he stepped off the boat in Dunkirk and whisked him straight off to Pignerol under the name of Eustache Dauger.

It would have been a good deal less complicated and more convincing if Barnes had argued that to bring Pregnani into existence Charles only needed the collaboration of Madame and the cooperation of Monmouth. In that case, he might have proposed that Louis XIV was just as much deceived as everyone else, that he made the mistake of engaging the man as his agent without probing his background and later, when he realized that the Pregnani identity was a complete fabrication, had the man arrested as a double agent. The priest's knowledge of the secret negotiations between England and France was a good enough reason for his imprisonment; and the need to keep his imprisonment secret, not only from Charles but also from the Society of Jesus, was a good enough reason for hiding his identity as completely as possible.

Of all the theories which trace the Iron Mask to the undercurrents of English politics in 1669 this one is certainly the best, and yet unhappily it must be rejected together with the rest. Pregnani did not disappear altogether in July 1669, nor indeed did he appear for the first time in the preceding January. Primi Visconti, the Venetian ambassador to Paris, who was himself something of a fortune-teller, knew Pregnani well enough to mention him in his *Mémoires sur la cour de Louis XIV*. According to him Pregnani did come from Naples, but only in as much as he was a Neapolitan by birth. Before his arrival at the French court, he had been at the Bavarian court and, on the recommendation of the Electress Adelaide, Louis XIV had given him a living at Beaubec near Dieppe in Normandy. He was indeed a Theatine priest, Visconti says, but altogether dissolute and in fact defrocked. What happened to him when he left England, Visconti does not explain, but it seems reasonable to assume that he stopped off at Beaubec on his way to Paris and this accounted for his delay in delivering Croissy's letter to Lionne. After that, with his reputation at the French court ruined by the Newmarket fiasco, he no doubt moved on, hoping to win patronage in some less hostile corner of Europe. What is certain is that he ended up in Rome where, Visconti says, 'he died, putrified by shameful diseases, in spite of numerous horoscopes which were found on his table according to which he predicted for himself that he would one day be Pope.'

CHAPTER ◇ ELEVEN

EUSTACHE DAUGER UNMASKED

'On 18 February 1639, was baptized Eustache, born on 30 August 1637, son of François Dauger, Master of Cavouet, Captain of the Musketeers of Monseigneur the Cardinal de Richelieu, and of Marie de Sérignan, living in rue des Bons Enfants.' So reads the baptismal certificate of Eustache Dauger as it appeared in the parish register of the church of Saint-Eustache in Paris. The actual document no longer exists, but this extract was recorded in 1864 by Augustin Jal in his *Dictionaire critique de biographie et d'histoire*. In the orthographical disorder of the seventeenth century the name 'Dauger' could take on various other forms: 'Daugier', 'Doger', 'Dogier', 'd'Auger', 'd'Augier', 'd'Oger', 'd'Ogier', 'Auger', 'Augier', 'Oger', 'Ogier'. Members of the same family, brothers and sisters as well as cousins, employed and accepted different spellings, but later documents reveal that Eustache himself preferred the form 'Dauger', as it appeared in his baptismal certificate. The name 'Cavouet' could also appear as 'Cavois' and 'Cavoie', but the only well-known member of the family, Eustache's younger brother Louis, who was a lifelong friend of Louis XIV, came to be known under the form 'Cavoye', and so established that spelling over any other.

The family Dauger claimed descent from Oger the Dane, or more properly Hogier the Ardennois, whose chivalrous exploits as one of the twelve peers of Charlemagne were glorified in French medieval romance. In ancient playing cards Hogier was portrayed as the Knave of Spades; being the bad luck card and called in French the 'Valet de Pique', this would make a fitting ancestral portrait for the unfortunate man who lived out his life as the Iron Mask and who, though a prisoner of evident consequence, was described at the time of his arrest as 'only a valet'. In the destiny of Eustache Dauger de Cavoye there was, it seems, as much irony as iron; by a curious turn of fate his grandfather

Adrien Dauger de Cavoye was known in his lifetime as 'Iron Arm'.

François, son of Adrien and father of Eustache, was a soldier of fortune, a swashbuckling character who came to Paris as a young man with nothing to his name except a reputation as a duellist. He had the good luck to be nominated Captain of the Cardinal's Guard in 1630 and the glory to die a hero's death in the King's wars at Bapaume in 1641. His wife bore him eleven children, nine of whom survived childhood. The eldest was only fifteen when François died; Eustache was four, and there were four children younger than he was. But even with so many small children to raise, Madame de Cavoye's situation was not desperate. She was lady-in-waiting to the Queen, Anne of Austria, and was favoured not only by her but also by Louis XIII and Richelieu. In March 1639 the King had granted her husband a monopoly on sedan-chairs, then recently introduced from England, and since the fashion for that mode of transport had caught on quickly, especially in Paris, it amounted to a significant revenue. As her children grew up, she was always able to afford the enormous sums of money necessary to furnish the boys with commissions and the girls with dowries.

There were six boys of which Eustache was the third, but by the time he was seventeen both his older brothers had, like their father, been killed in action, and so he had become head of the family. At that stage he was already an ensign in the French Guards, and four years later, when the war with Spain ended, he was a second-lieutenant. His comrades-in-arms were members of the most powerful families in the kingdom, heirs to the oldest names, the richest estates and the highest positions at court, while his field commander, the Comte de Guiche, who was one year younger than he was and his close friend, was the dazzling star of this young set: a romantic daredevil, handsome, wilful and debauched.

In April 1659, Eustache and Guiche were invited by the Duc de Vivonne to spend the Easter weekend with a small group of friends at the Château de Roissy-en-Brie. Another guest, Bertrand de Manicamp, travelled down with them from Paris and when they arrived on the evening of Maundy Thursday two other guests were already there: Mazarin's nephew and heir, Philippe Mancini, and a young priest called Etienne Le Camus, who was one of the King's chaplains. Seeing Guiche and his cronies arrive, Le Camus decided not to stay, retired at once to his room and left early the next morning. To take his place, Vivonne then invited Roger de Bussy-Rabutin, who though much older than the other guests could be relied upon to enjoy and enliven the party. How Eustache fitted into the group as a whole is not known. At least four of the company, Vivonne, Guiche, Mancini and Bussy-Rabutin, were intellectuals; at least three of them, Guiche, Mancini and

Manicamp, were homosexuals; and at least two of them, Guiche and Bussy-Rabutin, were rakehell hooligans.

Bussy-Rabutin arrived at the gallop on Good Friday morning which, being the day of sorrow and desolation in the Church, of obligatory fasting and abstinence, was not on the face of it a very appropriate day to start a party. The company moreover was well aware of its religious duties and prepared to go to great pains to observe them, eating nothing until dinner-time and then making do with fish. Being men of wit, however, they saw no reason why they should not spend the whole day drinking and, ingenious as they were, the fish served up for dinner was actually pork, the precaution being taken beforehand of baptizing a pig and naming it 'Carp', thus making it 'born again' as fish. The party continued until Easter Sunday, and what exactly happened in that time is not known. Hearsay reports hinted at things too shocking to print and Madame de Motteville, who like Eustache's mother was lady-in-waiting to the Queen Mother, maintained that 'the profanation of Good Friday was the least of the impieties committed.' They did things, she said, which were 'unworthy not only of Christians but of sensible people'.

Unfortunately, the only detailed account of the events was given by Bussy-Rabutin who had every reason to tone them down. According to him, it was just an elegant debauch with nothing more to it than a little cynical fine wit and irreverent good fun. To build up an appetite for their Good Friday 'fish', everyone except Bussy-Rabutin spent the afternoon hunting, and Guiche accompanied by Manicamp managed to chase and bring to bay an old gentleman whom they saw riding by on the road to Paris. When their quarry explained that he was Cardinal Mazarin's attorney, Guiche thought it excellent sport and dragged him by the scruff of his horse's neck back to the house. Here he was made to down several bumpers of wine before being dumped back in the saddle and sent reeling on his way. Dinner was a riotous affair with everyone drunk, defaming women and the world in extempore verse sung to the tune of pascal hymns, and they were three hours at table before staggering off to bed. The next day, Holy Saturday, began with Bussy-Rabutin and Vivonne going to wake Guiche and finding Manicamp in bed with him; it continued with a morning-after change of air in the park, an afternoon-after exchange of witty persiflage in the house, and ended with a late-night dinner even wilder than the night before. The day after that, Easter Sunday, the party broke up.

In all probability it was a word from the old attorney which set Cardinal Mazarin about their ears. The King ordered an enquiry, but Mazarin chose to go ahead and make an example of his nephew Mancini. He disinherited him and in May sent the captain of his guard to arrest him and take him to the prison of Brisach in Alsace. Word got about that the party had been a veritable orgy of obscenity, blasphemy, violence and depravity. There were rumours of horrifying crimes. A man had been killed and his thigh eaten. The Holy Eucharist had been desecrated. Things had happened too terrible to talk about. In June, Bussy-Rabutin received a letter under the King's seal commanding him to retire to his family seat in Burgundy; Vivonne was ordered to stay in Roissy; Guiche and Manicamp were banished to distant estates; and even Le Camus was deprived of his post and sent off to the provinces to do penance. Presumably Eustache was punished along with the others, but in effect there is no record of his disgrace beyond the fact that to distinguish him from his brothers he was commonly referred to thereafter as the 'Cavoye of Roissy'. No doubt his mother's feelings on the matter were similar to Cardinal Mazarin's. She was certainly concerned to preserve the good name of her family and did continue on excellent terms both with the minister and with the Queen Mother. In July Mazarin wrote to assure her that 'no one has told me the least thing that could harm you in my mind', and in the following January the Queen Mother wrote to her personally inviting her to the South of France for the King's wedding.

The disgrace was only temporary and none of the offenders had his future blighted by it, not even Mancini, who on the death of Mazarin in 1661 received as legacy the Duchy of Nevers which his uncle had bought in July 1659, even while he was languishing in Brisach. Eustache was allowed to become a full lieutenant in 1662, so by that time certainly he was no longer under a cloud. Just three years after that, however, he was involved in a much more serious affair, described officially as an 'unfortunate incident which happened to him at Saint-Germain', as a result of which his career appears to have been wrecked. On this occasion he had only one companion with him, the young Duc de Foix, and the sole account of what happened appears in a private letter written by Foix's friend the Duc d'Enghien on 19 June 1665. Enghien, son of the Prince de Condé, wrote regular letters full of court gossip to the Queen of Poland, to whom he was related by marriage and by whom he had been designated heir to the throne of Poland.

> A rather disagreeable incident happened recently involving M. de Foix. As he was leaving the old castle of Saint-Germain, he met a drunken page who struck him with his stick as he went by. M. de Foix cursed him, to which the page retorted and, it is even said, jabbed at his hand. M. de Foix lost his temper, drew his sword and gave the page five or six blows with the flat of it. A man

named Cavoye also drew his sword and struck him too. The page, stung by the thrashing, hit back with his stick and even tried to throw it at Cavoye, who stabbed at him and killed him. The place where the business occurred makes it rather awkward. The King has ordered an enquiry and in the meantime has forbidden either of them to appear before him. I do not know if there will be any unpleasant consequences.

One may be sure that Enghien was merely repeating the version he got from Foix and as it is the story sounds suspiciously like a cover-up. As a page, the boy could not have been more than fourteen years old and, even supposing that he had been drunk, it is unlikely that armed with a simple stick he would have stayed to fight two full-grown men with drawn swords. Even if he had done so, however, it is unlikely that an officer of twenty-eight who was sober, defending himself against a boy with a stick who was drunk, could have unleashed that kind of sword-thrust by accident. If another version of the incident existed in which it was the officers who had been drunk and the boy who had been attacked by them, it would make more sense. In the event, Foix belonged to an influential family and the charge of murder was not brought; there remained, however, the added complication referred to by Enghien – the fact that the King was actually in the palace of Saint-Germain-en-Laye when the killing occurred. The two young men had thus desecrated a place sanctified by the King's presence, and it was for this crime that they were eventually judged.

At the beginning of July, before Eustache's fate had been decided, Madame de Cavoye took ill and died. The Saint-Germain affair may have contributed to her death, but it did not play a part in her last will and testament since that document had been drawn up fourteen months before. Already at that time she had made up her mind that Eustache was unworthy of the family inheritance. She left behind three sons, all officers in the Guards, and three daughters, two married and one in a convent. Eustache's brothers were Armand, one year younger than he was, and Louis, two years younger. His married sisters were Henriette de Fabrègues, eleven years older than he was, and Anne de Clérac, three years younger. The will was read on 8 July and by it Madame de Cavoye bequeathed the family title and fortune to her youngest son, Louis. To her older sons she left 20,000 livres each, but attached to the will were 75 receipts for payments which she had made to cover debts amassed by Eustache; 'for good reasons and considerations known to her', she denied him access to the capital sum of his legacy, restricting his rights only to the interest. His inheritance thus amounted to 'an annuity of 1,000 livres' and this, it was specified, could only be used for 'food and upkeep'.

Armand, who like Eustache had been passed over for Louis, was disposed to argue the terms of the will, but on 15 August Eustache signed his acceptance and with it an agreement whereby in return for another 1,000 livres per year, he surrendered to Louis some small estates which had come to him ten years before as titular head of the family. Grim as it was for Eustache to be disinherited and disentitled in favour of his younger brother, it was only part of his sudden ill fortune. By that time judgement had been given on the Saint-Germain affair and he had been obliged 'by order of the King' to resign and sell his commission in the Guards. Thus in August 1665 Eustache Dauger, the Cavoye of Roissy, was a virtual outcast with no position and no apparent future. What friends he had to turn to in his misfortune we do not know, but already in April of that year Guiche had been exiled to Holland for misbehaviour and Bussy-Rabutin had been sent to the Bastille for libel; some months later, in December of that same year, Foix died of smallpox.

In July 1666 one of the three Cavoye brothers was forbidden the King's presence after a squabble with Lauzun, then known as the Marquis de Puyguilhem. Usually it is assumed that the Cavoye in question was Louis, though arguably it was Armand, and the fact that he had strong ties of friendship with Guiche suggests that it might even have been Eustache. The cause of the conflict was Guiche's sister, the Princesse de Monaco. Lauzun considered her to be his mistress and refused to accept that he did not have a monopoly on her favours. His jealousy even sparked a row with the King for which he spent four months in the Bastille. When he was released in December 1665 he seemed chastened, but in May 1666 he happened to be in a room where the Princess was sitting with other ladies on the floor and whether by accident or out of spite he stepped on her fingers. The Princess and her family were so sure that he had done it deliberately that the King had to intervene to protect him, even going so far as to send a personal message to Guiche in Holland, explaining that it was in his opinion a genuine accident. The Prince de Monaco, caught in a situation where there was little honour for him in any course of action, went to Holland to join Guiche; with him, he volunteered for active service with the Dutch fleet in the war against the English. While they were there, distinguishing themselves with acts of derring-do which made them the talk of the French court, their friend Cavoye harassed and baited Lauzun.

'There was a quarrel yesterday between M. de Puyguilhem and a man named M. de Cavoye.' So the Duc d'Enghien informed the Queen of Poland in a letter he wrote on 9 July 1666. 'Puyguilhem is the same person whom Your Majesty heard about in the business over Madame de Monaco. I think Cavoye, who is one of her friends, wanted to make trouble with Puyguilhem in order to please her and give her revenge, so he pushed into him rather roughly. Puyguilhem was combing his hair at the time and when he felt himself being pushed he hit Cavoye in the face with his comb and knocked off his wig. All this happened very near to the King who dismissed Cavoye because he was the aggressor and also because he doesn't have the same social rank as the other.' Soon after this incident, we learn from another of Enghien's letters, Cavoye, accompanied by the Chevalier de Lorraine, left France to join the Dutch fleet with Guiche and Monaco, and by August they too were distinguishing themselves with daredevil acts which filled the French court with admiration. Lorraine, like Guiche, was a brilliant and handsome young man, arrogant, dissolute and charming, made it was said 'as one paints the angels', a shameless womanizer and a notorious homosexual.

In August of the following year, Armand de Cavoye died, killed at the siege of Lille during the French invasion of Flanders. Ever since the death of Madame de Cavoye he had lived apart from his brothers, who whatever their differences had continued to share the same roof. The surviving brothers and sisters refused the inheritance because it seemed the dead man's estate would not cover his debts, though as things turned out he had only two creditors, one of whom was his brother, Louis. Eustache, it soon appeared, was also in debt to Louis. The sale of his commission in 1665 would have brought him at least another 20,000 livres, which properly invested would have raised his income to 3,000 livres per year, but in all likelihood he dissipated the capital and continued to spend wildly even when that was gone. By January 1668 he owed Louis 1,400 livres and was obliged to sign over that amount from his future revenue. In financial matters within the family, Louis' interests were always well cared for and the man he had to thank for that was his brother-in-law, Raymond de Clérac, who was the manager of his estate. According to Eustache, it was Clérac who was the author of all his woes.

In July 1668, just one year before the arrest of the Iron Mask, Louis went to prison for duelling and was kept behind bars for four years. A love affair, which he had been trying to start with a certain Sidonia de Courcelles, had turned into an affair of honour to be concluded with her husband. Louvois, who was also interested in the fair Sidonia, had then taken advantage of the quarrel to clear the field for himself. Both husband and lover were arrested and locked up in the Conciergerie. Duelling was a capital crime and so Louvois had every hope that the new situation would become permanent. However, the duellists were able to convince their judges that they had made up their differences without drawing swords, and two weeks later the Parlement ordered their release. Thwarted but not defeated, Louvois convinced the King that further investigation was necessary and continued detention advisable. Two years later the Parlement again sent an order to the Conciergerie authorizing the release of the two men, but by that time Louvois had moved them to the Bastille and the order was lost in the toils of bureaucracy. It was a further two years before Louis was released and by that time the fate of Eustache, locked up and forgotten, had long been sealed.

The writer who traced the prisoner named Eustache Dauger to Eustache Dauger de Cavoye was Maurice Duvivier, whose book on the Iron Mask was published in 1932. After searching the archives of the Cavoye family, Duvivier was able to establish that the last recorded reference to Eustache Dauger de Cavoye was January 1668, just eighteen months before the imprisonment of Eustache Dauger in Pignerol. What happened in the interval seemed anybody's guess, but to Duvivier one thing was certain: the mystery surrounding the disappearance of the Cavoye of Roissy in 1668 and the appearance of the Iron Mask in 1669 was one and the same. Duvivier was also sure that the key to this apparently insoluble mystery lay in the answer to another mystery. In his view the riddle of the Iron Mask involved two separate problems: firstly the reason why he was arrested and made a high-security prisoner in 1669; and secondly the reason why his name was suppressed and his imprisonment made top secret in 1680. To the mystery of 1680, Duvivier believed he knew the answer.

The event which caused the change in Eustache Dauger's status as a prisoner was Fouquet's death, reported by Saint-Mars on 23 March 1680. In the new instructions which Louvois sent on 8 April, Saint-Mars was told to clear the dead man's room, and it was presumably while he was doing this that he discovered something of significance in the pockets of Fouquet's clothes. What exactly it was, we do not know, but in a letter now lost which he wrote to Louvois on 4 May he gave the impression that he had found some papers. Louvois was not in Paris when the letter arrived. In his absence it was opened by one of his secretaries who informed the King and, at his command, wrote back to Saint-Mars on 16 May telling him to send the papers at once to Paris. Strange to say, Saint-Mars ignored this letter and made no further move until he received an answer from Louvois himself, written on 29 May, in which the minister naturally assumed that the papers in question were on their way. Even then Saint-Mars continued to prevaricate. Instead of obeying the order, he sent another letter and, though this too is now lost, the reply from Louvois, written on 22 June, makes it clear that there was a good deal more to the discovery than anyone in Paris had imagined. 'With regard to the loose sheet which accompanied your letter of the 8th, you were wrong not to give me that information the very first day you knew about it. Furthermore, I beg you to send me in a packet what you found in the pockets of M. Fouquet so that I might present it to His Majesty.' Evidently what Saint-Mars had found was not a bundle of papers at all, but an object of some kind, and he had wanted to prepare the minister for it before sending it to him.

Finally then, on 4 July, two months after his first report of the discovery and more than three months after the death of Fouquet, Saint-Mars sent what he had found in the dead man's pockets. His accompanying letter is now lost, but not the reply from Louvois which was written on 10 July. 'With your letter of the 4th of this month I received what was attached and I will make use of it as I should.' Louvois then went on to speak of Dauger and La Rivière: 'It will be enough to let the prisoners of the Lower Tower make their confessions once a year.' Then of Matthioli: 'As for Master Lestang I admire your patience, waiting for permission to treat a scoundrel as he deserves when he does not show you respect.' Louvois dictated this to a clerk as was his usual practice and at this point, so far as the clerk was concerned, the letter ended. Before he signed and sealed what the clerk had written, however, Louvois added another paragraph in his own handwriting: 'Tell me how the man named Eustache was able to do what you sent me, and where he was able to get the drugs he needed to do it. I hardly believe that you would have provided him with them.'

How to account for the odd behaviour of Saint-Mars, the strange reaction of Louvois? How to explain the cause of their secret concern, that mixture of drugs prepared by Dauger and found in the pocket of Fouquet after his death? Poison, says Duvivier. Dauger had poisoned Fouquet. Not only was Fouquet's death unexpected, Duvivier reminds us, it was sudden. On 6 April *La Gazette* spoke of apoplexy, but Madame de Sévigné, writing to a friend on 3 April, was more specific; she said that he had suffered 'convulsions and nausea without being able to vomit'. No one spoke of poison at the time, it is true, but even if his family had suspected it, there was little they could have done to prove it. Fouquet had been dead for three weeks before they were allowed to take his body away, and after that length of time an autopsy would have established nothing. At that stage, moreover, there appeared to be no motive for such a crime, and thus no suspect. It seemed that Fouquet's one-time enemies had nothing to gain from having him killed. Indeed they had so little to gain from having him remain in prison that they were about to set him free.

To all appearances that was the situation in 1680, but in Duvivier's view the realities of it were very different. Fouquet's release was a political manoeuvre in a power struggle which had developed between two government factions, both formerly Fouquet's enemies, one led by Colbert and the other by Louvois. It had been the intention of Louvois, Duvivier says, to bring Fouquet into his camp and push him to destroy Colbert just as Colbert had destroyed him; but Colbert, aware of the danger, had managed to have Fouquet assassinated before he could become a threat. The Cavoye family belonged to the Colbert faction, and it was on Colbert's orders that Eustache killed Fouquet. Colbert had always been the protector of the Cavoyes; Madame de Cavoye towards the end of her life had even chosen to live in the rue Vivienne where Colbert and many of his relatives lived, and it was only in the character of things that Louvois should have excelled himself as the oppressor of Louis de Cavoye. As for Eustache, it is altogether possible that officially Colbert never knew that he was a prisoner at Pignerol. Indeed an examination of the papers relating to Dauger's arrest give every reason to believe that he was deliberately kept from knowing.

These papers are three letters dated 19 July, one to Captain de Vauroy, the arresting officer, another to his superior, the governor of Dunkirk, and the other to Saint-Mars, all from Louvois, and two warrants dated 26 July, one for Dauger's arrest addressed to Vauroy and the other for Dauger's imprisonment addressed to Saint-Mars, both signed by the King and Michel Le Tellier, who was the father of Louvois and shared with him the post of Minister of War. It was normal procedure for all dispatches and documents to be recorded in a register which was confidential to the ministry of origin, and for all royal warrants to be recorded again in a Register of the King's Orders, which was seen by all ministers and countersigned by at least one. The letters to Vauroy and the governor of Dunkirk were not recorded in the Ministry Register, and though the letter to Saint-Mars was recorded, the name Eustache Dauger, given in the letter, was omitted. The royal warrants were recorded in the Ministry Register, though there again Eustache Dauger's name was omitted, but in the Register of the King's Orders they were not recorded at all.

In all likelihood, Duvivier argues, the arrest of Eustache was concealed from Colbert and the reason for this was that he was a Cavoye. Presumably Colbert discovered the truth only because Lauzun, who also was a Colbert man, made a secret passage to Fouquet's room and discovered Eustache there. Presumably too, it was Lauzun who, acting for Colbert, persuaded Eustache with promises of freedom and reward, to do the deed. At that date, the only human companionship Eustache had known in ten years of imprisonment had been with Fouquet, and yet he killed him. Whatever the motive, it was a monstrous act and could only have been carried out by a cold-blooded killer, who was already an expert in the use of poison. The man who was the Iron Mask, Duvivier concludes, was that kind of man.

In 1680 all Paris was talking of poison. A special tribunal, the Chambre Ardente, had been set up the year before to deal with a wave of suspected poisonings. In the course of the interrogations it had been revealed that an underworld traffic in poisons, in which people of the highest rank were implicated, had been in business for more than fifteen years. Duvivier, speculating that in the transcripts of this tribunal he might find some mention of Dauger, searched the government archives. Unfortunately the records are incomplete. Minutes were kept of 865 interrogations, but the King ordered a cover-up in the midst of the proceedings, dismissed the tribunal before its job was done and personally burned all documents which incriminated anyone intimately connected with himself. Duvivier nonetheless found something. In June 1679, during the final interrogation of a man called Belot, one of the King's bodyguards, convicted as a poisoner and sentenced to be broken that day on the wheel, the name Auger was mentioned. The magistrate asked Belot about his relations with 'Auger, the surgeon, who lived in the cour de Saint-Eloi', and if it was 'from Auger that he got the opium and other drugs he needed.' Belot replied that he knew Auger, but had not received any drugs from him. He said that Auger's mistress lived in the rue Soly above another convicted poisoner, La Cheron, who had been sentenced to the stake, and was the friend of yet another convicted poisoner, Duval, who was sentenced to the wheel. In the second phase of the interrogation, Belot was put to the torture and among other questions was asked 'what he knew about Auger and what business they had together.' In his agony he swore he knew nothing, and Auger's name was not mentioned again.

At first sight, any possible link between Dauger, as the poisoner of Fouquet, and Auger, the surgeon suspected of trafficking in poison, appears slight. When Belot was questioned about Auger, Dauger had been in prison for ten years and there seems no reason to believe that Belot was talking about someone he had not seen for so long. Nevertheless, as Duvivier demonstrates, he was not talking about a relationship of yesterday. He was referring to a time when Auger's mistress was living above La Cheron in the rue Soly, and yet when La Cheron was arrested in 1679 she was no longer living at that address. Duvivier also finds something of significance in the address Belot gives for Auger. La Cour de Saint-Eloi was the name of a villa in the village of Picpus on the outskirts of Paris and in the late 1660s this villa belonged to the Marquise de Brinvilliers, the most notorious poisoner of them all, brought to justice and executed three years before the tribunal was even set up. She had poisoned her father in 1666, killing him slowly over a period of eight months, having first tested the effects of her poisons upon sick people she visited in hospital. In 1670 she had gone on to poison her two brothers. If it was the late 1660s that Belot was talking about then, in addition to a possible link between Auger and Dauger, there was a definite link between Madame de Brinvilliers and Auger. Duvivier then squared his argument with evidence of a third link, one between Madame de Brinvilliers and Dauger. They were apparently related: a cousin of the Cavoye family was married to a cousin of Madame de Brinvilliers. At the time of her arrest Madame de Brinvilliers was carrying a written confession of all her crimes, including a list of sexual sins in which she specified an adulterous relationship with an unmarried cousin. The description is vague to say the least, but it would fit Dauger.

In February 1680, the interrogations of the poisoners had taken such a turn that it was necessary to enlarge the competence of the tribunal to deal with cases of sacrilege and profanation, witchcraft and devil-worship. In October, the Abbé Guiborg, sacristan of the church of Saint-Marcel, was questioned about a black mass he had said at the Palais Royal and in his reply he claimed that he had been engaged to do it by a surgeon. He did not know the name of this surgeon, but described him as 'a tall well-made young man', who had his practice in the Saint-Victor district and his home 'with his brother in the suburb of Saint-Germain in a big street opposite the great gate of the Charity Hospital.' In the following month a magician named Le Sage was also asked about this particular mass. Although no record exists of what he said, La Reynie, the chief of police who conducted the interrogation, wrote to Louvois on 16 November to say that the mass had been said for 'the late Madame and against Monsieur.' The date of the mass was not reported, but it is possible to fix it with some certainty. By 'the late Madame' was meant Henrietta of England, the first wife of the King's brother, and since she had died in June 1670 the mass had certainly taken place before that. What is more, the authorities clearly assumed that Le Sage knew all about the mass, though they were aware that he had been arrested in March 1668 and not set at liberty again until two years after Madame's death. It may be safely assumed that the authorities would not have questioned him unless the mass had taken place before March 1668 when he was in a position to know about it, and it is known as a matter of fact that Eustache Dauger was still at large at that time.

In Duvivier's view, of course, the unnamed surgeon who acted as go-between for Madame and Guiborg was the surgeon known to Belot as Auger and the prisoner known to us as Dauger. As evidence for this he turned once more to the address provided by the witness. The Charity Hospital was in the rue des Saints-Pères, and from early in 1668 Eustache Dauger had lived with his brother Louis in the rue de Bourbon which was a new street giving onto the rue des Saints-Pères. Neither the house-front nor the street-end was 'opposite' the gate of the hospital, it is true, but at that time the suburb of Saint-Germain-des-Prés was still predominantly open land with half-built streets and new mansions spreading into the countryside. It is perfectly possible that a view from the house could have given the impression that it was 'opposite' the hospital. In support of Duvivier's argument, it is also worth pointing out that most of the known companions of Eustache Dauger were part of the intimate circle of friends surrounding Monsieur and Madame: Guiche, Madame de Monaco, Manicamp, Foix, Mancini and, one might add, Lorraine. Monsieur had homosexual affairs with at least three of them: Guiche, Mancini and Lorraine; while Madame had a passionate heterosexual relationship with Guiche and a furtive homosexual liaison with Madame de Monaco.

When Le Sage was arrested in March 1668, it was with a partner in crime, the Abbé Mariette of the church of Saint-Severin, and they were brought to trial together at the Châtelet court on a charge of sorcery and sacrilege. Specifically they were accused of consecrating petitions and aphrodisiacs during holy mass, of making ritual conjurations and magical concoctions by the light of the moon, but both denied that they had done anything so serious. They said that a number of wealthy ladies had come to them, hoping by magic charms to increase their natural charms, and that they had exploited these women for money, giving them simple blessings or harmless powders. Among their clientèle had been several ladies of the court who had hoped with supernatural aid to win the King away from his then mistress, Louise de La Vallière, and according to Mariette these had included the Comtesse de Soissons, the Duchesse de Vivonne and the Marquise de Montespan. To allow the names of such illustrious ladies to be linked to such wretched proceedings, especially since the last-named appeared to have been successful in her endeavour, was a responsibility no judge would dare to assume, and as it was the presiding judges had even more pertinent reasons for curtailing the trial and hushing it up. The president of the Châtelet court was, by his wife, Mariette's first cousin. He refused to delve any further into the matter or to make any pronouncement on Mariette and referred the case to the Tournelle court with the recommendation that Le Sage be condemned to the galleys.

Mariette's cousin was not the only judge with a personal interest in the case. The president of the Tournelle court was, by a strange coincidence, the father of the Duchesse de Vivonne who, as it happens, was married to the brother of the Marquise de Montespan. In the new interrogations, Mariette did not mention the names of these two distinguished ladies again, and it was presumably because he did not that he drew such a mild sentence: banishment for nine years, altered to confinement in the asylum of Saint-Lazare, from which as things turned out he was allowed to escape that same year. Unfortunately for Le Sage, the provisory sentence that he should spend the rest of his life as a galley-slave was upheld, but as later events proved he too had powerful friends behind the scenes. In May 1673, he was released from his galley at Genoa. On whose authority, no one could ever find out, not even La Reynie, who rearrested him in 1679 and ordered an investigation.

This cover-up of 1668 is all the more significant when one knows that the Comtesse de Soissons was later exposed as a poisoner and had to flee the country, and that both the Marquise de Montespan and the Duchesse de Vivonne were later proved to be Satanists. To preserve the love of the King, Madame de Montespan lay naked on an altar with a chalice on her belly while the Abbé Guiborg performed the rites of a black mass between her open legs, slitting a baby's throat and mixing its blood with his semen. Madame de Vivonne did the same more than once in the hope of winning the King from Madame de Montespan and, when that proved ineffective, pledged her soul to the devil in a written contract. It was to hide such abominations that the King suppressed the tribunal in 1682 and burned all the incriminating documents. The truth only remains on record because, unknown to him, La Reynie kept private notes of some of the interrogations. It is difficult to establish exactly when it was that Madame de Montespan and Madame de Vivonne abandoned themselves to the horrors of the black mass. However, the fact remains that they were already involved with Le Sage before March 1668 and he was already involved with the Abbé Guiborg, who at that time was engaged by the mysterious surgeon to perform a black mass for Madame.

The final links in Duvivier's chain of argument reach all the way back to the Roissy affair in 1659, the host of that notorious party being the Duc de Vivonne, brother of Madame de Montespan and husband of Madame de Vivonne. One might include here also the extra link that in 1673, at the time of Le Sage's mysterious liberation at Genoa, Vivonne was Captain-General of the Galleys and acting Admiral of the Fleet. The Château de Roissy originally belonged to Madame de Vivonne's father, the president of the Tournelle court in 1668, and it came to Vivonne in the dowry of his wife. In Duvivier's view it was here, in the

home of that woman who later sold her soul to the devil, that all
Eustache Dauger's problems originated. The house was evil and in that
fateful Holy Week he too became evil. Whatever it was that horrified
people about the party, 'the profanation of Good Friday was the least of
the impieties committed', and Duvivier would have us believe that it
was something much more serious than the baptism of a pig. The rôle
played by Eustache in the party is not known, but that he took a key
part in whatever crime was committed is demonstrated by the fact that
the title of 'Roissy' was thereafter attached to his name. Significantly
too the only other person who was unable to be rid of that title was the
Abbé Le Camus, who later in life, as a prince of the Church, was called
by his enemies the 'Cardinal of Roissy'. Le Camus had not even stayed
for the party and yet people assumed, for all his denials, that he had
been there. From this, one might assume that, whatever the crime was,
it required the participation of a priest, something which is unnecessary
for the sacrament of baptism.

The priest who was there, Duvivier suggests, was very likely the
parish priest of Roissy, and he was most certainly a sorcerer and a
Satanist. The Abbé de Choisy, who was a contemporary of Dauger and
the rest, included the following story about this priest in his *Mémoires
pour servir à l'Historie de Louis XIV*:

> One of my friends, a Gascon, named Maniban de Ram . . . told
> me one day that the parish priest of Roissy had shown him visions
> in a glass: a young lady he knew in Toulouse who was weeping
> because he was far away. I laughed at his credulity, but he offered
> to let me witness it for myself, and I kept him to his word. He
> arranged a dinner-party at which the parish priest was to be the
> big attraction, and he invited some ladies who were curious. I
> arrived a quarter of an hour before dinner was served. I was
> announced and in I went. The sorcerer stiffened at the sight of me,
> I don't know why, and said in a whisper to Maniban that he
> would do nothing so long as I was there. No amount of
> persuasion could change his mind. Maniban was finally obliged to
> tell me so and, not wishing to disappoint the ladies by depriving
> them of their entertainment, I left. The next day they assured me
> that they had seen the devil or something like.

And thus the last of Duvivier's links falls into place, and his story of the
Iron Mask is ready to be told.

The parish priest of Roissy is a sorcerer in league with the powers of
darkness. Vivonne's wife knows him well, and through her Vivonne
comes to know him too. Vivonne is a man of reason and does not take

the priest's magic tricks seriously, but from time to time when he is staying at Roissy he invites him in to entertain his friends. No doubt it is at one of these performances that Vivonne's sister, Madame de Montespan, makes her first contact with black magic. In Holy Week 1659, Vivonne has some wild guests to amuse so he asks the priest to put on a special show. By the time the priest arrives, everyone is drunk and things get quickly out of hand. One of the guests is chosen by the priest to act a special rôle in the proceedings.

The guest chosen is one of Guiche's homosexual friends, a young infantry officer called Eustache Dauger de Cavoye. He is already a bad lot and the experience makes him worse. In the years that follow, he gets himself mixed up with other Satanists, the most depraved and corrupt elements of society, and through them with the criminal underworld of Paris. His vicious life involves him in numerous crimes, but his family always manages to cover up for him, until in 1665 he surpasses himself: he and another homosexual friend rape and kill a pageboy in the grounds of the King's palace. For this he is cashiered, and when his widowed mother dies of shame, he finds that she has disinherited him.

In his difficulties he turns to devil-worship for help and, when that fails to change his luck, to organized crime. With the contacts he has in the upper reaches of society, he is ideally placed to set up a secret traffic in magic and murder, supplying charms and potions, curses and spells, aphrodisiacs and poisons to the court. He can arrange anything from an abortion to a black mass, and among his clients he soon has several leading ladies of the court, including Madame herself. In the fashionable suburb of Saint-Germain he is Eustache Dauger de Cavoye, but in the teeming squalor of the Saint-Victor district he is Auger the surgeon, and no one suspects his double personality.

In 1668, however, someone informs on him. Two of his associates, Le Sage and Mariette, are taken in for questioning. They talk, and Madame de Vivonne is named. Her father, the judge, informs her and she passes on the word to Dauger. He decides to play safe and escapes to England. As it turns out, however, there are no more arrests. So far as he can gather, his accomplices are bribed not to speak and the investigation is closed. Knowing the two men as he does, he is nonetheless suspicious and it is more than a year before he thinks it safe to return. When he arrives in France, the police are waiting for him. His associates have betrayed him after all.

To his surprise, he is not interrogated. The King has given orders that under no circumstances is he to be allowed to talk about any dealings he may claim to have had with Madame. Louvois threatens him with death if he opens his mouth and then has him whisked off to

Pignerol. His imprisonment is kept secret to avoid it becoming known to his brother, Louis, and to Colbert. It is only when Lauzun discovers him at Pignerol and passes the word secretly to some trustworthy visitor that Colbert learns the truth. By that time, with the Chambre Ardente in session, there is every reason to believe the allegations made years ago by Le Sage and Mariette about the abortions, black masses and poisonings which Dauger arranged for Madame and her friends. Colbert, realizing that Dauger is a monster, ready to commit any kind of crime, persuades him, with a promise of freedom, to murder Fouquet.

At first no one suspects that Fouquet has been poisoned. What concerns Louvois is the discovery that Lauzun has made contact with Dauger and has probably informed Colbert and the Cavoye family of his whereabouts. What concerns the King is the need to suppress all knowledge of his sister-in-law's horrifying crimes, and his determination to do this is all the greater now that he knows, from the findings of the Chambre Ardente, that his mistress has been guilty of the same abominations. Dauger must be made to disappear without trace, and the stories he has told Lauzun made to appear without foundation. What better way to achieve this than to pretend that he has been released? It is not until three months after Fouquet's death that Louvois realizes Dauger poisoned him. He suspects that it was at the instigation of Colbert, but there is little he can do to prove that to the King. As for Dauger, the King's orders are formal: his identity must be kept secret so long as Lauzun and Louis de Cavoye are alive, and as events turn out they both outlive him.

Dauger's special case as an anonymous prisoner is due to the fact that he is a Cavoye, but his fate as a prisoner for life would be the same even if he had no family trying to protect him. Riff-raff involved in the same appalling crimes, vermin like Le Sage and Guiborg, suffer no worse a fate. If the law were allowed to take its course, they would end their vile lives on the scaffold, burned alive or broken on the wheel for devil-worship and murder; but their denunciations of ladies so intimately related to the King can never be made public. Their trials are simply not allowed to take place, and to assure their silence they are, like Dauger, forbidden to speak under pain of death and locked up for the rest of their lives.

However plausible Duvivier's story might seem, the fact that Dauger was a Cavoye is not in itself enough to explain why the King kept his imprisonment secret and forced him to wear a mask outside his prison cell. Whether or not he was all that Duvivier accuses him of being, 'sodomite and Satanist, cut-throat and poisoner', his family knew better than anyone that he was a reprobate who, like as not, was destined one day for the galleys or the scaffold. It is not in the least likely that Louis de Cavoye or anyone else would have questioned the King's reasons for locking him up. On the contrary, one has the impression that Louis de Cavoye would have been only too glad to see the last of his worthless, thriftless brother, especially since it meant 2,000 livres less per year to pay out from the estate.

To explain the mask, Duvivier's readers felt the need for another reason, and the first to propose one was Rupert Furneaux in his book *The Man Behind The Mask*, published in 1954. His theory was an old one, the most famous of them all, but in its application it was quite new. 'Purely as a surmise, it may be suggested that Eustache Dauger de Cavoye was masked because he resembled Louis XIV, whether or not this was the reason why he was first sent to Pignerol,' although the idea 'that he may even have impersonated him and was in consequence sent to Pignerol may be put forward as a guess.' Apart from the legend that the Iron Mask was the King's double, there is no reason to imagine that Eustache Dauger looked like him, but 'according to Saint-Simon,' Furneaux claimed, 'contemporaries remarked on the resemblance of his brother Louis to the King.' This is an overstatement. In fact Saint-Simon made no mention of any physical resemblance. He merely remarked that Louis de Cavoye 'had excellent taste and in that resembled the King.' As it happens, a portrait of Louis de Cavoye, brought to light by Adrien Huguet, whose book *Le Marquis de Cavoye* was published in 1920, does suggest some similiarity of appearance, though nothing more than one might expect to find in the portrait of a courtier who sought to ape his master. However and in any case, even if Louis de Cavoye did resemble Louis XIV, there is certainly no reason to assume that therefore his brother Eustache resembled him too.

Having hunted thus far, Furneaux abandoned the chase with a wild throw which even he recognized to be wide of the mark. He suggested that Eustache Dauger was the child of an adulterous affair between Madame de Cavoye and Louis XIII, and thus the illegitimate half-brother of Louis XIV. This of course takes no account of the fact that Madame de Cavoye was known to be the most faithful of wives and Louis XIII the most chaste of men, more likely to be suspected of impotence than of promiscuity. Nor does it take into account firstly the fact that to make sense of the resemblance, not only Eustache but also Louis de Cavoye would need to have been fathered in this way; and secondly the fact that after the example of his father, Henri IV (a precedent which Louis XIV was later to follow), Louis XIII could be confident that the illegitimate children of kings were an altogether acceptable feature of court life at the time.

In 1974, Marie-Madeleine Mast, in her book *Le Masque de fer*, took up the theory where Furneaux left off, arguing that the unfaithful wife was Anne of Austria and her paramour was the prolific François Dauger de Cavoye, father of eleven children by his own wife. Eustache was still the half-brother of Louis XIV, therefore, and still his spit and image, but this time it was Louis XIV who was illegitimate, the son of the Queen but not of the King.[1] Mast builds her theory on the curious circumstances surrounding the conception of Louis XIV. It was François Dauger, she maintains, the father of Eustache and Louis, who in 1637 was chosen to impregnate the Queen on command; the extraordinary rise to favour of the Cavoye family, which dates from soon after the birth of Louis XIV, was due entirely to this. From 1638 onwards the fortune of the family grew unchecked, reaching an importance out of all proportion to their station or ability, and though under the influence of Mazarin the Queen cast off all her old favourites, she continued throughout her life to protect Madame de Cavoye. Louis XIV showed the same special affection all his life for Louis de Cavoye, something which courtiers of higher birth and greater talent could never understand.

In August 1637, Anne of Austria was found guilty of treason and placed under house arrest at the Louvre. A miracle was needed if she was to save herself from repudiation and this occurred when a storm obliged the King to spend one night in her bed. According to Mast no other miracle was necessary. As a consequence of that night she became pregnant, gave birth to a son and was saved, but there was nothing miraculous about the actual conception. As captain of Richelieu's guard, François Dauger de Cavoye had access to the Louvre whenever he wished; as husband of the Queen's lady-in-waiting, he could be persuaded to doff more than his hat in the Queen's service; and as father already of seven children he could be counted on to serve her effectively in what it was she required of him. It was when Eustache Dauger discovered the true nature of his father's glory and sought to use it to his own advantage that he was arrested and imprisoned. The secret which Dauger could not be allowed to disclose, Mast would have us believe, was that Louis XIV was not the son of Louis XIII and that therefore his claim to the throne was spurious. Whether anyone would have believed Dauger even if he had disclosed this secret is another matter.

From Duvivier's apparent discovery in 1932 that the prisoner was Eustache de Cavoye to Mast's conclusion in 1974 that François de Cavoye was the father of Louis XIV, passing by way of Furneaux's theory in 1954 that Eustache de Cavoye and Louis XIV were look-alikes, much ground had been covered, but even before the publication of Furneaux's book the line of investigation opened up by Duvivier had been proved wrong. Since the publication of his book no less than three documents had come to light demonstrating that Eustache Dauger and Eustache Dauger de Cavoye were not after all the same man. The coincidence of the names was extraordinary, but it was only a coincidence. At the beginning of 1668, Eustache Dauger de Cavoye had been locked up at the request of his own family in the asylum of Saint-Lazare and there, in spite of his appeals, he had been made to remain until his death sometime between 1680 and 1689.

Two of these documents were letters written by Eustache Dauger de Cavoye himself, and they were both published in 1953 in an article by Georges Mongrédien which appeared in the *Revue XVIIe Siècle*. The first, dated 20 June 1678, was addressed to Eustache's eldest sister, the Marquise de Fabrègues.

> My Dear Sister, If you only knew how I suffer, I have no doubt at all that you would do your utmost to get me out of the cruel persecution and captivity in which I have been kept under a pretext for more than ten years by the tyranny of my brother M. de Cavoy. He deprived me of my freedom, the sole possession I had after he tricked me into making over my estate to him, and now he would have me die insane so that he might freely enjoy the possessions he so cunningly took from me. I beseech you, dear sister, for the love of Jesus Christ, do not abandon me in this state, with the salvation of my soul in jeopardy, for I will never make my confession so long as I am here, unable as I am to forget the cruel treatment I receive every day from the most ungrateful of men who listens only to the malicious counsel of Clérac, who is the author of all my woes. Let yourself be touched, dear sister, by the prayers of a poor unfortunate who drags out a miserable existence which without your pity will soon end. If you refuse me this grace you will have to answer for the salvation of my soul before God and you will have reason to regret that you did not help a brother who had no one to turn to but you. If you have in you the goodness to help me then I beg you to do all that you judge necessary for my liberty and for my affairs even if it means approaching the King. Hoping for this favour, I am, with all my heart, yours, Eustache de Cavoy. This twentieth of June 1678.

Eustache makes no mention here of where he was imprisoned, but the second letter, a petition to the King written a year later, states quite clearly that he was in Saint-Lazare and had been there all along.

> To the King. Sire, Cavoy who has been detained under a royal warrant in the prison of Saint-Lazare for eleven and a half years

begs Your Majesty most humbly to do him the grace of hearing his just complaints against the Master of Cavoy, his brother. Having tricked me into making over my entire estate to him in return for a very modest pension, he made Your Majesty believe that I was leading a disreputable life in Paris and that I was causing him shame by my misconduct. This apparently was the pretext he used to impose upon Your Majesty's good faith, if indeed he ever did address himself to Your Majesty to ask for such a warrant. I cannot believe that he did so, because fair-minded as you are, Sire, you would not without a hearing have wished to help a younger brother imprison his elder brother when he had just signed over to him all his property. Such an extraordinary proceeding will surely win the compassion of Your Majesty who has always been the refuge of oppressed innocence. I hope so and all the more so since I have no protection other than your justice to turn to. As long as my brother, who was killed at the siege of Lille, was alive, no one ever dared to restrict my liberty. His death was the beginning of my troubles and gave the opportunity to the Master of Cavoy to sell all the lands and all the property which were set aside to ensure my pension and which belonged to me by right as the eldest of the house. Do me the grace, Sire, to examine the causes of so long and so unjust a detention, and if Your Majesty does not care to look into the matter himself I beg him most humbly to refer me to my proper judges or to the heads of my family that they might decide whether I deserve so cruel a treatment. Have the kindness, Sire, to revoke the warrant against me so that I might at least enjoy freedom as the sole possession left to me. Here I am barely furnished with the necessities of life and am denied those comforts which might lessen the sorrows and the pains which I have borne for so long and which have weakened my health and exhausted my spirit to such an extent that I have scarcely more strength than I need to conjure Your Majesty in the name of Jesus Christ to make them end. Upon that hope all my faith is set, trusting in the justice of my cause and still more in the justice of Your Majesty, and continuing my wishes and prayers for the prosperity of Your Majesty in arms and for the preservation of His Sacred Person and of all the Royal Family, Cavoy.

The third document, published as early as 1938 in an article by Antoine Adam which appeared in the *Revue d'Histoire de la Philosophie*, was a funeral ode written for Eustache by another inmate of Saint-Lazare, the Comte de Brienne. The poem is not dated, but it was written in a notebook filled with verse which Brienne completed in February 1689. Brienne was a poor poet, but he was not a madman. During his detention at Saint-Lazare, which lasted from 1674 to 1692, the Abbé de Choisy used to visit him regularly to get material for his *Mémoires pour servir à l'Histoire de Louis XIV*. He was a man of exceptional gifts and education, shabbily treated by the King and his own family. As the eldest son of the Secretary of State for Foreign Affairs, he had received his father's charge in reversion only to have it taken from him a few months after he succeeded to the post. He was two years older than Eustache and knew the Cavoyes well. He had been present at the brawl which took place between Lauzun and one of the Cavoyes in 1666 and had lifted his cloak to hide the squabblers from the King. His elegy leaves no doubt about the fate of Eustache Dauger de Cavoye. Imprisoned by his brother and his brother-in-law, ignored by his sister and by the King, he had lived out his life with lunatics and outcasts and had drunk himself to death.

> Here in this coffin at Saint-Lazare lies
> Cavoye, whose saint's name was Eustache,
> An intransigent gent overcome by drink
> And death, which took him by surprise.
> Indolent, surly, disorderly, grim,
> He was the genuine tortoise-type,
> But he stuck his neck out for another drink
> And apoplexy poleaxed him.
> So handsome he looked in his dirty white dress.
> Pity he never would listen to me.
> If he had, at least he'd have lived to die
> A natural death nonetheless.

Since the publication of these three documents, die-hard supporters of the Cavoye theory have done their utmost to invalidate them, claiming that Brienne's poem must have been a forgery and that Cavoye's letters must have been written not from Saint-Lazare but from Pignerol. However, a fourth document, as yet unpublished, which was brought to the author's attention by Stanislas Brugnon, establishes the authenticity of the three published documents as incontrovertible. This final piece of evidence is a letter signed by Louis XIV himself which can be consulted in the register of the King's Orders in the National Archives in Paris. The document reads as follows:

Letter from the King to the General Superior of the House of Saint-Lazare. In the name of the King. Dearly Beloved, We are writing this letter to tell you that it is our intention that M. de Cavoye should have communication with no one at all, not even with his sister, unless in your presence or in the presence of one of the priests of the mission designated by you for that purpose. Let this be done without fail. For such is our desire. Given at Saint-Germain-en-Laye, the 17th day of the month of August 1678. Signed 'Louis' and 'Colbert'.

1.   *not the king*: in 1987, thirteen years after Madame Mast's book appeared in French, this same theory appeared in English in a book by Harry Thompson.

CHAPTER TWELVE

THE MANY FACES OF EUSTACHE DAUGER

If Eustache Dauger was not Eustache Dauger de Cavoye, then who was he? Before Duvivier's authorative but mistaken identification, only two other theories had been proposed. Jules Laire, in his book *Nicolas Fouquet*, published in 1890, had been the first to recognize that the prisoner in the mask of black velvet who died in the Bastille in 1703 was the man called Eustache Dauger arrested in 1669; who Dauger was and what he had done he did not know, and since it was of little significance to his theme he did not bother to follow it up. 'In all likelihood,' he remarked, 'Dauger was the kind of man who takes on a shady job: robbery, abduction, perhaps worse; and whose silence is ensured, once the job is done, by imprisoning him.' He made no attempt to hunt out Eustache Dauger's name in the events which preceded his arrest and it was not until 1931, just one year before Duvivier published his sensational discovery, that Emile Laloy made the first tentative steps in this direction.

From documents, Laloy discovered that 'Daugers' was the name of the King's major-domo in 1652 and that 'Daugé' was the name of the chaplain of the Archbishop of Sens in 1670. Aware that in the orthographical confusion of that time 'Daugers', 'Daugé' and 'Dauger' could have been variant spellings of the same family name, he imagined a young man named Eustache Dauger who was the son of Daugers, the King's major-domo, and nephew of Canon Daugé, the Archbishop's chaplain and who, following in his father's footsteps, was a member of the King's household in 1668 and 1669. The existence of such a person was purely hypothetical, but the events and circumstances which it brought into play were full of possibilities. The Archbishop of Sens was the uncle of Louis de Montespan, whose wife was the celebrated mistress of the King, and Canon Daugé was a tried and trusted friend of the Montespan family; in 1670, Montespan's mother actually named him, along with the Archbishop, executor of her will.

The King's adulterous relationship with Madame de Montespan began in July 1667, but for many months only their most intimate friends knew about it. Montespan himself was in the south of France at the time, engaged, at least ostensibly, in leading his own company of light cavalry against Spanish marauders in the Pyrenees. His troops were little better than brigands and, riding at their head with a shapely peasant-girl wearing breeches and a sword beside him, he terrorized French and Spanish alike, bullying and brawling, drinking and looting. In February 1668, he came to Paris to give his wife power of attorney to handle their affairs in his absence and then hurried back to the south. At that time it was still not realized that Madame de Montespan had become the King's mistress. 'The King loves La Montespan,' the Marquis de Saint-Maurice, who was the Savoyard ambassador at the time, reported to Turin on 3 February. 'She doesn't dislike him, but she holds firm.' Six months later, however, Montespan knew the truth and returned to Paris in a fury. He drove up to Saint-Germain in a hearse with stag's horns on the roof instead of plumes and denounced the King as an adulterer. He slapped his wife in public, insulted anyone he suspected of aiding them in their illicit union, and let it be known that he had deliberately contracted syphillis so that he could pass it on to the King.

It was generally suspected that Montespan had been incited to cause this uproar by his uncle, the Archbishop of Sens, who joined in the attack himself from the pulpit. Preaching at Fontainbleau when the court was there, he denounced a woman in the congregation who was living openly with another woman's husband, made her do public penance and then ordered the church laws on adultery to be published in all the parishes of his diocese. In September, Montespan was arrested and the Archbishop, fearing the same fate, kept to the sanctuary of his cathedral, sleeping in a bed put up for him behind the altar. Montespan was liberated after a couple or weeks, but banished to the south of France and the Archbishop though not arrested was confined to Sens.

The King, it is certain, was greatly alarmed by the furore. Montespan was capable of anything. Presumably he did not know then that his wife was expecting the King's child, but once he did he was certainly reckless enough to abduct his wife, pregnant as she was, or later, after the birth, to abduct the child. If one can imagine Eustache Dauger as a member of the King's household with close ties of loyalty to the Montespan family, one might also imagine him playing spy and agent against the King. No doubt he would have been the one who first informed the Archbishop of the King's adulterous relationship with Madame de Montespan. No doubt he would have discovered eventually that she was pregnant and later that a child had been born in secret. The birth took place in March 1669 and the child was raised in hiding. Perhaps, in the summer of 1669, he managed to find out where the child was hidden, but before he could pass on the information to the Montespan family or while he was himself attempting to abduct the child, he was arrested. Plausible as the story might be, however, there is not a grain of evidence that this particular Eustache Dauger ever existed.

The name 'Eustache Dauger' was in fact 'Eustache d'Auget'; so at least P.M. Dijol would have us believe in the book called *Nabo* which he published in 1978. His Eustache, like Laloy's, was only a valet, but with a face which made him instantly recognizable: he was black. The valet's true name was Nabo, but he was called Eustache because the governor of Dunkirk gave him to his wife on the day of Saint-Eustache; he was called d'Auget because he had been taught to play the guitar by Paul Auget, the Director of the King's Music. Since he was a Moor from North Africa, his guards naturally nicknamed him 'Ali' and since he was a prisoner of consequence they also gave him the title of Marquis; thus he came to be known within the prison walls as the 'Marquis Ali', which on his burial certificate was rendered 'Marchiali'. Dijol is quite sure of all this because his mother-in-law revealed it to him on her death-bed in 1970. She was the last of the Desgranges family, descended from the father-in-law of the youngest son of Saint-Mars, who apparently on his own death-bed had, for some mysterious reason, confided the secret of his mysterious prisoner to the in-laws of his dead son.

Dijol's story, for all its extravagant claims, is based upon a modicum of fact. Nabo the Moor was real enough, and the crime he committed was certainly of sufficient gravity to merit the fate of the Iron Mask. On 16 November 1664, Queen Maria-Teresa, the wife of Louis XIV, gave birth to a black daughter. The child was said to be a month premature and so the usual witnesses were not present. The Grande Mademoiselle in her *Mémoires* reported what she heard about it from Monsieur, who was there: 'that the daughter born to the Queen resembled a little Moor, given her by M. de Beaufort, who was very pretty and who was always with her; that when it had been remembered that her child might come to look like him he had been taken away from her but it was then too late; that the little girl was monstrous and would not live.' The mere presence of the Moor, it was imagined, had made the child turn black. Officially both the Queen and her daughter were very ill. There were no visitors and the child's death was announced on 26 December. What became of the little Moor who 'had been taken away' is not known.

In the popular view, the child's death was only pretended. The Princess Palatine writing in 1719 observed: 'one cannot get it out of people's heads that the child is still living and that she is in a convent at Moret, near Fontainbleau'. This was a reference to the mysterious woman known since as 'the Mooress of Moret'. In 1695 Madame de Maintenon, who married Louis XIV after the death of Maria-Teresa, acted sponsor for a black girl who took the veil at the Benedictine Convent of Moret. The King himself endowed the girl with 20,000 crowns and she took the name of Sister Louis-Marie-Thérèse. Madame de Maintenon visited her regularly thereafter, taking various members of the royal family along with her, and everyone at the convent, including her superiors, treated her with the greatest respect. It was said that she always claimed to be the daughter of the King, even though Madame de Maintenon assured her that she was not.

The little Moor was one of the wedding gifts received by the Queen at Saint Jean-de-Luz in June 1660. He was dwarf just two feet three inches high and, being ten or twelve years old, was presumably fully grown. The Queen was delighted with her pet black dwarf and by October of the same year he was already her favourite companion, riding up beside the coachman of the royal carriage and climbing inside to join her and the King when it was raining. According to Dijol, he had unusual musical talents and because of this was handed over to Paul Auget who taught him to play the guitar. These talents must have been discovered early and developed rapidly because Auget, who was sixty-eight years old, died that same year; although his place as Music Director was taken by the celebrated Lully, it was from the uncelebrated Auget that the Moor took his name.

The Queen bore the King a son in November 1661 and in November 1662 a daughter, who died after two weeks. The King meanwhile had a romantic affair with Madame, his sister-in-law, and then under the pretext of hiding that liaison from his mother and brother began a passionate relationship with Madame's lady-of-honour, Madame de La Vallière. Madame, scorned and furious, turned to the Comte de Guiche for help, and with the Comtesse de Soissons and her lover the Marquis de Vardes sought a means to break up the relationship. Together they decided to send a letter to the Queen as though from her father, the King of Spain, informing her of the King's attachment to Madame de

La Vallière. Vardes composed the letter and Guiche translated it into Spanish. The letter reached the Queen, Dijol asserts, on 17 February 1664. She was so deeply hurt by the news that she turned to her black page for comfort and conceived that day the black daughter who was later known as the Mooress of Moret.

The point of Dijol's story is that the Moor was the father of the Queen's black daughter, something which fortunately for his argument can be accepted without his story. To keep the record straight, however, it should be recognized that the tale, as he tells it, is a concoction. Though such a letter was written and sent, it was not sent at this time and the Queen in any event did not receive it. Guiche went to Poland in September 1663 and did not return to France until June 1664. The letter was sent sometime in 1662 and it was delivered to the Queen's lady-in-waiting, who finding it suspicious took it not to her mistress, but to the King. In 1664, moreover, the Queen was well aware of her husband's affair with Madame de La Vallière. She had known about it as early as November 1662 when she is reported to have pointed out her husband's mistress wearing diamond earrings in a crowd of court ladies. Exactly what the circumstances of the conception were, we do not know but, for what it is worth, it was precisely at this time that the King suddenly decided to change all the Queen's ladies-of-honour.

Dijol would have us believe that the King really did believe that a black man's presence could blacken the skin of a child in the womb and so it was only in June 1666, when the Queen was pregnant again, that he had the Moor removed from the palace. The Queen made such a fuss over losing her pet that the King decided to get rid of him for good. According to Dijol, he sent him to the Company of the Islands of America in Dunkirk, which had a monopoly on the French slave-trade, in the expectation that he would be shipped to America and sold. The president of the company, however, who was the governor of Dunkirk, realized that as a court page the boy had more value in Europe and so kept him for his own household. No one in Paris suspected that the Queen's black page was in Dunkirk until in 1669 preparations were begun for a visit from the King. Madame was to go to Dover in May 1670 to speak with her brother Charles II of England. Louis XIV and his court were to accompany her to Dunkirk and wait there until she returned. In June 1669 someone, sent from Paris to make arrangements for the forthcoming royal visit, recognized the Moor and reported back to Louvois. Afraid that if the boy were allowed to remain he would meet the Queen again, the minister had him arrested and taken off to Pignerol. It was to avoid any possible complications, Dijol concludes, that the governor of Dunkirk was not informed of the arrest.

Saint-Mars must have been surprised to receive a black prisoner since, so Dijol claims, he already had a black man locked up in his prison. La Rivière, the valet of Fouquet, was also black. In February 1661 *La Gazette* reported the baptism of a convert from Islam named La Rivière. He was an African from the Cape Verde Islands, aged about thirty, and his godmother was Madame Fouquet, the mother of the Superintendent of Finance. According to Dijol, La Rivière was a groom at a fashionable riding school in Paris and being a skilful rider was often asked to give lessons to people of rank, including Madame de La Vallière. Towards the end of 1665, when Madame de La Vallière became pregnant, the King was alarmed about the possibility of La Rivière changing the colour of her baby's skin so he rid himself of the man by packing him off to Pignerol with the son of his godmother. Why the King thought it necessary to send the poor man to the far reaches of his kingdom, or why, having chosen to send him so very far away, he did not banish him to some even more distant place – to America for instance where he had given orders to send the Moor – Dijol does not say. Nor does he explain how the King could have decided that a gentleman like Fouquet could be properly served by a man whose job it had been to look after horses.

As it was, when Fouquet died in 1680, the King was once again in difficulties, afraid that some word might reach Paris about the two black valets who were at Pignerol and that the Queen, hearing about them, would have her suspicions aroused. Lauzun knew that Eustache d'Auget was a prisoner, but the true danger lay elsewhere. The Abbé d'Estrades, who as ambassador to Turin had played such an important part in the kidnapping of Matthioli, was the son of Comte Godefroy d'Estrades, the governor of Dunkirk, and therefore had almost certainly met Eustache d'Auget before his arrest. If Lauzun told the Abbé that d'Auget was a prisoner, he might pass on the information to his parents, and through them the secret might reach the Queen. It was to forestall this possibility that Louvois gave orders to pretend that the two black valets had been liberated. Ironically, however, the Abbé d'Estrades already knew that Eustache d'Auget was a prisoner. Apparently he had kept the secret to himself, because Saint-Mars trusted him enough to go on keeping him informed. On 25 September 1681, when Saint-Mars wrote to d'Estrades to inform him of his appointment to Exiles, he included a word about the two black valets as well as about Matthioli: 'I will have in my charge,' he wrote, 'two blackbirds that I have here, who have no other name than the gentlemen of the Lower Tower. Matthioli will stay here with two other prisoners.'

To give Dijol his due, the basic theory he has to offer answers a number of major questions left unanswered by other theoreticians, not least the reason why the mysterious prisoner was obliged to wear a mask. In seventeenth-century France there were so few black men that a state prisoner who was black would have attracted a great deal of attention. His theory also explains why the prisoner was described as 'only a valet' and forbidden to speak of what he had done in the past. As valet to the Queen, he had been responsible, however one cares to view that responsibility, for giving her a black daughter. It is reasonable to presume that, as long as the Queen was alive, the King was concerned to keep her pet's imprisonment secret. Since when she died in 1683 her black daughter was nineteen years of age and no doubt already convinced that she was the daughter of the Queen, it is also logical to suppose that the King thought it wise to continue the imprisonment and the secrecy. One might go further and conclude that if, as seems likely, the King had enough gumption to realize that a black child born to his wife must have been conceived by a black man, then it is even more reasonable to suppose that he would have wished to keep that man locked up and silent for the rest of his life. Unfortunately, however, Dijol's theory raises one problem more difficult than any of the problems it resolves: his candidate for the Iron Mask was a dwarf. If the prisoner in the mask had been only two feet three inches tall, then the witnesses who actually saw him, like Du Junca and the peasants at the Château de Palteau, would certainly have mentioned it. None of them did, of course, and what descriptions do exist are in agreement that on the contrary he was a fine figure of a man, tall and well-built.

According to Pierre-Jacques Arrèse, whose book *The Iron Mask* was published in 1969, it is not the identity of Eustache Dauger which is the important factor in the case, but the secrecy surrounding it. Who he was and what he had done were irrelevant. His significance was invented by the authorities to create the existence of a top-security prisoner whose identity was a mystery; a man unknown whose place could one day be taken by someone else who was well known and could in this way be made to disappear. No doubt he was really just a valet and whatever he had done would normally have got him hanged. He was forbidden to speak about his past, not because it contained some terrible secret, but precisely because it contained nothing of any consequence; such a disclosure would have raised suspicions about the motives of those responsible for the pretence. The plan to use him in this way was worked out and set in motion in the summer of 1669, the date at which he was sent to Pignerol. By that time, the man who was one day to take his place had already been in Pignerol for four and a half years: the man hated and feared alike by Louis XIV and all his ministers: the former Superintendent, Nicolas Fouquet.

Arrèse's theory is thus a revamping of the old theory first presented by Paul Lacroix, and much of his argument is based upon the confusions and uncertainties surrounding Fouquet's death. In his view, it was the death of Eustache Dauger which Saint-Mars reported in the letter he wrote to Louvois on 23 March 1680, and it was then that the minister was told to go ahead with the prepared substitution of one prisoner for the other. Presumably the original plan had been to choose the moment for the exchange and thus create the most favourable circumstances for its success, but Dauger's sudden death left no alternative. The plan had to be adapted to the situation as given, or abandoned altogether. The chief difficulty, so far as the authorities were concerned, was that as soon as Fouquet's death was announced, his family would ask to have the body. This in fact happened and to allay any suspicion it was necessary to grant that permission immediately; however, written authorization was deliberately delayed and did not reach Saint-Mars until nearly four weeks after the death, by which time, Arrèse assumes, the family would not have wished to open the coffin. Thus in spring 1680, Fouquet became the mysterious prisoner known later as the Iron Mask, while Eustache Dauger, the miserable nonentity who had acted the rôle of the original prisoner, was buried in his place.

That the mysterious prisoner arrested in 1669 was 'only a valet' was also the view offered in 1970 by Jean Christian Petitfils in his book *L'Homme au Masque de fer*. His theory was the development of a line of investigation first suggested by Theodore Jung, who ironically was himself unaware that the man he called 'Eustache Dauger, Danger or d'Augers' was the Iron Mask. Petitfils also insisted that the prisoner's name was Danger (or d'Angers) and not Dauger. 'It is because of a reading error made by the first investigators that the majority of historians, without themselves referring to the documents, have called him Eustache Dauger', he maintained, and throughout his book he gave the prisoner's name as Eustache Danger. The argument developed by Petitfils is one of the best recent contributions to the subject, made without sensationalism, trickery or distortion, and, though he often treads ground well-worn by others, the debt he owes to Jung or anyone else is finally minimal.

As other writers before him, Petitfils would have us recognize that there is a difference between the government attitude to the Iron Mask before his stay on Sainte-Marguerite and after. At some stage during the eleven years he was there, he ceased to be the prisoner of consequence he had been, and where once the authorities had shown great anxiety and vigilance on his account, they came to show no particular concern or interest. It is evident for instance from government dispatches that whereas the prisoner's security was a major consideration in the decision to transfer Saint-Mars from Pignerol to

Exiles, it was no longer an important issue when Saint-Mars was invited to move to the Bastille. In fact it is even possible that there was no intention of having Saint-Mars bring his prisoner with him to the Bastille until Saint-Mars himself proposed it.

The difference in treatment of the prisoner before and after Sainte-Marguerite is particularly noticeable in the way he was transported from one prison to another. For the journey to Exiles he was shut up inside a closed litter and for the journey to Sainte-Marguerite in a sedan-chair covered with oil-cloth. On the journey to the Bastille, however, he was merely given a loo-mask to wear and allowed to sit in an open litter with Saint-Mars. Though the journey was much longer than the previous ones, the open litter was not escorted, as were the closed litter and the sedan-chair, by a company of troops; Saint-Mars had no other guard with him than half a dozen members of his prison staff. It was no doubt for this reason that before setting out for Paris he applied for a royal warrant to empower him to requisition lodging for himself and his prisoner en route, but the authorities thought even this precaution excessive. 'His Majesty does not consider it necessary,' Barbezieux informed him on 4 August 1698, 'to issue you with the authorization you request for lodging on your way to Paris. It will suffice for you to lodge and pay as comfortably and securely as you can wherever you judge it appropriate to stay.' Clearly the prisoner's security was no longer a top priority.

The same change of attitude can be found in all matters relating to the prisoner's day-to-day life. Whereas at Pignerol, Exiles and Sainte-Marguerite special high-security cells had to be built for him to ensure that he would be completely sealed off from the world, even from the eyes and ears of the sentries who guarded him, at the Bastille he was lodged like any other prisoner in a normal prison cell. Until he and La Rivière became secret prisoners he was allowed to see a confessor four times a year and after that on strict orders from the minister only once a year; at the Bastille the minister himself imposed no restrictions at all. When he first arrived at Pignerol it was Saint-Mars who took him whatever he needed for the day and later, as a secret prisoner at Exiles and on Sainte-Marguerite, the minister was concerned that only the senior-lieutenant should deputize for Saint-Mars when he was ill or absent. At the Bastille, however, the prisoner was given over entirely to the care of a sergeant.

What happened to alter the prisoner's status is not at all evident. No record exists of any conscious change of attitude directed by a minister. What did change, however, as Petitfils points out, was the actual minister. In July 1691, when the prisoner had been on Sainte-Marguerite for four years, Louvois died and was succeeded by his son,

The government ministers responsible for the Iron Mask's detention. *Left to right*: 1) Louvois, from the prisoner's arrest in 1669 until 1691. Artist unknown. 2) Barbezieux, from 1691 until 1698. After a painting by Mignard. 3) Pontchartrain, from 1698 until 1699. After a painting by Cavin. 4) Chamillart, from 1699 until the prisoner's death in 1703. Engraving by Duflos. (*Photographs Bibliothèque Nationale*).

Barbezieux. It was after this date, Petitfils maintains, that government concern for the prisoner's security declined. Neither Barbezieux before the move to the Bastille, nor Pontchartrain after it, ever showed the kind of obsessive concern that Louvois had always shown. Petitfils is thus brought to the conclusion that Louvois had some personal reason for keeping the prisoner under such tight security.

Under the absolute rule of Louis XIV, Petitfils reminds us, what passed for the will of the King was only too often some minister's interpretation of the King's intention, made according to his own will, and no one abused his ministerial powers more in this regard than Louvois. In his case it even happened that matters of personal interest unrelated to state affairs were conducted in the name of the King. In 1668, for instance, when he wanted to make Sidonia de Courcelles his mistress, he had her husband and Louis de Cavoye, who was her lover, held in prison on a charge for which they had been acquitted. Two years later he contrived to bypass a court order for their release and keep them in prison for another two years. When the lady in question refused nevertheless to become his mistress, he hounded her into prison too, and from there into permanent exile. This, as Petitfils points out with examples of even more outrageous conduct, was not at all an exceptional way for Louvois to behave, and so it is not on the face of it impossible that Eustache was the victim of just such a misuse of power. The official papers relating to his arrest and imprisonment make it clear that apart from Louvois, his father Le Tellier and his confidential agents, Vauroy and Saint-Mars, no one but the King could possibly have known of Eustache's fate; and for the King to have been aware was not even necessary since Louvois had access to royal warrants already signed and sealed in blank. The evidence, such as it is, establishes the fact that Eustache's imprisonment could have been arranged by Louvois for personal reasons and the truth kept hidden from everyone else in the government, including the King.

Louvois knew, and in all likelihood was the only one who did know, the truth of Eustache's identity and crime. He referred to him as 'only a valet' and described his secret as 'how he was employed before coming to Pignerol'; hence Petitfils thinks it reasonable to assume that Eustache had been 'employed' as a 'valet' under circumstances which Louvois wished to hide. Who his master had been was evidently an important part of the secret, and leads one to suppose that if that had been revealed, the crime itself would have been exposed. Presumably the crime was known, and the perpetrator thought to be a valet in the service of someone in particular. Presumably also this valet had escaped capture and had disappeared. A state prison was the last place anyone would have thought to look for such a man and if Eustache was that man then the only motive Louvois could have had for hiding him in such an extraordinary way was that he himself had instigated Eustache to commit the crime.

When Jung wrote about 'Eustache Dauger, Danger or d'Augers', he stated flatly that after all his researches he was sure that 'there exists no trace of this person anywhere.' Then he went on to give what little he had turned up that might be relevant, including a story he claimed to have had from the historian Pierre Clement that there was 'a valet of Colbert who ran away, totally disappeared, and who was accused of having wished to poison his master in 1669.' In fact Clement's reference, which was given in a book entitled *La Police sous Louis XIV*, derives from a note made in 1679 by La Reynie about a possible conspiracy to poison Colbert in 1676. Certainly at that time poisons had been acquired to use against Colbert and for many years he had been suffering from bouts of recurring illness which La Reynie thought might have been the consequence of an earlier attempt to poison him. In his view, the poisons were probably administered by 'a servant who had been bribed and used.' La Reynie gives no date for 'the time when M. Colbert was ill,' but Petitfils, like Jung, traced its first appearance to a much earlier date than 1676.

Throughout the summer and autumn of 1668, Colbert had been in poor health, tortured by repeated attacks of gout, but in December under treatment from the King's own apothecaries his condition began to improve. However, on 27 December he became suddenly ill again with stomach pains as a result of some medicine he had taken. Petitfils would have us believe that it was 'a violent burning of the stomach', but there is in fact no evidence for this. On 28 December Colbert described his own condition thus: 'Today I feel very out of sorts, the result I think of a physic I took yesterday which taxed me very much.' Though after a week or so he appeared to recover, Petitfils claims that the effects of the 'physic' were serious and long-lasting. 'Since I have a weak stomach,' Colbert wrote to one of his brothers in November 1672, 'I have for some time now followed a carefully regulated diet. I eat according to my own schedule and I take only chicken with soup for lunch and in the evening a piece of bread and more soup.' Whether or not it occurred to anyone that the medicine he took on 27 December 1668 was poisoned, the suspicion was not voiced at the time and there was no enquiry. At that time poisoning was thought to be rare in France, the work of foreigners, especially Italians. It was not until seven years later that the Brinvilliers trial gave the first serious hint of an underworld traffic in poison, with murders committed at all levels of French society. One of the chief features of this wave of poisonings was that in many cases the valets and servants of the victims had been bribed or blackmailed to administer the poison.

The absence of a prime minister under Louis XIV caused fierce rivalry amongst his ministers, chief of whom were Colbert, the Controller of Finance, and Le Tellier, the Minister of War. In the struggle for ascendancy, each minister brought his family and friends to power around him, while the King sought to keep the reins of government in his own hands by playing one clan off against the other. It was in 1662, when Louvois was twenty-one, that he became his father's associate and executive in the Ministry of War. He and Colbert were implacable enemies from the start. Saint-Simon, among others, maintains that Louvois was so determined to overthrow Colbert in the King's opinion that he kept up a deliberate campaign to ruin the country's economy, inciting the King to unnecessary extravagance in peace and the army to unnecessary destruction in war. His tactics were only too successful at first. In spring 1667 he was in high favour and Colbert, accused in the King's ear of embezzling 'ten millions a year', was close to disgrace. Since Colbert was the only serious obstacle in his way, it seemed that Louvois at the age of twenty-six was about to realize supreme power. Then, unexpectedly, the wind turned. 'Stories against M. Colbert are still going the rounds,' Saint-Maurice reported home towards the end of 1668, 'but he is completely in favour. M. de Louvois wants to get the better of him and they are at daggers drawn. Something unpleasant is sure to happen to one or the other. M. de Louvois has become unbearable with his abrupt, touchy behaviour. He is rude to everyone who speaks to him.'

The picture of Louvois left by his contemporaries leaves no doubt as to his capacity for murder. According to Saint-Simon, he was in every way 'arrogant, brutal and boorish'. According to La Fare, he was 'savage and bloody', a man 'whose sole aim was to be master' and who was capable of destroying everything around him by his extreme 'ferocity, pride and rashness'. According to the Princess Palatine he was 'hard and brutish'. She thought him 'detestable', called him 'horribly vicious', and claimed that 'it was nothing for him to burn, poison, lie and cheat.' That he had secret contact with the criminal underworld of Paris, including those who dealt in poison and black magic arrested in the late 1670s, is an established fact. According to Primi Visconti, La Voisin, the notorious witch who was the mistress of Le Sage, 'boasted that it was by her art that Madame de Montespan and Louvois kept themselves in favour.' It is by no means inconceivable therefore that in December 1668, when Colbert unexpectedly came back into favour with the King, Louvois should have decided to take advantage of his illness to do away with him. Colbert was a very sick man, worn out by months of suffering. If his illness had taken a sudden turn for the worse and he had died, no one would have suspected foul play.

Thus Petitfils arrives at his hypothesis. Eustache Danger is one of

Colbert's valets, bought by Louvois and furnished by him with poison to use against his master. Danger adds the poison to Colbert's medicine on 27 December 1668, but the dose is not strong enough and Colbert survives. Danger leaves Colbert's service then or soon after, presumably because he is under suspicion for what he has done or as a result of some second attempt in which he failed to get the poison into the medicine. With or without the help of Louvois he then goes into hiding in England, but in July 1669 he believes, or is led to believe, that it is safe to return to France. Louvois, who with or without his knowledge has followed his movements closely, has him arrested and bundled off to prison the moment he lands in Dunkirk. For Louvois it is a great relief to know that the agent of his crime is safely locked up and silenced for ever. If Danger had fallen into the hands of La Reynie and had been made to talk, Louvois would certainly have been incriminated.

Thus Danger, who is 'only a valet', is arrested by a confidential agent of Louvois under circumstances of the greatest secrecy and is then taken all the way across the country to the custody of another of Louvois' confidential agents. He is forbidden to speak to anyone about what he did and is held under conditions of the highest security. Eight months after his arrival, everyone is so curious to know who he is that Saint-Mars has taken to inventing preposterous stories about him. Then to everyone's surprise, just one year after his arrival, Louvois himself decides to go to Pignerol. 'They say that M. de Louvois is going to Pignerol to see what has to be done in that place to improve the fortifications,' reports Saint-Maurice on 25 July 1670, and he continues: 'I hardly think that he would undertake such a long journey in the heat of the summer and that he would separate himself from the person of the King for such a long time just for the supposed fortifications.' At Pignerol, Louvois changes the garrison, giving no reason for his action and taking the precaution of allowing no contact between the newly-appointed officers and those they replace. Presumably the new garrison does not know that in the state prison there is a mysterious prisoner held incommunicado in a specially built cell, and so there is no more curiosity.

Though permission is given for Danger to act as valet to Fouquet, under no circumstances is he to be allowed contact with Lauzun. Since Fouquet was imprisoned more than seven years before the attempt on Colbert's life, he is not likely to know anything about a valet who was under suspicion and, since he was imprisoned by Colbert, he is not likely to feel much concern for Colbert if Danger tells him about it. Lauzun by contrast is, in Saint-Simon's words, a 'long-standing friend' of Colbert and will know his household well enough to recognize

Danger as the suspect valet who disappeared. If Lauzun learns the truth from Danger, he will sooner or later somehow or other get the information to Colbert. Unknown to Saint-Mars and Louvois, however, Lauzun manages to communicate with Fouquet's cell by way of the chimney, makes contact with Danger and discovers the secret.

Lauzun's loyalties being first and foremost to himself, he decides to offer Louvois a deal: his liberty in return for his silence. On 27 January 1680 he writes to Louvois saying that he has information for him which 'is in your interest' to have delivered by 'word of mouth.' It is 'of an importance for you above anything you could imagine' and 'you alone should be informed.' He wants his friend Barrail sent to Pignerol to act as messenger and eventually Louvois agrees. Barrail arrives on 17 March, but as things turn out Fouquet dies while he is there, and Saint-Mars discovers the communicating hole. A full report of the new situation reaches Louvois from Saint-Mars just before Barrail arrives to deliver the message that Lauzun knows all about Danger and will keep the secret to himself only if he is liberated.

Louvois does not reply to Lauzun directly. He tells Saint-Mars to inform him that, since Fouquet is dead, Danger's services are no longer required and so he has been released. Lauzun is thus left to deduce that the story he got from Danger is a ridiculous lie and that Louvois has more serious matters to concern himelf with than his foolish attempt at blackmail. Danger, he is to believe, was not even a prisoner at Pignerol but was, like La Rivière, a simple valet hired to serve a prisoner and paid off when that prisoner died. Louvois is playing a game of bluff and to succeed in it he has to play the game with everyone at Pignerol; thus Danger from then on becomes a secret prisoner to be hidden away as well as silenced. Lauzun, however, is a wily bird and Louvois can never be sure that he has succeeded in deceiving him. A year later, when Lauzun is allowed to leave Pignerol and live under surveillance at Bourbon and Chalon, Louvois has all his mail intercepted, and when finally he is allowed to return to Paris, summons him to a private meeting before he has time to visit Colbert. To everyone's surprise, the two men, hostile to each other though they always have been, stay talking together from half past ten until midnight. What they discuss is not known and no one can possibly imagine. Presumably in the course of their conversation Louvois refers to the story told by Danger and either does a deal with Lauzun or in some devious way contrives to smother any remaining suspicions he might have.

Petitfils acknowledges that his contribution is 'only a hypothesis', but maintains, with no small justification, that 'no other explanation takes better account of the singular features which surround the arrest and imprisonment of Eustache Danger.' It explains, one might add, why later governments were always unable to dig up any information on the prisoner and so fell back on the story of Matthioli. But what it does not explain is why, being the kind of man he was, Louvois chose to give himself so much trouble and anxiety. A knife in Danger's back on a dark street one night and all his problems would have been over. Paris and London were full of men who, for a small fee and no questions asked, would have taken on such a job. If Louvois could hire a valet to assassinate a government minister, he could certainly hire someone to assassinate a valet.

CHAPTER THIRTEEN

THE VALET IN THE FACE-SAVING MASK

'Not even a Hindu god', it has been said of the Iron Mask, 'ever underwent so many transformations, so many incarnations', and looking back at the welter of theories produced so far, the multitude of candidates presented in these pages, it may seem that unless and until more relevant and reliable documents are uncovered the mystery will never be solved. Ill-served though we are, I would nonetheless venture to propose that we already have all the information we need to solve the mystery. I would even suggest that the mask has been lifted many times already but, because those who lifted it could never understand why the face behind it should have been masked in the first place, the mystery has been allowed to continue. It is the mask which fascinates and mystifies us, drawing our attention to the prisoner even while rendering him anonymous, and among all the contradictions which rise to baffle us in the Iron Mask story it is this contradiction at the heart of the mystery, the fact that the masked prisoner was made noticeable by the very means used to hide his identity, that none of the theories advanced so far has ever been able to resolve. My own theory does not pretend to answer all the questions posed, but this particular contradiction it does explain. Illogical as it may seem, I suggest that the prisoner known to the world as the Man in the Iron Mask was a nonentity whose face without the mask would have meant nothing to anyone and, irrational as it may seem, I suggest that the mystery surrounding him, including the fact that he was once even made to wear an actual mask of steel, was the fabrication pure and simple of his gaoler Saint-Mars.

Little is known about the prisoner but, though for the moment we cannot say much about who he was, we can say a great deal about who he was not. He was not for instance Eustache Dauger or Eustache d'Auget. His name was Danger or d'Angers, as Petitfils maintained back in 1970. Most theorists since that time, like Mast and Dijol, have ignored this claim but, at the International Symposium on the Iron Mask held in Cannes in 1987, Bernard Caire removed all remaining doubt on the matter with an analysis of the handwriting of the original warrants and dispatches. Furthermore, this man called Danger was neither well-born nor well-known. For all his importance as a prisoner, he was not in himself a person of any significance. The fact that Louvois described him as 'only a valet', that Saint-Mars thought he would make 'a fine valet' for Lauzun, that he was given to Fouquet 'as a servant' and 'to serve as a valet', and that La Rivière was described as 'his colleague', is evidence enough: in seventeenth-century France only a valet would have been required, or indeed prepared, to act as a valet.

If further proof of the prisoner's humble condition is needed, it is not lacking. When in July 1669 Louvois told Saint-Mars to make ready for Danger's arrival he was quite specific about the man's social status: 'you will prepare the furniture necessary', he wrote, 'taking note of the fact that since the prisoner is only a valet he will need nothing of any significance', and later, when Saint-Mars moved Danger from Exiles to Sainte-Marguerite, he informed Louvois that all the prisoner's belongings including his bed had been so old and broken that they had not been worth the expense of transporting them. By contrast the overall cost of what furniture, linen and clothes were judged necessary to prepare a prison apartment for a gentleman like Lauzun amounted to more than 4,000 livres and included the provision of 460 livres worth of table-silver and such things as twelve lace nightcaps, four pairs of gloves and a Bergamo tapestry. In 1681, when Danger and La Rivière were the only prisoners Saint-Mars had, Louvois wrote to him: 'You may buy new clothes for your prisoners, but clothes for that kind of people should be expected to last three or four years.' For Danger's upkeep at Pignerol, Saint-Mars was allowed 4 livres per day and at Exiles 5 livres per day, the same as for La Rivière; the allowance he was given merely for feeding Lauzun and his servant amounted to 20 livres per day. Just to provide Lauzun with sheets and towels cost the equivalent of Danger's entire upkeep for more than four months[1].

It has been argued that if Danger had been only a valet, the authorities would not have wasted so much time and money keeping him in prison. A valet, as Pagnol put it, 'could have been hanged in five minutes with a rope for forty sous'; but Pagnol was wrong. Though the power of Louis XIV and his ministers was supreme, it was nonetheless governed by law and there was no place in the legal order for them to save government time and money by killing people. As it was, La Rivière, who was certainly nothing but a valet, was not killed when it was discovered that he knew too much, and Matthioli's valet, who was kidnapped to stop him talking about the circumstances of his master's disappearance, was not killed either. Both were kept in prison, like Danger at a cost of 5 livres per day, La Rivière until his death from dropsy seven years later and Matthioli's valet until his death more than fifteen years later.

The valet Eustache Danger was certainly the prisoner who ended his days wearing a mask in the Bastille in November 1703, but when he was arrested and imprisoned in August 1669 there was no concern to hide his face. Captain de Vauroy was simply ordered to arrest him on sight and take him immediately to Pignerol where Saint-Mars was ordered 'to keep him under safe custody preventing him from communicating with anyone by word of mouth or in writing.' The order for reimbursement issued to Vauroy for his journey from Dunkirk to Calais and from there to Pignerol makes it clear that he had with him only three constables to serve as escort and that the group travelled on horseback by regular roads, stopping to eat and sleep and change horses at the ordinary post-houses along their way. The danger to the State which the prisoner represented was real enough, but it had nothing to do with his face. He knew something which the authorities were afraid he might reveal and he was arrested and imprisoned to stop him talking. 'You must make sure,' Louvois warned Saint-Mars, 'that the windows are so placed that they do not give on to anywhere accessible to anyone and that there are enough doors closing one upon the other that the sentries will not be able to hear anything. You personally must take the wretch whatever he needs for the day once a day and you must never listen to anything he tries to tell you, no matter what the pretext might be.' The following month, the prisoner was allowed the services of a doctor and of a priest, and still the only concern voiced by Louvois was that he should 'speak to no one'. That the doctor or the priest would see his face was a matter of no significance at all and later, when he was allowed to leave his cell to serve Fouquet and even to walk with him in the citadel, the question of hiding his face was never raised.

What Danger's secret knowledge was we do not know. It was something which the authorities believed Fouquet could be trusted with, but not Lauzun. Louvois writing to Fouquet about the risk of Danger revealing the secret to others declared: 'you know how important it is that no one has knowledge of what he knows', and according to Bernard Caire the secret was something which Danger had seen. In the letter from Louvois to Fouquet 'regarding what Eustache may have said of his past life to his colleague', Louvois asked 'if the man named Eustache, given to you as a servant, has not spoken in front of your other valet of how he was employed before coming to Pignerol.' From an examination of the original first draft of this letter Caire discovered that the minister had first dictated 'of what he had seen', then changed his mind, had the clerk cross it out and write in its place 'of how he was employed'. As things are, we know precious little about the secret and even that little is not without its contradictions; for all the concern to stop Lauzun discovering what it was, it was something which apparently he could nevertheless be persuaded not to believe.

In April 1680 the security measures surrounding Danger were changed. La Rivière, suspected of having learned whatever forbidden knowledge it was that had cost Danger his liberty, lost his liberty too. Both became secret prisoners, their names suppressed in all subsequent correspondance, while word was put about in Pignerol that they had been released. The reason for this change was the discovery made by Saint-Mars at the time of Fouquet's death that Lauzun had been visiting Fouquet in secret and so had probably met and talked with Danger. The purpose of the subterfuge was to deceive Lauzun into believing that Danger, like La Rivière, had never been more than an ordinary valet, engaged at Pignerol to serve Fouquet, and that in consequence any revelations he might have made were pure inventions. Presumably the increased security around Danger included the precaution that his face should not be seen, but it was a measure which applied equally to La Rivière. Moreover it was necessary only for so long as Lauzun or anyone capable of informing him was in a position to discover that the two valets had not been set free. In April 1681, Lauzun was released from Pignerol; the following September Saint-Mars left for Exiles with the two secret prisoners, hidden 'in a litter' by order of Louvois; and in the following November, the crisis over, Louvois informed Saint-Mars that once again he could allow his prisoners the services of a doctor and of a priest. Far away from Lauzun and his friends at Pignerol, the security measures surrounding the prisoners could become the same as they had been for Danger at the time of his arrest and the only concern voiced by the minister thereafter was that they should be 'unable to speak with anyone not only from outside but even from among the garrison of Exiles.'

Since Danger and La Rivière had been secret prisoners at Pignerol, it was important that they should not be recognized when they left for Exiles and it was for this reason that Louvois ordered Saint-Mars to have them 'leave the citadel of Pignerol in a litter'. So far as the minister was concerned, the use of a litter was quite sufficient to meet the demands of the situation. This form of conveyance was a box-like structure built on a framework like a stretcher with shafts front and back to which horses or mules were harnessed. Being curtained with leather or oilcloth, it could easily be kept closed from the outside. Moreover, since it was a common means of transport at the time, it was not likely to attract undue attention; and as it happened it appears to have attracted no attention at all. According to Ettore Patria, who contributed a study of the Exiles period to the Cannes Symposium in 1987, no one in the region of Exiles had the least suspicion that Saint-Mars had brought any prisoners with him; and the Savoyard governor of nearby Susa, who kept his superiors in Turin constantly informed on what was happening over the border, of the doings of the French in general and of Saint-Mars in particular, did not at any time realize that there were prisoners in the fort.

In all the time Saint-Mars was governor of Exiles, nothing happened to trouble the security of his two prisoners and the simple directive in force when they arrived, 'that no one should be able to communicate with them', remained unchanged, reiterated by Louvois in almost identical form from year to year. And yet, though the security status of the two prisoners did not change in the five and a half years they were there, it was during the transfer from Exiles to Sainte-Marguerite that the secret prisoner, who we know was 'only a valet', became the mysterious prisoner known to the world as the Man in the Iron Mask. In January 1687 La Rivière died, in the following month Saint-Mars went to Sainte-Marguerite to make a tour of inspection and in April it was common knowledge in the region of Cannes that a mysterious prisoner of great importance was going to be brought to the island. In May the prisoner arrived in a sedan-chair on the shoulders of four porters who, in relay with four others, had carried him over mountain roads for twelve days, and in September it was reported in Paris that the prisoner in the chair had arrived 'with a steel mask on his face'. What had happened to transform Danger from being one of the two secret prisoners in a litter who arrived in Exiles unnoticed in September 1681 into being the well-publicized sensation he was on his arrival at Sainte-Marguerite in May 1687 has nothing to do with any order issued by Louvois. The idea of using a sedan-chair and a mask of steel was the responsibility solely and simply of his gaoler Saint-Mars and he chose to transport his wretched prisoner in that way not for reasons of state, but for reasons of his own. To understand how Saint-Mars could have become capable of such a thing, a brief recapitulation is necessary.

It was no secret in Pignerol that Saint-Mars had been sent from Paris to take charge of a prison where there was only one prisoner. Pignerol was no ordinary prison. It had been upgraded to a state prison under the command of Saint-Mars for the sole purpose of guarding Fouquet and when after four and a half years Saint-Mars received another prisoner, the assumption was naturally made that the second prisoner was as extraordinary as the first. On 31 August 1669, just one week after Eustache Danger's arrival, Saint-Mars reported to Louvois that 'many people here believe he is a Marshal of France and others say a President'. Word got out that transformations were being made in the Lower Tower to provide a special high-security cell for this new prisoner and Saint-Mars, finding himself the focus of everyone's interest, enjoyed the attention. On 12 April 1670 he wrote to Louvois: 'There are sometimes people who are so curious to know about my prisoner and why I am having such fortifications built for his security, that I am obliged to tell them preposterous stories to make fun of them.' Who the secret prisoner was, no one could say, but two and a half years after his arrival the belief that the state prison of Pignerol was reserved for prisoners of only the highest rank and importance seemed confirmed by the arrival of a third prisoner, every bit as exceptional as the first: the King's favourite, Lauzun. Judging by what evidence there was, it seemed reasonable to assume that the mysterious prisoner was someone of birth, position and influence who could count on powerful supporters to attempt his liberation.

Saint-Mars knew differently. The secret prisoner was 'only a valet'. His importance lay not in anything he was, but in something he knew. No doubt it struck Saint-Mars as ironical that, while his two other prisoners were served by valets, he personally was obliged to fetch and carry for this man who was 'only a valet'. But apart from occasional bouts of illness, Danger gave no trouble. Unlike the prisoners of rank, he was meek and acquiescent. Indeed he was so obedient and sensible that in February 1672 Saint-Mars thought he could trust him enough to put him with Lauzun as valet and spy. Louvois did not approve of the idea, but Saint-Mars saw little sense in trying to persuade valets to serve in his prison when one of his prisoners was actually a valet and eventually in January 1675 he won the minister's approval to have Danger act valet to Fouquet. Seven years later in the isolation of Exiles, he must have pondered with amazement the strange turn of fate which had transformed him from the commander of the state prison of Pignerol, the celebrated keeper of Fouquet and Lauzun, into the governor of a run-down fortress in the middle of nowhere, the gaoler of two wretched valets.

The name Saint-Mars was the sword-name of Benigne d'Auvergne, assumed by him when as a boy of fourteen he was enrolled as an army cadet. Both his parents died when he was a child and he was raised by an uncle, Gilles de Biot de Blainvilliers, who packed him off to the army at the age of twelve. In 1650, when he was twenty-four, he was given a place in the First Company of the King's Musketeers and, though he was thirty-four before he was promoted corporal and thirty-eight before he was made sergeant, he could flatter himself that to achieve rank at all in the Musketeers, where every man was a gentleman, was a mark of some distinction for a man with neither birth nor money behind him. It was as a sergeant that, in December 1664, he was appointed governor of the State Prison of Pignerol and he was recommended for that post by the commander of his company, d'Artagnan, who recognized in him all the qualities necessary for a gaoler. He was the perfect subordinate, ready to carry out the orders of his superiors no matter how arbitrary, and to the letter, without question, hesitation or scruple. He was moreover a man who knew his place in society and the place of others, the rights and duties of class and office: an ideal warden for prisoners of rank. As it happened, the honours and responsibilities of his new post brought out the worst in him as well as the best; he was vain, ambitious, ruthless and rapacious, but his masters quickly came to believe that he could be kept in line and firmly handled so long as they valued his services and proved it with hard cash.

Soon after his arrival in Pignerol, he became friendly with a certain Damorezan who was the military commissioner there and a trusted agent of Louvois. Damorezan had married the daughter of an apothecary named Collot who had two other daughters, as beautiful by all accounts as they were stupid. Saint-Mars married one and a secretary of Louvois, named Dufresnoy, married the other. After this union in triplicate of the Collot sisters with Louvois men, Damorezan, Dufresnoy and Saint-Mars, it was not altogether a surprise when one of the sisters went on to union with Louvois himself. In 1670, Madame Dufresnoy became the mistress of her husband's master and, since her husband was accommodating, everyone in the family, including Saint-Mars, could reap the benefit. Four years later, Louvois had the woman of his bed created Lady of the Queen's Bed, which for all the smothered laughter it produced at court, gave her immense standing and influence. She was flattered on all sides and responded, according to La Fare, 'with all the insolence that can be derived from beauty and prosperity when combined with low birth and limited intelligence.'

The 24th of August 1669 was a providential day for Saint-Mars: he received not only the custody of Eustache Danger, but also possession of the Château de Palteau. An uncle, Cantien Garrot, died that day and left him both the château and the governorship of Sens. Fortune chose to make Saint-Mars a man of substance, but a wise man will make more opportunities than he finds. Within ten years of his appointment to Pignerol, he had exploited every possible channel for advancement and had made himself not only rich but noble. As well as being governor of Pignerol prison and a sergeant in the Musketeers, he had half a dozen lucrative positions as non-resident governor of towns and forts elsewhere in France and was captain of his own Free Company. It was to be expected that on top of his regular salary and frequent bonuses he would, like all other gaolers, make money out of the allowances supplied for his prisoners, but he quite surpassed all precedent in the field. With prisoners of rank, where the allowance for food alone was in the region of 7,000 livres a year, there was a great deal of money to be made, but no sum however petty was too small for Saint-Mars to pass up, and he stole from all his prisoners, even those with a minimum allowance. What the authorities objected to was not this, however, but his continual attempts to gain even more from the government by claiming false expenses. Louvois indulged his greed with enormous gifts of money and even so was obliged to admonish him repeatedly for cheating on his day-to-day accounts. By 1673, he had enough property to apply for and receive letters of nobility.

The driving force behind Saint-Mars was not a need to make money, however. No doubt at the beginning a fear of poverty played some part in his voracious appetite, but the desire to enjoy the wealth he amassed played no part at all. Throughout his life he never spent more than a few days in the magnificent house he owned at Palteau, nor on any of the other estates he managed to acquire. He lived out his life in prisons, a virtual prisoner himself, and preferred to finish his days in the Bastille rather than in Palteau. What impelled him to make money, and to go on making money when he was already rich, was the desperate and deluded belief that a man of substance is a man of standing; his striving for wealth became an obsession as a direct consequence of his frustrated need for prestige. 'My lord,' he wrote to Louvois on 27 February 1672, 'I take the liberty to inform you that what could make me live here in health would be a little honour. I have been a sergeant for so long that I am the doyen of the lot . . . If you don't have the kindness, my lord, to remind His Majesty of my seniority, I will die what I am.' To quieten him, Louvois sent a bonus of 6,000 livres by return post, but money was not enough and on 18 December 1675 Saint-Mars repeated the same plea: 'I beg you in grace, my lord, to accord me some mark of honour or else allow me to go and break my head in the army.' Again Louvois put him off with a large sum of money, but in the following year a promotion was finally granted. To be elevated to the rank of Second Lieutenant in the Musketeers was certainly an honour, but, when the recipient had been made to wait until the age of fifty, it must have seemed too little and too late. Honour was a good deal more difficult to acquire than money and unhappily for Saint-Mars there

The Château de Palteau, seat of the estate which Saint-Mars owned but never occupied, as it is today. It was here that Saint-Mars stopped for the night with his prisoner on his way to the Bastille in September 1698, and the peasants saw that 'whenever the prisoner crossed the courtyard he had the black mask on his face'. *Inset:* Saint-Mars interrogates Renneville at the Bastille in 1702. Illustration from *L'Inquisition Française*, published in 1715. (*Photograph Bibliothèque Nationale*)

were honours of rank and status which no amount of money could buy.

Saint-Mars, the self-made man, was far and away the most influential member of his family, as is proved by the fact that so many of his relatives turned to him for a job. When he took up the post at Pignerol, he brought with him two cousins, both former musketeers, to serve as his lieutenants, one of whom was Blainvilliers, the son of his guardian. Later when he had established himself he found positions in the prison guard for two of his nephews, sons of his sister Marguerite, who had married a man of little means by the name of Eloi de Formanoir de Corbé. He stayed at Pignerol for sixteen years during which time his wife bore him two sons, the eldest of whom had Louvois for godfather.

In the eyes of his own family and the lowly creatures he employed, Saint-Mars was all that he wished to be, a member of the wealthy and powerful élite, but, in the eyes of the élite, he was an upstart. The governor-general of the city of Pignerol, himself a marquis, resented the fact that such a low-born, low-grade officer was not answerable to him, and so refused to accept him in society. The snub hurt Saint-Mars where he felt it most, his inflated self-esteem, but taking the stand that at Pignerol he was no-one's subordinate served to give him standing of a kind anyway; and as things turned out, for his last three years at Pignerol he was in his element. The French acquisition of Casale, with all the complications which that entailed, brought him into close relationship with men of mark like d'Estrades and Catinat, and the opening of the prison to the families and friends of Fouquet and Lauzun brought him into regular contact with visitors of quality. At his request, Louvois even authorized him to play host to these visitors and have them dine with Fouquet and Lauzun at his own table in the company of Madame de Saint-Mars. To all appearances he had made the grade, had become a man of position and influence, accepted by people of birth and breeding, and he enjoyed the rôle immensely.

In retrospect, those were palmy days. Exiles by contrast was a grim, isolated spot where he felt neglected, thwarted and depressed. Technically, in his new job, he was the governor of a fort not a prison, but the fort was too far behind the frontier and the times to have any military significance. Without prisoners of rank to give him importance, without friends of rank to give him reassurance, he lacked direction and purpose. He did not like anything about the Exiles job, except the money, and his health as well as his spirits suffered. Dufresnoy, the accommodating husband, thrived meanwhile, but not Damorezan. Like Saint-Mars, he had been swindling the government for every penny he could get, and in 1683 a warrant was issued for his arrest on a charge of embezzlement. Fortunately for him, Louvois tipped him off in time and he was able to take refuge with Saint-Mars before escaping to Turin. After the achievement and promise of Pignerol, Exiles was a wretched and humiliating anticlimax. Anyone else in such a post, aged almost sixty as Saint-Mars then was, would have recognized that he had been put out to grass, but Saint-Mars pestered his superiors for a better post and even sent his wife to Paris to petition Louvois on his behalf.

The transfer to Sainte-Marguerite was a merciful reprieve, and Saint-Mars exploited it at once and to the full. From the moment he arrived on the island to carry out his preliminary inspection, he sought to make up the ground he had lost at Exiles by impressing everyone with a show of his importance. The secrecy and security surrounding Danger had once intrigued and excited the people of Pignerol. Their curiosity had been aroused by circumstances beyond the control of Saint-Mars, but he had enjoyed the attention it brought him, the aura of mystery and significance he acquired as the secret prisoner's keeper. On Sainte-Marguerite that situation was repeated, but this time because Saint-Mars deliberately aroused that curiosity, spreading stories about his prisoner's importance before anyone had any reason to know that the man even existed. Tourists like the Abbé Mauvans, stopping off at the island while the prisoner was still actually at Exiles, heard all about the 'unknown prisoner' who was to be 'transported with such great precaution' and who would get 'a pistol-ball in the head' if ever he tried 'to speak out his name'. They also heard about the new prison which was being built for him 'connected to the governor's lodging' so that the governor himself would 'be almost his only gaoler and guard'.

As implied in this version of things, the important thing about the prisoner was his identity and, since the authorities were prepared to kill him if he attempted to reveal his name, there was every reason to believe that his identity was one which even ordinary people could be expected to know. Such an impression of the prisoner's importance was altogether false. In the first place it was not true that there was an order to kill him if he should try to reveal his name. The only government order with any resemblance to this pretence was given at the time of the prisoner's arrival at Pignerol when Louvois warned Saint-Mars that he must 'threaten to kill him' if ever he tried to speak about anything other than the bare necessities of life; as it was the prisoner had gone on to reveal his secret to Fouquet, La Rivière and Lauzun without suffering any such dire consequence. Moreover, the name Eustache Danger would have meant nothing to anyone anyway, except perhaps Lauzun, and it was not even certain that seven years after his last meeting with him Lauzun would have remembered the name of a mere valet. Even before moving to Sainte-Marguerite with his prisoner, Saint-Mars had the people of the region agog with expectation, convinced that his prisoner was someone of such fame and consequence that the authorities would stop at nothing to conceal his identity; and in May, when finally he arrived with his prisoner, he staged a show sensational enough to satisfy those expectations.

To transport Danger from Exiles, the most discreet form of conveyance would have been a litter, as demonstrated by its success for the journey to Exiles, but Saint-Mars wanted something else. 'I think the most secure mode of transport for conducting him to the islands would be a sedan-chair covered in oilcloth,' he wrote to Louvois. 'It will be less troublesome than a litter which can often get broken.' Outside of major cities, the use of sedan-chairs was in effect, albeit not in principle, restricted to people of only the highest rank, but Louvois, having no reason to suspect that Saint-Mars would be anything but discreet, did not object. In all probability he assumed that it was his intention to escape notice by avoiding main roads and towns and there was no doubt that a sedan-chair would have been more manageable than a litter on small roads or cross-country. In the event, however, Saint-Mars chose to go by main roads and through main towns, stopping two days in Briançon and long enough in Grasse for the prisoner's appearance to make such an impression that tales of 'the guise under which he was seen' were reported to the Abbé Mauvans. If in the region of Cannes any doubts had remained that the fort of Sainte-Marguerite was to receive a prisoner of the highest importance, they were dispelled the moment the prisoner arrived in Grasse, carried in a sedan-chair by two teams of porters who, so far as anyone could discover, had carried him all the way from Pignerol. Far from trying to pass with his prisoner unnoticed, as presumably Louvois supposed he would, Saint-Mars had done everything to draw attention to him and give the impression that he was both famous and noble.

Nor was that all. At the International Symposium held in Cannes in 1987, Stanislas Brugnon produced a document which until that time had been unknown to investigators of the Iron Mask mystery. A letter, unsigned but thought to be by Louis Fouquet, the Bishop of Agde, and written from Paris on 4 September 1687, a mere three months after the arrival of Saint-Mars and his prisoner at Sainte-Marguerite, it gives news of that arrival in even more sensational terms than those reported by the Abbé Mauvans:

> Monsieur de Cinq-Mars (sic) has by order of the King transported a state prisoner from Pignerol to the island of Sainte-Marguerite. No-one knows who he is: there is an interdiction on speaking his name and an order to kill him if he should pronounce it . . . He

was enclosed in a sedan-chair with a steel mask on his face, and all that one could learn from Cinq-Mars is that this prisoner was at Pignerol for many years and that all the people one believes to be dead are not.

Until this letter was uncovered by Brugnon, it was generally believed that the mask of iron was a myth invented or at least popularized by Voltaire. Now we know that it was not a myth at all, that Saint-Mars made use of just such a mask when he moved his prisoner from Exiles to Sainte-Marguerite. It seems scarcely imaginable that Saint-Mars could have gone so far in his pretence as to make the valet Danger wear a mask of steel, and yet this letter leaves no doubt about it. That Louvois could have ordered Saint-Mars to draw attention to his wretched prisoner in such a spectacular way is not within the realms of possibility. If hiding his face had indeed been necessary, then a sack pulled over his head would have done the job just as well, but that we know was not the real purpose of the mask. Saint-Mars had received no order telling him to hide the prisoner's face. The only concern ever voiced by Louvois was that the prisoner should be kept from speaking to anyone. If for extra security he had chosen to recommend anything at all it would have been a gag, not a mask. The idea of masking the prisoner was a ploy thought up by Saint-Mars to advertise the supposed secret of his prisoner's identity, and he chose to do it in such a theatrical way because he knew a steel mask would have greater impact on those who saw it than would a normal mask. From the suspense-publicity mounted before ever the prisoner left Exiles to the shock appearance of the star-product himself, with the altogether convincing sight of a sedan-chair and the altogether stupefying glimpse of a mask of steel, Saint-Mars conducted his campaign with all the flash and flair of a modern promoter. No wonder his invention, created to impress his public in 1687, survived as myth to bamboozle the public ever after.

Three days after reaching the island, Saint-Mars wrote to Louvois to announce that all was well. In fact his prisoner had been almost suffocated and rendered even more ill than usual by twelve days of sedan-chair and steel mask, but Saint-Mars was still enjoying the triumph of his new-found image. His choice of words betrays him: 'I can assure you, my lord, that no one in the world saw him and that the way in which I guarded and conducted him throughout the journey left everyone guessing as to who my prisoner could be.' One must suppose that Louvois, reading these words, imagined that Saint-Mars had expressed himself badly, but we know that what he said was an accurate description of the situation he had gone to such pains to create.

The way he had guarded and conducted his prisoner had indeed set everyone guessing as to who he might be, and later he could not resist revealing the high success of his endeavour. 'Throughout the province,' he wrote to Louvois in January 1688, 'they say that my prisoner is M. de Beaufort or that he is the son of the late Cromwell.'

Years before in Pignerol, when people had been curious to know why a special cell was needed for Danger, Saint-Mars had amused himself by telling 'preposterous stories' about him and one can only wonder whether a new batch of 'preposterous stories' was not responsible for this particular rumour that his prisoner was the Duc de Beaufort. The letter uncovered by Brugnon states quite specifically that Saint-Mars not only said that his prisoner had spent many years in Pignerol, but also implied that he was someone whom everyone believed to be dead. The Duc de Beaufort had disappeared at the siege of Candy just two months before Danger had been imprisoned at Pignerol, and rumours that Beaufort was not dead but in prison were still circulating at court as late as 1682. As a preposterous story it was not after all so preposterous, and Saint-Mars would have been aware of the possible deductions people were likely to make on the strength of such a suggestion. That the former keeper of Fouquet and Lauzun should also be the keeper of Beaufort was not in itself impossible; and Beaufort, being grandson of the King's royal grandfather and himself 'King of the Market', was certainly noble enough and famous enough to be the mysterious prisoner who was treated in such an exceptional manner – masked with steel and carried all the way from Pignerol, a distance of more than 200 miles, in a sedan-chair. It was Lamotte-Guérin, the successor of Saint-Mars on Sainte-Marguerite, who assured Lagrange-Chancel that the prisoner was Beaufort.

For a man as vain and ambitious as Saint-Mars, however, bluffing his way to the admiration and deference of the people around him was not enough. His dream was to be what he once had been, the keeper of prisoners of rank and consequence who were known to be in his charge; men of fame and former power living on in the faded gold of lost privilege and office, who received visits from their still gilded families and friends; who, though out of favour, retained influence and sympathy at court, who got themselves and their gaoler talked about; and who, knowing where their immediate best interests lay, were ready to flatter their gaoler with the consideration and respect he yearned to have. Following the orders of Louvois, he set about building new prison cells and in January 1688, when they were finished, he wrote to Louvois to describe them: 'They are large, handsome and well-lit, and as for their excellence as prisons I do not think there could be any safer and sounder in Europe. This is especially so with regard to the danger of prisoners communicating orally with someone nearby or far off, and that could never be said for any of the places where I had charge of M. Fouquet after his arrest.' The reference to Fouquet is significant; Saint-Mars had space for another prisoner and was reminding the minister of his past glory in the hope that he would trust him with another prisoner of rank. 'With relatively few precautions one can even have prisoners taking walks about the island without fear that they might escape or pass messages.' Since only prisoners of rank would ever be allowed such a privilege, the hint was obvious. 'I take the liberty, my lord, to inform you in detail of the excellence of this place in the eventuality that you may have prisoners you wish to keep in complete security but with a reasonable degree of freedom.' Saint-Mars could exploit the mystery of Danger to give himself an appearance of importance, but to re-live the great days of Pignerol he needed more prisoners like Fouquet and Lauzun.

It would be wrong to underestimate the concern for Danger's security, which was shown by those responsible for his arrest and imprisonment, the fact that he was kept incommunicado from the beginning and, after his contact with Lauzun, incognito as well; the fact too that having been given in custody to Saint-Mars there seemed to be no question, at least until 1698, of entrusting him to anyone else. But it would be equally wrong to overestimate his importance with the claim that Saint-Mars built a special prison on Sainte-Marguerite to accommodate him and that it cost a great deal of money. That prison was certainly special, though it cost no more than the regular yearly allowance which Saint-Mars received for feeding a prisoner of rank like Fouquet or Lauzun, and it was not made solely for him. Saint-Mars initially constructed two cells and then added four more, all of which shared the same exceptional features of security. It was a model prison, deliberately planned by Saint-Mars, and possibly even intended by the minister, to serve for future prisoners of rank. As things turned out, however, those hopes for a prisoner of fame never materialised and that was at least partly the reason why there did materialise the fame of the prisoner known later as the Iron Mask.

Though the move to Sainte-Marguerite was for Saint-Mars a happy deliverance, it came too late. He was already sixty-one years of age and, when after a few years it became clear that the only other prisoners he was going to get were Protestant ministers and old lags from Pignerol, his aspirations for the future became centred upon his sons. For both boys he planned army careers and, as they came of age, he bought them commissions in the Dragoons. Such was the wealth that he had amassed, wheedling his superiors and cheating his prisoners, that he could afford to launch them well. In 1693, however, his eldest son, aged twenty-two and already a lieutenant-colonel, was killed in action and his youngest son, still only seventeen, was seriously wounded. Four years later his wife died, and when in the following year he was offered the most prestigious prison-command in France, the governorship of the Bastille, he hesitated to take it. He was too old to change his ways, too old to benefit from such an accolade. Through all the years of waiting he had bluffed and bought his way to an appearance of importance which he had been prepared to settle for. Not that he was wiser and more content. On the contrary, his urge to make money had become a compulsion and Barbezieux was able to persuade him to take the job by a description of the fabulous revenues it carried: over 21,000 livres per year for himself and whatever prison staff he employed, the amount he paid to them being left completely to his own discretion, and on top of that, to use the minister's own words, 'the profit normally made on what is given for the upkeep of the prisoners, which being what it is, cannot be anything but considerable'.

For Danger, in the meantime, the years spent on Sainte-Marguerite, eleven of them in all, were dragged out with no apparent change. He continued to live in solitary confinement, having contact with no one except Saint-Mars and his lieutenants, a doctor when he was ill and at set times a confessor. However, though the minister's orders regarding his custody did not change, the minister himself did and the consequences of that were significant. On 16 July 1691 Louvois died and was succeeded by his son Barbezieux who had been only two years old at the time of Danger's arrest and clearly did not care to lose sleep over an old problem which to all intents and purposes had been resolved. For instance, in his view, Danger was less important than at least one, if not all, of the prisoners who were then at Pignerol: Dubreuil, Herse,[2] Matthioli and Matthioli's valet. On 20 March 1694, when preparations were being made to move these prisoners to Sainte-Marguerite, he wrote to Saint-Mars: 'since you know that they are more important, at least one of them, than those who are at present on the islands, you must give them priority and put them in the most secure of your prison cells.' The only occasion on which Barbezieux ever showed concern over Danger was in 1697 when he was annoyed to hear that Pontchartrain, the Controller of Finance, had been questioning Saint-Mars about his prisoners and the reasons why they had been arrested. In fact he was not upset because of any risk this might have posed to Danger's security; he simply resented the interference of another minister in his domain. As it was, Saint-Mars was at that time answerable to Pontchartrain for a number of prisoners in his charge, those arrested as Protestants, and in the event he became answerable to Pontchartrain for all his prisoners, including Danger, when he moved to the Bastille the following year.

Danger's importance in the eyes of the authorities in Paris diminished so much in the time he was on Sainte-Marguerite that, when in 1698 they offered Saint-Mars the post of governor of the Bastille, the idea of transferring him too did not occur to them. Saint-Mars received the offer in a letter from Barbezieux written on 1 May and he replied on 8 May. This reply is now lost, but from what Barbezieux said when he in turn replied on 15 June it seems reasonable to deduce that, along with his acceptance of the post, Saint-Mars pleaded the importance of his longtime prisoner and the necessity of transferring him as well. 'I have been a long time replying to the letter which you took the trouble to write to me on the 8th of last month,' Barbezieux explained, 'because the King did not inform me of his intentions sooner. You can make your dispositions to be ready to leave when I instruct you to do so, and (you can)³ bring with you your longtime prisoner under safe guard.'

The fact that the King took a month to grant his permission gives reason to believe that he did not consider the prisoner to be as important as Saint-Mars made him out to be, and this is confirmed by a letter from Barbezieux to Saint-Mars written on 4 August. 'His Majesty has not judged it necessary to send the order you requested to commandeer lodging on your journey to Paris: it will suffice for you to find and pay for the most convenient and secure lodging possible in the places you decide proper to stay.' Saint-Mars and his prisoner were to travel to Paris by regular roads stopping at ordinary post-houses along the way, just as Captain de Vauroy had done on his journey with Danger to Pignerol. Nor did Saint-Mars have more than half a dozen men to serve as escort and they were the motley crew who later at the Bastille were to be described by Renneville as nothing better than a gang of louts and bullies, thieves and thugs: Corbé, Rosarges, L'Ecuyer, Ru, the Abbé Giraut and possibly Jacques La France. For the transfer from Pignerol to Exiles and from Exiles to Sainte-Marguerite, Saint-Mars had been at the head of his own Free Company, a troop of over forty men, but these he had been obliged to leave behind on the island. So far as the King and his minister were concerned, major security measures were no longer necessary for Danger's safekeeping. Far from being more important than he had ever been before, as the move to the Bastille in a mask would seem to imply, Danger was a good deal less important. The length of his captivity, which by that time was twenty-nine years, had reduced the danger his secret represented and without the intervention of Saint-Mars he would have finished his days on the island of Sainte-Marguerite under the custody of Lamotte-Guérin.

In more romantic theories than the one I propose, much has been made of the wording of the official order which Barbezieux sent to

Saint-Mars on 19 July. 'The King sees fit that you leave the islands of Sainte-Marguerite and come to the Bastille with your longtime prisoner, taking care to avoid him being seen or known to anyone.' There, it has been said, is proof that the prisoner's face was so well known or in some way so exceptional that it had to be masked, but in the context of the correspondence which preceded and succeeded this letter, and in the light of all we know about Danger's personal insignificance, no such conclusion is possible. Arguably the words 'taking care to avoid him being seen or known to anyone' were a conventional turn of phrase in common use for such orders and therefore not to be taken literally, but even if that were not the case it seems certain that Barbezieux did not mean them to suggest that Saint-Mars should cover the prisoner's face with a mask. No such order was ever given and indeed from what we know of the prisoner such an order would have been absurd. In all probability the reason why Barbezieux expressed himself in this way arose from his lack of interest rather than his concern, it being a phrase he was echoing from something Saint-Mars himself had said. Years before in Pignerol, Saint-Mars had indeed been ordered to avoid Danger being seen or known to anyone. The same order had applied to La Rivière, of course, and its purpose had been to deceive Lauzun into the belief that they had been liberated, but no doubt Saint-Mars had embroidered upon this story to persuade Barbezieux of Danger's importance. Though Barbezieux and the King were certainly aware that the prisoner's identity was not of major importance, they would have seen no reason to contradict an old man like Saint-Mars in what after all appeared to be nothing more than an excess of concern. If they had been genuinely afraid lest the prisoner should be 'seen or known to anyone', they would not have left Saint-Mars to find lodging for him wherever he could, including common post-houses, on his way to Paris.

And so to the Bastille Saint-Mars brought his longtime prisoner, hiding his face in a mask of black velvet as if otherwise the mystery-man would have been recognized. The change from steel to velvet was a necessity in view of the more sophisticated spectators he could expect to find in Paris. A steel mask there would have caused such a sensation that the King and his ministers would have come down on him for an explanation, but a velvet mask, though sure to attract attention, was not without precedent. Saint-Mars almost certainly knew that a similar mask had been used just three years before to cover the face of a prisoner brought to the Bastille. On 21 March 1695 *La Gazette d'Amsterdam* published the following report: 'A lieutenant of the galleys accompanied by twenty horsemen has conducted to the Bastille a masked prisoner, brought from Provence in a litter and closely guarded throughout the journey, which leads one to believe that he is someone of importance, especially since his name is kept secret and those who brought him say that it is a secret from them.' Saint-Mars knew this line of thinking well: he had been exploiting it for years, and if like the lieutenant of the galleys he chose to mask his prisoner, it was with the deliberate intention of leading people to believe that the masked man was someone of unusual importance, proof to the world that he himself was, and always had been, a gaoler of unusual importance.

As it happens, the identity of the earlier masked prisoner is known, and he was not important at all. It was a certain Gesnon Fillibert, a captain of the galleys who was a Protestant, suspected of trying to reveal war-secrets to the English fleet then cruising in the Mediterranean. He was arrested at sea out of Genoa and was brought to Paris in a mask because he had to be taken by way of Lyon where his family lived; the authorities did not wish his father, who was a banker, to know about his arbitrary arrest. According to Du Junca, he arrived at the Bastille 'in a litter with his face hidden' on 15 February 1695 and was liberated on 15 October 1697. Though the effect of Danger's mask was the same as that of Fillibert, the reason he wore it was not. Danger's mask was not to hide who the wearer was, but to hide who he was not. He was not a Marshal of France nor a President of the Parlement. He was not Richard Cromwell nor the Duc de Beaufort. He was not in himself anyone of any significance, but it was necessary for the image of his gaoler that he should appear to be so. Hiding the prisoner's face with a mask was the gaoler's way of saving his own face.

As governor of the Bastille Saint-Mars no longer needed to bluff his way to an image of importance, but the game begun at Sainte-Marguerite had to be played to the end or his pretence would have been discovered. Nor at that stage was he capable of changing his ways, let alone his game. Though in Paris he had finally become all that he had always longed to be, the honour came too late for him to enjoy the respect and consideration which his new post gave him. Seventy-two years old, as then he was, a widower, often ill and almost without friends, deaf and infirm, back-bent and trembling, he no longer had the force or the will to remake or rethink his life; imprisoned in his own masquerade, like poor Danger in his mask, he was obliged to live out his remaining years the swaggering mythomaniac he had allowed himself to become, the vainglorious old fool who in 1702 boasted of pretended past exploits in such a ridiculous way in front of Renneville:

> He told me that he had left Holland the day after the birth of King William . . . because the day before, when everyone was celebrating, he had picked a quarrel with seven Dutchmen, had

killed four and disarmed the other three . . . From there he had
embarked for Lisbon where he had carried off the prize in a
famous tourney. After that he had moved to the court of Madrid
where he had won acclaim in a bullfight, carrying off the prize for
that too and the admiration of all the ladies, who had wellnigh
drowned him in a deluge of perfume-eggs filled with scented
waters. And every fourth word he uttered was an oath to assert
this big talk which was so at odds with his puny size.

The idea of keeping a prisoner masked in prison was altogether
unprecedented in France, but for Saint-Mars it was a logical extension
of the idea of having his prisoner masked for the journey. In this way he
could be sure that under day to day circumstances which he could no
longer personally control, he would be able to keep up the pretence that
his prisoner's hidden identity was significant. On Sainte-Marguerite,
all his prisoners had been sealed off behind his own quarters, making it
possible for him to supervise and restrict all movement and contact. At
the Bastille, such personal control was impossible. The staff including
Du Junca had been greatly impressed by his arrival with a mysterious
prisoner. Without comment from him they had assumed that a mask
was needed to keep the man's identity secret, and with just a word from
him they had learned that the man had been in his personal custody ever
since Pignerol and the days of Fouquet and Lauzun. Saint-Mars was not
the type to risk losing the magic of such a powerful first impact and was
careful to keep Du Junca away from the prisoner from the outset. Du
Junca owed his appointment to the King and, unlike the sorry creatures
employed by Saint-Mars, he was neither a fool nor a knave. If he had
been allowed into contact with the prisoner, he would sooner or later
have seen through the hoax and raised questions. As it was he accepted
the situation without question or resentment and to all appearances
without curiosity, his lack of interest being due no doubt to his
realisation that the prisoner was not of much consequence anyway. He
must certainly have recognised that the man was not of high rank.
Even if he never saw him close enough to know that he was dressed in a
suit 'expected to last three or four years', he did know that he had no
valet to serve him and that he was to be looked after by the drunken
clown Rosarges, as stupid as he was ignorant and as brutal as he was
dishonest.

Nonetheless, the older members of the Bastille staff had once been
accustomed to the everyday sight of someone masked and under guard.
François de Besmaux, the predecessor of Saint-Mars, had in earlier days
kept his wife masked and guarded in public, at least that was the claim
made in 1700 by Courtilz de Sandras in the third volume of his

Mémoires de M. d'Artagnan. Before ever he became governor of the Bastille, Besmaux had lived in constant fear that someone might try to steal his money and his wife. He put his money in a strong-box and, according to Courtilz de Sandras, would have put his wife in one too if he could, or at least kept her locked up in a chastity-belt; 'but since that was even less permitted than the other, he bought one of the biggest masks in Paris with one of the biggest chin-pieces and obliged her to wear it on her face all the time.' It was because he judged that the Bastille was the safest place to hide away his wife and his money that he bribed and swindled his way to the governorship, and thereafter his poor wife was as much a prisoner as any of the inmates. 'He did not want her to go out except to attend mass at the Sisters of Mary which was nearby nor to spend the least amount of money. Moreover she was only allowed out in her big mask with its big chin-piece, for all the world as if she were afraid of a sunburn, and two soldiers of the Bastille accompanied her even in her devotions.' Presumably Saint-Mars knew all about his predecessor's masked wife because in June 1663 he had been second-in-command to d'Artagnan when he had moved Fouquet to the Bastille. At that time Besmaux had been alarmed because the thirty or so musketeers who installed themselves in his prison to guard Fouquet were all fascinated by his masked wife and, as Courtilz de Sandras claimed, 'there was no chin-piece proof against their great appetite though it were double the thickness and bigger again than the one she was wearing.' It was of course the mask which attracted Saint-Mars and his fellow-musketeers, it being their understandable assumption that if she had not been beautiful Besmaux would not have masked her. In his use of a mask for his prisoner, Saint-Mars was deliberately seeking a similar response: the assumption that if his prisoner had not been easily recognisable he would not have masked him.

At the Bastille, Saint-Mars came under a new master, the Controller of Finance, and the secretary of that minister, a man called Desgranges, cultivated his friendship. After more than thirty years in the provinces, Saint-Mars had few friends in Paris. Desgranges flattered him with shows of respect and attention in society and indulged him at the ministry by wangling gifts of government money and closing his eyes to irregularities in his accounts. 'It is known,' the Marquis de Sourches commented wryly in his *Mémoires* for 14 June 1699, 'that the King has given a bonus of 5,000 livres to old Saint-Mars, the governor of the Bastille, to compensate him for what he did to feed the prisoners more economically than his predecessor managed to do.' For Desgranges it was a sprat to catch a mackerel. In 1700 the son of Saint-Mars and the daughter of Desgranges were married, and even though Saint-Mars outlived his son and there were no grand-children, he included his son's widow in his will. When Saint-Mars died in 1708, at the age of eighty-two, the fortune he left behind was enormous. Each of his three nephews received a titled estate: Palteau, Dimon and Blainvilliers; and the daughter of Desgranges received the rest: furniture, arms, silver and 'jewels of great value', as well as coffers containing 'more than 600,000 silver francs in cash'. No one mourned his loss. Only the heirs showed any concern at his passing, and what concerned them was the extent of their share in the inheritance.

For Saint-Mars himself in the last years of his life, it was probably not the legacy of his wealth that concerned him most; to the vile and servile Corbé, whom he detested anyway, went the magnificent house and estate of Palteau. In all likelihood what he valued more was something he had been unable to buy and so at one time had been obliged to invent: a means to attain the awe and admiration of society. As governor of Sainte-Marguerite he had managed to impress the people around him by making a display of secrecy and importance over one of his prisoners who, whatever significance he might have had in the eyes of the authorities, would have gone unnoticed by the rest of the world. As governor of the Bastille he kept up that pretence and saw the image he had invented for the prisoner outlive the prisoner's death. During the remaining years of his own life, he may even have come to realise that the myth would live on after his death too and carry his name with it to impress the world when he had gone. If the idea occurred to him, it no doubt gave him pleasure; but even he could not have imagined how, in the years that followed, coincidence and circumstance would combine to inflate the myth to archetypal proportions and make his name as famous in history as anyone in his age.

Surrounded as he was by creatures of his own mark and making, he was not alone in his exploitation of the mystery which enveloped the imprisoned valet. Blainvilliers, as an old man swinging the lamp to impress his grand-nephew, was playing the same game, as was Louis de Formanoir telling the preposterous story he had concocted around a pair of steel tweezers. Since it is unlikely that either of these men ever dealt with the prisoner directly, they may have believed that he was all that Saint-Mars made him out to be, but Lamotte-Guérin for his part knew differently. As senior lieutenant on Sainte-Marguerite, he had served the prisoner in his cell and so had seen how poorly he was dressed and how meagrely his cell was furnished. When he informed Lagrange-Chancel that the prisoner was served on dishes of silver, he was deliberately contributing to the myth, and when he maintained that the mystery-man was the Duc de Beaufort, he might have been reporting what Saint-Mars had said, but he certainly knew that it was not the truth.

Memories of the masked prisoner, confused with memories of Fillibert and Besmaux's wife, were already a tradition at the Bastille by the time Voltaire heard them. It is just possible that the story reported by the Princess Palatine in 1711 included details remembered from the masked and guarded excursions of Besmaux's wife, but it seems wellnigh certain that the description of the prisoner's mask given by Voltaire in 1751 was derived directly from some recollection of that poor woman's mask. An important feature of that mask had been its chin-piece, and in Voltaire's account the chin-piece was an essential feature of the prisoner's mask of iron; in fact, we know that the mask actually worn by the prisoner at the Bastille was an ordinary loo-mask which covered only the upper part of his face. The transition from velvet to iron was once difficult to explain, but not today, knowing as we now do that the prisoner was actually seen on his way to Sainte-Marguerite with his face hidden by a mask of steel. Most of Voltaire's information was based on local tradition picked up in the region of Cannes, and it was there no doubt that the name Iron Mask[4] originated.

Voltaire, like Saint-Mars, had a direct hand in the creation of the myth of the Iron Mask, but like all great myths it arose from circumstances and evolved by processes which were accidental, from semblance and coincidence, by rumour and tradition. Saint-Mars was not responsible for the original conjectures about marshals and presidents, just as the eventual confusions with Fillibert and Besmaux's wife were not of Voltaire's making. Consciously and deliberately they nourished the myth's growth: Saint-Mars gave it life, Voltaire gave it form, and in due time Dumas gave it immortality; but the story of the masked prisoner grew with a momentum of its own, accumulating and assimilating whatever stories it touched: Louvois at Pignerol removing his hat in the presence of Fouquet; Madame Le Bret in Paris buying lace and fine linen for Madame de Saint-Mars; Salves on Sainte-Marguerite trying to pass messages on shirts and plates. Possibly some dim memory of Fillibert disembarking from a galley at Marseilles, masked and under guard, led to the tradition still popular today that the Iron Mask was imprisoned for a time in the Château d'If; and no doubt a vague recollection of special precautions taken at the Bastille, when some prisoner was thought to have died of cholera or plague, led to the tradition that, when the Iron Mask died, the order was given to burn everything in his cell and scrape the walls and floor, for fear that he had left some message or sign.

In the mystery of the Iron Mask there is finally more irony than iron: he was a nonentity who became famous precisely because he was a nonentity; but though one can explain how the myth developed, one cannot explain it away. Even the best attempts to disentangle the truth and uncover the prisoner's identity have only added to the lore of the mystery. From Griffet to Brugnon, from Soulavie to Pagnol, the fact-finding as much as the fiction-making has served the same process which Saint-Mars, Voltaire and Dumas served. No solution is finally satisfying because the mystery is itself a resolution, an image formed in the collective thought-patterns of Europe in the eighteenth century and still charged with meaning today. The prisoner is no one, a man without a face or identity, type of the unknown political prisoner, victim and nonentity; but out of thirty years of his life have come three hundred years of living myth: he is anyone and everyone, a man with many faces and many identities, archetypal projection of lost liberty and void identity, of failed potential and fouled fortune. When all that there is to say about the Iron Mask has been said, when the evidence for the actual prisoner has been presented and the errors, deceptions, inventions and confusions which went to make his image have been exposed, the iconic transfiguration wrought by the mask rests nonetheless unchanged, the mystery and fascination of his iron face unimpaired.

In April 1786, a section of the underground quarries of Paris were consecrated to serve as a catacomb, and the transport began of all the bones in the cemetries and charnel-houses of Paris. The graves of Saint-Paul were emptied along with the rest, and for fifteen months cart-loads of jumbled skeletons were poured down chutes into the subterranean passageways. There went the remains of the masked prisoner, and with them the remains of Saint-Mars and Louvois, of Avedick, Molière, Cavoye and six million others, sundered and sorted by thigh-bone and skull into six thousand cubic metres of stacked bones. The myth and the mystery of the Iron Mask is as much this simple fact as the simple fiction that three years later his skeleton was found still masked and chained in some abandoned dungeon in the depths of the Bastille.

1.   These figures are taken from original documents in the records of the Royal Treasury, brought to the author's attention by Stanislas Brugnon.
2.   *Herse*: Little is known about him except that he was imprisoned at Pignerol in 1687 and that the allowance for his upkeep was the same as for his fellow prisoners. Official corrrespondence shows that in 1689 he tried to commit suicide and in 1692 to escape.
3.   The grammatical sequence in French, more obvious than in English, leaves no doubt that *you can* governs *bring* as much as it governs *make*.
4.   *Iron Mask*: the first published use of the name was made in 1750 by Charles de Fieux de Mouhy in a sensational novel which though called *Le Masque de fer* had nothing to do with the masked prisoner guarded by Saint-Mars. The preface to Mouhy's book is not without interest however, To give some pretence of verisimilitude to the extravagant story he was to relate, he gave examples of four more Iron Mask stories, all fictions presented as fact:

The Turks tell the story that one of their emperors, wishing to be sure upon his throne, had his eldest son locked up in the Seven Towers, and fearing that the gentleness and majesty manifest in the features of that prince might seduce his guards and fill them with compassion, he covered his face with an iron mask made in such a way that it was impossible even for the most skilled craftsman to break or open it. There is also a tradition that in the time of Cromwell, a Scots prince was sent to the islands of the archipelago, and in order that he would not be recognized the method just described was employed. In the time of Dom Pedre, the cruel King of Spain, a father used the same device on one of this sons who had dishonoured him by a shameful act. At Stockholm they say that a prince named Jean Theull, who was jealous of his wife, made use of this method to achieve his ends: the day after his marriage, he put a sleeping-powder into his wife's drink, and while she was asleep he enclosed her face in an iron mask made almost like a helmet: when his unfortunate princess awoke he made her believe that the misfortune which had happened to her was a punishment from Heaven for having gloried too much in her own beauty and inspired love in men other than himself.

POSTSCRIPT

That the myth of the Iron Mask is still capable of new growth, with proliferations as fantastic as ever flourished before, will be apparent to any visitor to Cannes who troubles to take the narrow street which climbs steeply from the bus-station beside the port to the Tower of Mont Chevalier, on the hilltop above the old town. At an abrupt right-angle bend half-way up this street, one comes upon another tower not immediately recognizable as such because it is attached to an apartment building of the same height. This tower is of white stone, recently restored, and has an arched gateway, closed by an iron-strapped door, giving on to the street. Above the arch there is a barred window and below this window, fixed to the keystone of the arch, is a mask-like head of iron, larger than life-size. A marble plaque on the wall of the apartment building reads as follows:

> Tower of the Mask. 12th century. Watchtower of the Citadel, defended against the sieges of the Berbers by the valiant militia of Le Suquet. The Iron Mask escaped from the island of Sainte-Marguerite to take refuge here (the prisoner of the Bastille being nothing more than an unfortunate stand-in). In the course of circumstances which remain mysterious he died here after a long period of meditation and prayer, having forgiven his persecutors. Dimitte et Dimittemini. (Forgive and you will be forgiven. Luke vi 37.) Passer-by halt your step and meditate upon the sufferings of this tormented man whose ghost on certain nights haunts this place.

On the tower itself there is another plaque which reads: 'The historical discoveries made in this tower as well as its restoration are due to Comte Michel de Lacour, 10 rue Mont Chevalier, Résidence de la Citadelle, Cannes.' The address given is that of the apartment building. The Count lives on the top floor with direct access to the tower through a sliding bookshelf in his living-room. The eight-foot tall white marble statues which crown the tower, a Venus inspired by Botticelli's *Birth of Venus* and a Neptune copied from Giambologna's

Neptune-fountain in Bologna, were placed there by the Count himself, who had them made in Italy for that special purpose.

The tower has been in the possession of the Count's family for many years, as has also a splendid oil-painting, handsomely displayed in the entrance to his apartment, which represents the Iron Mask in the manner of a portrait. In this picture the celebrated prisoner is shown in front of a barred window, wearing a red velvet robe with white lace at wrist and throat, his head covered by a cowl of black velvet which hangs to the shoulder in a fringe of tassels and black lace. The cowl is altogether unusual in design; as well as openings for the eyes it has an opening below the nose to expose the mouth and chin. To anyone familiar with portraits of Louis XIV, the small eyes and full lips, the thin moustache and double chin, are immediately recognizable. The painting is unsigned, but the Count believes it to be the work of Nicolas de Largillière or of Hyacinthe Rigaud, both famous portrait-painters of the time of Louis XIV.

The story of the Count's 'historical discoveries' appeared in the national press in January 1978. The facts as reported by the Count, excluding any deductions he made or anyone else might make from them, are as follows. In spring 1977 he embarked upon major restoration work of the tower, and in the course of this his workers discovered an underground chamber containing the skeleton of a man, incomplete but including the skull, along with a gentleman's high-heeled silk shoe of the time of Louis XIV, fragments of black lace and velvet, part of a walking-stick with a silver pommel and a book of meditation published in 1675.

The Count took the fragments of velvet and lace to a dressmaker who, having pieced them together, made a copy of the original article of clothing, which turned out to be a cowl identical to the one worn by the Iron Mask in the oil-painting. The Count then had a study made of the skull, and a comparison made between the findings of that study and the waxwork of Louis XIV's head which the sculptor Antoine Benoist modelled from life. The scientists who made the comparison found enough characteristics in common to uphold the thesis that the owner of the skull and the subject of the waxwork were identical twins.

Soon after he had disturbed the bones, the Count became ill and his neighbours came to him with stories of strange noises heard and strange lights seen in the tower at night. The Count returned the bones to the chamber and had it sealed up again, while one of his neighbours brought a priest to exorcise the place. The Count recovered, but the nocturnal manifestations continued.

The silk shoe, the silver pommel and the book of meditation are all displayed in the Count's living-room, as is the copy of the mask-like cowl. But the fragments of velvet and lace which remained of the original cowl, like the skull and bones, can no longer be seen; having made the copy of the cowl, the dressmaker threw the original fragments away.

It was the mask engaged your mind,
And after set your heart to beat,
Not what's behind.

W.B. Yeats

GENERAL CHRONOLOGY OF EVENTS MENTIONED IN THE TEXT

1610   Henri IV assassinated. Marie de' Médicis becomes Regent.

1614   Birth of Guise.

1615   Marriage of Louis XIII and Anne of Austria. Birth of Fouquet.

1616   Birth of Beaufort.

1617   Louis XIII assumes power.

1619   Birth of Colbert.

1622   Birth of Molière and of Roux.

1624   Cardinal de Richelieu becomes Prime Minister.

1625   Death of James I. Charles I succeeds and marries Henrietta of France. Buckingham woos Anne of Austria.

1626   The Chalais Conspiracy. Birth of Saint-Mars, of Richard Cromwell and of Marguerite de Carteret.

1627   Founding of the Company of the Holy Sacrament. Birth of Mademoiselle.

1628   Buckingham assassinated.

1630   Day of the Dupes. François de Cavoye nominated Captain of the Cardinal's Guard. Birth of Charles II.

1631   Founding of *La Gazette*.

1632   Birth of Lauzun.

1633   Birth of James II.

1635   Outbreak of war between France and Spain. Birth of Brienne.

1636   Spanish invasion of France.

1637   Anne of Austria under house-arrest at Louvre. Birth of Eustache de Cavoye.

1638   Birth of Louis XIV and of Armand de Cavoye.

1639   French occupation of Alsace. François de Cavoye granted monopoly on sedan-chairs. Birth of Louis de Cavoye.

1640   Birth of Monsieur and of Matthioli.

1641 Death of François de Cavoye. Birth of Louvois.

1642 Death of Cardinal de Richelieu. Mazarin becomes Prime Minister. Outbreak of English Civil War. French occupation of Roussillon. Death of Joseph Béjart. Possible birth-date of Armande Béjart.

1643 Death of Louis XIII. Anne of Austria becomes Regent. Beaufort imprisoned at Vincennes. Molière forms acting company with Madeleine Béjart. Birth of Pontchartrain.

1644 Gondinet appointed physician to Anne of Austria. Birth of Madame, Henrietta of England. Date of birth given by James de La Cloche.

1645 Battle of Naseby. Molière and company leave Paris. Possible birth-date of Armande Béjart.

1646 Charles II visits Jersey for two months.

1648 Beaufort escapes from Vincennes. Outbreak of French Civil War. Birth of Corbé.

1649 Execution of Charles I. Birth of Monmouth. Charles II visits Jersey for five months.

1650 Saint-Mars becomes a musketeer. Birth of William III.

1651 Mazarin banished. Birth of Chamillart.

1652 Mazarin returns. Beaufort kills brother-in-law. End of French Civil War. Beaufort banished. Birth of Madame, Princess Palatine.

1653 Mazarin re-established as Prime Minister. Fouquet becomes Superintendent of Finance. Oliver Cromwell becomes Lord Protector.

1654 Louis XIV crowned.

1656 Marriage of Jean La Cloche and Marguerite de Carteret.

1657 Comtesse de Soissons becomes Louis XIV's mistress. Birth of Avedik.

1658 Death of Oliver Cromwell. Richard Cromwell succeeds. Molière and company return to Paris. Besmaux appointed governor of the Bastille.

1659 The Roissy debauch. Richard Cromwell abdicates. Treaty of Pyrenees ends war between France and Spain.

1660 Restoration of crown to Charles II. Richard Cromwell leaves England. Marriage of Louis XIV to Maria-Teresa. Nabo given as wedding present.

1661 Death of Mazarin. Marriage of Monsieur and Henrietta of England. Louise de La Vallière becomes Louis XIV's mistress. Party at Vaux-le-Vicomte. Fouquet is arrested. Colbert becomes Controller of Finance. Death of Auget. Lully succeeds as Director of the King's Music. Birth of Dauphin.

1662   Louvois joins Le Tellier as Minister of War. Maria-Teresa realizes that Louise de La Vallière is Louis XIV's mistress. Marriage of Molière and Armande Béjart. Bellings' mission to Rome.

1663   Fouquet transferred to Bastille. Lionne replaces Brienne as Secretary for Foreign Affairs. Beaufort succeeds father as Grand Admiral. Louise de La Vallière bears first child to Louis XIV. Montfleury attacks Molière. Marriage of the Montespans. Founding of *La Gazette d'Amsterdam*.

1664   Molière's first *Tartuffe* is banned. Maria-Teresa gives birth to a black daughter. Madame de Cavoye makes her will. Fouquet sentenced and transferred to Pignerol. Death of Guise.

1665   Great Plague of London. Saint-Germain brawl. Death of Madame de Cavoye. Eustache de Cavoye disinherited and cashiered. Lauzun spends four months in the Bastille. Molière's *Dom Juan* is banned.

1666   Death of Anne of Austria. Marquise de Brinvilliers poisons her father. Fight between Lauzun and Cavoye.

1667   French invasion of the Spanish Netherlands. Work begins on Versailles. Athénais de Montespan becomes Louis XIV's mistress. Colbert accused of embezzlement. La Reynie becomes Lieutenant of Police. Molière's second *Tartuffe* is banned. Death of Armand de Cavoye. Birth of Vermandois and of Barbezieux.

1668   Jan: Anglo-Dutch Alliance against France.
Feb: French occupation of Franche Comté.
Mar: Le Sage and Mariette arrested.
Apr: James de La Cloche joins Jesuits in Rome. Sweden joins England and Holland against France in Triple Alliance.
May: Roux in London betrayed by Morland. Treaty of Aix-la-Chapelle: France cedes Franche Comté, but keeps gains in Flanders.
Jul: Louis de Cavoye imprisoned in Conciergerie.
Aug: Roux visits Switzerland. Montespan in Paris makes protest against his wife's adultery.
Sep: Montespan arrested and banished. Le Sage sentenced to the galleys, Mariette to Saint-Lazare.
Oct: La Cloche leaves Rome.
Dec: Mariette escapes from Saint-Lazare. Roux returns to London and meets Veyras. Colbert, back in favour, falls ill after taking medicine. La Cloche returns to Rome.
Month unknown: Eustache de Cavoye locked up in Saint-Lazare.

1669   Jan: Charles II begins secret negotiations with Louis XIV. La

Cloche arrives in Naples with companion who continues to Malta.

Feb: La Cloche marries. Pregnani arrives in London. Molière's third *Tartuffe* is authorized.

Mar: Secret birth of Athénais de Montespan's first child by Louis XIV. La Cloche imprisoned in Naples. Pregnani visits Newmarket.

May: Roux kidnapped in Switzerland.

Jun: Beaufort disappears at Candy. Roux interrogated and executed in Paris. Croissy suggests extraditing Veyras and Martin. La Cloche is released.

Jul: La Cloche dies in Naples. Pregnani returns to France. Lauzun insults Athénais de Montespan and defies Louis XIV. Warrant issued for arrest of Danger.

Aug: Danger imprisoned at Pignerol.

Sep: Death of Henrietta of France.

Dec: Discovery of plot for Fouquet's escape.

1670   Publication of *Elomire*. Secret Treaty of Dover. Death of Madame, Henrietta of England. Louvois visits Pignerol and changes garrison. Madame Dufresnoy becomes mistress of Louvois. Marquise de Brinvilliers poisons her two brothers. Mademoiselle proposes marriage to Lauzun.

1671   Death of Lionne. Pomponne succeeds as Secretary for Foreign Affairs. Marriage of Monsieur and Princess Palatine. Kéroualle killed in action. Lauzun imprisoned at Pignerol. Birth of eldest son of Saint-Mars.

1672   French invasion of Holland. Louis de Cavoye released from prison. Discovery of plot for Lauzun's escape. Oldendorf under surveillance in Brussels. Death of Madeleine Béjart.

1673   Death of Molière and d'Artagnan. Capture of Oldendorf. James publicly recognized to be Catholic. Le Sage released from galleys. Saint-Mars acquires letters of nobility. Marquise de Brinvilliers tried *in absentia* and sentenced to death.

1674   French reconquer Franche Comté. Royal apartments at Versailles are completed. Athénais de Montespan granted legal separation. Louise de La Vallière takes the veil. Madame Dufresnoy becomes Lady of the Queen's Bed. Brienne locked up in Saint-Lazare. Dominican monk transferred to Pignerol. Execution of Rohan. Birth of Regent.

1675   Vivonne becomes marshal.

1676   Dubreuil imprisoned at Pignerol. Armande Béjart traduced for incest. Execution of Marquise de Brinvilliers. Birth of Lagrange-Chancel and of second son of Saint-Mars.

1677   Armande Béjart remarries. Matthioli in Verona contacted by French.

1678   The Popish plot. Court moves to Versailles. Eustache de Cavoye writes to his sister. Matthioli in Paris signs agreement for sale of Casale.

1679   Peace of Nijmegen: France keeps Franche Comté and gains in Spanish Netherlands. Pomponne dismissed; Croissy succeeds as Secretary for Foreign Affairs. Le Sage rearrested. Chambre Ardente set up to investigate poisonings. Fouquet's wife and daughter allowed to live with him. Matthioli and servant kidnapped and imprisoned at Pignerol. Eustache de Cavoye writes petition to Louis XIV. Monmouth banished to Holland. Marie-Angélique de Fontages becomes mistress of Louis XIV. Death of Gondinet.

1680   Chambre Ardente widens investigation to include sorcery. Comtesse de Soissons escapes to Holland to avoid arrest. Exclusion Bill passed by Commons. Richard Cromwell returns to England. Fouquet dies. Danger and La Rivière become secret prisoners. Marriage of Dauphin. Death of Morelhie.

1681   Lauzun released from Pignerol. Casale bought and occupied by French. Saint-Mars moves to Exiles with two prisoners. Death of Marie-Angélique de Fontanges.

1682   Versailles becomes seat of government. Louis XIV suppresses Chambre Ardente. Monmouth returns to England. Report of Matthioli's imprisonment at Pignerol published in Cologne. Story of Beaufort's imprisonment in Constantinople told in Paris.

1683   Rye House plot. Monmouth expelled to Holland. Death of Colbert: Seigneley and Le Peletier succeed him in office. Death of Vermandois and of Maria-Teresa.

1684   Morganatic marriage of Louis XIV and Françoise de Maintenon.

1685   Death of Charles II. Succession of James II. Rebellion and execution of Monmouth. Revocation of Edict of Nantes. Death of Le Tellier.

1686   Esoteric paintings made in Monastery of Cimiez. League of Augsberg against France.

1687   Saint-Mars moves to Isle Sainte-Marguerite with one prisoner, wearing a mask of steel. Story published in Leyden that prisoner of Saint-Mars is Matthioli.

1688   The Glorious Revolution: William III and Mary II accede to the throne; James II escapes to France. Outbreak of war between France and Austria. Destruction of Palatinate. Armande Béjart libelled for incest.

1689	Le Peletier retires: Ponchartrain succeeds as Controller of Finance. First Protestant minister imprisoned on Sainte-Marguerite.
1690	Du Junca becomes King's Lieutenant at the Bastille. Death of Seigneley.
1691	Siege of Cuneo. Arrest of Bulonde. Athénais de Montespan enters convent. Death of Louvois; Barbezieux succeeds as Minister of War.
1692	Publication at Cologne of *Les Amours d'Anne d'Autriche avec C.D.R.*.
1693	Death of Mademoiselle and of eldest son of Saint-Mars.
1694	Prisoners of Pignerol transferred to Sainte-Marguerite. Death of Mary II. Birth of Voltaire.
1695	The Mooress of Moret takes the veil. Imprisonment of Fillibert in the Bastille.
1696	Barclay's conspiracy. French abandon Pignerol. Death of Croissy. Torcy becomes Secretary for Foreign Affairs. Birth of Maréchal Richelieu.
1697	Treaty of Ryswick: Louis XIV recognizes William III. La Reynie retires as Lieutenant of Police and is replaced by d'Argenson. Death of Besmaux and of Madame Saint-Mars.
1698	Saint-Mars moves to the Bastille with one prisoner wearing a mask of velvet. Portland's embassy to Versailles. Disappearance of Barclay. Death of Brienne. Birth of Griffet.
1699	Fériol becomes ambassador to Constantinople. Pontchartrain becomes Chancellor; Chamillart succeeds as Controller of Finance. Death of Pomponne.
1700	Publication of *Mémoires de M. d'Artagnan*. Marriage of youngest son of Saint-Mars.
1701	Death of Barbezieux; Chamillart succeeds as Minister of War, while continuing to be Controller of Finance. Death of Monsieur, of James II and of Montespan.
1702	Beginning of War of Spanish Succession. Renneville imprisoned in the Bastille. Avedik becomes Patriarch of Constantinople. Death of William III. Succession of Anne.
1703	Death of masked prisoner. Avedik imprisoned in Syria.
1704	Publication of Grimarest's *Vie de M. de Molière*. Avedik returns to Constantinople.
1705	Death of Rosarges.
1706	Destruction of Nice castle by the French. Avedik kidnapped and confined at Mont-Saint-Michel. Death of Du Junca.
1707	Death of Athénais de Montespan.
1708	Death of Saint-Mars. Desmarets becomes Controller of Finance.

1709 Chamillart retires. Voysin becomes Minister of War. Avedik transferred to the Bastille. Louis XIV destroys records of Chambre Ardente. Death of Bulonde and of La Reynie.

1710 Avedik abjures his faith. Death of Louise de La Vallière. Birth of Louis XV.

1711 Madame, Princess Palatine, learns story of masked prisoner. Richelieu imprisoned in Bastille for short time. Death of Dauphin and Avedik.

1712 Death of Richard Cromwell. Birth of Palteau.

1713 Renneville released. Death of Ru and of Marguerite de Carteret.

1714 Pontchartrain retires. Death of Anne. Succession of George I.

1715 Publication of Renneville's *L'Inquisition Française ou l'Histoire de la Bastille*. Death of Louis XIV.

1716 Richelieu again in the Bastille. Regent's daughter becomes Richelieu's mistress. Death of Louis de Cavoye.

1717 Voltaire imprisoned in the Bastille.

1718 Voltaire released.

1719 Death of Françoise de Maintenon. Richelieu again in the Bastille.

1720 Lagrange-Chancel imprisoned on Sainte-Marguerite.

1721 Death of Chamillart, of Desmarets and of d'Argenson.

1723 Death of Lauzun, of Renneville and of the Regent. Succession of Louis XV.

1727 Death of Pontchartrain.

DETAILED CHRONOLOGY OF EVENTS RELATIVE TO THE LIFE OF THE IRON MASK IN PRISON

1664 Dec: Saint-Mars becomes governor of Pignerol prison with Fouquet as his sole prisoner lodged in the Angle Tower.

1665 Jun: Angle Tower damaged by explosion of powder-magazine. Fouquet transferred to La Pérouse.

1666 Aug: Angle Tower repaired. Fouquet returned with two valets: La Rivière and Champagne.

1669 Jul: Saint-Mars ordered to prepare a high-security cell for Eustache Danger who is to be furnished with nothing more than simple necessities because he is only a valet, is to be threatened with death if he tries to speak of anything but his basic needs and is to have contact with no one except Saint-Mars himself.
Aug: Danger is imprisoned at Pignerol, lodged as securely as possible until a special cell can be prepared.
Dec: Saint-Mars discovers plot to liberate Fouquet. Valcroissant detained. La Fôret hanged.

1670 Mar: Louvois learns that Valcroissant, La Fôret, Champagne or La Rivière contacted Danger, but were unable to get him to talk.
Apr: Danger moved to a special cell.
Jun: Valcroissant sentenced to the galleys for five years.
Aug: Louvois visits Pignerol.
Oct: Garrison of town and citadel of Pignerol changed.

1671 Dec: Lauzun imprisoned at Pignerol.

1672 Feb: Saint-Mars asks permission to have Danger serve as valet to Lauzun. Permission refused.
Jul: Saint-Mars discovers plot to liberate Lauzun.
Aug: Heurtaut commits suicide.
Sep: Plassot, Mathonnet and Madame Carrière detained.
Oct: Mathonnet and Madame Carrière released.

1673 Jan: Laprade becomes lieutenant.
Jul: Plassot released. Saint-Mars discovers supply of poisons among Plassot's abandoned belongings.

1674 Apr: The Dominican monk imprisoned at Pignerol.
Sep: Champagne dies.

1675 Jan: Saint-Mars receives permission to have Danger serve as valet to Fouquet, but only when La Rivière is absent.
Mar: Louvois reiterates his concern that Danger should not serve as valet to Lauzun and should have contact with no one but Fouquet.

1676 Feb: Lauzun attempts to escape.
May: Dubreuil imprisoned at Pignerol, lodged with the Dominican monk who has become insane.
Nov: Louvois advises Saint-Mars to cure the monk's insanity by flogging him and chaining him to the wall.

1677 Nov: Lauzun allowed visit from brother and sister.
Dec: Fouquet and Lauzun allowed to walk together for two hours every day.

1678 Nov: Louvois asks Fouquet for a confidential report on what Danger may have said of his past life to La Rivière.
Dec: Saint-Mars also provides a report.

1679 Jan: Fouquet and Lauzun allowed to visit each other and receive visitors, but precautions taken to avoid Danger meeting Lauzun or having contact with anyone except Fouquet and La Rivière. Villebois becomes lieutenant.
May: Matthioli and his valet imprisoned at Pignerol. Matthioli called 'Lestang'. Fouquet allowed to take charge of his family affairs and to have his wife live with him. Lauzun allowed the use of four horses for exercise within the citadel.
Dec: Authorization given to prepare a room above Fouquet's apartment where his daughter can stay. Fouquet discovers her relationship with Lauzun, sends her away and breaks contact with Lauzun.

1680 Jan: Lauzun persuades Louvois that he has a confidential message of personal significance to transmit to him and can only entrust it to his friend Barrail. 'Lestang' and Dubreuil both reported to be insane.
Feb: 'Lestang' claims to be a close relative of the King.
Mar: Barrail visits Pignerol. Fouquet dies. Saint-Mars discovers a communicating-hole between the apartments of Fouquet and Lauzun.
Apr: Danger and La Rivière become secret prisoners, Lauzun and everyone else being told that they have been liberated. Fouquet's body is given to his family.
Jun: Lauzun's valet is liberated.

Jul: Louvois receives from Saint-Mars a parcel containing something found in Fouquet's clothes and asks how Danger acquired the drugs he needed to do it.

Sep: The name 'Lestang' is dropped and Matthioli is referred to by his proper name. He is put with the monk and threatened with the bastinado. Saint-Mars takes possession of his diamond ring.

1681   Apr: Lauzun is released.

May: Saint-Mars is notified of his transfer to Exiles with the two prisoners of the Lower Tower.

Jun: Saint-Mars is told to take Matthioli's baggage with him to Exiles.

Sep: Catinat and his valet pose as prisoners at Pignerol before leaving for Casale. Saint-Mars moves to Exiles transporting his two prisoners in a litter. Villebois takes charge of the four remaining prisoners at Pignerol. Blainvilliers is transferred to Metz and replaced by Boisjoly.

1682   May: Louvois advises Villebois at Pignerol that the best cure for Dubreuil's insanity would be a flogging.

1684   Apr: Louvois asks Saint-Mars at Exiles to tell him what he knows 'of the birth of the man named La Rivière and the circumstances by which he was put in the service of the late M. Fouquet.'

1685   Jun: One of the two prisoners at Exiles wishes to make his last will and testament. (La Rivière?).

1686   Sep: Saint-Mars reports that one of his two prisoners is suffering from dropsy. (La Rivière?).

1687   Jan: One of the two prisoners at Exiles dies. (La Rivière?). Saint-Mars is notified of his transfer to Sainte-Marguerite.

Feb: Saint-Mars visits Sainte-Marguerite.

Mar: Saint-Mars returns to Exiles.

Apr: Mauvans and Mazauges visit Sainte-Marguerite.

May: Saint-Mars arrives at Sainte-Marguerite with one prisoner transported in a sedan-chair covered with oil-cloth.

Aug: Herse imprisoned at Pignerol.

Sep: It is reported in Paris that the prisoner in the sedan-chair was wearing a mask of steel.

1689   Jan: Herse at Pignerol attempts suicide.

Apr: Protestant minister Cardel imprisoned on Sainte-Marguerite.

1690   Jan: Protestant ministers Salves and Valsac imprisoned on Sainte-Marguerite.

1691   Aug: Louvois dies and is succeeded by Barbezieux who tells

Saint-Mars to continue the same security procedure for the prisoner who has been in his custody for twenty years.

1692 May: Protestant minister Malzac imprisoned on Sainte-Marguerite.

Jul: Villebois dies. Laprade replaces him at Pignerol. Lamotte-Guérin becomes lieutenant on Sainte-Marguerite.

Dec: Herse at Pignerol attempts escape.

1693 Aug: Protestant minister Gardien imprisoned on Sainte-Marguerite.

Dec: Boisjoly retires. Matthioli and his valet at Pignerol caught hiding messages in the linings of their clothes.

1694 Jan: Corbé becomes lieutenant. Barbezieux to Saint-Mars: 'M. Laprade, to whom the King has entrusted the custody of the prisoners who are detained by order of his majesty in the prison of Pignerol, reports that the one who has been in prison there the longest has died, and that he doesn't know his name. Since I have no doubt you will remember it, I beg you to inform me of it in cipher.' (Death of the Dominican monk?).

Apr: The four prisoners of Pignerol are transferred to Sainte-Marguerite. Laprade becomes governor of Besançon.

May: Barbezieux to Saint-Mars: 'The valet of the prisoner who has died, you can put into the vaulted cell as you propose.' (Death of Matthioli?).

1695 Feb: Fillibert imprisoned in the Bastille.

1697 Oct: Fillibert released.

Nov: Barbezieux, annoyed that Pontchartrain has been asking questions about the prisoners on Sainte-Marguerite, informs Saint-Mars that he has no reason to tell anyone what it was that his longtime prisoner did.

1698 May: Saint-Mars notified of his transfer to the Bastille.

Aug: Saint-Mars leaves Sainte-Marguerite with his longtime prisoner and another whom he leaves at Lyon. Lamotte-Guérin becomes governor of Sainte-Marguerite.

Sep: On his way to Paris, Saint-Mars stops off with his prisoner at the Château de Palteau. The prisoner, who is wearing a mask of black velvet, is transported in a litter with Saint-Mars. On their arrival at the Bastille the masked prisoner is put into the First Chamber of the Basinière Tower until nightfall and then moved to the Third Chamber of the Bertaudière Tower. The King's Lieutenant, Du Junca, is allowed no contact with him. He is looked after by Rosarges, a sergeant from Sainte-Marguerite.

Nov: Permission is given for the prisoner to make confession and receive communion whenever Saint-Mars thinks fit.

1699   Sep: The Third Room of the Bertaudière Tower is occupied by a prisoner named Falaiseau.

1702   May: Renneville imprisoned in the Bastille.

1703   May: Possible date of Renneville's encounter with the prisoner. Nov: The masked prisoner dies in the Bastille and is buried in Saint-Paul cemetery.

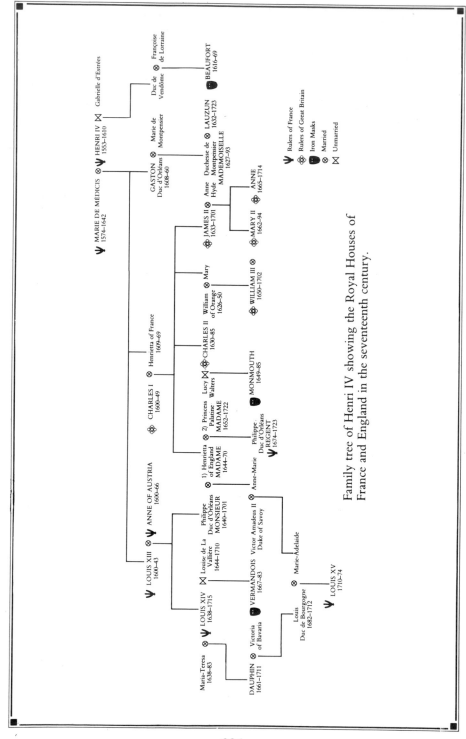

Family tree of Henri IV showing the Royal Houses of
France and England in the seventeenth century.

294

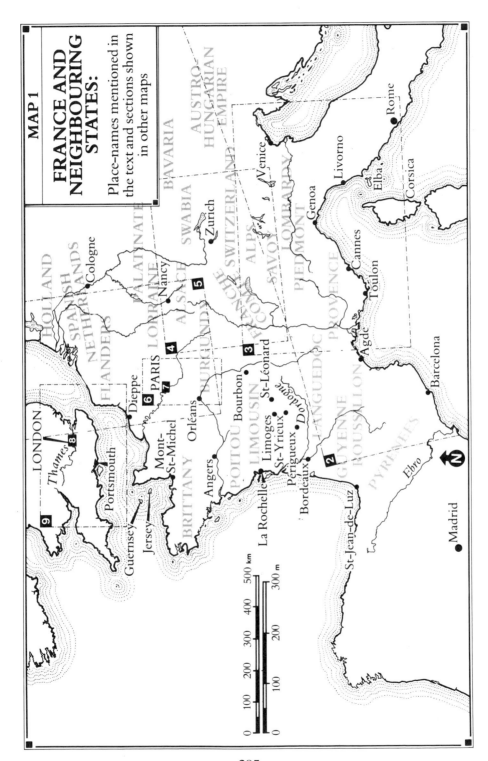

MAP 1

FRANCE AND NEIGHBOURING STATES:

Place-names mentioned in the text and sections shown in other maps

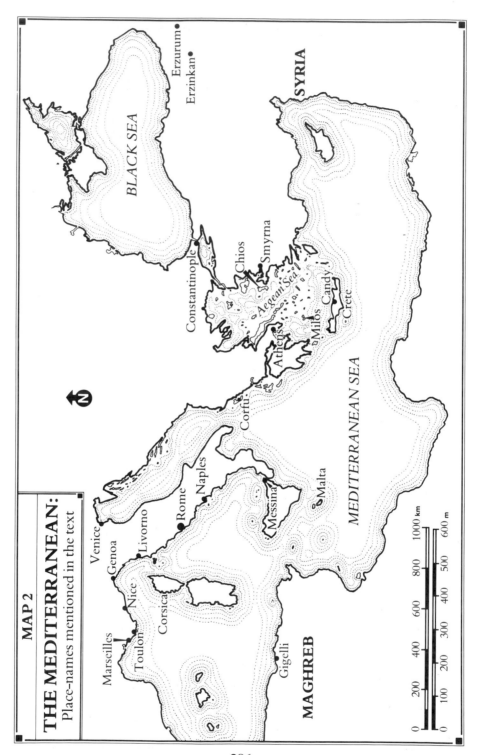

MAP 2

THE MEDITERRANEAN:
Place–names mentioned in the text

BLACK SEA

Erzurum
Erzinkan

SYRIA

Constantinople
Chios
Smyrna

Aegean Sea

Candy
Milos
Athens
Crete

Corfu

MEDITERRANEAN SEA

Venice
Genoa
Nice
Livorno
Corsica
Rome
Naples
Messina
Malta

Marseilles
Toulon

Gigelli

MAGHREB

0   200   400   600   800   1000 km
0   100 200 300 400 500 600 m

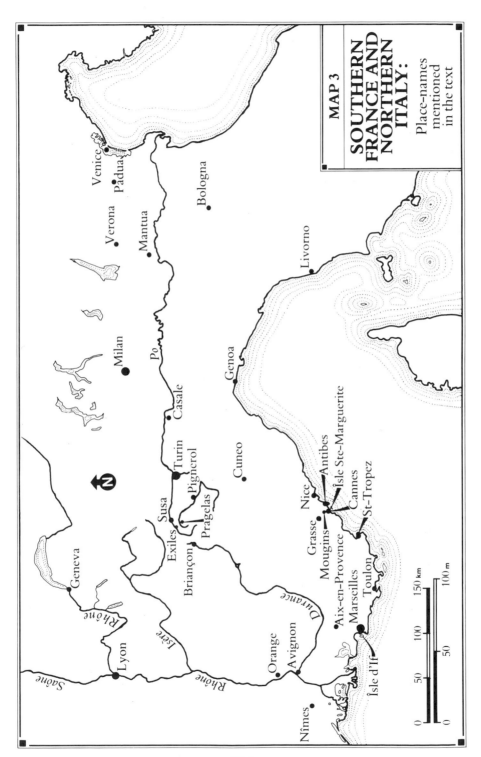

Venice

Padua

Verona

Mantua

Bologna

Milan

Po

Livorno

Genoa

Casale

Turin

Pignerol

Cuneo

Susa

Prágelas

Exiles

Briançon

Isle Ste-Marguerite

Antibes

Cannes

St-Tropez

Nice

Grasse

Mougins

Durance

Aix-en-Provence

Marseilles

Toulon

Geneva

Rhône

Isère

Lyon

Saône

Orange

Avignon

Rhône

Île d'If

Nîmes

150 km

100 m

100

50

50

100

50

0

0

297

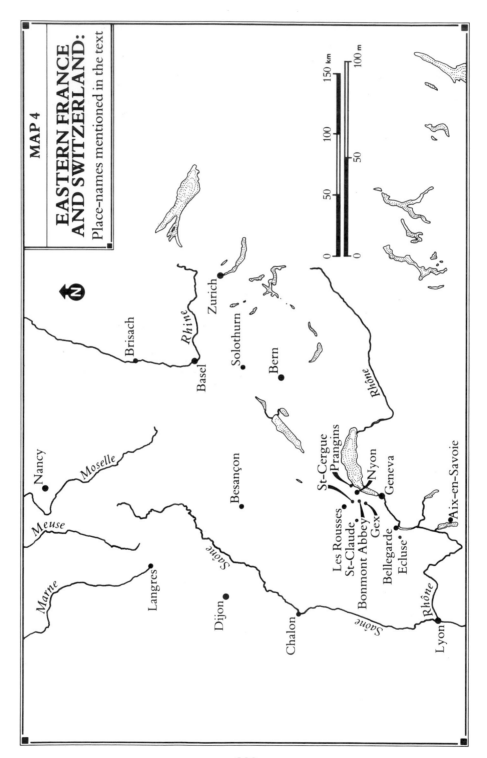

MAP 4

**EASTERN FRANCE
AND SWITZERLAND:**
Place-names mentioned in the text

MAP 5

NORTHERN FRANCE, SPANISH NETHERLANDS AND HOLLAND:

Place-names mentioned in the text

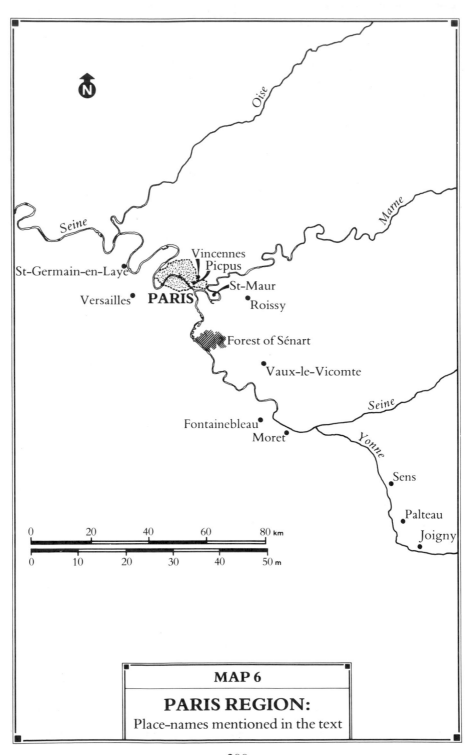

N

Seine

Oise

Marne

Vincennes
Picpus
St-Germain-en-Laye
St-Maur
Versailles
PARIS
Roissy

Forest of Sénart

Vaux-le-Vicomte

Seine

Fontainebleau
Moret

Yonne

Sens

Palteau

Joigny

| 0 | 20 | 40 | 60 | 80 km |

| 0 | 10 | 20 | 30 | 40 | 50 m |

MAP 6

PARIS REGION:

Place-names mentioned in the text

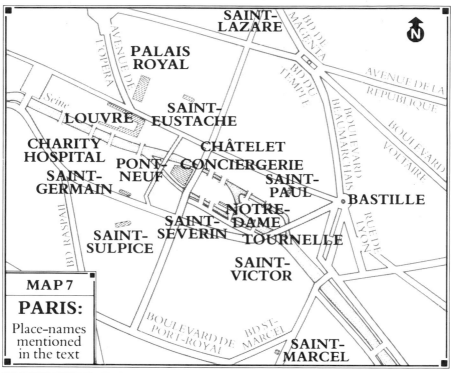

MAP 7

PARIS:

Place-names mentioned in the text

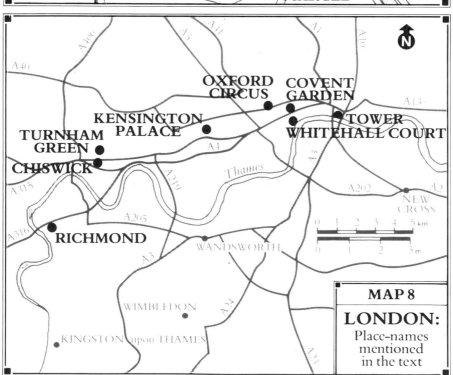

MAP 8

LONDON:

Place-names mentioned in the text

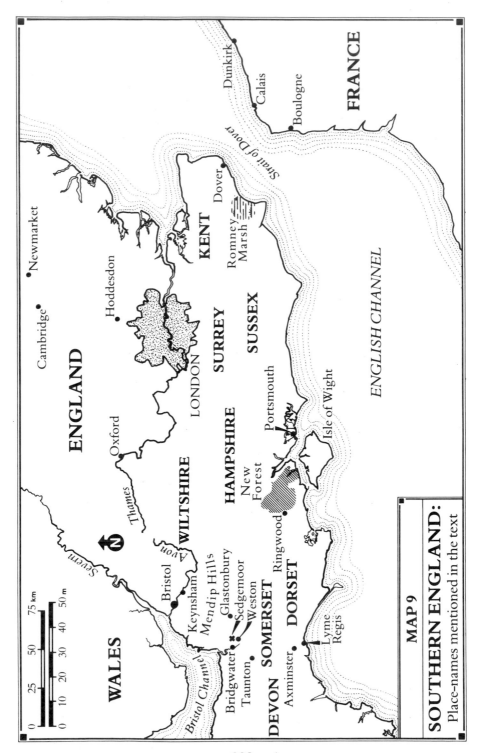

MAP 9

SOUTHERN ENGLAND:
Place-names mentioned in the text

BIBLIOGRAPHY

Adam, Antoine. *Revue d'Histoire de la Philosophie*. Paris, 15 October 1938.

Anonymous. *Mémoires secrets pour servir à l'Histoire de Perse*. Amsterdam, 1745.

Antier, Jean-Jacques. *Les grandes heures des Iles de Lérins*. Paris, 1975.

Arrèse, Pierre-Jacques. *La Masque de fer*. Paris, 1969.

Barine, Arvède. *Revue de Paris*. Paris, 1 July 1905.

Barnes, Arthur Stapylton. *The Man of the Mask*. London, 1912.

Bartoli, Camille. *J'ai découvert l'inconcevable secret du Masque de fer*. Nice, 1978.

Bazeries, Etienne & Burgaud, Emile. *Le Masque de fer, Révélation de la correspondance chiffrée de Louis XIV*. Paris, 1893.

Bournon, Fernand. *La Bastille*. Paris, 1893.

Broglie, Isabelle de. *Le duc de Beaufort, roi des Halles ou roi de France*. Paris, 1958.

Cabanès, Docteur. *Légendes et Curiosités de l'Histoire: Deuxième Série*. Paris.

Carey, Edith. *The Channel Islands*. London, 1904.

Charpentier, ——. *La Bastille dévoilée, ou Recueil de pièces authentiques pour servir à son histoire*. Paris, 1790.

Chéron, A. & Sarret de Coussergues, G. de. *Coussergues et les Sarret*. Brussels, 1963.

Courtilz de Sandras, Gatien de. *Mémoires de M. d'Artagnan*. Paris, 1700.

Decaux, Alain. *Les Grands Mystères du Passé*. Paris, 1964. *Grands Secrets, Grandes Enigmes*. Paris, 1970.

Delort, J. *Histoire de L'Homme au Masque de fer, accompagnée des pièces authentiques et des fac-similés*. Paris, 1825. *Histoire de la détention des Philosophes*. Paris, 1829.

Depping, G. *Correspondance administrative du règne de Louis XIV*. Paris, 1850. *Revue bleue*. Paris, 18 July 1896.

Dijol, Pierre-Marie. *Nabo, ou le Masque de fer*. Paris, 1978.

Dutens, Louis. *Mémoires d'un Voyageur qui se repose*. Paris, 1806.

Duvivier, Maurice. *Le Masque de fer*. Paris, 1932.

Fréron, Elie. *L'Année Littéraire*. Paris, 1759 & 1768.

Funck-Brentano, Frantz. *Légendes et Archives de la Bastille*. Paris, 1898. *Le Masque de Fer* Paris, 1933.

Furneaux, Rupert. *The Man Behind the Mask*. London, 1954.

Gérin-Ricard, Lazare de. *Le Masque de fer, La solution de l'énigme*. Marseilles, 1956.

Griffet, Henri. *Traité des différentes sortes de preuves qui servent à établir la vérité de l'histoire*. Liège, 1769.

Grimm, Frédéric-Melchior. *Correspondance Littéraire*. Paris, 1753–1790.

Henri, Robert. *Les grands Procès de l'Histoire*. Paris, 1925.

Huguet, Adrien. *Le Marquis de Cavoye*. Paris, 1920.

Jung, Theodore. *La vérité sur le Masque de fer, (les Empoisonneurs) d'après les documents inédits des Archives de la Guerre et autres dépôts publics*. Paris, 1872.

Kunstler, Charles. *Paris Souterrain*. Paris, 1953.

La Barre de Raillicourt, Dominique de. *Les Cahiers de l'Histoire*. No. 2. Paris, 1960.

Lacroix, Paul. *L'Homme au Masque de fer*. Paris, 1837. *Revue Universelle des Arts*. Paris/Brussels, 1855.

La Force, Duc de. *Lauzun, Un Courtisan du Grand Roi*. Paris, 1946.

Laloy, Emile. *Mercure de France*. Paris, 15 August 1931.

Lang, Andrew. *The Valet's Tragedy, and other studies*. London, 1903.

Las Cases, Emmanuel de. *La Mémorial de Sainte-Hélène*. Paris, 1833.

Lenotre, G. *Dossiers de Police*. Paris, 1935.

Loiseleur, Jules. *Le Masque de fer devant la critique moderne*. Paris, 1867.

Loquin, Anatole. *Un secret d'état sous Louis XIV. Le Prisonnier Masqué de la Bastille, son histoire authentique*. Paris, 1900.

Macaulay, Thomas Babington. *History of England*. London, 1849 & 1855.

Marchand, Prosper. *Dictionnaire Historique, ou Mémoires Critiques et Littéraires*. La Haye, 1758.

Mast, Marie-Madeleine. *Le Masque de fer*. Paris, 1974.

Mongrédien, Georges. *Le Masque de fer*. Paris, 1952. *Revue XVIIe Siècle*. No. 17/18. Paris, 1953.

Mossiker, Frances. *The Affair of the Poisons*. London, 1969.

Mouhy, Charles de Fieux, Chevalier de. *Le Masque de fer, ou les aventures admirables du Père et du Fils*. La Haye, 1750.

Pagnol, Marcel. *Le Secret du Masque de fer*. Paris, 1965.

Papon, Jean-Pierre. *Voyage Littéraire de Provence*. Paris, 1780.

Petitfils, Jean Christian. *L'Homme au Masque de fer*. Paris, 1970. *Lauzun, ou l'insolite séduction*. Paris, 1987.

Rabinel, Aimé-Daniel. *La Tragique Aventure de Roux de Marcilly*. Toulouse, 1969.

Raphélis, Jean. *Annales de la Société Scientifique et Littéraire de Cannes et de l'Arrondissement de Grasse*. Tome XXI. Cannes, 1969.

Ravaisson, François. *Archives de la Bastille*. Paris, 1868 & 1879.

Renneville, René-Augustin-Constantin de. *L'Inquisition Française ou l'Histoire de la Bastille*. Amsterdam, 1715.

Roux de Fazillac, Pierre. *Recherches historiques et critiques sur l'Homme au Masque de fer d'òu résultent des notions certaines sur ce prisonnier*. Paris, 1800.

Saint-Foix, Germain-François-Poullain de. *Essais Historiques sur Paris*. Paris, 1776.

Soulavie, Jean-Louis. *La Vie Privée du Maréchal de Richelieu*. Paris, 1791.

Taulès, Pierre, Chevalier de. *L'Homme au Masque de fer*. Paris, 1825.

Thompson, Harry. *The Man in the Iron Mask*. London, 1987.

Topin, Marius. *L'Homme au Masque de fer*. Paris, 1870.

Various. *La Maschera di Ferro e il suo Tempo. Atti del Convegno Internazionale di Studio, Pinerolo 28-29 Sett. 1974* (including contributions by Arrèse, Dijol, Mongrédien, Patria, Petitfils et al.) Pinerolo, 1976.

Vernadeau, Pierre. *Le Médecin de la Reyne*. Paris, 1934.

Voltaire. *Le Siècle de Louis XIV*. Berlin, 1751, et al.

N.B. The proceedings of the International Symposium on the Iron Mask held in Cannes in September 1987 will be published at some future date by l'Office Municipal de l'Action Culturelle de Cannes. It should include contributions by Brugnon, Caire, Dijol, Noone, Patria, Thompson, et al.

INDEX

References to illustrations are in italic type, to maps in bold type; n indicates a reference to a page note.